ALSO BY BENJAMIN CARTER HETT

Burning the Reichstag:
An Investigation into the Third Reich's Enduring Mystery

Crossing Hitler:
The Man Who Put the Nazis on the Witness Stand

Death in the Tiergarten:
Murder and Criminal Justice in the Kaiser's Berlin

THE DEATH OF DEMOCRACY

The Death of Democracy

Hitler's Rise to Power and the
Downfall of the Weimar Republic

BENJAMIN CARTER HETT

HENRY HOLT AND COMPANY   NEW YORK

Henry Holt and Company
Publishers since 1866
175 Fifth Avenue
New York, New York 10010
www.henryholt.com

Henry Holt® and 🏰® are registered trademarks of
Macmillan Publishing Group, LLC.

Copyright © 2018 by Benjamin Carter Hett
All rights reserved.
Distributed in Canada by Raincoast Book Distribution Limited

Library of Congress Cataloging-in-Publication Data is available.

ISBN: 978-1-25016-250-2

Our books may be purchased in bulk for promotional, educational, or business use. Please
contact your local bookseller or the Macmillan Corporate and Premium Sales Department at
(800) 221-7945, extension 5442, or by e-mail at MacmillanSpecialMarkets@macmillan.com.

Designed by Kelly S. Too

Printed in the United States of America

3 5 7 9 10 8 6 4

To everyone who fights for freedom,
human rights, democracy, peace, and tolerance.

And the King shall answer and say unto them, Verily I say unto
you, Inasmuch as ye have done it unto one of the least of these my
brethren, ye have done it unto me.

Matthew 25:40

CONTENTS

Cast of Characters   xi

Important Political Parties in the Weimar Republic   xvii

Introduction   1

1. August and November   15

2. "Don't Believe Him, He's Telling the Truth"   35

3. Blood May and the Creeper   62

4. The Hunger Chancellor   94

5. State of Emergency   131

6. The Bohemian Private and the Gentleman Jockey   162

7. Coordination   184

8. "We Have to Get Rid of Him"   208

Notes   237

Acknowledgments   267

Index   269

CAST OF CHARACTERS

Prince Max von Baden (1867–1929): Hereditary prince of the Grand Duchy of Baden and chancellor of the German Reich in October and November 1918.

Max Bauer (1869–1929): Colonel, artillery expert, and staff officer before and during the First World War. Adviser on politics and economics to General Erich Ludendorff. First author to formulate the "stab in the back" myth, in early 1919.

Herbert von Bose (1893–1934): An intelligence officer and conservative activist who became press secretary to Vice-Chancellor Papen in 1933 and 1934.

Otto Braun (1872–1955): Social Democratic politician and prime minister of Prussia most of the time from 1920 to 1932, and then with limited powers until early 1933.

Aristide Briand (1862–1932): French politician, prime minister on a number of occasions, and foreign minister from 1925 to 1932. Worked with Gustav Stresemann to bring peace and Franco-German reconciliation.

Heinrich Brüning (1885–1970): One of the leaders of the Catholic Center Party in the Weimar Republic and one of the republic's most important statesmen. Chancellor from March 1930 to May 1932.

Rudolf Diels (1900–1957): A Prussian civil servant, recruited to the police section of the Prussian interior ministry in 1931 to prepare reports on Communist violence. In 1932 he shifted his allegiance, first to Papen and then to the Nazis. Named head of the Prussian secret police, which, by 1933, grew into the Gestapo, he was forced out in the spring of 1934.

Friedrich Ebert (1871–1925): Leader of the Social Democratic Party of Germany during the First World War. First head of the government after the German Revolution of 1918, or "November Revolution," and president of the Weimar Republic from 1919 to 1925.

André François-Poncet (1887–1978): French ambassador to Germany from 1931 to 1938.

Wilhelm Frick (1877–1946): One of the earliest Nazi activists. Interior minister under Hitler from 1933 to 1943.

Joseph Goebbels (1896–1945): Head of the Nazi Party in Berlin from 1926 to 1945. Propaganda director for the Nazi Party from 1930 and minister of popular enlightenment and propaganda from 1933. A highly talented propagandist and one of the most intelligent of Hitler's inner circle, he is said to be the only one Hitler found a stimulating conversationalist.

Hermann Göring (1893–1946): One of Hitler's first followers and part of the Nazi inner circle. Speaker of the Reichstag in 1932, and then both Reich "minister without portfolio" and Prussian interior minister in 1933.

Wilhelm Groener (1867–1939): A staff officer during the First World War and, in 1918, Erich Ludendorff's replacement as first quartermaster general. Served as defense minister from 1928 to 1932 and also as interior minister from 1931 to 1932. Kurt von Schleicher was his particular protégé.

Franz Gürtner (1881–1941): Bavarian politician and member of the German National People's Party. Minister of justice in the cabinets of Franz von Papen and Kurt von Schleicher from 1932 to 1933 and then under Hitler until 1941.

Kurt von Hammerstein-Equord (1878–1943): A senior military officer who was commander in chief of the German Army from 1930 to 1934. An anti-Nazi, he was eventually forced out of his command.

Konrad Heiden (1901–1966): Social Democratic journalist. Went into exile in France and the United States after 1933 and wrote the first important biography of Hitler.

Wolf-Heinrich Count von Helldorff (1896–1944): Scion of an aristocratic Saxon family, commander of the Berlin Sturmabteilung, or SA, in 1931, and then police chief of Potsdam (1933–1935) and Berlin (1935–1944) under the Nazis. Gravitated toward the resistance as early as 1938, and was executed following the failure of the Valkyrie plot in 1944.

Heinrich Himmler (1900–1945): Commander of the Schutzstaffel, or SS, starting in 1929, at a time when it was a small corps of bodyguards within the larger SA. Transformed the SS into the most powerful organization in Nazi Germany, one that eventually encompassed all police and security services, some of the armed forces, and some important economic institutions.

Oskar von Hindenburg (1883–1960): Army officer and son of field marshal and German president Paul von Hindenburg. A friend and regimental comrade of Kurt von Schleicher, Oskar was one of his father's most influential advisers during the last years of the Weimar Republic. Due to his educational and intellectual limitations, he was known to insiders as "the son not foreseen in the constitution."

Paul von Hindenburg (1847–1934): Career army officer who retired in 1911 but was recalled to service at the outbreak of the First World War. Credited with the crucial victory of the Battle of Tannenberg in 1914, saving East Prussia from Russian invasion. Commander in chief of the German Army from 1916 to 1919. Elected president of the German Reich in 1925 and reelected in 1932. Appointed Adolf Hitler chancellor in January 1933.

Adolf Hitler (1889–1945): Leader of the National Socialist German Workers' Party from 1920 to 1945. Led Beer Hall Putsch in Munich in 1923. Author of *Mein Kampf*. Chancellor of Germany from 1933 and "Chancellor and Führer" from 1934 to 1945.

Alfred Hugenberg (1865–1951): Industrialist, media magnate, and leader of the right-wing German National People's Party after 1928. Served briefly in Hitler's cabinet in 1933.

Edgar Julius Jung (1894–1934): Right-wing, "young conservative" intellectual and political activist. Known for his critique of democracy, *The Rule of Inferiors* (1927). Speechwriter for Franz von Papen in 1933 and 1934, he was at the heart of the resistance activities run from Papen's office.

Erich Ludendorff (1865–1937): Senior army officer, first quartermaster general of the army from 1916 to 1918. One of the architects of the "stab in the back" myth, he was the most important theorist of "total war" and its meaning for a "totalitarian state."

Karl Mayr (1883–1945): Staff officer and immediate superior of Adolf Hitler in 1919. Ordered Hitler to become involved with the German Workers' Party.

Otto Meissner (1880–1953): State secretary in the office of the president under Friedrich Ebert and Paul von Hindenburg, and continuing under Hitler.

Hermann Müller (1876–1931): Social Democratic politician, chancellor in 1920 and from 1928 to 1930, when he led a "great coalition" that was the last fully parliamentary government of the Weimar Republic.

Eugen Ott (1889–1977): Staff officer in the defense ministry under Kurt von Schleicher. In late 1932, he prepared a crucial report on a war game showing that the army would be overwhelmed by a simultaneous Nazi and Communist uprising and a foreign invasion.

Franz von Papen (1879–1969): Army officer before and during the First World War and Center Party politician. Chancellor in 1932 and vice-chancellor under Hitler in 1933 and 1934. Thereafter, ambassador to Austria and Turkey until 1945.

Ernst Röhm (1887–1934): Professional army officer who was an early follower of Hitler and one of Hitler's few friends. Commander of the SA from 1930 to 1934.

Alfred Rosenberg (1893–1946): German émigré from Estonia. An early activist with the Nazi Party, he was known as the Nazis' philosopher. He was the author of *The Myth of the Twentieth Century* and editor of the Nazis' newspaper, the *Völkischer Beobachter* (Nationalist Observer).

Kurt von Schleicher (1882–1934): Career army officer. Head of the army's ministerial office for liaison with politicians from 1928 and influential adviser to Paul von Hindenburg. Defense minister in 1932 and chancellor from December 1932 to January 1933.

Carl Schmitt (1888–1985): Right-wing jurist and political theorist, important adviser to Kurt von Schleicher and Franz von Papen, and then known as the "crown jurist" of the Third Reich.

Carl Severing (1875–1952): Social Democratic politician. Prussian interior minister from 1920 to 1926 and from 1930 to 1932, Reich interior minister from 1928 to 1930.

Gregor Strasser (1892–1934): Nazi activist, organizer, and political strategist, he broke with Hitler in December 1932.

Gustav Stresemann (1878–1929): Leader of the German People's Party, chancellor in 1923, and foreign minister from 1923 to 1929. Generally held to be Weimar's greatest statesman, he worked with Aristide Briand to bring Germany back into the European and world community.

Fritz Günther von Tschirschky (1900–1980): Scion of an aristocratic Silesian family, he was "adjutant" and intelligence adviser to Franz von Papen in 1933 and 1934 and one of the central figures in the resistance activities run from Papen's office.

IMPORTANT POLITICAL PARTIES
IN THE WEIMAR REPUBLIC

Arranged from most left-leaning to most right-leaning:

Communist Party of Germany (Kommunistische Partei Deutschlands): Dedicated to the overthrow of the existing social, political, and economic order, it was generally the party of the unemployed, unskilled, and poorest industrial workers. It was particularly strong in major cities such as Berlin and Hamburg, and subject to firm control by the Comintern (Communist International), and thus by Joseph Stalin's regime in the Soviet Union.

Independent Social Democratic Party of Germany (Unabhängige Sozialdemokratische Partei Deutschlands, "the Independents"): A faction of the Social Democratic Party that split off during the First World War to oppose continued support for and funding of the war effort, it had a base in more radical workers and left-wing intellectuals. After 1922, most of its members either returned to the Social Democrats or joined the Communists, and the party ceased to be significant.

Social Democratic Party of Germany (Sozialdemokratische Partei Deutschlands): Formed in 1875, it is the longest continuously active German political party. Its leaders became the leaders of Germany through the Revolution of 1918, and it was the party most firmly committed to the democratic republic, although after 1920, it did not often serve in national administrations. Its base was in skilled and unionized workers, and from 1912 to 1932 it was the largest political party in Germany in both membership and Reichstag deputies.

German Democratic Party (Deutsche Demokratische Partei): Growing out of the prewar left-liberals and committed to democracy and civil liberties, it represented intellectuals, independent professionals, and small business. It was very successful in the first Weimar election in 1919 but thereafter quickly lost support. It moved to the right after 1930 and changed its name to the "State Party" (Staatspartei) but became all but irrelevant, earning 1 percent of the vote in the last elections.

Center Party (Zentrum): The party that represented most German Catholics, it occupied the ideological center ground and was the indispensable party in the Weimar Republic, involved in all administrations until 1932 and providing most of the chancellors. One of the committed democratic parties, it moved to the right in the last years of the republic.

Bavarian People's Party (Bayerische Volkspartei): The Bavarian sister of the Center Party, similarly a party meant to represent Catholics. Bavaria has historically sought greater autonomy within Germany, and the Bavarian People's Party was accordingly more interested in federalism and considerably more conservative than its national sister: it backed Paul von Hindenburg for president in 1925 against the Center's candidate Wilhelm Marx.

German People's Party (Deutsche Volkspartei): A right-liberal party with a base particularly in big business, important largely because its leader, Gustav Stresemann, was one of the leading statesmen of the Weimar Republic, serving as chancellor in 1923 and foreign minister from 1923 to 1929.

German National People's Party (Deutschnationale Volkspartei, "German Nationals"): Formed in 1918 out of a merger of the prewar German Conservatives, Free Conservatives, and various antisemitic parties, it was the establishment right-wing party, representing aristocratic landlords, army officers, senior civil servants, and some sections of big business. Through the 1920s, the German Nationals were divided over whether they should pragmatically accept the republic, but after Alfred Hugenberg became leader in 1928, they turned increasingly to fundamental opposition.

National Socialist German Workers' Party (Nationalsozialistische Deutsche Arbeiterpartei, "the Nazis"): Emerging from the German Workers' Party that was formed in 1919, it was a fringe party until the late 1920s, when it began to win significant support, first in Protestant rural areas. When Adolf Hitler took over as the party's leader in 1920, he added "National Socialist" to its name. From July 1932, it was the largest German political party, and from July 1933, it was the only legal political party until the end of the Second World War.

THE DEATH OF DEMOCRACY

Introduction

The first signs of something happening come a few minutes past nine o'clock on an icy winter evening in Berlin. Hans Flöter, a theology student, is walking home from an evening of study at the State Library on Unter den Linden. Crossing the square in front of the massive Reichstag, he hears a window breaking. Flöter alerts Karl Buwert, a police officer walking his beat in front of the building. Civic duty done, Flöter continues on his way home. Werner Thaler, a typesetter at the Nazi newspaper the Völkischer Beobachter *(Nationalist Observer), also approaches Buwert: moving closer to the building and looking through a first-floor window, the two men think they see someone inside carrying a torch. Buwert fires his revolver at the glow, but without much result.*

Alarming news keeps coming. A young man wearing high military-style boots and a black coat appears at the Brandenburg Gate police station at 9:15 to report that the Reichstag is on fire. The police carefully note the time and the message, but in the excitement, they forget to take the man's name. His identity remains a mystery to this day. Within a few minutes the glow of flames is clearly visible through the glass cupola over the Reichstag's plenary chamber. At 9:27 the chamber explodes. Firefighters and police find themselves faced with a catastrophic fire at the heart of the building.

Two minutes before this, the police have arrested a strange young man lurking in a corridor near the burning chamber. His papers show that he is Marinus van der Lubbe, journeyman mason, age twenty-four, of Leiden, Holland. Van der Lubbe is naked to the waist and sweating profusely. He gladly confesses to being the arsonist. No one at the time thinks he could be the only one.

The firefighters rush to work, drawing water from the nearby River Spree as well as from hydrants around the building. They are able to train their hoses on the burning chamber from all sides. With the hoses in place, the blaze is brought under control within seventy-five minutes.

Even as the fire is spreading, Germany's leaders arrive at the Reichstag. The first is Hermann Göring, the Nazi interior minister of the state of Prussia. A few minutes later, a black Mercedes limousine delivers the new chancellor, Adolf Hitler, and his chief propagandist, Joseph Goebbels. The urbane, aristocratic vice-chancellor Franz von Papen is there, immaculately dressed as always, and seemingly unruffled. Rudolf Diels, the handsome thirty-two-year-old chief of the secret police, was disturbed while on a date ("a most unpolice-like rendezvous," as he will later put it) at the elegant Café Kranzler on Unter den Linden. As Diels tells it, he arrives in time to hear a tirade from the new chancellor. Hitler already seems to know who has set the fire. Standing on a balcony looking over at the burning chamber, his face reflecting the glow of the flames, the chancellor rages, "There will be no mercy now . . . Every Communist official will be shot where he is found. The Communist deputies must be hanged this very night!"

Soon, Göring puts out an official press release reflecting Hitler's wishes. After describing the extensive damage to the building, Göring's statement calls the fire "the most monstrous Bolshevik act of terror in Germany to date," and the "beacon for a bloody uprising and civil war."

But a dramatically different explanation begins to spread just as quickly as the official story. It is not yet midnight when an Austrian reporter named Willi Frischauer, Berlin correspondent for the Wiener Allgemeine Zeitung (Vienna General News), cables his paper: "There can be little doubt that the fire which is consuming the Reichstag was the work of hirelings of the Hitler Government." Frischauer thinks that these "hirelings" probably made their way into the Reichstag through a tunnel connecting the build-

ing to the official residence of the speaker of the Reichstag. The speaker of the Reichstag is Hermann Göring.

Reporters tell stories about crimes. Governments make arrests. Even as the firefighters struggle with the burning chamber, two separate waves of arrests begin. The Berlin police, working from carefully prepared lists, begin rounding up Communists, pacifists, clergymen, lawyers, artists, writers—anyone at all whom they judge likely to be hostile to the Nazis. The police bring their prisoners to Berlin's police headquarters at Alexanderplatz and book them, everything proper and official. At the same time, though, the Nazi Stormtroopers of Berlin carry out an arrest action of their own. The Stormtroopers have lists, too, but they do not register their prisoners officially. They bring them to abandoned basements, warehouses, even a water tower, where the prisoners are beaten and tortured in a hundred different ways, in many cases killed. Soon Berliners have a new name for these places: "wild concentration camps."

It is Monday, February 27, 1933. We might say it is the last night of the Weimar Republic, the last night of German democracy.

WHEN THE REICHSTAG burned, Adolf Hitler had been chancellor of the German Reich for precisely four weeks. He had come to office in a constitutionally legitimate, even democratic way. His party had emerged from two elections in the previous year with the largest number of seats in the Reichstag, Germany's parliament. At the end of January, Germany's president, the venerable eighty-five-year-old field marshal Paul von Hindenburg, had reluctantly but properly called on Hitler to take on the chancellorship and form a cabinet. Hindenburg had reserved for himself the appointment of ministers to the key portfolios of defense and foreign affairs, and it was also part of the deal that Franz von Papen, who had briefly been chancellor in 1932, would serve under Hitler as vice-chancellor. Papen was Hindenburg's protégé, despite being Catholic—a faith with which the resolutely Lutheran field marshal was far from comfortable.

Hitler's new cabinet came into office on January 30 looking much like other administrations of the democratic Weimar Republic, if a bit more oriented to the right than even Papen's "cabinet of barons" of the previous year. Hitler's government was still a coalition, with key ministries being held by representatives of the establishment right-wing German National People's Party and the conservative veterans' organization the Steel Helmet, with a sprinkling of nonpartisan establishment figures. Apart from Hitler himself, the Nazis held only two other cabinet positions: the veteran Nazi activist Wilhelm Frick was Reich interior minister, and Hitler's right-hand man, Hermann Göring, was minister without portfolio (a member of cabinet without departmental responsibility). At the time, few people appreciated the crucial importance of one detail: Göring also became the interior minister of the giant state of Prussia, which comprised three-fifths of Germany's land and people. Prussia had fifty thousand men in its state police forces, making the Prussian police half the size of the German Army.

To almost all seasoned observers, Hitler's political position on January 30 looked weak. It was *designed* to be weak. Like the three chancellors before him, he had been put into office by a small circle of powerful men who had Hindenburg's ear. They sought to take advantage of Hitler's demagogic gifts and mass following to advance their own agenda. They knew that without someone like Hitler to serve as a front man, they, and their goals, stood no chance of anything more than minuscule electoral support. They assumed they had Hitler squarely under control. Why should they not? These were men such as Vice-Chancellor von Papen and President von Hindenburg, aristocrats bred to leadership and army officers experienced in command. Hitler was the nameless son of a minor Austrian customs official, with little formal education. He made grammatical mistakes in his mother tongue. In four years of almost continuous service on the Western Front, he had never risen above the rank of private first class (*Gefreiter*) because, as one of his officers explained later, he was judged to lack the leadership qualities of a sergeant. Mingling class, rank, and North German prejudices, Hindenburg referred to Hitler contemptuously as "the Bohemian private." Sure, Hitler could excite lower-class mobs at a rally or a beer hall, but he was not a gentleman. He could not possibly govern.

This was a view held with remarkable unanimity across the German political spectrum. "We have hired him," Papen wrote confidently of

Hitler. "In a few months we will have pushed him so far into the corner that he will squeak." The independent Nationalist politician Gottfried Treviranus wrote years later that everyone he knew expected Hitler to "exhaust himself on the phalanx of Hindenburg, the army, and the constitution." Friedrich Stampfer, editor in chief of the Social Democratic paper *Vorwärts* (Forward), asked a foreign correspondent if he seriously believed that "this roaring gorilla can govern," adding that Hitler's government would last no longer than three weeks. A young carpenter and furniture maker named Max Fürst—whose political sympathies were far to the left and whose roommate, the radical lawyer Hans Litten, had earned notoriety by cross-examining Hitler in a Berlin courtroom two years before—thought that "it probably couldn't get any worse than the Papen administration."

Everyone knew, of course, about the intemperate tone of Hitler's rhetoric. In his speeches and in his rambling memoir *Mein Kampf*, he had raged against "the Jews" and "the Marxists." The men who had put together Germany's new democracy after the Armistice of 1918 were nothing but "November criminals," whose peace settlement was a betrayal of the German nation and its heroic army. Hitler had spoken openly about the need of a war to conquer *Lebensraum*, or "living space," in "the east." Especially in the most recent years, his movement had meted out brutal violence to its opponents, and Hitler had threatened still more if he were to come into power. "Heads will roll in the sand," he had told a court, testifying under oath in 1930 at the sedition trial of three army officers who were also Nazi activists.

But power always made radical leaders act reasonably, didn't it? This was an almost universal experience in political life. In 1933, after fifteen years of political responsibility, Germany's Social Democrats were a pale, timid shadow of their revolutionary pre-1914 selves. And they were dramatically less popular with the electorate, their vote share in national elections having fallen from nearly 39 percent in 1919 to 20 percent in 1932. President Hindenburg's inner circle calculated that bringing the Nazis into the government would do to Hitler's party precisely what the Weimar Republic had done to the Social Democrats. In early 1933, many Germans shared this assumption. One well-connected and thoughtful

observer, surprised by the moderation of Hitler's first speech as chancellor, wondered if "the Chancellor Hitler might think differently than
the vote-catcher Hitler did?"

Yet even the first weeks of Hitler's chancellorship provided more to
worry about than Papen's government had ever offered. There was more
violence, not least from the Nazi Stormtroopers the new government had
recruited en masse into the police forces. Opposition newspapers and
political events were closed down. It became increasingly difficult for
other political groups to campaign at all. Yet it was the Reichstag fire that
truly changed the course of events.

Hitler's cabinet met at eleven o'clock the morning after the fire. Reich
interior minister Frick presented a text bearing the title "Decree of Reich
President von Hindenburg for the Protection of People and State," known
informally ever after as the "Reichstag Fire Decree." The decree expressed
Hitler's theory that the Reichstag fire marked the start of a Communist
uprising. The state needed emergency powers to defend itself. The decree
suspended the civil liberties contained in the German constitution,
legalizing the imprisonment without trial of anyone the regime deemed
a political threat and effectively abolishing freedom of speech, assembly
and association, confidentiality of the post and telegraphic communica-
tions, and security from warrantless searches. It also gave the Reich government the power to replace any federal state administration if "the
necessary measures are not enacted for the reestablishment of public
security and order." The cabinet approved the decree, and later that day,
Hindenburg signed it into law.

This decree was, in the words of the distinguished legal scholar Ernst
Fraenkel, the "constitutional charter" of Hitler's Reich. It was the legal
basis for all the arrests and deportations, for the concentration camps
and the infamous secret police, the Gestapo. It also allowed the Nazis
effectively to abolish Germany's federal system and extend their rule
over all the states of the union. For most Germans alive in 1933, the
Reichstag fire and the decree marked a crucial turning point. Walter
Kiaulehn, a seasoned Berlin reporter, concluded an elegiac book about
his native city written after the war with the words, "First the Reichstag
burned, then the books, and soon the synagogues. Then Germany began
to burn, England, France and Russia . . ."

How COULD THIS happen?

This is one of the great questions in all of human history. For we know too well the consequences of Hitler's ascent to the chancellorship: the most devastating war the world had yet seen, accompanied by a campaign of mass murder so sweeping and unprecedented that legal scholar Raphael Lemkin had to coin a new word for it: *genocide*.

The question of how this could happen takes on a special, agonizing force against the background out of which Hitler and Nazism grew: the Germany of Weimar. Here, surely, was some kind of apex of human civilization. The 1919 constitution of the Weimar Republic created a state-of-the-art modern democracy, with a scrupulously just proportional electoral system and protection for individual rights and freedoms, expressly including the equality of men and women. Social and political activists fought, with considerable success, for even more. Germany had the world's most prominent gay rights movement. It was home to an active feminist movement that, having just won the vote, was moving on to abortion rights. Campaigns against the death penalty had been so successful in Germany that, in practice, the ax was never used. At the beginning of the Republic, workers had won the eight-hour day with full pay. Jews from Poland and Russia were drawn to Germany's tolerance and openness.

Germany led the world in more than politics and social activism. Even before 1914, Pablo Picasso had told a friend that if he had a son who wanted to paint, he would send him to Munich for training, not to Paris. Germany's Expressionist and "New Realist" painters (Ernst Ludwig Kirchner, Emil Nolde, George Grosz, Otto Dix) were producing some of the most exciting and troubling art of the age. The Bauhaus school turned out architects and designers whose ideas still influence their fields today. If you cared about music, no country could rival Germany's remarkable orchestras, ensembles, and soloists. And here, too, Germans were making the future, whether in the difficult classical works of Richard Strauss and Paul Hindemith, or in the exciting modern hybrids of Bertolt Brecht and Kurt Weill. Movies? Berlin could claim to be a second Hollywood, and with directors such as Fritz Lang, G. W. Pabst, or

F. W. Murnau, one that worked at a higher artistic level than the American original. The presence of writers like Alfred Döblin, Franz Kafka (who took up residence in Germany at the end of his life), and brothers Thomas and Heinrich Mann meant that Germany could match any other country in literature as well.

Germany's reputation in science and scholarship was unrivalled. In the 1920s, around a third of the world's physics journals were written in German, and of course Albert Einstein held a professorship at the University of Berlin while his friend, the Nobel Prize–winning chemist Fritz Haber, directed the Kaiser Wilhelm Institute for Physical Chemistry and Electrochemistry in the suburb of Dahlem. It was probably the excellence of German science and German universities that explained why the country led the world in industries such as chemicals and pharmaceuticals, and competed strongly with American cars for quality if not quantity.

If Germany had long prided itself on being the "land of poets and thinkers," then in the 1920s it seemed to surpass even itself. And yet somehow, out of this enlightened, creative, ultramodern democracy, grew the most evil regime in human history. Hitler's Reich utterly destroyed the creativity of Weimar, and destroyed it permanently. Many Germans still mourn what they have lost. "The uncertain Germans do not frighten Europe any longer, but nor do they fascinate anyone," the publisher Wolf Jobst Siedler lamented in 2000. We still puzzle over how this could have happened. That barbarism could issue from high civilization seems to confound our deepest beliefs and intuitions.

Hitler's Germany is unique among all regimes in human history in at least one respect: serious historians are unanimous in judging it a catastrophe with no redeeming features. There is no other regime, not even the Soviet Union under Joseph Stalin, that can claim such a dubious distinction. But that is also where agreement ends. Hitler's Germany is a kind of historical Rorschach test: we project onto it whatever we believe to be the worst conceivable political features. What you think those might be depends on who you are. Not everyone sees it the same way. This kind of projection affects explanations of how Hitler's regime came about, and this means that historians have always offered contradictory narratives of the fall of the Weimar Republic.

Was the problem with Germany in 1933 that it was not democratic enough or that it was too democratic? Did Nazism happen because of unchecked elite power or because the German masses were incapable of functioning as responsible citizens? Were the Nazis mired in the past, or were they dangerously modern? Was Nazism a specifically German problem or a manifestation of a wider crisis? Is this a case of history being made by a few "great men," or were deep structural factors at work in bringing Hitler to power? Were Christians, especially German evangelical Christians, a critical support group for the Nazis, or did Hitler's rise come in the teeth of traditional Lutheran, Calvinist, and Catholic German values? Was Hitler's rise inevitable—the great British historian A. J. P. Taylor once called it as surprising as a river flowing into the sea—or was it so chancy and unlikely that it almost didn't happen?

Ever since 1933, historians, philosophers, lawyers, psychologists, politicians, artists, writers, musicians, socially critical comedians, and many others have sought to explain Hitler's rise. Their answers have piled up. Most are enlightening. Why return to this problem again? What is still to be said?

There are several answers to this question.

First, historical knowledge works like a slow accretion of sediment. There is always a new layer being added. This is especially true of German history in the twentieth century. So much critical source material was held for so long in inaccessible archives, especially in the former East Germany and the Soviet Union, that the end of the Cold War brought major advances in what we know about the Nazi era. Historians are still finding, working through, and digesting these newly available materials.

One of the results of this process has been that much of what we thought we knew about Nazi Germany appears now as the residue of Nazi propaganda, or of the years just after World War II. In the late 1940s and early '50s, thousands of important players in Hitler's Reich needed to retell and reshape their stories in order to survive war crimes trials and "denazification" proceedings. Many distinguished scholars have held to the idea that Hitler was somehow an "unperson," a "man without qualities," never really alive unless he was addressing a rally. This is nothing but an unconscious reflection of the Nazis' propaganda notion that Hitler sacrificed all personal life to devote himself to his people.

Generational change is also a part of the story. In each era, we see the past differently, according to how we see ourselves and our own experiences. One era will notice things about the past that another will not. This is one reason that history is, and has to be, constantly rewritten.

In the 1990s, for instance, we basked in the glow of the end of the Cold War and the seemingly final triumph of democracy and liberal capitalism. Today, much has changed in our world. We are more worried about "globalization" and the stimulus it has given to right-wing populism. The bloom is off the revolutionary rose of 1989–1991, and the instabilities of the post–Cold War order are much more apparent. We are beset by an international refugee crisis and deeply aware of the myriad political problems it can cause. We have seen a new kind of terrorism take center stage across much of the world. All this means that, in many ways, our time more closely resembles the 1930s than it does the 1990s.

It is time, then, to tell the story of the fall of Weimar and the rise of Hitler in a new way. This book will put German affairs into their international context and examine their international influences. The Nazis, like other authoritarian but populist movements of their time, were a response to an overwhelming triumph of global liberal capitalism at the end of the Great War. The postwar Anglo-American order had linked doctrines of financial austerity (symbolized by the payment of debts and reparations and the return to the gold standard) with the stability of democracy itself. Political logic pushed opponents of austerity to become opponents of liberal democracy as well. The Nazis responded to other disruptions of the world they lived in, most of them traceable to the war. How should national borders be squared with ethnic identification? How should countries manage the rights of minorities? What should be done with refugees and other migrants?

If they were fundamentally a protest reaction against globalization and its consequences, the Nazis were themselves also shaped by general European and global trends. They drew consciously on influences from Russia, Italy, and Turkey, from the British Empire and the United States. Even the violence and terror of their Stormtroopers were tied to broader influences.

The Nazis would have been unthinkable without the First World War. In part, this was because so many Nazi leaders and activists had served in the trenches, become accustomed to violence, and were unable to settle down to civilian life. But the actual experience of combat was not what most heavily influenced the politics of the Weimar Republic. It was the way Germans came to remember the war's beginning and the war's end that really counted. The beginning and end, August 1914 versus November 1918, brilliant summer versus gray autumn, ecstatic unity versus bitter division, dreams of victory versus the reality of catastrophic defeat—these concepts ran through nearly everything that happened in Weimar and fundamentally shaped the way Germans thought about their political life. It is not an exaggeration to say that the answer to all questions about Weimar lies somewhere in the First World War.

The global situation and the legacy of the war help explain why the Nazis could find a wide popular following in Germany. But a wide following—around a third of the electorate before 1933—could never by itself have put Hitler in power. For that, Hitler had to win over the conservative establishment: above all President Paul von Hindenburg and his advisers, and the army, which held the keys to power. These conservatives could have stopped Hitler in his tracks. Instead, they chose to use him, although the Nazi-conservative alliance was always an awkward one.

This is where the individual personalities in the story become important. After 1930, German politics became increasingly deadlocked. It was impossible to assemble a stable majority in the Reichstag to pass legislation and support an administration. By the middle of 1932, the Nazis and the Communists, the two parties most committed to the destruction of the democratic system, together held a majority of Reichstag seats. But they came from opposite ends of the political spectrum and could never work together. President von Hindenburg and the chancellors he appointed bypassed the Reichstag. They relied on the emergency powers provision of the Weimar constitution to govern through executive orders. This meant that a small group of leaders could wield unusual power, and their individual goals and quirks took on a much greater significance.

President von Hindenburg, born in 1847, was a man of a different time: a Prussian aristocrat, Germany's most revered soldier, a devout Lutheran with a deep suspicion of Catholics and a loathing for Social Democrats. The constitution gave him the power to hire and fire chancellors, and from the time of his election to the presidency in 1925, he looked for ways to move the Republic politically to the right while preserving his reputation as a German hero and unifier.

Among Hindenburg's closest and most influential advisers was another military man, General Kurt von Schleicher. Schleicher was the head of the army's "Ministerial Office," which in practice meant he was the army's main political lobbyist. No one was ever quite sure what they were getting with Schleicher. He was sarcastic, devious, a schemer, always up to something, although that "something" was often mysterious. In reality, Schleicher, like Hindenburg, sought to create a more authoritarian and military regime out of Weimar's democracy. In the critical years from 1929 through 1932, it was Schleicher above all who made and unmade chancellors and administrations, and who played a crucial role in the Republic's downward spiral.

Schleicher's foil was the man who held the Weimar chancellorship for the longest continuous term: the Catholic union official and economist Heinrich Brüning. Where Schleicher was witty, flippant, and inscrutable, Brüning was earnest and solemn, a cool rationalist who struggled to grasp the irrationality of the world he was forced to confront. It was Brüning's fate to be chancellor during the worst years of the Great Depression, from 1930 to 1932. But finding a way out of the Depression was not Brüning's goal. He wanted to return Germany to full sovereignty. This meant getting out from under the burden of reparation payments that the 1919 Treaty of Versailles had imposed. To achieve this end, Brüning was willing to make Germany's economic crisis even worse.

Brüning's successor as chancellor was Franz von Papen, another former army officer and aristocrat, whose résumé in public life did not extend beyond ownership of a newspaper and back-bench service in the Prussian state parliament. Papen had served in the cavalry, and riding a horse was probably his outstanding skill. For this he was widely known as "the gentleman jockey." Papen was an elegant dresser, a charming conversationalist, and a fluent French speaker who wanted to see better Franco-German relations. Even his closest supporters would never have claimed that he possessed the gravitas of Brüning. Yet, after a few months in office, he grew to enjoy the privileges of power. In the end, it was his rage at losing power and his injured vanity that set up the last act in the downfall of Weimar democracy.

And, of course, there was Adolf Hitler. Hitler is a strong candidate for the most historically important individual of the twentieth century. But he is frequently misunderstood. In 1919, when he entered politics, Hitler had no experience and seemingly no gifts. For the next fourteen years he was constantly mocked and underestimated. He looked like a waiter in a railway station restaurant, people said, or a hairdresser. Structural factors in the economy and international affairs did much to make Nazism possible, but why did the context pick *this* man, of all people, to rise to such unprecedented power?

Certainly, Hitler brought some unusual talents to the game. He had a rare ability to captivate a crowd with his voice. Much less obvious to contemporaries was his uncanny intuition, his ability to read what people felt and wanted to hear, and to predict what they would do next. He was a skilled actor who could modify his behavior to fit the moment and the audience. He, like several of the people in his inner circle, was a clever political strategist who could see the ways in which the Nazis might come to power—and just as important, the ways they *couldn't*—and plan accordingly.

But even these talents cannot fully explain Hitler's success. The key to understanding why many Germans supported him lies in the Nazis' rejection of a rational, factual world. Hitler himself, in the words of his biographer Joachim Fest, was "always thinking the unthinkable," and "in his statements an element of bitter refusal to submit to reality invariably emerged." The realities that Germans faced after 1918 were all but unacceptable: a lost war that had cost the nation almost two million of her sons, a widely unpopular revolution, a seemingly unjust peace settlement, and economic chaos accompanied by huge social and technological change. Millions of Germans retreated into conspiracy theories: that a "stab in the back" (*Dolchstoss*, literally, "a dagger thrust"), not straightforward military defeat, had ended the war; or that they were beset by conspiratorial cliques of Communists, capitalists, Jews, and Freemasons. Hitler could give voice to this flight from reality as could no other German politician of his time.

Hostility to reality translated into contempt for politics, or, rather, desire for a politics that was somehow not political: a thing that can never be. The workings of democracy seen up close—the necessary deal-making, favors, compromises—are seldom inspiring. The Weimar Republic was certainly no exception. A large number of political parties, each representing well-defined social interests, competed for power and the spoils of power, compromising and making deals when they could. Often enough they could not, so the turnover of administrations was rapid: twenty-one in fourteen years. For a democracy to work, all parties have to acknowledge that they have at least some minimal common ground and that compromises are both possible and necessary. By the 1930s, however, there was very little of this spirit left as German society grew ever more bitterly divided. Defenders of the Republic often seemed like little more than defenders of a corrupt system. Opponents of democracy, preaching an "antipolitics" of unity and resurrection, could look like they were operating on higher moral ground. Hitler was thrilled when the racist theorist Houston Stewart Chamberlain called him "the opposite of a politician." The Nazi code word for the Weimar Republic was *the system*. It was a short step from this contempt for "the system" to the belief that a providential leader could lift the nation out of its soulless dead end. This was Hitler's appeal from the beginning to the end. Not to everyone, of course—the divisions in German society never went away. But Hitler's message convinced as many Germans as he needed it to.

There was nothing the Nazis did in the years after 1933 that was not prefigured in their rise to power. Shrewd observers could see what was coming: "Dictatorship, abolition of the parliament, crushing of all intellectual liberties, inflation, terror, civil war," wrote the novelist Friedrich Franz von Unruh in 1931, in an acclaimed series of articles for the newspaper the *Frankfurter Zeitung* (Frankfurt News). Hitler "starts from the recognition that there must be a new war," added the sharp-eyed liberal politician Theodor Heuss, who missed nothing of the Nazis' embrace of irrationality, either. Unruh was wrong about only one thing: that Hitler's seizure of power would be greeted by millions of determined opponents. For this, tragically, the Weimar Republic's reality deficit had grown too large.

1

August and November

Prince Max von Baden spends most of the day waiting impatiently for news from Kaiser Wilhelm II.

Prince Max is a trim man who seems to look into every camera lens with the baleful expression of someone who has seen a lot, been impressed by little, and bears few illusions about his fellow men and women. He has an unusual reputation as a liberal German prince. This was why he was named chancellor of the German Reich in October, at the age of fifty-one. Later, he will record his experiences in a dry tone, betraying irritation with almost everyone he had to deal with: the Kaiser, the generals, the moderate and radical socialists.

Prince Max's problem is that the Kaiser—Germany's hereditary emperor, whose family has ruled from Berlin since the fifteenth century—cannot make up his mind to abdicate the throne. Germany is falling further into the grip of revolution and every minute counts. Max's repeated phone calls to the Army's headquarters at Spa in Belgium, where the Kaiser has gone, are met only with stalling. The prince wants to save what he can of the old order. He knows that the revolution is winning. It can't be "beaten down," but "it might perhaps be stifled out." The only thing to do is contain the revolution by naming Friedrich Ebert, the leader of the moderate Social Democrats, as chancellor by royal authority.

Ebert will soon be chancellor one way or another, Max reasons, if not by royal appointment then by revolution in the streets. "If Ebert is presented to me as the Tribune of the People by the mob, we shall have the Republic," *he tells himself. A still-worse fate is possible. If the mob makes the more radical independent socialist Karl Liebknecht chancellor instead of Ebert,* "we shall have Bolshevism as well." *But if, in his last act, Kaiser Wilhelm names Ebert,* "then there would still be a slender hope for the monarchy left. Perhaps we should then succeed in diverting the revolutionary energy into the lawful channels of an election campaign."

Prince Max doesn't know about the drama playing out at the Kaiser's headquarters. At Spa, Field Marshal Paul von Hindenburg, the supreme commander of the German Army, understands two things clearly: the Kaiser has to abdicate, and Hindenburg himself must escape blame for pushing him to this realization. The Kaiser is toying with the idea of leading his army back to Germany to crush the revolutionaries. Hindenburg understands that this will lead to a disastrous civil war. He does not want to be responsible for such a thing. But Hindenburg is also a monarchist, and he knows that other monarchists might blame him for not standing by his king. Hindenburg is the hero of Tannenberg, one of Germany's few great victories in this lost war. He cannot let his reputation be tarnished now.

He solves the problem by giving the job to his second in command, First Quartermaster General Wilhelm Groener. Groener tells the Kaiser bluntly that the army will return peacefully to Germany under its commanders, "but not under the command of your majesty, because it no longer stands behind your majesty." *Hindenburg quietly begins arranging the Kaiser's escape to neutral Holland, where he will be safe.*

These events set a pattern. More than a decade later, Hindenburg will still be wrestling with the problem of potential civil war. He will still be trying to find a way to keep the army out of domestic strife while preserving his own reputation. He will still be unloading unpleasant tasks on his subordinates.

With no decision from Spa, Prince Max runs out of patience and decides to take matters into his own hands. He will announce Wilhelm's abdication himself. Prince Max summons Ebert and asks if he is prepared to govern in accordance with "the monarchical constitution."

Ebert is an unusually conservative Social Democrat and would have preferred to retain the monarchy, but events have gone too far. "Yesterday I could have given an unconditional affirmative," he tells Prince Max. "Today I must first consult my friends." Prince Max asks him about considering a regency, someone to serve as placeholder for a future monarch. Ebert replies that it is "too late." Behind Ebert, as Max's jaded pen records, the other Social Democrats in the room repeat in unison: "Too late, too late!"

Meanwhile, Ebert's colleague Philipp Scheidemann stands on a balcony of the Reichstag and calls out, "Long live the Republic!" This is taken as a declaration that Germany has in fact become a democratic republic, although Scheidemann will later say he meant it only as a "confession of faith" in the idea.

At the royal palace, a half mile or so east of the Reichstag, the radical Karl Liebknecht declares Germany a "socialist republic." By this time, the Kaiser has finally abdicated as emperor of Germany.

In the late afternoon, Prince Max has a final meeting with Ebert. Ebert now asks the prince to stay on as "administrator," a regent by another name. Prince Max replies stiffly, "I know you are on the point of concluding an agreement with the Independents [the more radical Independent Social Democrats] and I cannot work with the Independents." As he leaves, he turns to say one last thing: "Herr Ebert, I commit the German Empire to your keeping!"

Ebert responds gravely, "I have lost two sons for this Empire."

It is November 9, 1918.

Two days later, an armistice negotiated between German politicians and Allied military officers goes into effect. The First World War is over. For most Germans, defeat comes suddenly and shockingly. Among them is a wounded soldier convalescing from a poison gas attack at a hospital in Pasewalk, a small Pomeranian town about seventy-five miles northeast of Berlin.

"So it had all been in vain," he writes. "In vain all the sacrifices and deprivations . . . futile the deaths of two millions who died . . ." Had Germany's soldiers fought only to "allow a mob of wretched criminals to lay hands on the Fatherland?" He has not wept since the day of his mother's *funeral, but now the young man staggers back to his ward and buries his "burning head in the blankets and pillow."*

His name is Adolf Hitler, Private First Class.

IF YOU LOOK closely, you will find that almost everything about the Weimar Republic was really about the First World War.

There had never been a war like it, with such high casualties concentrated in such a relatively short period of time. Germany suffered 1.7 million soldiers killed in just over four years, more than any country except Russia. Civilians, including women, had been mobilized for industrial and other war work as never before. Wartime pressures forced the state to demand ever more labor and sacrifice from its people. This made it crucial to maintain public support. The new mass media opened up myriad possibilities for the state to "sell" the war, usually through highly emotional and largely untrue versions of the meaning of the conflict, or the nature of the enemy. Wartime propaganda left a deep imprint on the German people, as it did on people in other countries.

The war dragged its way from the summer of 1914 to the late autumn of 1918, but the real moment of decision came halfway through, toward the end of 1916. Shocked by the completely unexpected costs of the war and the growing unrest at home, the governments of all the warring countries faced the same decision: they could push to win outright, or they could accept the stalemate and negotiate peace. To win, they would have to take on more debt, accept still more casualties, and redouble efforts to extract labor and sacrifice from what they now called "the home front." In all the important cases, governments decided to push for victory. More resolute leaders came to power everywhere. In December 1916, the energetic David Lloyd George replaced the burned-out H. H. Asquith as prime minister of Great Britain. In November 1917, the fierce Georges Clemenceau ("the Tiger") came to power as French prime minister with the simple, grim promise "I make war." In Germany, the process was subtler. In the second half of 1916, the two supreme army commanders, Field Marshal Paul von Hindenburg and General Erich Ludendorff, steadily imposed their authority not only on the conduct of the war but on management of the home front as well. They marginalized Kaiser Wilhelm's civilian government and replaced it with their own "silent dictatorship." There was a paradox here, one that pointed to Germany's future. Hindenburg and Ludendorff had been appointed to the Supreme Command in the summer of 1916, against the Kaiser's wishes and as a result of popular pressure. Their dictatorship was therefore a kind of populism.

More ruthless leadership could not change the basic facts of modern total war. Total war demanded the labor or fighting power of every citizen. In turn, this gave citizens unprecedented bargaining power with the state, which was forced to make ever more extravagant promises about the wonderful world that would come with victory. Great Britain, for instance, entered the war with its government talking only of the sanctity of treaty rights and the defense of "brave little Belgium" against the German onslaught. But it is hard to ask hundreds of thousands of young men to die, and their loved ones to mourn them, for the sanctity of treaties. So, by 1918, Lloyd George had joined with U.S. president Woodrow Wilson in calling for a "League of Nations," dubbing the struggle "The War That Will End War" (a phrase coined originally by British science-fiction writer and social critic H. G. Wells). Lloyd George promised extensive social reform and, in the words of one of his cabinet ministers, to make Germany pay by squeezing it "until the pips squeak." Total war fostered a new kind of nationalism, more populist and egalitarian and less deferential to elites and traditional symbolism.

In Germany, the government felt forced to promise democratic reforms, particularly to change the voting rules for Prussian state elections, which had been heavily weighted toward the wealthy. Gustav Stresemann, a Reichstag deputy who would go on to be foreign minister in the Weimar Republic and one of the Republic's most important statesmen, told his parliamentary colleagues in 1917 that the war had changed the relationship between the people and the state. The postwar state, he said, would have to become more democratic. Even the "Patriotic Auxiliary Service Law," which Hindenburg and Ludendorff introduced in 1916, could look like democratic progress, although it drafted workers into war industries. The democratic parties in the Reichstag had cooperated in drafting the law. It included provisions for workers to be represented in management decisions.

Other wartime developments pointed to a more ominous future. The German government promised its people that victory would bring a new kind of imperial grandeur. Germany would become the dominant power in Europe, annexing territory from Belgium and France, and still more from the western lands of the Russian Empire. This vision was briefly realized when Russia dropped out of the war in 1918 and the Germans controlled, directly or indirectly, what is now Poland, the Baltic States, Belarus, and Ukraine. A new political party that formed in 1917, the Fatherland Party, called for continuing the war until Germany had won a complete victory, crushing political moderates at home and establishing itself as the dominant power in Europe and "up to the Gates of India." One Fatherland Party member was Alfred Hugenberg, a steel executive and media baron who, in the Weimar Republic, would go on to lead the main establishment right-wing party, the German National People's Party. Another was a Munich toolmaker and locksmith named Anton Drexler. In 1919, to keep the Fatherland Party's vision alive, Drexler would found something called the German Workers' Party. In another year, after recruiting the young war veteran Adolf Hitler to its ranks, the German Workers' Party would change its name to the National Socialist German Workers' Party—the Nazis.

Just as the war pushed some Germans to the extreme right, it pushed others to the extreme left. One of the victims of wartime disillusion was the Social Democratic Party. The Social Democrats had been the largest party in prewar Germany and the largest socialist party in the world, with a million members. In 1912, they had won the largest share of seats in the Reichstag elections. Although their socialist ideology should have committed them to peace, they had loyally supported Germany's war effort, and their Reichstag deputies had voted for all necessary war spending. Partly as a result, their membership plummeted during the war, down to a quarter million by 1917. That year, a faction of the Social Democratic Party split away to oppose all further military spending. The new faction became known as the Independent Social Democratic Party. By the end of 1917, it could count 120,000 members—nearly half the membership of the mainstream Social Democrats. The Independents were the root from which, after 1918, Germany's Communist Party would grow. The German workers' movement was now permanently divided.

Yet the political center could still hold. In July 1917, the three most democratic parties in the Reichstag (the Social Democrats, the left liberals, and the Catholic Center Party), together controlling nearly two-thirds of the seats, passed a resolution in favor of a negotiated peace without annexations or forced reparation payments. The resolution could not bind Hindenburg and Ludendorff, but it could frighten them. After all, the Reichstag majority presumably expressed the views of a majority of Germans. It was in the immediate aftermath of this resolution that the generals arranged the formation of the Fatherland Party. They also brought about the dismissal of the hapless head of government Chancellor Theobald von Bethmann-Hollweg, whom they judged too weak to control the unruly Reichstag democrats.

The real significance of the Peace Resolution was that it clearly defined a democratic block in German politics. The three parties behind it would become the pillars of Weimar democracy after 1918—in fact, they became known as "the Weimar coalition." From 1917 until 1933, German politics would be dominated by the struggle between this democratic block and the nationalist block, those conservatives and right-wing liberals who stood behind a more aggressive pursuit of the war.

By the late summer of 1918, the German Army was exhausted. Defeat was looming on the Western Front. Hindenburg and Ludendorff understood this perfectly well—Ludendorff called an Allied attack at Amiens on August 8 "the black day of the German army"—and in late September, they told the Kaiser it was time to seek an armistice with the western powers. Cagey as always, the generals refused to negotiate the armistice themselves, instead handing the job to the democratic leaders from the Reichstag. Disastrously, Woodrow Wilson played along, refusing to negotiate with the German "militarists." An armistice is usually negotiated by the respective military commanders on both sides. In this case, democratic politicians carried the ball for Germany. Later, they would carry the blame.

In the autumn of 1918, the German armed forces stood everywhere on foreign ground, still occupying most of Belgium and much of northern

France and controlling vast stretches of eastern Europe as well. Not a square foot of Germany was occupied by enemy troops. Unlike in the Second World War, the technology of bombs and aircraft had not developed to the point that Allied air forces could do significant damage to German towns. The German wartime press had been heavily censored and had carried nothing but news of victories and promises of more to come. Only an unusually imaginative or well-informed civilian could have understood that Germany was on the verge of defeat. Yet, suddenly, its leaders had asked for an armistice. It is little wonder that most Germans found defeat difficult to grasp.

Before an armistice could come into effect, though, Germany was shaken by revolution. It began with a naval mutiny, led by sailors who saw no point in the suicide mission against the British that their commanders were ordering. In a war-weary, exhausted, and hungry country, revolution spread from town to town and even to army units in France. In the space of a few days in early November, all the ancient royal houses that had still ruled Germany's federal states, such as the Wittelsbachs in Bavaria and the Wettins in Saxony, and finally even Kaiser Wilhelm himself in Berlin, were forced into abdication. On November 9, the Social Democrats and the Independent Social Democrats took power in the capital. These two parties had split only the year before. Now the revolution pushed them temporarily back together.

The country's new leader, Friedrich Ebert, found himself at the head of something called the "Council of People's Deputies," a body made up of three Social Democrats and three Independents. For the moment, this was what Germany had for an executive branch of government. The problems Ebert faced were overwhelming: a lost war, an army of millions to be brought home and demobilized, a population starving under the effects of the British naval blockade, and uncertainty about what kind of peace terms the victorious Allies would impose.

Ebert and the Social Democrats had a clear idea of what they wanted to do. They wanted Germany to become a parliamentary democracy along Western lines. Far to the east, the revolution in Russia was a fearful example of what could happen if things went wrong: civil war, famine, state terror. Ebert hated social revolution (meaning a revolution like that in Russia, overturning not just the political leadership, but also property ownership and class relations) "like sin," he said. He and his party wanted to hold elections quickly for a national assembly that would draft a new constitution.

Yet not everyone saw the Russian Revolution as an example to fear. For some, it was an inspiration. And in late 1918, there were still several different kinds of revolutions going on in Germany. A "Greater Berlin Workers' and Soldiers' Council" had formed on the model of the soviets in Russia. Its executive committee claimed power over the Council of People's Deputies, and its members sought a radical transformation of Germany along Russian Bolshevik lines. Some of the more radical Independents wanted the same thing, as did other left-wing groups such as the Spartacus League, led by the socialist intellectuals Karl Liebknecht and Rosa Luxemburg.

Under these circumstances Ebert's coalition was not fated to last long. The major tension involved relations with the army. On his first day in office, Ebert reached an agreement with General Wilhelm Groener, who had replaced Ludendorff as first quartermaster general of the army. Groener agreed that the army would support Ebert's government and not the Greater Berlin Workers' and Soldiers' Council. In return, Ebert agreed to leave the army and its officer corps intact. In December, a left-revolutionary military unit called the "People's Marine Division" occupied Berlin's royal palace and took some Social Democratic politicians hostage. Ebert relied on his agreement with Groener and gave the army authority to go after the rebels. The Independents broke with Ebert over this decision. The breach between the constitutional and revolutionary wings of the workers' movement was growing wider.

The revolutionary wing was also reorganizing itself. At the turn of the year, the left wing of the Independents joined with several other radical groups, including the Spartacus League, to form the Communist Party of Germany, modeled on the Soviet Russian original. On January 4, Karl Liebknecht announced a revolutionary uprising against Ebert's government. The uprising soon became known as the Spartacus Revolt. Once again, Ebert turned to Groener. With the aid of the army and the new Freikorps (Free Corps), paramilitary squads consisting mostly of demobilized veterans and students frustrated that they had missed the war, Ebert's government crushed the revolt. Free Corps men arrested and murdered both Rosa Luxemburg and Karl Liebknecht. This sequence of events (leftist uprising and bloody Free Corps response) repeated itself later, in the spring of 1919, in Berlin and Munich (in the latter case, with about six hundred leftists killed).

On January 19, Germans voted for a national assembly. Ebert's Social Democrats won nearly 39 percent of the vote—a record that no German party, including Hitler's, would surpass in a free election until West German chancellor Konrad Adenauer's overwhelming third victory in 1957. The other parties committed to creating a new democracy, the Catholic Center Party and the left-liberal German Democratic Party, earned 19.7 percent and 18.6 percent of the vote, respectively, meaning that more than three-quarters of Germans had cast their votes for progressive, democratic politics.

Between early February and August 1919, amid extraordinary continuing turmoil, political uprisings, and bitter controversy over the terms of the peace treaty, the national assembly drafted a state-of-the-art constitution for a modern democracy. The main architect of the Weimar Constitution was a law professor named Hugo Preuss. A few years later, Preuss told two American interviewers that he had felt pressure simply to copy the American Constitution. "The convention was held while Wilson was at the zenith of his career," he said. "Then came Wilson's fall from power [Preuss presumably meant Wilson's congressional defeat over the peace treaty], the deadlock between the President and Congress; and it was plain that your system had faults which we should try to avoid." It was ironic that he had drafted a constitution to avoid deadlock: by 1930, deadlock would be exactly what it produced. Yet Preuss had sound reasons for thinking his system could avoid such a problem.

The new constitution did take some elements from the United States: the powerful office of the president and the enumeration of basic individual rights. At the same time, it spelled out the rules for a parliamentary government along British lines—another irony, given that the British have never written these rules down in a formal constitution. Some of it drew on German history. Some of it was truly innovative.

At the heart of the constitution was the Reichstag, a parliament to be elected at least every four years by all men and women over the age of twenty. The striking and innovative element of these elections was that they were to be proportional. This meant that voters would vote for a party list of candidates, rather than one candidate in an individual district, as is done in elections for the British House of Commons or the U.S. House of Representatives. Each party would then receive the number of seats in the Reichstag that corresponded to its share of the popular vote.

Proportional systems are common in Europe today. Germany still has one. They have the advantage of producing a parliament that exactly reflects the voters' choices. The British system, by contrast, gives a big advantage to parties that can achieve around 40 percent of the vote or that have strong regional centers of power, and it penalizes parties that have modest support evenly distributed throughout the country. Even in American congressional elections, generally fought out between only two parties, the outcome often does not reflect the national popular vote. The disadvantage of a proportional system is that it tends to produce a parliament with many different party delegations, some of them small. This can make it hard to produce stable administrations. The Weimar Republic suffered greatly from this ailment.

The reason lay in the combined effects of Articles 52 and 54 of the constitution. Article 52 said that the Reich government—meaning the executive branch—would consist of the chancellor and the chancellor's cabinet. Article 54 said that the chancellor and the cabinet needed the confidence of the Reichstag, and had to resign if they lost it. In practical terms, this meant that an administration needed to maintain the support of a majority in the Reichstag. A chancellor and his cabinet would have to resign if more than 50 percent of the members voted against them, signaling a loss of confidence. This is a basic principle of parliamentary government. It sounds logical and reasonable. It is meant to ensure democratic control over the executive. In Weimar, it opened the door to nearly permanent crisis and, in the Republic's last years, deadlock and near–civil war conditions.

The other major figure in the Weimar Constitution was, of course, the president. The president was to be elected by all the people in elections separate from Reichstag elections. The president's term of office was seven years.

The president was the head of state. The constitution outlined his general duties to dedicate his "whole strength" to the "welfare of the German people," to "keep them from harm," and to preserve the constitution and the laws. It was his job to represent the country internationally. He was responsible for approving treaties and alliances, and it was to him that foreign ambassadors were to "present their credentials." In domestic politics, it was his privilege to appoint a chancellor (which didn't change the fact that the chancellor still needed majority parliamentary support). The president also appointed cabinet ministers, although here he was supposed to follow the chancellor's suggestions.

Nothing about the presidency turned out to be more controversial than the emergency powers the constitution assigned it.

Article 48 became the most important, some would say the most infamous, provision in the Weimar Constitution. It said that the president could "take the necessary measures," including "with the help of the armed forces," if "public security and order become seriously disturbed or endangered." It also allowed the president to "oblige" a state government to fulfill its constitutional duties were it failing to do so, again "with the help of the armed forces." There was a check on this power: whatever the president did under Article 48 could be overturned by a majority vote in the Reichstag.

There was yet another irony in the role the constitution assigned the president. One of the debates among the constitution's framers had been about whether the new system should give more weight to the power of the parliament or to that of the president. Preuss had, at first, been an advocate of the supremacy of parliament. But he came around to thinking that a strong, unifying presidency would be better able than a fractious parliament to overcome Germany's divisions of religion (Catholic versus Protestant), social class, and region. There was an even more important factor. Preuss, like most of the other framers, was a liberal, not a socialist. In the conditions of 1919, it looked as if the socialists might have a permanent majority in the new Reichstag. Preuss feared that permanent socialist dominance might create an "authoritarian state in reverse." Here again, a strong president—armed with emergency powers to rule above the parties if necessary—would, Preuss thought, form an essential defense of democracy.

In 1925, Preuss's American interviewers asked him if he thought the president could abuse his powers. Preuss said no. In the final analysis, he said, the president was subject to the Reichstag. All his orders, including under Article 48, had to be countersigned by the chancellor or a minister—and of course, the chancellor or minister would have to have the confidence of the Reichstag. It did not occur to Preuss, nor to any other framer of the Weimar Constitution, that an opponent of democracy could be elected to the presidency and might then try to subvert the system. Still less did anyone imagine that parties hostile to the democratic system would form a majority in the Reichstag. This is a good example of why noted American jurist Oliver Wendell Holmes Jr. said that, to be safe, laws must be drafted with the "bad man" in mind, not the good.

In any case, written laws on their own seldom mean very much, or, rather, they can mean many things, which amounts to the same thing. Laws cannot apply themselves. What matters is the whole cultural and political context in which fallible humans are going to execute them. The Weimar Constitution would have to operate in a political culture substantially shaped before the First World War.

You couldn't exactly call Germany before 1914 a democracy, but it wasn't exactly undemocratic, either. Under the constitution of 1871, Germany was ruled by a hereditary emperor, or Kaiser. For the Empire's last thirty years, from 1888 to 1918, this was Wilhelm II. Like the president of the United States, the Kaiser appointed all the personnel in his administration, chiefly a chancellor to head the government and secretaries for the various departments. They served only at the Kaiser's pleasure. Yet Germany also had an elected parliament, the Reichstag, for which all men aged twenty-five or over had the right to vote. This was a very democratic arrangement at a time when many countries, including Great Britain, still tied the right to vote to taxation or property ownership. No law could be passed without the Reichstag's approval, and the Reichstag's influence on the administration grew steadily over the German Empire's forty-seven-year history.

In fact, in the years between the founding of the new Germany in 1871 and the outbreak of war in 1914, the political momentum had moved in favor of liberal or democratically oriented parties. By contrast, the right-wing parties steadily lost ground. The social groups they represented (the elites of the aristocracy, the military high command, the senior civil service, and big business, but also many humbler rural and agricultural communities) could see their country moving away from them. New groups were coming to prominence in German society. Some of them had long been the poorest and most vulnerable: industrial workers and minorities such as Jews. Right-wing politics began to take on an angrier, often more despairing and desperate tone. At the founding of the German Empire in 1871, loyalty to the monarchy and the Church had been the hallmark of conservatism. The leading conservative newspaper, the *Kreuzzeitung* (Cross Newspaper), bore on its masthead the motto "Forward with God for King and Fatherland." But by 1914 much of the far right had become so frustrated and angry with the rise of liberal and socialist forces that it was turning against tradition. It was becoming a frankly antisystem, almost revolutionary movement, sometimes even venting its anger on the Kaiser.

The right was also losing a culture war. In part, this war was over newer forms of art and literature: socially critical theater, novels that dealt frankly with sex, Expressionist painting. In part it was about anxiety over new forms of media, such as films and mass-circulation newspapers, their pages filled with sports, crime, and scandal, rather than politics and diplomacy. Sometimes it was about social changes. The growing feminist and gay movements were challenging straight male identities. In 1906, a talented con man named Wilhelm Voigt, better known as the "Captain of Köpenick," used a fake officer's uniform and good acting skills to convince a credulous squad of soldiers to help him rob a suburban town hall. His audacity and subversion of the codes of military discipline made him an instant folk hero and media superstar. But many Germans wondered how a criminal could earn such adulation in the land of Bach, Kant, and Goethe. Reflecting on all this, one newspaper moaned in 1908 that "a thoroughly shattering internal or external catastrophe will be needed for the moral recovery of our people."

The catastrophe came in the shape of the First World War. Yet the war did not change the basic elements of German political culture. It accentuated them. Germans entered the postwar era already well accustomed to mass political mobilization and with firmly set patterns of political allegiance. And their political right felt itself more than ever to be fighting a desperate, and likely losing, battle in culture as well as politics.

GERMANS WERE MUCH more deeply affected by the war's end and aftermath than by the course of the war itself. The conservative intellectual Edgar Julius Jung wrote that "the birth hour for me of a new picture of the world was the ghastly time of the breakdown of the fronts, the November Revolution and the occupation of my homeland."

The main element of the postwar order for Germans was the Treaty of Versailles, signed on June 28, 1919. Its terms gave German border territory to Poland, Denmark, Belgium, and France, limited the size of the German army and navy, prohibited an air force, and forbade union with Austria. It also excluded Germany from the new international organization, the League of Nations. But what really got Germans' attention were Clause 231, the "War Guilt Clause," which assigned to Germany sole responsibility for the war's outbreak, and Clause 232, which obliged Germany to pay reparations to the victors. The treaty did not define a specific sum for these reparations. In the time-honored bureaucratic manner, the statesmen at Paris assigned the task to a committee. For the next thirteen years, the payments would be regularly renegotiated.

A persistent myth has it that the Treaty of Versailles was excessively harsh, and that its harshness explains the rage that gave rise to the Nazis. Actually, the treaty was the mildest of the post–First World War settlements. Experts on German and diplomatic history generally agree that it did not cause all the troubles of interwar Europe. Certainly, almost all Germans perceived the treaty to be unjust, which didn't necessarily make it so. What matters is that Germans were divided on how to respond to it: should they try to overcome it by resistance, including armed resistance, or by patient diplomacy?

At least as important as the treaty in fostering postwar division were two myths about the war. One, "the myth of 1914," concerned the war's beginning. The other, the myth of the "stab in the back," was about its ending in revolution and defeat. These myths existed in a dialectical

relationship to each other: unity versus division, patriotism versus treason, victory versus defeat, right versus left, August versus November.
"The very fact that the war began in brilliant summer weather and the
revolution in cold, wet November fog was a severe handicap for the latter," wrote German journalist and historian Sebastian Haffner, who was
an eleven-year-old schoolboy in Berlin at the end of the war. Even the
democrats, said Haffner, felt the force of this contrast. "They never really
wished to be reminded of November 9 and have never celebrated it. The
Nazis who countered November 1918 with August 1914 always had an
easy victory." Although the November Revolution meant that the killing was over and "husbands restored to wives, and life restored to men,"
there was no sense of joy, "only a bad mood, defeat, anxiety, senseless
gunfights, confusion, and bad weather." Certainly, the war had brought
catastrophe. But "its outbreak was associated in almost everyone's memories with a number of unforgettable days of great exaltation and inten-
sity," while the revolution awakened only "dark memories in the minds
of most Germans."

As Haffner's words suggest, this contrast between August and November fundamentally defined the politics of the Weimar Republic. Neither
myth had much basis in reality, the second even less than the first, but
among the Weimar Republic's more fatal defects was that millions of its
people deeply believed things that were verifiably untrue.

According to the myth of 1914, the outbreak of war had brought
sudden, ecstatic unity to the German people. The old and often bitter
divisions between social classes, political parties, religions, and regions
vanished in an upsurge of ardent patriotism. The future playwright Carl
Zuckmayer, still in his teens, was in Holland with his family as war
loomed. On a train heading home to Mainz, he watched a cavalry officer
who had just parted from his wife. The young officer's fate "was my fate
also," Zuckmayer wrote years later. "There was no longer any separation,
any distance." These feelings overpowered him "with an almost religious
force."

Zuckmayer's account is a typical expression of the optimistic mood
of 1914, although even he described several weeping women who presumably did not share it. In fact, such feelings were concentrated among
upper-middle-class young men like Zuckmayer. The idea of a universally

shared outburst of war enthusiasm among Germans is a myth in every sense of the word. There were no opinion polls in 1914, so to gauge how people felt, historians rely on mass demonstrations and newspaper editorials. As for the first, at least as many Berliners took to the streets to protest the outbreak of war as did to cheer it. On July 28, up to one hundred thousand people attended public antiwar meetings in the capital. For the second, newspaper opinion ranged mostly between hope that the war could be contained to general criticism of war's barbarity. Very few papers showed real enthusiasm for what was coming. As the war progressed, with the growth of the Independents on one side and the Fatherland Party on the other, Germans became only more divided. But perhaps for that very reason, the dream of a time when differences melted away and all Germans were united in a common struggle took powerful hold. It was an ideal to which many Germans longed to return, a kind of nationalist lost Eden. The memory of 1914 was invoked by politicians of all stripes during the Weimar years, but it would prove to be the Nazis who really capitalized on it.

The supreme commanders Hindenburg and Ludendorff, and other officers in their orbit, were chiefly responsible for the birth of the "stab in the back" myth. After August 1918, these men recognized that Germany had lost the war militarily, and the only rational thing to do was to negotiate a way out of it as best they could. They were shrewd enough to recruit the Center Party's Matthias Erzberger, the main sponsor of the 1917 Peace Resolution, for this disagreeable task, with an emotional appeal to his patriotic duty. Erzberger, moved to tears, complied and negotiated the Armistice. His reward was to be vilified and libeled by the right. In 1921 he was assassinated.

In the spring of 1919, an army colonel named Max Bauer published a pamphlet titled *Could We Have Avoided, Won, or Broken Off the War?* Bauer had been Ludendorff's main adviser on politics and economic management. His answer to the question in his pamphlet's title was clear: Germany could easily have won the war at the outset. Even later, the prospects had been good. "It was lost," he said, "only and exclusively through the failure of the homeland. Especially the revolution sealed Germany's fate in the most difficult moment."

In November 1919, Hindenburg and Ludendorff appeared together to testify at a hearing of a national assembly committee formed to investigate the causes of Germany's defeat. Both officers wore civilian clothes. They explained publicly that to appear in uniform would show too much respect to the parliamentarians who were to hear their evidence. When the chairman of the committee, a liberal named Georg Gothein, tried to question Hindenburg, the field marshal ignored him and read a statement that Ludendorff had drafted. Gothein tried to interrupt, but Hindenburg coolly went on reading. "In spite of the superiority of the enemy in men and matériel," said Hindenburg, "we could have brought the struggle to a favorable issue." Instead, "divergent party interests began to manifest themselves with us. These circumstances soon led to a disintegration of our will to conquer." Collapse then became inevitable, and "the Revolution was merely the last straw." Hindenburg's statement closed with what would become its most memorable line: "The German army was stabbed in the back."

The myth of 1914 and the myth of the stab in the back had important things in common. Each rested on the idea that willpower was decisive in war, not, as Hindenburg put it, men and matériel. And each could support a conservative, antidemocratic political strategy. In right-wing thinking, the unity of August 1914 was the answer to a breakdown such as November 1918. The ultimate form of this idea was the Nazis' concept of *Volksgemeinschaft*, or "people's community." The Nazis expressly claimed that their *Volksgemeinschaft* would be a re-creation of the spirit of 1914.

The idea that the democrats were responsible for the lost war, and that the Treaty of Versailles was the fruit of a democratic conspiracy against the army—a "stab in the back"—thus began as a lie that the military high command used to excuse its own conduct of the war. Nationalists picked it up to delegitimize democrats. Democrats tended to respond, as the historian Jeffrey Verhey writes, with "that tone of disbelief rational people feel when faced with profound irrationality." Yet millions of Germans believed in the stab in the back anyway. They didn't care if it was rational. It fit their deeper ideological outlook, perhaps even their psychological needs. They *wanted* to believe it.

The fundamental problem of Germany's first democracy was that there was no general social consensus on why the war had been lost or how to respond to the postwar settlement. Those who accepted the outcome of the war acknowledged that Germany had been overwhelmed by a coalition better endowed with resources, manpower, and sea power. British and American capitalism and imperial reach shaped the postwar world. Anglo-American power created globalization long before anyone used the word. The imbalance in world power after the First World War was breathtaking. The Washington Naval Treaty of 1922 provides a revealing snapshot. In the world of the 1920s, cost and technical sophistication made battleships the clearest expression of national might. The Washington Treaty fixed the ratio of battleship construction among the world's major powers for Britain, the United States, Japan, France, and Italy, respectively, at 10:10:6:3:3. No other country rated at all.

So the Germans could accept Anglo-American globalization, work to accommodate themselves to it, and eventually try to make it benefit them. Or, against all odds and perhaps against all reason, they could rebel against it. This was the fundamental foreign policy choice that faced the Weimar Republic throughout its existence.

The cleavages of democrat/nationalist and acceptance/nonacceptance of the outcome of the war tended to line up. Accommodation to the world order was the reflex of Germany's democratic politicians, whereas rebellion was the path of the nationalist right.

The implications were clearly spelled out by no less a figure than General Ludendorff, first in his testimony before the national assembly committee, then in his war memoirs and, a few years later, in his remarkable book *Der Totale Krieg* ("Total War"), revealingly translated into English under the title *The Nation at War*. Even more revealing, and unintentionally accurate, was the English translator's version of Ludendorff's German term *totaler Krieg*. The translator rendered this not as "total war," its literal meaning, but as "*totalitarian* war." A totalitarian society was precisely what Ludendorff had in mind. If Germany had lost the First World War because of a breakdown in discipline on the home front, then the primary task was for the state to control society so effectively that this breakdown could never occur again. Dissent should be brutally crushed. All people should be mobilized in one way or another for the war effort, whether in industry or the armed services. Control of ideas and effective propaganda were vital. Only a dictatorship could do all this, and so, for nationalists who refused to accept the postwar order, German democracy was never an option.

Ludendorff's former adviser Max Bauer put the point bluntly: "To govern means to dominate."

In the early 1920s, Ludendorff began to work with—and pass his ideas on to—that young soldier from the hospital in Pasewalk, Private First Class Adolf Hitler.

2

"Don't Believe Him, He's Telling the Truth"

The officials are worried about his security.

There have been warnings that Communists might attack him. Huge crowds have gathered outside the massive criminal court at 91 Turmstrasse in the Berlin district of Moabit. Most of the people in the crowds are Nazi Stormtroopers, but you can never be sure that a Communist hasn't worked his way in there somewhere. The police—they are there by the score, too—gradually push the demonstrating Nazis into the side streets.

The courthouse has stood at the corner of Turmstrasse and Rathenower Strasse since 1906. They still call it the "new" criminal court. At the other end of the block, where Rathenower Strasse meets Alt-Moabit, is the "old" court, which dates back to the 1870s. In between are remand cells, connected to the two courthouses by secret passages. This is how they bring him in, neatly avoiding the crowds out front.

He wears no uniform today, but rather a standard civilian-issue blue suit. Only the swastika pin in his buttonhole indicates his political role. Moving quickly, the guards bring him and Wilhelm Brückner, his adjutant, to courtroom 664, on the third floor. When he enters, the four Nazi defendants leap to their feet, raise their right arms, and shout, "Heil Hitler!" Thereafter, they refuse to sit down. "Upright and zealous," the Nazi paper

Der Angriff observes with satisfaction, "they showed their Führer *that even in the slammer they were not to be brought low."*

It is May 8, 1931. A subpoena has brought Adolf Hitler, the leader of the National Socialist German Workers' Party, to testify at the trial of the four Nazi Stormtroopers for attempted murder. He faces a difficult challenge. A few months before, the Stormtroopers fired blindly into a crowded dance hall where a Communist hiking club was holding a party. They wounded three young men, who are now represented by the twenty-seven-year-old radical socialist lawyer Hans Litten. Litten wants to use Hitler's own evidence to show that Nazi violence is not just a matter of hot-headed youths getting carried away. It is planned and systematic—and flows from Hitler's direct orders.

Answering Litten's questions will force Hitler into a dilemma. He does, in fact, regularly encourage the Stormtroopers to commit violence. That is their point. But the electoral success the Nazis have been enjoying since the September 1930 election comes from appealing to middle-class voters. To gain this success, the Nazis swear up and down that they are loyal to the Weimar Constitution and the laws of Germany. Middle-class voters—or so it is assumed, anyway—don't like rowdy political activists. Too much Nazi violence might scare them away again. But too much loyalty to the constitution angers the rowdy, revolutionary Stormtroopers, who dream of a violent coup d'état. Whichever way Hitler presents his party's program, he might lose one wing of its supporters—or expose himself to a prosecution for perjury.

This isn't Hitler's only problem as he enters the Moabit courtroom. He hates situations he cannot control, where his cultivated aura of omniscient power might be shown up as hollow. Also, he has deep insecurities about his level of education. Hans Litten, by contrast, is the brilliant product of a prominent family. He was an effortlessly superior law student. In court, he is a precocious master of legal argument, fearless in confrontations with judges, witnesses, and opposing attorneys, and tireless in the pursuit of evidence. He has a photographic memory. To top it off, he is partly Jewish.

The examination lasts three hours. Litten's calm, relentless questioning steadily wears Hitler down. On this day, as on many others, the photographer Leo Rosenthal has smuggled his camera into court. Rosenthal specializes in bootleg courtroom pictures. His sharp eye catches Hitler in a revealing posture: hunched forward, shoulders tense, his expression strained and worried. No mighty Führer there.

The climax comes in an exchange over a pamphlet written by the Nazi Party's propaganda director, Joseph Goebbels. The pamphlet is a quick guide to Nazi ideology for new party recruits. It includes the promise that if the Nazis cannot come to power through elections, "then we will make revolution! Then we will chase the parliament to the devil and found the state on the basis of German fists and German brains!" If Hitler's party is legal, Litten wants to know, how could such a thing be written by the party's designated propagandist and published by the party's official publisher? In the morning session, Hitler evades this question by denying that the party ever approved the pamphlet. Then, over the lunch break, Litten learns that the pamphlet is still being sold at Goebbels's meetings and at all party bookstores. Can Hitler explain this? Hitler cannot. He roars with helpless, inarticulate rage. Litten calmly presses him for an answer.

Then the judge, Kurt Ohnesorge, throws Hitler a lifeline. Ohnesorge is one of the many Weimar jurists who belong to the establishment conservative German National People's Party. It's not that he likes these rowdy Nazis. It's that if he has to choose, he prefers them to the Socialists and Communists. "That has nothing to do with this trial," he says, disallowing further questioning. Hitler is shaken and embarrassed. But he is saved.

The shrewdest commentary on this moment comes from the lawyer and liberal newspaper columnist Rudolf Olden. Writing the next day in the Berliner Tageblatt *(Berlin Daily News), Olden sighs that "Hitler swears and swears to his legality," yet "few believe him." Does Hitler actually want anyone to believe him? The answer, Olden thinks, is that the Nazis' core supporters, especially the young men of the Stormtroopers, do not want to believe him. They prefer talk of violent revolution. But there are disillusioned former Nazis who thought they had joined a revolutionary movement and now believe in Hitler's fidelity to the constitution. They "turn from him in disappointment."*

Olden recognizes Hans Litten's subtle strategy: if Hitler can be made to insist under oath on the legality of his party, and renounce the incitement to violence that he always telegraphs to the Stormtroopers, perhaps it will cost him the rest of his support. Olden sums up the message Litten hopes to send Germans: "Don't believe him anymore, he is telling the truth." Yet

Olden's expectations for his fellow Germans are low. "The people do not catch on that fast," he writes.

Indeed they don't, and Hans Litten will pay for this day in court. A little less than seven years later, thirty-four years old but broken from years of beatings, torture, and hard labor, he will die in something new— something called a concentration camp.

ADOLF HITLER LIED all the time. Yet he also said clearly what he was doing and what he planned to do. This is the essential paradox of Adolf Hitler.

We can see this paradox at work in the memories of people who were close to Hitler. Hans Frank, later Hitler's lawyer and governor of occupied Poland, remembered that when he first heard Hitler speak in 1920, he felt that "here was someone who meant what he said, who didn't want to convince you of anything he didn't believe entirely himself." While working as a reporter in Munich, Konrad Heiden, a Social Democratic journalist and Hitler's first important biographer, witnessed Hitler speaking many times. "At the highpoints of his speeches," Heiden wrote, "he is seduced by himself, and whether he is speaking the purest truth or the fattest lies, what he says is, in that moment, so completely the expression of his being . . . that even from the lie an aura of authenticity floods over the listener." On the other hand, Hitler's finance minister, Count Lutz Schwerin von Krosigk, observed, "He wasn't even honest towards his most intimate confidants. . . . In my opinion, he was so thoroughly untruthful that he could no longer recognize the difference between lies and truth."

In *Mein Kampf*, Hitler addresses his lack of candor with remarkable candor. The less honest a political message, Hitler wrote, the better. Politicians went wrong when they told small and insignificant lies. The small lie could easily be discovered, and then the politician's credibility would be ruined. Better by far to tell "the big lie." Why? In "the greatness of the lie there is always a certain element of credibility," Hitler explains, "because the broad masses of a people can be more easily corrupted in the deeper reaches of their hearts" than consciously or deliberately. "In the primitive simplicity of their minds they more readily fall victims to the big lie than the small lie, since they themselves sometimes lie about small things but would be too ashamed of lies that were too big."

These primitive and simple people would never think to make up "colossal untruths," and they could not imagine that other people might do so. Facts didn't matter at all. "Even when presented with the true facts (*ja selbst bei Aufklärung*)," these ordinary people "will still doubt and waver and will continue to take at least some of [the lie] to be true. For the most impudent lie always leaves something lingering behind it, a fact which is known only too well to all great expert liars in this world."

Hitler's argument then took a curious turn. Having just advocated the telling of huge lies for political gain, he blamed the people he imagined to be his main enemies for being the *real* liars. "From time immemorial," he wrote, "the greatest experts on the possibilities for the application of untruths and slanders were the Jews." The great philosopher Arthur Schopenhauer, said Hitler, had called "the Jew" "the Great Master of Lies." If you did not realize the "truth" of Schopenhauer's insight, or if you did "not wish to believe it," you would "never be able to lend a hand in helping Truth to prevail." What truth it was you might be helping to prevail, which you would presumably do by telling lies yourself, remained unclear.

Another striking fact emerges from these passages: Adolf Hitler had nothing but contempt for the German people. This may sound surprising. Everyone knows that Hitler was an extreme nationalist. He dreamed of making Germany great again, expanding its wealth and territory, and he sought to found an empire on the superiority of the Germans' human matériel. Were Germans not the master race? Yet, if you look carefully at Hitler's words, you notice that from the beginning of his political career to the end, he thought the German people were ignorant, weak, and foolish.

"The mass of the people are lazy and cowardly," he writes in *Mein Kampf*. There was no point in trying to reach them with sophisticated messages about tariffs or tax levels or the minutiae of foreign treaties. It was the mistake of "bourgeois" (middle-class liberal) politicians to try to do this, to deliver learned and dry policy lectures. Ordinary people couldn't understand these things and wouldn't bother to try. To sink into the minds of average people, a message had to be simple. It had to be emotional—hatred worked well—not intellectual. And it had to be endlessly repeated.

Indeed, Hitler vented his frustration over the "quality" of the German people at various times throughout his political career. *Mein Kampf* contains a colorful passage about the corrupting influence of urban poverty on a working-class family. In his so-called *Second Book*—a 1928 sequel to *Mein Kampf* that was published only after the Second World War—he complains that the German people do not "have the average quality of, for example, the English," although if "the Englishman . . . may never reach the dangerous depths of our people" neither would he "reach the illustrious heights." As the Second World War started to go wrong for him, a typical and often-repeated observation was that "if the German people turned out to be weak, they would deserve nothing else than to be extinguished by a stronger people; then one could have no sympathy for them."

There is a second paradox about Adolf Hitler that is at the heart of his puzzling political success. Here was someone, historians always tell us, who was utterly closed off from other human beings. He loved only his mother. Everyone else was just someone to use. He had no close male friends, or, if he did, he broke with them eventually, or even had them killed. He had no close romantic relationships with women. (His mistress Eva Braun was only another person he used.) People who spent a lot of time with him said that he always remained remote and unknowable.

Yet this man had a remarkable intuition for the thoughts, hopes, fears, and needs of other people—both as individuals and as crowds. Ernst Hanfstaengl, Hitler's longtime foreign press chief, described this quality with a technological analogy: "As soon as some person of interest—and there was no one he did not find interesting for a time—joined his company, you could almost see him mobilizing his internal machinery," Hanfstaengl recalled. "The asdic pings of inquiry would go out and within a short time he had a clear image of the wavelength and secret yearnings and emotions of his partner." Hitler's interlocutor would then begin to imagine "that there lay in Hitler immense depths of sympathy and understanding." Hanfstaengl concluded that Hitler "had the most formidable powers of persuasion of any man or woman I have ever met."

As Hanfstaengl noted, this wasn't just a trick Hitler could pull with crowds. He made a favorable impression on a string of seasoned world statesmen, such as the British prime ministers David Lloyd George and Neville Chamberlain. Some of this had to do with his acting ability— one of his great talents, along with speaking. Hitler could appear quiet, modest, and reasonable when it suited him. Similarly, his famous outbursts of rage or his tears of emotion were often just performances, done for effect, as was his trick of shaking hands with supporters while looking deeply into their eyes for a long moment, which seldom failed to leave a powerful and lasting impression.

Hitler practiced tirelessly in order to achieve the effects he wanted, both on crowds and on individuals. His personal photographer, Heinrich Hoffmann, took picture after picture of Hitler in speaking pose, so that he could refine every hand gesture and facial expression. His biographer Konrad Heiden, who relied on many high-level sources within the Nazi Party, wrote about how Hitler prepared to meet an important visitor with the help of his devotee Rudolf Hess. First, Hitler sent Hess to meet the visitor so that Hess could deliver a full report back to Hitler and the two could rehearse the encounter, with Hess playing the role of the visitor. The guest would expect "natural authority," Hess told Hitler. "It is alright for you to speak for a long time. Your will is unshakeable." So he should speak with a firm voice without yelling? Hitler asked. "Certainly," said Hess. Hitler tried the approach, while Hess urged him to speak "more calmly, no passion, commanding. You want nothing from him. Fate speaks . . ." Eventually, Hitler was satisfied with the approach, and after speaking for a few more minutes, he broke off and told Hess, "So, I think we have it now."

Doubt, mystery, and debate endure over most of the things we would really like to understand about Hitler, even after the publication of countless biographies. In *Mein Kampf*, Hitler claims to have learned his antisemitism as a young man in Vienna. He writes that the war was the great experience of his life, and that he served in it with courage and distinction. The shattering news of the Armistice made him decide to enter politics, he explained, to bring retribution to the "November criminals" who had betrayed Germany's war effort and imposed an illegitimate government on the country.

Recent research has picked apart Hitler's account at almost every point. But how, then, do we make sense of the man?

Adolf Hitler was born in Braunau am Inn, Austria, on April 20, 1889. His father, Alois Hitler, was an official in the Austro-Hungarian customs service. A poor farm boy without higher education, Alois had climbed a very long way up the social scale. Hitler's mother was the former Klara Pölzl, twenty-three years younger than Alois and, in fact, his niece as well as his third wife. Hitler was the couple's fourth child but the first to survive infancy.

Right at the beginning we find one of those points of uncertainty with significant implications. Hitler's father was born out of wedlock. Extensive research has never brought full clarity on the identity of Alois's father. His mother was Maria Anna Schicklgruber, and Alois bore the name Schicklgruber until he was thirty-nine. The most likely candidate for his father is one of the Hiedler brothers, Johann Georg and Johann Nepomuk. Johann Georg married Maria Anna after Alois's birth, but never gave his name to his wife's child. It was only after Johann Georg's death that Johann Nepomuk arranged for Alois to be legally declared Johann Georg's son, and only then did Alois change his name to Hiedler, though he spelled it "Hitler." Such spelling variations were common in rural Austria in those days.

Modern research has effectively refuted an old suggestion, endorsed by Hans Frank, among others, that Alois's father came from a Jewish family in Graz for whom Maria Anna had worked as a domestic servant. Yet Hitler himself seems to have feared it was true, and it affected his actions. It may have been behind his obsession with the purity of blood, including his own, and the prohibition in the 1935 Nuremberg Laws of "Aryan" women serving as domestics in Jewish households. Hitler repeatedly ordered Gestapo investigations into his own lineage, which never produced a conclusive result. Most remarkable was the fate of Döllersheim, the Austrian village where his father had been born and his grandmother buried. Immediately after the German annexation of Austria in March 1938, Hitler turned Döllersheim over to the army as an artillery range. The village was evacuated and then the army obliterated it with shell fire, along with its cemetery.

Hitler said later that his father's change of name was the biggest favor

Alois had ever done him. It is hard to imagine rapturous crowds yelling "Heil Schicklgruber"—at least outside of a satire like Charlie Chaplin's film *The Great Dictator.*

Alois's job and general restlessness meant that the Hitler family moved frequently—to Passau, on the German side of the border (where Hitler acquired the Bavarian accent he would have for the rest of his life) and then to Linz, in Austria. Much mythology to the contrary, Hitler seems to have had a reasonably happy early childhood. That Alois was authoritarian and occasionally violent did not distinguish him from many other fathers of that era. For the most part, Adolf did well in school. As Hitler told it later in *Mein Kampf,* the main conflict with his father involved Adolf's future. He dreamed of becoming an artist, whereas, he said, Alois wanted him to be a civil servant. This is another of Hitler's stories about himself that is unlikely to be true. If Alois had wanted Adolf to be a civil servant he would have sent the boy to an academic high school, a gymnasium, which prepared boys for university entrance. Instead, he sent Adolf to a *Realschule,* more of a vocational high school. Probably this amounted to meeting Adolf halfway, allowing him to prepare for a career as an architect.

Of course, this was not how Hitler's life unfolded. Alois died in January 1903, when Adolf was thirteen. A much greater trauma for Hitler was the death of his mother nearly five years later. Klara was diagnosed with breast cancer early in 1907 and died in December. The doctor who treated her recalled that Hitler had taken care of his mother with extraordinary devotion and that he had never seen anyone so grief-stricken as Adolf was when Klara died.

Hitler moved to Vienna, planning to enroll in the Academy of Fine Arts. The school twice rejected his application, marking the start of a seven-year period in which Hitler drifted. He had some savings, and drew an allowance from his aunt, but gradually the money ran out. After a few years he had to earn his own living, which he did by painting postcards and street scenes of Vienna, living in a men's home on the northern edge of the city. In 1913, he moved to Munich but found himself in trouble for evading his Austrian military service.

All the accounts of his life in these years that have come down to us are in various ways unreliable. Some consist of recollections of him from other residents of the men's home or from those who peddled his paintings. Hitler intended *Mein Kampf* to show that he was a budding genius and to underscore his political message by using himself as a didactic example, in the time-honored manner of autobiographers from St. Augustine to Malcolm X. We can safely say, however, that without the coming of the First World War, Hitler would probably have drifted for the rest of his life and died an obscure postcard painter eking out a living in Vienna or some south German town.

But the First World War did come. When Germany declared war in August 1914, Hitler recalled, "I sank down upon my knees and thanked Heaven out of the fullness of my heart for the favor of having been permitted to live in such a time."

Hitler had only contempt for the religious and national diversity of the Austro-Hungarian Empire, and he refused to serve in its armed forces. By contrast, in August 1914 he volunteered right away for the Bavarian Army. (Bavaria, like Saxony, maintained an army separate from the main Prussian-German Army.) Hitler was still an Austrian citizen, and the Bavarians should have refused him. But in the confusion of the war's outbreak, he slipped through and was assigned to the Bavarian Reserve Infantry Regiment 16, known informally as the "List" Regiment, after its first commander. On October 29, Hitler's battalion went into action near Ypres, Belgium. After four days of combat, he wrote later, only 611 of 3,600 men remained. The commander, Colonel Julius List, was among the dead.

Hitler wrote about his reaction to this baptism of fire in a surprisingly minor key: "A feeling of horror replaced the romantic fighting spirit. Enthusiasm gradually cooled and exuberant exultation was choked by the fear of death." All soldiers, he said, had to wrestle with "a struggle between the drive for self-preservation and the call of duty. I too was not spared this struggle." When death was "on the hunt," he went on, "an undefined Something rebelled" and would try to convince "the weak body" that it was really "reason," but "it was actually just cowardice."

Less surprising was his resolution of this personal crisis. Eventually, he wrote, "the internal strife was over and the call of duty carried the day. Already in the winter of 1915–16 this inner struggle was resolved in me. The will was finally absolute ruler." The triumph of the will over the physical reality of the world—one could also say the stubborn refusal to acknowledge that physical reality—would become one of the enduring themes of Hitler's life and political career. It was telling that he treated "cowardice" and "reason" as opposites.

Hitler held a specialized job in the army: he was a *Meldegänger*, or "regimental dispatch runner." This meant that he carried messages from the regimental command to the command posts of the regiment's several battalions. In late 1916, Hitler was wounded and was granted a period of convalescent leave in Germany. In late 1918, he was caught in a gas attack, which was why the signing of the Armistice on November 11 found him in the hospital in Pasewalk. Otherwise, except for rare and brief periods of leave, he remained at the Western Front for the duration of the war. Just after his unit's first engagement, he was promoted to *Gefreiter*, or "private first class." He was never promoted again. He was, however, awarded two medals for bravery: the Iron Cross Second Class and, later, the particular honor of the Iron Cross First Class, as high a decoration as someone of his rank could win.

There is some debate about the meaning of this record. The historian Thomas Weber has recently argued that Hitler's service was not the brave and dangerous experience he claimed. Regimental dispatch runners were based at headquarters, not in the trenches, so it was a safer and more comfortable job than that of front-line riflemen. The officers at headquarters gave out medals to soldiers they knew, not necessarily soldiers who were brave, which could explain Hitler's decorations. To be sure, being a dispatch runner was a dangerous enough job. Hitler was sometimes in the forward trenches, and even those in the rear areas had to fear artillery fire. If we were talking about anyone but Hitler, it would seem petty to criticize his service for having been slightly less potentially deadly than that of a rifleman. The biographer Volker Ullrich comes to a balanced conclusion: "When we weigh up all the sources, we can conclude that Hitler did not stand out as particularly brave but neither did he occupy a 'shirker's job' guaranteed to keep him out of harm's way."

Mystery also surrounds why Private Hitler was never promoted after 1914. In the armies of the Great War, hardly any soldiers who were at the front in 1914 were both still alive and still at the front in 1918. If they were, they had been promoted at least to junior officer status. Fritz

Wiedemann, who was the List Regiment's adjutant in 1916 and 1917, testified after the Second World War that the regiment's officers had judged Hitler lacking in the "leadership qualities" necessary to be a sergeant—Wiedemann's statement all the more amusing because his exact words in German were that Hitler had lacked "Führer" qualities. This provoked laughter in the Nuremberg courtroom. Yet the testimony of Max Amann, a sergeant in the regiment and later the Nazis' publisher, suggests that Hitler himself turned down promotion to junior officer. It is possible that Hitler understood that officer casualties were proportionately higher than those of other ranks and that he wanted to avoid a more dangerous post.

For our story, two things are important about Hitler's service. The first is that however average he may have been in dedication and courage, he was able to turn his four years at the front into a triumph of self-promotion. It is hard to imagine that he could have made his way in postwar German politics without being able to invoke his status as a humble soldier of the Great War.

The second is that he claimed the war had brought him to a political awakening. Hitler makes this point clearly in *Mein Kampf*. He presents himself as the dedicated and courageous soldier who, like his comrades, suffered and bled for four years at the front only to be betrayed by the "November criminals" who brought surrender and revolution. This chapter of Hitler's memoir ends with a clear declaration of a far-right political program. The sacrifices of the war could not have gone only to put "despicable criminals" in power. That the "criminals" were at once both socialists and Jews was clear from his statement that "There is no such thing as coming to an understanding with the Jews. It must be the hard-and-fast 'Either-Or.'" The passage closes with the simple declaration "For my part I then decided that I would take up political work."

Yet there is a more complex reality behind Hitler's political direction. Hitler actually began the postwar era as a *supporter*, not an enemy, of the revolution and the Social Democrats. In the spring of 1919, his fellow soldiers twice elected him to their Soldiers' Council, one of the institutions of the revolution. From reliable electoral data we know that about three-quarters of the men in Hitler's unit voted for the mainstream Social Democrats in the January 1919 election. They would not have voted for Hitler if they did not think he held their views. During a short-lived Communist uprising that created a "Soviet Republic" in Munich in the spring of 1919, Hitler's comrades voted him deputy battalion representative. For the brief life of the Soviet Republic, Hitler's job was to serve as a liaison to the soviet's Department of Propaganda. There is film footage and a still photograph showing him marching in the funeral procession of the Bavarian Independent leader Kurt Eisner, wearing a black mourning armband and another red one in support of the socialist government.

How do we square this with Hitler's later record? It is possible that at this early point he could accommodate himself to any government with a collectivist ideology, of the right or left. More likely, it was simple opportunism. Private Hitler did not want to return to his prewar life of poverty and isolation. The army had become his home as well as his employer, and if staying in it meant serving a radical socialist government, so be it.

It is much the same with Hitler's attitude toward Jews. In *Mein Kampf,* he claims that he developed his antisemitism in prewar Vienna. He illustrated the point with a story of encountering a foreign-looking "phenomenon" in Vienna's inner city, with "long kaftan and black locks." His first thought, so he claimed, was to wonder, "Is this also a Jew?" Hitler watched the man "stealthily and carefully; but the longer I stared at this foreign face and examined it feature by feature, the more the first question reshaped itself in my mind . . . Is this a German?" Driven by this experience, Hitler began to study the "Jewish question" and, he writes, to recognize the "destructive" influence of Jews in all aspects of politics, social life, journalism, and the arts. "Gradually," he writes, "I began to hate them."

Many of Hitler's toxic expressions of hatred for Jews after 1919 can be traced to specific newspapers, pamphlets, and books that he read in Vienna before 1913. Certainly, he absorbed the distinctive Viennese antisemitism of that time. But there is no evidence that he actually held these views until later, while considerable evidence points to his many friendships with Jews, both in Vienna and in the army during the war, and his respect for Jewish culture in general. The hatred seems to have remained latent, like a photographic image waiting for developing solution.

Troops sent by the Social Democratic government in Berlin brutally crushed the Munich soviet in May 1919, and a right-wing state administration took office in Bavaria. A committee began investigating the army's role in supporting the soviet. Hitler was still desperate to stay in the army, but now his recent record of supporting the soviet had become a liability. He began serving the investigators by informing on fellow soldiers who had supported the left-wingers. Max Amann testified after 1945 that before being discharged from the army, he had faced questioning from Hitler about his role in the soviet. We do not know if Hitler informed voluntarily or whether the investigators used his record to pressure him into turning "state's evidence." In either case, the most expedient way for Hitler to cover his flirtation with communism was to leap to the other end of the political spectrum. Yet even in September 1919, as he worked for the committee, a memo he wrote for a superior included "socialism" and "democracy" among the ideals that "make men strive for higher things."

By then Hitler was working under Captain Karl Mayr in the army's counterrevolutionary propaganda unit in Munich. That month, Mayr asked Hitler to draft a reply to a letter about the "danger" of Jews. Hitler's letter reveals a set of ideas that would stay with him. "The Jew," he wrote, was a "leech" interested only in money and never in ideas. Jews were a separate race, not a religious group. Germany's aim must be the "removal" of "the rights of the Jew" and ultimately "the removal of the Jews altogether." Both goals were "possible only under a government of national strength."

Hitler's shift from revolutionary socialism to the antisemitic far right is important for understanding not only him but also what was happening in Germany in 1919. In the first half of the year, Germans lived in what the theologian Ernst Troeltsch called "the dreamland of the armistice," maintaining optimistic illusions about what the postwar world would look like. It was in this period that three-quarters of voters supported democratic parties in the elections to the constituent assembly. But in the course of 1919, Germans learned the terms of the Treaty of Versailles, on which the Allies would accept no negotiation. Later, Hindenburg and Ludendorff began articulating the "stab in the back" myth, and the central government, aided by the Free Corps, violently suppressed the far-left uprisings that rocked Berlin and Munich. It was suddenly a darker world. But the darkness was a product more of the aftermath of the war than of the war itself.

These experiences certainly did not make all Germans swing politically to the right. Nor did they mean German democracy was already doomed to fail. What did happen is that a disillusionment with democracy and the postwar order began to spread. The outcome of the 1920 Reichstag election points to this reality: the Social Democrats' vote fell by nearly half, from almost 39 percent to 21 percent. Their lost supporters moved largely to the Independents and the Communists, while the liberal German Democratic Party's vote bled away to the more right-wing German People's Party and the *much* more right-wing German Nationals.

It seems that for Germans the war was very much like Hitler's time in Vienna: a series of experiences whose meaning could fluctuate until defined by something that happened later. In 1919 the revolution and the terms of the peace treaty began to give the war a darker and more divisive meaning.

SOMETHING MOMENTOUS HAPPENED in the life of Private Hitler as well.

In the course of his work for Captain Mayr, Hitler began giving lectures to groups of soldiers on such themes as "Peace Conditions and Reconstruction," "Emigration," and "Social and Political-Economic Catchwords." As he recalled, "I started out with the greatest enthusiasm and love. For all at once I was offered an opportunity of speaking before a larger audience; and the thing that I had always presumed from pure feeling without knowing it was now corroborated; I could 'speak.'"

By chance, Hitler had discovered something at which he really excelled: whipping an audience into a frenzy with a display of his own intensely felt anger. For even at this stage, Hitler's "lectures" were filled with rage, particularly toward Jews. Although no texts of these lectures survive, from what we know of their subjects and from his own and others' descriptions of them, it is likely he was beginning to link "the Jews" with the loss of the war and the harshness of the conditions that the Versailles peace settlement had imposed on Germany. Hitler's commander actually told him to tone down his antisemitism, lest his lectures be perceived as nothing more than antisemitic agitation.

Captain Mayr began to develop considerable respect for this man—he wrote to him using the salutation *sehr verehrter Herr Hitler* ("very esteemed Mr. Hitler"), an unusual way for a captain to address a private in any army—and began sending him out as an informer to meetings of the many small political parties that sprang up in Munich. In September 1919, Hitler went to observe a group called the German Workers' Party. His mission did not include participating in the discussion. But one speaker advocated Bavaria's separation from Germany, and in his rage at such treachery, Hitler forgot his role and rose to pour a torrent of abuse over the unfortunate man, who thereafter reportedly looked like a "wet poodle." "Man, he's got a mouth on him," party chairman Anton Drexler is said to have observed. "We could use him."

Hitler, still in the army, became a member of the German Workers' Party and began speaking regularly at meetings in beer halls around Munich. His reputation steadily grew, as did the profile of the party and the crowds at its meetings. On February 24, 1920, the party staged its first mass meeting in the large *Festsaal* (Festival Hall) of the famous Hofbräuhaus in the center of Munich. This gathering attracted a crowd of two thousand (perhaps a fifth of them left-wing opponents). For the occasion, Hitler and Drexler had drafted an official party program of twenty-five points—and a little later, at Hitler's urging, changed the party name to the *National Socialist* German Workers' Party. Thereafter the party was known for short as the "Nazis," just as the Social Democrats were sometimes called the "Sozis."

Hitler was not the first speaker that night, but he was the most effective. A Munich police report gives us a good sense of what he had to say. Everywhere, said Hitler, people were in need, in misery, hungry. "How long will this go on, everyone wonders, and what is done about it by officials? Nothing! Because the government is too cowardly to tell the people the truth." The government just told the people over and over: work harder. "But they forget to say that all this work brings no benefit to us, but to our enemies" as "this Peace Treaty spawns ever new and enormous suffering." Hitler turned to another favorite target, Matthias Erzberger, the politician who had signed the Armistice and urged acceptance of the Versailles Treaty. Once, he said, German officials had been famous for their integrity. But how could you expect honesty from any government that included a traitor such as Erzberger? Hitler played deliberately on the fact that Erzberger, who was Catholic, bore a name that sounded Jewish to many Germans. The police report recorded "stormy applause" for Hitler's remarks. "We find it incomprehensible," Hitler continued, "that this gentleman is not yet sitting in a penitentiary." "Lively applause" followed this outburst, too.

Workers, said Hitler, were always being told they should simply emigrate from Germany to Russia. "Wouldn't it just be more practical," said Hitler, "if the Eastern Jews just stayed there, if there are so many jobs?" Here Hitler was playing on the migration of Jews from the former Russian Empire into Germany, a much-discussed feature of German life in the years following the war. Again, his words received "lively applause." "You can imagine what kinds of jobs they are, if these people are emigrating!" he added sarcastically. (Applause, and cries of "Down with the Jew press! Out with it!") "For the crimes of the fraudsters and usurers fines are pointless," Hitler continued, as the crowd yelled, "Beat them! Hang them!" Hitler's reading of the twenty-five points drew applause but also interruptions from opponents, and the police observer thought a brawl might break out at any time. Hitler concluded, "Our motto is only struggle. We will go our way unshakably to our goal."

Konrad Heiden was one of the few people to recognize Hitler's importance from the beginning, and as a young journalist in Munich, he was a frequent spectator at Hitler's early beer hall events. Although Heiden was a Social Democrat, Hitler understood the propaganda value even of his critical attention, and there was a rumor in those days that Hitler would not begin to speak until he knew Heiden was in the audience. Heiden grasped one of the reasons for Hitler's rhetorical success: the magnificent voice that poured out of this otherwise unremarkable man. "Between these two shoulders, modestly drawn together, there is a speech-organ whose tone is virtually the epitome of power, firmness, command and will," Heiden wrote. "Even at rest[,] a rich thunder, in excitement a siren-like howl," a "signal of merciless danger" but also with "flexible human undertones of intimacy, indignation or contempt."

With his steadily growing ego and flair for self-promotion, Hitler always told the story of the Nazi Party's early days with himself as the hero, the political genius and natural leader who went his own way. But he would have amounted to nothing without the circumstances in which he found himself: a pervasive sense of humiliation and fear among Germans (always the most dangerous political emotions), coupled with economic misery. The lost war, the humiliating peace terms, the uncertainty and violence of the revolution and its aftermath (especially in Bavaria) had created a unique mood that Hitler was uniquely able to capture. He convinced thousands who heard him speak that he, and only he, offered a path to salvation, not because he was logically persuasive, but because of the intense conviction with which he offered simple solutions to bewildering problems. The answer to the "Betrayal" of 1918 was to drive out the "November Criminals": the socialists and the Jews. Germany needed to be built up again to the great power status it used to enjoy. Only then could it reverse the terms of the postwar order. He always played on the contrast between August 1914 and November 1918: the first, the great symbol of Germany united and powerful; the second, the moment of its defeat and betrayal at the hands of internal enemies.

Certain of Hitler's character traits became clear in this early period and would go on to shape the kind of leader he became and the movement he led. Most obvious was the mixture of insecurity and its natural complements: intolerance of criticism and bombastic claims to sole authority. The insecurity had been a feature of his personality since his youth. His boyhood friend August Kubizek remembered that after his rejection by the Academy of Fine Arts in Vienna, Hitler would "fly into a temper at the slightest thing." He "cursed the old fashioned fossilized bureaucracy of the Academy where there was no understanding for true artistry. He spoke of the trip-wires which had been cunningly laid . . . for the sole purpose of ruining his career. But he would show these incompetent, senile fools that he could go ahead without them." Kubizek was in Vienna to study music. When his teacher sent him some private pupils, Hitler only grew angrier, envious of his friend's success. "Now one could see, he said . . . there was a great conspiracy against him." Altogether, said Kubizek, "I had the impression that Adolf had become unbalanced."

Hitler was also touchy about his limited education and knowledge.

"Like most basically ignorant people," Ernst Hanfstaengl remembered, "he had this complex about not needing to learn anything." Kubizek once asked Hitler if he planned to go on studying from books alone. "He looked at me, surprised, and barked: 'Of course, you need teachers, I can see that. But for me they are superfluous.'" He routinely voiced scorn for intellectuals and experts. The vast majority of "people who consider themselves educated," he said, were nothing but "a superficial demimonde, pretentious and arrogant bunglers, who don't even realize how laughably amateurish they are." His own expertise, he liked to suppose, was sufficient for all occasions. He once announced that the only book that would ever really matter was the one he was going to write after he "retired." Yet he craved recognition from experts. He was excited and flattered when a University of Bonn psychology professor gave a lecture on concepts from *Mein Kampf.* This was, Hitler said, a "great joy."

THE YEAR 1923 could and should have been a disaster for Hitler, but it ended up bringing an odd sort of victory. Starting with the French occupation of the Ruhr Valley, Germany's industrial heartland, to enforce reparation payments early in the year, Germany experienced the worst string of crises since the war. There were far-left uprisings again in the Ruhr and in central Germany, radical governments came to power in the states of Saxony and Thuringia, and a separatist movement was active in the Rhineland. As inflation became hyperinflation, the country effectively ceased to have a currency system at all. That the exchange rate stood at 17,000 marks to one U.S. dollar in January was bad enough, but that rate became 4.6 million to one dollar in August, 98.9 million in September, 2.2 billion in November, and 4.2 billion in December.

In this atmosphere, and with the example of Mussolini's "March on Rome" of the year before, Hitler decided the moment had come for a coup d'état against the government in Berlin. It began at a mass meeting on November 8 at the Munich beer hall known as the Bürgerbräukeller. For this effort, the Nazis joined with a number of other right-wing groups, and the First World War commander Erich Ludendorff. The next day, however, the uprising failed completely when police opened fire on Hitler and his followers, several of whom were killed or wounded.

Hitler was arrested on November 10. The following spring he, along with Ludendorff, the paramilitary leader Ernst Röhm, and a number of conservative leaders and officers who had been complicit in Hitler's efforts, stood trial before a special court in Munich.

This was where defeat turned to victory. Hitler was clearly guilty of high treason and should have been given a heavy sentence for what had come to be known as the Beer Hall Putsch. As he was not a German citizen, the court should also have ordered his deportation. Yet the judges clearly admired the lead defendant. One of them was heard saying, "What a tremendous chap, this Hitler!" after Hitler's first courtroom speech. Wearing his Iron Cross, Hitler was given full scope to display his speaking talent. The trial received prominent news coverage throughout the country, making Hitler a national celebrity. The court gave him a nominal five-year sentence, but it was understood that he would be released early. In view of his military service for Germany, the court expressly refused to order Hitler's deportation.

Prison in fact proved to be something of a rest cure for Hitler. His "cell" was more akin to a comfortable apartment. Followers came to pay homage, and so many gifts of chocolate, cake, and other delicacies poured in that Hitler gained considerable weight. There is a legend that while in prison Hitler dictated *Mein Kampf* to his devoted acolyte Rudolf Hess. In fact, Hitler first sketched out his ideas in longhand and then typed the manuscript painfully with the hunt-and-peck method. But the book was certainly a product of his time in prison.

The Germany that Hitler found upon his release from prison in December 1924 was a very different place from what it had been a year earlier. This new Germany would prove a much more difficult environment for his movement than the crisis-racked country of the early 1920s. Much of the change had to do with a man who was in every important way Hitler's polar opposite, the dominant figure of German politics in the second half of the 1920s: Gustav Stresemann.

CHANCELLOR FOR JUST a few months in 1923, but foreign minister from 1923 to 1929 (through nine successive administrations, including his own), Stresemann left the greatest mark on the Weimar Republic. Not that his record wasn't controversial. There was debate about him at the time, and that debate has echoed through the years. Was he a "good German," seeking peace and reconciliation abroad along with democracy at home? Or was he a wolf in sheep's clothing, just another aggressive nationalist, one who covered his expansionist schemes with peaceful rhetoric? There was an element of truth in both views. But for Stresemann—as for his most important opposite number, the French foreign minister Aristide Briand—Germany's national interest *required* peace, reconciliation with France, and integration into the world economy.

Opinions about Stresemann as a man varied widely as well. The British journalist Claud Cockburn found him "entertaining provided that you did not believe in him." He had "a wonderful act in which he pretended to be not only fat, which he was, but good-hearted and a little muzzy with beer into the bargain. In reality he was as quick and sharp as a buzz-saw." Theodor Heuss, another Weimar liberal politician, who later became the first president of West Germany, said that he "could not stand" Stresemann. On the other hand, the novelist Thomas Mann called him "this extraordinary man" with a "power of understanding which was simultaneously full of vitality and refined by illness." Viscount D'Abernon, the British ambassador in Berlin in the early 1920s, gave the most nuanced opinion. Stresemann's "capacity for arousing animosity was quite exceptional," he wrote, perhaps because "his mind was too rapid to give an impression of solidity—his enunciation too resonant and the phrases too brilliant to suggest reflection or measure." His talents "earned him a reputation for defects from which he was entirely free— recklessness, and lack of conviction."

Stresemann was born in Berlin in 1878. His father ran a beer distribution business, making Stresemann's background a modest one by the standards of European foreign ministers of the time. But although Stresemann was the youngest of seven children, the family was sufficiently well off to send him to university. He studied political economy at the Universities of Berlin and Leipzig, where he earned a doctorate with a thesis on, of all things, Berlin's bottled beer industry. He was a good student and would have liked to pursue an academic career. But he also needed to make a living, so upon graduating, he worked as an organizer of industrial trade organizations in Saxony and entered politics as a National Liberal.

When he started working, the young woman he wanted to marry turned him down because his future prospects were too uncertain. She made a mistake. With brains, ambition, and hard work, Stresemann rose quickly in both business and politics. He was elected to the Reichstag in 1907, at the age of twenty-eight, in an upset, defeating a Social Democrat who had held the district in a poor part of Saxony. Stresemann was the youngest member of the Reichstag elected that year.

Throughout his life, Stresemann's views were marked by the tension between his liberalism and his nationalism. During the war, he became an advocate of territorial annexations and unrestricted submarine warfare, but also of democratic reforms, which meant he was increasingly caught between the two major Reichstag blocs: the nationalist right, wanting victory without reform, and the left, wanting peace and democratization. Yet the end of the war seemed to bring a change. Stresemann began furiously denouncing the Kaiser's regime and the general staff, expressing admiration only for Prince Max von Baden, the Social Democrats, and Friedrich Ebert. An effort to unite the prewar left-liberals and National Liberals failed, and Stresemann ended up as the leader of a reformed version of the old National Liberal Party, now called the German People's Party.

For the first two years of the Weimar Republic, Stresemann and his party were part of the nationalist-right opposition, hostile to the Treaty of Versailles and the Weimar Constitution. But Stresemann was clearly evolving from wartime nationalist to peacetime advocate of reconciliation, and in his brief chancellorship and his long service as foreign minister, he would lead his country through a similar process. The landmarks of his time in office are remarkable. There was the end of hyperinflation and the stabilization of the German economy in 1924. That same year, the Dawes Plan, arranged by the American banker Charles Dawes, rescheduled Germany's reparations payments, and put the Reichsbank, Germany's central bank, partly under Allied control. In return, the French ended their occupation of the industrial Ruhr district. In 1925, at the Swiss town of Locarno, Germany, France, Belgium, Britain, and Italy recognized the western borders the Paris peace conference had given Germany, and Germany, France, and Belgium agreed never to go to war with one another. A complicated formula was worked out so that Germany, conspicuously, did not have to make a similar agreement about its eastern borders with Poland and Czechoslovakia. The Locarno Treaties cleared the way for Germany's entry into the League of Nations in 1926. Germany was even given a permanent seat on the League's Council (equivalent to the United Nations Security Council today). Two years later, at the initiative of Aristide Briand and U.S. secretary of state Frank Kellogg, France, the United States, Germany, and most other major countries signed the Kellogg-Briand Pact renouncing war as an instrument of state policy. The year 1929 saw yet another reparations payment renegotiation, the Young Plan, which once again lowered Germany's annual payments, though it extended them to the 1980s. Briand took the first steps toward European integration through a set of proposals that he introduced in a speech at the League of Nations. There were agreements for the end of the Allied occupation of the Rhineland and talk about returning the Saar region, which had been under French administration, to German control. All in all, in this brief period, Germany shed its pariah status and returned to its place as a respected and important force in European and world politics.

This is not to say that Stresemann alone was responsible for these developments. Complex factors of domestic and international politics and economics played an important part. Capable officials and diplomats supported Stresemann's work, as did the parliamentary delegations of the democratic parties. The Locarno Treaties were largely motivated by financial pressure, not idealism: without the political stability they brought to western Europe, American banks would have been unlikely to lend money to either France or Germany.

And then there was the relationship between Stresemann and Briand. The French foreign minister had also come from a humble background and had once been an advocate of territorial annexation. Like Stresemann, in the postwar years Briand came to realize that a durable European peace settlement could come only through Franco-German reconciliation. The two men also shared an edgy sense of humor. On one occasion, as the German chancellor Hans Luther delivered a speech about the scale of Germany's problems, Briand interrupted to say, "If you go on, we will all start to cry." Luther was irritated, but when Briand responded with an exaggerated frightened expression, Stresemann erupted in laughter. British foreign secretary Austen Chamberlain later described his colleagues as "a great German and a great Frenchman, who, from amidst the blood-soaked ruins of the past, sought to raise a new temple of peace."

Stresemann recognized the personal parallels between himself and Briand, and recognized as well their common political challenge: making reconciliation palatable to the hard-line nationalists at home. After one meeting in 1926, Stresemann wrote to his son, "Briand said of our conversation, in the language which is only natural to the French, that our souls were as white as the snow on Mt. Blanc." He and Briand had talked for five hours and shared four bottles of wine, but Stresemann added that "We both have to overcome glaciers" in Paris and Berlin. For Briand, the glacier was named Raymond Poincaré, his conservative nationalist rival, who was prime minister for much of the time that Briand was foreign minister. For Stresemann, it meant above all Alfred Hugenberg.

Like Stresemann, Alfred Hugenberg rose from a humble background and entered politics after doctoral studies in political economy and success in business. There the similarities ended. Hugenberg was born in Hanover in 1861. His father, a civil servant, died young, leaving the family impoverished. Hugenberg grew up to be a militant nationalist and a deep believer in the Social Darwinist notions so widespread at the turn of the twentieth century. In 1891, he became one of the founders of the Pan-German League, a nationalist lobby group that would play a baleful role in German politics up to the time of Hitler. In the same year, he earned his doctorate with a thesis on state assistance to farmers and Germany's need to expand its territory, ideas he would pursue throughout his career. After a time as a civil servant, Hugenberg found a position on the board of directors of a bank, and from there, in 1909, he jumped to be chairman of the board of the mighty Krupps steel and armaments concern. On his watch, Krupps's dividends rose from 8 percent in 1908 to 14 percent in 1913.

In 1916, Hugenberg purchased the August Scherl company, one of Germany's large media empires. Scherl owned a string of newspapers and magazines, of which the most important was the *Berliner Lokal-Anzeiger* (Berlin Local Advertiser), which had a daily circulation of roughly 250,000 copies. The other two Berlin-based press empires, Mosse and Ullstein, were owned by Jewish families and advocated liberal politics. August Scherl was not Jewish, and his papers were conservative. In the 1920s, Hugenberg added a news wire service, the Telegraph Union, to his holdings and also purchased the film studio UFA (*Universum Film Aktiengesellschaft*), making himself by far the most important media entrepreneur in Germany. He used these outlets to advance his brand of radical right-wing, nationalist, antidemocratic politics.

Hugenberg became one of the leading figures in the German National Party in the early 1920s, at a time when the German Nationals looked like they might be able to emerge as the single major party of the right. He was not particularly antisemitic, nor did he hanker after the lost monarchy. But in the 1920s he was the most important radical opponent of the Republic, and of Stresemann's policies of accommodation to the postwar settlement.

In the mid-1920s, even the German Nationals had been starting to make their peace with the new democracy. They participated in the administrations of Chancellors Hans Luther in 1925 and Wilhelm Marx in 1927–28, accepting as the price of admission Stresemann's policies on Locarno and the League of Nations. But not Hugenberg. He wanted the party to pursue a relentlessly radical course. In the elections of 1928, the German National vote dropped from 20.5 percent to 14.3 percent. With the moderates weakened, Hugenberg's bid to take over the party leadership succeeded. For Hugenberg, it didn't matter if the party lost votes and members. He feared his party had become nothing but a "mush" of middle-class elements, united only by fear of the Social Democrats. Instead, he wanted a "bloc" in which "the iron clamp of worldview holds us together," and "weak and fluid" elements firm up. Other German Nationals, he said, either had to step aside or give in to his views.

Gustav Stresemann understood that for Germany's new democracy, foreign and domestic policies could not be separated. The goals he sought abroad would stabilize the democratic system at home, whereas another war would only make Germany's divisions even worse and democratic politics impossible. "The new Germany and its recovery," he said in 1926, "can only be based on peace," and peace in turn was possible only through reconciliation with France. He wanted to see closer European economic integration, but he also thought in global terms and did not want that integration to come at the expense of trade and financial ties to Britain and the United States.

That Stresemann achieved an unusual degree of success was evident even to his most committed opponents: later, Hitler would tell his own foreign minister Joachim von Ribbentrop that he "could not have achieved more" than Stresemann had. Yet the progress he made was never easy. His dealings with Briand, Austen Chamberlain, and others were always haunted by mistrust, uncertainty, and grievances from the war. Even as the "spirit of Locarno" spread over Europe in the second half of the 1920s, difficulties were mounting. By the end of 1928, Hugenberg's position in the German National Party and the power of his media empire were Stresemann's main worries. When Hugenberg won the German National leadership, Stresemann wrote to a friend, "The beginning is dark but the end may be civil war." By then, the once-warm relations between Stresemann and Briand had also cooled. Something else changed in 1929. That July, Stresemann told a French journalist that Adolf Hitler, who "preached rebellion not only against the peace treaties but also against the social order," was now a bigger worry for him than Hugenberg.

By that time, Stresemann had been in visibly poor health for a year. On October 2, 1929, he suffered a severe stroke. The next day, a second stroke killed him. He was only fifty-one years old. His loss was recognized immediately by all observers, in Germany and around the world, as a crippling blow to the Weimar Republic and to European peace. No one knew this better than Aristide Briand. It is said that upon receiving the news, Briand cried out, "Order a coffin for two."

AT THE TIME of Stresemann's death, Hugenberg was busy organizing a campaign to fight the emerging Young Plan for restructuring Germany's war reparations payments. The idea was to obtain enough signatures to force a vote in the Reichstag and a national plebiscite. One of the elements of his campaign was an attempt to get the Reichstag to pass a law declaring the collection and payment of reparations in any form by a German official an act of treason. Hugenberg succeeded in enlisting Adolf Hitler, whose party had recently doubled its vote in a state election in Stresemann's former political base of Saxony, as an ally. On September 30, in his last speech, Stresemann had suggested that Hugenberg actually understood that the Young Plan was going to pass no matter what he did. His real goal was to forge an alliance with the Nazis to fight the Republic on a broader front. Once again, Stresemann warned of the dangers of civil war.

The Stresemann era had been a hard time for Hitler. His most important gift was to tap into the anger of people who felt they were the victims of political humiliation and economic hardship. He could do this so well because he felt that anger himself. But he was a crisis politician; he could not modulate. In December 1925, with the Republic well on the road to recovery from the disasters of 1923, he could speak only of the ongoing "German collapse." Seven years after the end of the war, he told a Munich audience, "we can say that we have sunk lower and lower." In April 1926, he described "a decrepit industrial sector with twelve million unemployed," when in fact at any one time that year no more than two million Germans were unemployed. At the high point of the "spirit of Locarno," he went on linking international affairs to the misery of Germans. The Dawes Plan and the Locarno Treaties, he suggested, were simply different expressions of German humiliation and subordination to the other major powers. Stresemann was nothing but a traitor.

The failure of the Beer Hall Putsch had shown Hitler that he could not come to power against the police and the army, only with them. This would mean fighting the Republic on its own terms, through its constitution, by winning elections. Perhaps he was already thinking of how he might be able to trick and subvert the conservative establishment. Working with Hugenberg against the Young Plan was an effective first step.

But Hitler needed things to be a lot worse for Germany than they were in the autumn of 1929. Fortunately for him, forces were at work that would make this happen.

3

Blood May and the Creeper

The police have been prepared for weeks. Altogether, they will deploy between thirteen thousand and fourteen thousand officers on the streets of the capital city. Some have been brought in as reinforcements from other towns. Later, looking back on the events of the year, the Prussian interior minister Carl Severing will lament that there has been "scarcely a day" in which "somewhere in Germany . . . political opponents [were] not shot at, beaten or stabbed." A young carpenter and left-wing activist named Max Fürst is probably right when he says, "[T]he final battle [has] begun."

Despite all the threats and the tension, the day begins quietly enough. In the morning, a few small groups gather in working-class neighborhoods and begin walking to the center of Berlin. All are stopped by the police before they get very far. But as the day goes on, conflict between police and demonstrators begins to escalate. First the police use their truncheons. Then they fire warning shots.

Max Fürst and his young wife, Margot, are among the demonstrators. Max is twenty-three, Margot only sixteen, a slight young woman who, Max says, always looks "forlorn and skinny." Margot's appearance is deceptive. Years later, when she risks her life to save a friend from a concentration camp, she will prove to be a woman of extraordinary moral and physical courage, toughness, and intellect. But here, even the police show her no mercy. Max tells how he and Margot are repeatedly attacked by officers wielding truncheons. They manage to evade them time and again. Once, as a policeman stands behind them and raises his truncheon to strike at Margot, Max just manages to deflect the blow with his arm.

Still the situation escalates. Many unions have held rallies in closed halls. When the rallies end, more people pour onto the streets. The first death comes just before noon, at Hackescher Market. The police claim that protesters attacked an officer and pulled him to the ground. They respond. Several officers fire blindly into the crowd. One demonstrator is hit by three bullets and killed. Four more are injured.

One of the centers of protest is around Kösliner Strasse, in gray, poverty-stricken Wedding, a district of slum tenements north of the central city. During the afternoon, the police repeatedly clear the street of protesters But the residents, who are among the poorest and most vulnerable of Berliners, yell insults at them and, by some accounts, throw stones and bottles. With pistols drawn, the police order residents to stay inside and close their windows.

One man does not respond quickly enough to this order. He is a plumber named Max Gemeinhardt, a member of the Social Democratic Party and its paramilitary organization, the Reich Banner. Gemeinhardt seems to want to talk to the police and stays at his open window. An officer aims directly at him and fires. The bullet catches Gemeinhardt in the forehead. He is the first to die in Wedding. But not the last.

Some protesters respond to the police violence by putting up barricades in Wedding's narrow streets. The police bring in more firepower—machine guns and rifles in addition to pistols. They use armored cars to clear the barricades, and gradually give up any pretense of shooting only in self-defense. They fire wildly into crowds, and aim at other people standing at windows. At around 10:00 p.m., one man is shot through the front door of his building. As his widow later explains, he had been at home and had taken no part in the demonstrations. When the shooting let up, he had decided to go to his mother's nearby apartment, where his seventeen-year-old son had spent the day. Just before he opened the door, a bullet hit him in the arm. Two more bullets struck him in the back. None of his wounds was necessarily fatal, but, says his widow, the doctors could not get through to him because of the shooting, and the police didn't care. The victim "lay in his own blood for about an hour," she says. By the time any help could reach him it was too late.

The same kind of thing happens around Hermannplatz, in the district of Neukölln. A seventeen-year-old boy named Paul Pande wants to go out to buy cigarettes, and on the way, he stops to chat with some people on the street. His mother starts to worry and comes down to get him. Without warning, the police start shooting. Paul's mother, still inside the door of her own building, is hit. She is taken to the hospital, where she soon dies.

It is May 1, 1929: May Day. Soon, much of the press is calling it "Blood May." By any standard, it is an extraordinary outpouring of violence against peaceful citizens. Why does it happen? Part of the answer lies in the attitude of the police to the poorest and most disadvantaged Berliners. The police hate and fear areas such as Neukölln and Wedding, seeing them as nests of criminals and Communists—the police do not always distinguish between the two. The Berlin correspondent for the Chicago Daily News catches the tone when he reports a characteristic police comment on these areas: "We would like to smoke out the whole nest. We would like to go at it very differently, but we are not allowed to."

Since 1889, workers across Europe and even in America have celebrated May Day as their day. Socialist parties and labor unions organize workers' marches and demonstrations. Before 1918, the Social Democratic Party was the keeper of this tradition in Germany. In 1929, two things are different.

One is that the Social Democrats are in power in the state of Prussia and in Germany as a whole. They have to take responsibility for the safety and security of the people of Berlin, which serves as both the state and national capital. Political violence in Berlin has been escalating, especially between the political parties at the extreme ends of the spectrum: the Nazis and the Communists. To contain the violence, Berlin's authorities have banned all outdoor political demonstrations. Because these authorities are Social Democrats, the representatives of workers, many people expect them to make an exception for May Day. But the authorities judge it irresponsible and inconsistent to do so.

This leads to the second difference. Before 1918, Germany's political left was united in the Social Democratic Party. In 1929, the left is bitterly split between the Social Democrats and the Communists. The split was born in *the division between the Social Democrats and the Independents during the war. It was exacerbated by the revolutionary violence of 1918 and 1919, when Friedrich Ebert's government turned the Free Corps loose on left-wing radicals and Rosa Luxemburg and Karl Liebknecht were murdered, along with hundreds of others. The two left-wing parties represent very different groups. The Social Democrats are the party of workers who are inside the system: skilled, relatively well paid, unionized. The Communists are the party of the underclass: the unskilled and the unemployed, the poorest and most vulnerable. These are the people who live in places like Wedding and Neukölln. Unlike the moderate, reformist, and now governing Social Democrats, the Communists are expressly committed to revolution on the Soviet Russian model. And they hate no party, maybe not even the Nazis, more than they hate the Social Democrats. For the Communists, the Social Democrats are not just enemies. They are traitors.*

In 1929, the Communists insist on holding their traditional May Day protests. All the better if it embarrasses the Social Democratic authorities who insist on upholding the ban on marches. In the run-up to May 1, their rival media outlets scream accusations. The Social Democrats are trying to create a "dictatorship in Prussia," say the Communists. The Communists delight in comparing the Social Democrats to the Kaiser's officials, who took the same position on political demonstrations. The Social Democrats reply that "the Communist Party needs corpses" for its propaganda.

There are enough of those. The official report for May 1 lists nine dead and sixty-three badly wounded among the workers and activists, along with twenty-five wounded policemen. The violence worsens over the next two days. By May 3, the police have killed thirty-three civilians, wounded ninety-eight more, and arrested well over a thousand. The police suffer forty-seven officers injured, none dead. The only bullet wound suffered by an officer is self-inflicted. The dead of Blood May are, in the words of the journalist Carl von Ossietzky, victims of the "prestige battle between the Social Democratic and Communist parties."

Communists against Nazis, Communists against Social Democrats, police against workers—all are part of the bitter divisions that, by 1929, are tearing at German society.

THE ROMANISCHE CAFÉ was the place where Berlin's artists and intellectuals met—the great, and those who thought they were great. For this reason, it earned the nickname "Café Megalomania." Yet the guests did not meet on equal terms. The journalist Matheo Quinz compared it to a "bathing establishment with a big pool for swimmers and a small one for nonswimmers." The doorman decided which guests were assigned to which section of the café. The swimmers' pool was for the wealthy, which meant film directors and actors, advertising executives, and a few unusually successful artists. In the nonswimmers' pool were writers, journalists, the rest of the artists, political activists, even Talmudic scholars. There were further divisions: the Communists had their table, the art dealer Alfred Flechtheim presided over another, the Talmudic scholars naturally had yet another. The various small groups and cliques did not mix much. Only the reporter Egon Erwin Kisch had "the astounding capacity of conducting excited conversations at all the tables at the same time," while also reading all the newspapers and keeping an eye on all the women.

The Romanische Café was also a hard-nosed establishment. Any artists the doorman did not know "simply [did] not exist." The house would permit only a few guests, such as playwright Bertolt Brecht, to linger all day over one drink. Most would be told to settle up and leave. The historian Eric Weitz calls it "the perfect symbol of Weimar politics and society—lively, democratic, engaged, and divided and divisive, unable to speak beyond its own circle."

Divisions, increasingly bitter, increasingly irreconcilable, in matters of politics, religion, social class, occupation, and region, were the hallmark of the Weimar Republic. Markus Wolf, for many years the head of Communist East Germany's foreign intelligence service, was the child of an active Communist family in the 1920s. Many years later, he remembered feeling that the political battles between right and left had been "like a gang fight," and that the Nazis were "profoundly, even tribally different from our family."

Because the Republic ultimately gave way to Hitler's dictatorship, it is natural to focus attention on the division between Weimar's democrats and its antidemocrats. No doubt for the politicians in Berlin, the cleavage between democrats and antidemocrats was the most important one. Yet, for the country as a whole, the picture is more complicated. There were no opinion polls then, and so we can't be sure what was in the minds of German voters in each election. But we do know a lot about the various groups of people and the regions that supported the Republic's many political parties.

One of the most important cleavages in Weimar politics involved "political confessionalization." This is a bit of historians' jargon that means that people are often conditioned into voting as they do by the influence of their social surroundings: by their neighbors, colleagues, churches, clubs, newspapers, and other media. Once political confessionalization has taken hold, voters are deeply resistant to changing their preferences. It is similar to being socialized into a church community, which is where the term comes from.

There were three "confessionalized" camps in Weimar Germany: the socialist camp (basically made up of the Social Democrats and the Communists), the Catholic camp (the Center Party and its Bavarian sister, the Bavarian People's Party); and the Protestant middle-class camp (consisting of the conservative German Nationals, the liberal German Democratic Party and German People's Party, and various fringe groups like the Small Business Party).

The crucial point is that for all the top-level political instability in the Weimar Republic—thirteen chancellors and twenty-one different administrations in just over fourteen years—these *camps* remained stable from 1919 to 1933. Each camp was a broad tent, containing democratic and antidemocratic elements. Voter movement generally took place *within* each of the camps, not across camp boundaries. The Social Democrats lost some voters to the Independents early on and to the Communists later, but (after the unusual peak of 1919) the socialist camp's vote settled into a predictable range of about 35 to 40 percent of the total. The Catholic vote moved within an even narrower range—a few points on either side of 15 percent. When the Nazis began to attract a significant number of votes, what really happened is that they took over the Protestant middle-class camp, which hovered a few points ahead of the socialists, from the high 30s to the low 40s. Hitler himself showed that he understood this basic element of German politics when he told a follower in 1925: "We shall have to hold our noses and enter the Reichstag against the Catholic and Marxist deputies." Until 1932, his party never drew very well from voters already "confessionalized" into the socialist group, and still less well from the Catholics. And even at the height of Nazi electoral success in 1932 and 1933, Nazi inroads into those other camps were limited.

The stability and strength of the three camps point again to the pervasive divisions in Weimar German society. Yet there is something else. The fact that Weimar voters stayed within their camps means that the socialization process that put them in these camps in the first place explains their votes as much as formal political ideology—perhaps even more so. Catholics voted for the Center Party or the Bavarian People's Party because they believed it was the proper, Catholic thing to do. Urban workers voted for the Social Democrats or the Communists out of allegiance to their social class. And the Nazis succeeded because their program fit a basic worldview already held by middle-class Protestants.

The confessional divisions in German politics were amplified by the division between Germany's rural and urban citizens—and above all, between Berliners and everybody else.

Our image of Weimar Germany is almost exclusively about Berlin: the art of George Grosz, the music of Kurt Weill and Bertolt Brecht, the architecture of Erich Mendelsohn, Christopher Isherwood's cabaret singer Sally Bowles, a large and open gay community, and sexual experimentation of all kinds. But in 1925 only 4 million of the 62.5 million Germans lived in Berlin. More than a third of the population lived in rural communities, defined as villages with fewer than two thousand inhabitants. Their lives differed enormously from the hypermodern experience of Berlin.

Cities in the early and mid-twentieth century were marked by sharper class differences than we know today. Also, Europeans (then and now) have a different understanding of social class from Americans. Americans generally define class by income. Europeans see it as a much more complex matter of milieu, outlook, and relationship to the economy. A working-class person is someone who brings only his or her own labor to the marketplace, while a middle-class person is someone who owns a business or carries on an independent profession such as law or medicine—whatever his or her income. In the 1920s and 1930s, the line

between the working class and the middle class was immediately apparent from clothing, accent, height, and, as George Orwell memorably
wrote, smell. This urban social structure in turn gave rise to modern
urban politics, with its clear distinction between the parties of the
working class on one hand and of the middle class on the other.

This social structure was absent in rural villages. Instead, the countryside had what the historian Shelley Baranowski calls "the rural
myth." According to this myth, farming was the most admirable form
of work, and rural life was wholesome and authentic, fostering social
stability, harmony, and peace. Certainly, the rural myth depended on
hierarchies, particularly those of aristocratic landlords over agricultural
laborers. Educated professionals such as pastors and schoolteachers held
a middling rank. Yet the hierarchy was supposed to be eased by a sense
of community: everyone in the hierarchy knew his place, and also knew
his duties and responsibilities. Inevitably, maintaining such beliefs
depended on having an "other." Cites were the enemy: they represented
"republicanism, pluralism, mechanization, Americanization, sectari-
anism, experimentation in education, and moral decay, particularly in its
confusion of the proper boundaries between the sexes," in Baranowski's
words.

Religious belief was a huge component of rural identity. In the countryside, church affiliation held up much more strongly than in cities. In
the heavily Protestant Prussian east, the creation of Poland after the First
World War increased the importance of Protestant identity because
Poland defined itself as Catholic. This led to an even greater tendency to
see the core meaning of being Prussian as being Protestant.

Rural people had understandable reasons to be unhappy with the
Weimar Republic. The strength of the Social Democrats meant that
the urban working classes wielded more political clout than had been the
case before the war. This meant that governments made greater efforts
to keep food prices low. Export industries also gained influence, which
made foreign trade deals to reduce tariffs more likely. Rural people would
have benefited more from tariffs on imports and higher food prices. A
1929 trade deal that would have brought in food imports from Poland,
of all places, caused such outrage in rural areas that it could never be
ratified. In 1927 and 1928, world food prices, already in decline, suddenly

fell much faster. Some farmers could not pay their taxes. Others went bankrupt.

The First World War had another important effect on rural areas. It had been necessary to keep large numbers of factory workers at home to produce the guns, planes, and everything else modern war required. This meant that the German Army, like all European armies, had drawn its recruits more from rural areas than from the cities—so farm boys did most of the dying. Rural resentment of cities—above all of Berlin, the supposed home of intellectuals and profiteers, who had been sheltered from the war—grew accordingly.

Berlin's artistic and cultural experimentation had little appeal for more conservative people in the countryside. Nor was this the only thing to dislike about the big city. Berlin was a major industrial center, home to huge manufacturers of electronic goods such as AEG and Siemens, along with makers of machinery, textiles, and much else. As in most countries, ever since industrialization began in the nineteenth century, many Germans had demonized the factory and yearned for a return to farming life. Berlin was also Germany's financial center, and banks and stock exchanges were not popular among people who did not make their living through them.

The social composition of Berlin was distinct from the rest of the country. Berlin had Germany's largest Jewish community, about 7 percent of the city's population, far outreaching the 1 percent of all Germans who were Jewish. Since Berlin was a manufacturing center, it was naturally home to a large number of industrial workers, who were likely to vote for the Social Democratic or Communist parties. In almost all Weimar elections, the Social Democrats and the Communists together won a majority of Berliners' votes. The Nazis, and others on the right, called the city "Red Berlin."

So it is not surprising that for many Germans Berlin became the symbol of everything they hated about the Weimar Republic. The city's name was a kind of shorthand: to be against Berlin was to be against the Weimar order. "Berlin is not Germany," said the Bavarian writer Ludwig Thoma. "In fact it's the opposite—it's corrupted and polluted with Galician filth." "Galician" was code for Jewish, since so many Jewish migrants had come from the Polish region of Galicia. Similarly, the conservative journalist Wilhelm Stapel called Berlin the "cesspool of the Republic." "All too many Slavs and all too many altogether uninhibited East European Jews have been mixed into the population of Berlin," he said, adding that this "embarrassing mixture" determined the character of the city. Stapel disliked "the insolent self-righteousness and the endless cackle of irony" he thought the migrants brought with them, and the arrogance of Berlin intellectuals who thought they had to "Berlinerize" the countryside. What was the cure for Berlin? In part, it was the German cultural tradition of Kant and Goethe; in part, the "iron resolve" of the Lutheran Church. The "peasant of the German countryside," said Stapel, was beginning to rebel.

Disapproval of big-city sexual mores and experimentation took up a lot of space in rural and Church criticisms of Berlin. This was not just about prudishness. There was something deeper at work. For German Protestants, the male-centered family was the core of the social order. Fathers should rule not just at home, but in politics and economic life as well. This meant that all different arrangements of sexual relations or family structure were a direct threat to fundamental political and social power.

Some Berliners responded with condescension or even contempt for their country-dwelling fellow citizens. The poet and children's book author Erich Kästner imagined tourists from the countryside overwhelmed by Berlin's busy and cosmopolitan Potsdamer Platz (home to Europe's first traffic light, among other things) doing "everything wrong" and smiling "painfully" until "they are run over." The journalist Kurt Tucholsky described the "philistines," the "farcical figures" in outdated clothes who populated the rural worlds of Silesia, East Prussia, and Pomerania. He urged Berliners to "speak out" and bring Berlin's light to the dark provinces. Still, he was coolly realistic about the prospects. "The prestige of large democratic newspapers, or artists, and of liberal associations in fact bears no relation to their actual power," he wrote. The "power of reaction—always there and working more skillfully and, above, all, less respectfully"—functioned silently and with the support of "the stock market and the merchant class."

Wilhelm Stapel was correct in writing that the peasantry was beginning to rebel. In 1928, amid the economic crisis that had hit German agriculture, a radical rural protest movement emerged. Calling itself the Landvolk (Country People), it began in the rural northern Prussian province of Schleswig-Holstein, and spread across the rural areas of the north and east. The Landvolk wanted new tariffs on food imports, easier credit, and cuts to social welfare programs (which tended to go to cities). The movement was politically far to the right and used terrorist tactics to make its point, setting off bombs in government buildings. In 1929, in the ultimate symbolic strike against the hated Republic and its hated capital city, the rebels set off a bomb in the Reichstag. The police discovered links between the Landvolk and the then-still-obscure Nazi Party. Soon, the Nazis would succeed in capturing the Landvolk's constituency.

CHRISTIAN GERMANS' ATTITUDES toward Jews also played a role in the country's political divisions.

In the decades before the First World War, antisemitism became the trademark of Germany's political right. It was, as historian Shulamit Volkov has written, a "cultural code," the glue that held together a package of beliefs.

German nationalism was the most important of those beliefs, but there was also worship of power, strong value placed on "manliness" and "virility," social elitism, racism, and misogyny. The nationalist right was hostile to democracy, liberalism, and socialism. It hated cities and loved the countryside. Its values were military rather than commercial, and its reverence for military codes of honor often slid into antimaterialism and anticapitalism. From here it was only a short step to antisemitism. Antisemitism in politics tended to be populist: It claimed to be the cause of the farmer against the grain dealer, the small business owner against the department store. It was anti-elite, anticapitalist, antimodern.

At the other end of the spectrum, *anti*-antisemitism was strongly linked to democratic or socialist political allegiance, pacifism, and feminism. The most famous example is the great prewar Social Democratic leader August Bebel, who proclaimed antisemitism "the socialism of fools." There were many others like him: the historian Theodor Mommsen said that antisemitism involved hatred not only of Jews but of "education, freedom and humanity." The philosopher Theodor Lessing, himself an advocate of feminism, wrote in 1910 that women and Jews possessed a moral superiority based on common oppression.

This use of antisemitism as a code and the role it played in defining the nationalist right grew more pronounced after 1918. Antisemitic outbursts in prewar Germany had generally been responses to crises within a local community or a particular trade. But after 1918, the crises were multiple and nationwide—defeat, revolution, civil war, hyperinflation, unemployment—and the antisemitic responses were correspondingly greater. The Weimar political structure was not necessarily good news for Germany's Jews. Because antisemitism was populist, the prewar, mildly authoritarian German state had tended to oppose it, and the limited power of political parties made it hard for antisemitic activists to gain influence. All this changed in the new democracy. The Weimar Communist Party could sometimes sound as anti-Jewish as anyone else, but generally, antisemitism remained confined to, and defined by, the nationalist right. It functioned a bit the way the issue of abortion functions in defining Democrats and Republicans in contemporary America. For most people, being pro- or anti-Jewish was far from the most important question. But the symbolism of the question made it the point you had to accept, the price of entry to one side or the other.

Once the code was established, antisemitic rhetoric could operate effectively without any mention of Jews at all, as it did in many of Hitler's speeches as he moved closer to power. When Hitler talked about "international finance spiders," or complained that "Today international high finance is Germany's lord and master," his audiences would understand whom he was really talking about.

WEIMAR DEMOCRACY WAS built on foundations that were hardly promising: a catastrophic lost war and a hated peace settlement, followed by extraordinary political and economic turbulence. Yet, against all the odds, the Republic survived and, in the Stresemann era, even flourished. Weimar's unlikely survival and integration into the international community is a forceful reminder that the Republic was not doomed from the start, contrary to another persistent myth.

It was the very stability and success of the Republic that forced its

opponents into a more embittered, desperate, and intransigent posture—
and ultimately into strategies of overcoming democracy that proved
successful. From the middle to the late 1920s, four key insurgencies from
four different directions went to work to undermine German democracy.
Each contributed its part to that democracy's downfall in the early 1930s.

The most obvious of the insurgencies was the extreme nationalist
movement. For most of the 1920s, it was Alfred Hugenberg and the German Nationals who led this insurgency. But they were certainly not
alone. Hitler had his moment in 1923 and 1924, and by 1929, he seemed
to be making a comeback. At the same time, the Landvolk's violent
nationalist protest began to erupt in rural areas.

From the other end of the political spectrum came the Communists, who were just as dedicated as the nationalist right to overturning
the democratic system. In 1928, the Sixth Congress of the Communist
International, run by the Soviet Union and known as the Comintern, proclaimed the doctrine that world capitalism had entered a "third
period" of crisis and revolution. Moscow expected that big business,
desperate to defend itself against revolutionary workers, would turn to
fascists for support. It would also turn for help to Social Democrats,
fraudulent friends of the workers and, in fact, supporters of the capitalists. Communists were supposed to denounce Social Democrats as "Social
Fascists" and to work against them just as much as they worked against
fascists. The Comintern's policy ensured that the breach between the left-
wing parties that had begun with the war and the Spartacus Revolt would
outlast Weimar democracy.

There were two other powerful groups in Germany, big business
and the armed forces, which had different reasons to want the same
thing: the exclusion of the Social Democrats from any share of power.
This meant in practice finding a way to shut down or at least limit the
power of the Reichstag to make laws and shape the formation of a cabinet. Businessmen and soldiers wanted a more authoritarian form of rule.
Higher wage settlements, in many cases instituted by the state-mandated
arbitration scheme, were an increasing irritant for big business. And the
Social Democrats' unwillingness to vote for military expenditures angered
the armed forces. In the later 1920s, both army and business shifted to a
new level of political activity: they formed interest groups, lobbied

sympathetic political parties, and sought a legal strategy for the undermining of democracy.

All these insurgencies took on a new resolution and level of activity
during the "good" years of Weimar, and precisely in reaction to those
good years.

Something else helped them. All societies and all democracies have
divisions: divisions of class, region, religion, gender, ethnicity, and so on.
No democracy can function for long, however, unless ultimately the
divided groups are willing to compromise with one another. But two
important factors made this necessary element of democratic life difficult in Weimar Germany. One was structural. The pressures of war
had divided German society along lines of economic self-interest. In the
Weimar political system, there was a party for every interest group,
which had incentives to lobby and legislate only for its own group's
benefit. People from other groups (workers or employers, farmers or industrialists) were alien, unknown, and in any case represented in their own
distinct party. So the political parties never developed much desire, or
even ability, to "reach across the aisle."

There was also an ideological, almost philosophical dimension to this
problem. Common to all camps in Weimar Germany, democratic as well
as antidemocratic, was a strong cultural prejudice against compromise. On
several occasions in the 1920s, the German Nationals in the Reichstag
made the painful decision to support a policy in the national interest
that directly contradicted their ideology. These votes could have led to
the party's gradual acceptance of the democratic republic. For a while,
around the time of Locarno, this seemed to be happening. Yet, rather
than celebrating the German Nationals' larger vision, democratic politicians mocked their "broken spine," and felt that "if the nationalist voters
stay true to [German Nationals] after this conduct, no party will envy
[them] such voters."

Defenders of democracy were particularly worried when the Social
Democratic Reich president Friedrich Ebert died suddenly in 1925 and
the resulting presidential election was won by Field Marshal Paul von
Hindenburg, who six years before had been one of the main architects
of the "stab in the back" myth.

Paul von Beneckendorff und von Hindenburg was born in Posen in

October 1847 into a family that could trace its military record back to the thirteenth century. For the son of such a Prussian family there was only one possible profession. It is said that when he was a child, his nurse would quell any complaints by yelling, "Silence in the ranks!" He joined the Prussian cadets at the age of eleven and was commissioned as a lieutenant in 1866, just in time to take part in the Battle of Königgrätz, in which Prussia's defeat of Austria assured Prussian dominance of the coming unified Germany. Four years later, in the war against France, he served again with distinction. He was awarded the Iron Cross and was chosen by his regiment to be present at the founding of the German Empire at Versailles. Thereafter, he passed a successful but unspectacular career in the peacetime army, and retired in 1911.

That would have been it for Hindenburg's historical role, had not the First World War intervened. On August 22, 1914, at the age of sixty-six, his life was transformed literally overnight. He was recalled to service to command German forces facing the Russian invasion of East Prussia and immediately thrown into action. The result was one of the few decisive German victories of the war, the Battle of Tannenberg, which put a permanent end to any Russian hopes of advancing into Germany. Hindenburg reaped enormous credit for a victory that had largely been the work of his talented subordinates, his chief of staff General Erich Ludendorff and Lieutenant Colonel Max Hoffmann. Hoffmann later commented that Hindenburg had made about the same contribution to victory as had Hoffmann's little daughter. But from the time of Tannenberg on, Hindenburg was an icon, the savior of Prussia and of Germany. Nothing could dim the heroic aura that surrounded him.

Tall, striking with his perfect military posture, and vigorously healthy until the very end of his life, Hindenburg habitually displayed a solemn expression that most Germans read as a sign of melancholy depth and commitment to duty. He looked like a man who had faced tragedy with resolve, courage, and equanimity, and in the years he was at the center of German affairs (from Tannenberg until his death in 1934), this appearance contributed greatly to the cult that developed around him. Hindenburg embodied German history, and perhaps for this reason he had a masterful, intuitive grasp of how to deploy his symbolic weight in politics.

He married Gertrude von Sperrling in 1879, and they had four children, three of whom survived to adulthood: Irmengard, born in 1880; Oskar, born in 1883; and Annemarie, born in 1891. Hindenburg was devoted to his family and had little social life beyond it: what few close friends he had had died by the time he became president. He was a deeply religious Lutheran with a slight suspicion of Catholics. For someone of his class and background it was hardly surprising that he was a believer in the Prussian code of duty, frugality, honor, and sacrifice. Equally unsurprising, his political views were strongly conservative. His unease with Catholics made him at best an awkward partner of the Center Party. His dislike of the Social Democrats ran much deeper, although he got on well with some individual Social Democrats, such as the long-serving Prussian prime minister Otto Braun, who shared his passion for hunting. Hindenburg was always mystified and sometimes amused when Social Democrats showed that they shared the widespread German reverence for him. Once, when a delegation of Social Democrats visited him at his wartime headquarters to congratulate him on his seventieth birthday, Hindenburg joked that he was becoming so popular with the "comrades" that he would soon have to buy a red cap.

Time and again, he proved himself to be stolid and unflappable. As a young soldier at the Battle of Königgrätz, he came literally within a hairsbreadth of dying as a bullet passed through his helmet and just missed his skull. He calmly went on with his duties. Of his experiences in the Franco-Prussian War, in which his unit took fearsome casualties, he wrote, "I myself do not understand how I could stay so cold-blooded through the whole action." The high command appointed him to lead the German forces on the Eastern Front in the First World War precisely because his calmness would steady the crisis of the Russian invasion and balance the more strategically talented Ludendorff's excitable temperament.

Hindenburg was far from an embodiment of the cultivated ideal so common among Germans. He had no time for literature, apart from Schiller's play *Wallenstein*, which depicts the life of a famous military commander from the Thirty Years' War. He read mainly history and military history, because they were useful for a senior officer. That schools squandered the time of young people by teaching them Latin and Greek only irritated him. His musical taste ran no farther than marches. When he traveled, which he did frequently in his brief retirement between 1911 and 1914, he took interest only in the military potential of the landscape. His real passion was hunting, and he followed it actively until the very last years of his long life.

Yet Hindenburg did not fit the stereotype of a dull and stolid general, nor was he as weak-minded and persuadable as many legends claim. His horizons were wider than those of most Prussian aristocrats of his time. As a young officer, he made a point of attending lectures given by the nationalist historian Heinrich von Treitschke at Berlin University. He was a military modernizer who sought to take full advantage of new technology. His writing was precise and accurate. As president, he read very carefully the briefing materials and documents given to him for signature. To prepare for meetings, he kept notebooks of points he wanted to discuss, and then recorded the results of the meetings so he could give the appropriate instructions. His painstaking preparations made it hard for his advisers to manipulate him.

Even as a regimental commander in Oldenburg in the 1890s, he had demonstrated another enduring characteristic: delegating as much work as possible to subordinates. This practice became notorious, even a sensitive point, during his long wartime partnership with Ludendorff. Many senior officers at the German Army's Supreme Command headquarters had a chance to observe how little work Hindenburg did and how much Ludendorff was obliged to make up for him. The admiral and chief of the naval staff, Magnus von Levetzow—later the chief of police in Berlin under the Nazis—observed a revealing moment while on a visit to headquarters late in the war. At dinner, Hindenburg did little more than tell cheerful anecdotes. Finally, Ludendorff got up and said he had to get back to work in the operations section. Fearing a loss of face in front of the visiting officers, Hindenburg reluctantly added, "I should probably go, too." But Ludendorff told him, "That's not necessary, Herr Field Marshal." Looking a little embarrassed, Hindenburg sat down again with the excuse that he had talked to the operations officers earlier.

Hindenburg was comfortable with the wartime arrangement in which he nominally served under his king and emperor, who had to take ultimate responsibility for what happened. He hated having to make important and possibly unpopular decisions on his own. This persistent desire to avoid responsibility would emerge at the time of the Armistice in 1918 and become one of the themes of his presidency.

When Hindenburg decided to run for president as the candidate of the nationalist right in 1925, the democratic parties were faced with a difficult problem. Hindenburg was too revered a figure for them to mount a frontal assault on him, so the democratic campaign stressed respect for Hindenburg while pouring scorn on those who stood behind him. When Hindenburg eked out a narrow win over the Center Party leader Wilhelm Marx, with 48.3 percent of the vote to Marx's 45.3 percent in the second round of the election, democrats were understandably alarmed.

At first, Hindenburg's scrupulous adherence to the constitution and his willingness to accept the policies of Foreign Minister Gustav Stresemann astonished his critics. In the Reichstag elections of 1924 and 1928, the votes for the far right steadily declined. The Nazi vote fell dramatically, from 6.5 percent in May 1924 to 3 percent in December 1924, and to 2.6 percent in 1928. Meanwhile, support for the Social Democrats rose from 20.5 percent in May 1924 to 26 percent in December to nearly 30 percent in 1928. After the 1928 election, President Hindenburg properly asked the Social Democratic leader Hermann Müller to form an administration. The result was a "Great Coalition" of the democratic parties, from the Social Democrats on the left to Stresemann's moderate right, probusiness German People's Party.

Paradoxically, the death of Weimar democracy began with the democratic outcome of this election.

Even in 1928, a good deal of political disaffection was hidden in the vote totals. Fully a quarter of the electorate had voted for fringe parties, defined as those receiving less than 5 percent of the vote. These were voters who had shed their allegiance to the main parties.

Despite being a party that served the interests of a small, wealthy, and powerful elite, the German Nationals had tried valiantly to invent a populist conservatism. The party's full name, the "German National People's Party," gave the idea: it was the product of a merger of two prewar parties, the German Conservatives and the Free Conservatives. Stresemann's National Liberals had made a similar move by adopting the new name "German People's Party." The plan seemed to be working when the

1924 elections brought the German Nationals vote shares of 19.5 and 20.5 percent. But in 1928, the party's vote fell by 6 percentage points. This setback stimulated Alfred Hugenberg's rise to the party leadership and prompted him to think about making an ally of the dynamic new Nazi movement as a possible path to power.

Big business was also becoming increasingly reluctant to reach compromises with labor. In the wake of the 1918 revolution, unions won full recognition as bargaining partners and a standard eight-hour workday at full pay. The national government set up an arbitration system for industrial wages. These were among Weimar's most distinctive and important accomplishments.

But in the 1920s wage settlements increased rapidly, while worker productivity did not. (In a healthy economy, steady gains in productivity— that is, how much each worker can produce in a given amount of time— pay for both increased wages and corporate profits.) In 1928, hourly wages rose 10 percent (adjusted for inflation) while productivity actually dropped by 4.8 percent. In 1930, the Reich Association of German Industry insisted that the "sharpest criticism" was merited against "a politically dictated economic system that wavers back and forth between capitalism and socialism," and in which, as a result, capitalism got blamed for the "mistakes of socialism." The German political system had to recognize that "there can be no compromise between socialist and capitalist economic methods." The industrialists called for cuts in public spending and wages, and a rollback of government regulation.

As business leaders well knew, this was a program that could be achieved only through the exclusion of the political left, especially the Social Democrats. They began to back groups such as the "League for the Renewal of the German Reich," which aimed at moving the political system away from democracy and toward authoritarianism. Business lobbying of the German People's Party explained the party's much more intransigent posture toward its Social Democratic coalition partners in 1929 and 1930. This was the beginning of Weimar democracy's ultimately fatal political deadlock.

And then there was the army.

A GOOD CASE can be made that General Kurt von Schleicher was the most important actor in the last five years of the Weimar Republic. Seldom has an historical figure borne such a fitting last name. *Schleichen* means "to crawl." A *Schleicher* is a "skulker" or a "sneak." Kurt von Schleicher was a champion manipulator and intriguer, always creeping from door to door, whispering in important ears.

Schleicher was far from a stereotypically severe, humorless Prussian officer. He was down to earth and informal. One of his staff officers, Vincenz Müller, remembered liking the "open and frank" atmosphere in Schleicher's office. German humor often plays on regional accents and dialects, and Schleicher's specialty was cracking jokes in the tough, sarcastic dialect of working-class Berlin, which he could speak fluently. The aggressive sarcasm of Berliners is known as "Berlin snout," and colleagues were not always sure if Schleicher was refreshingly honest or just full of snout. When Müller mentioned that he was engaged to be married, Schleicher reacted with mock horror. "Have you really thought that through?" he asked. He then assured Müller it was a joke. "You'll get used to this kind of remark from me," he said. On another occasion, Schleicher listened as a supporter of Adolf Hitler waxed rhapsodic about Hitler's leadership qualities and political gifts. "Yes, it's just a pity that he's crazy," Schleicher replied. This remark got back to Hitler, who never forgave Schleicher for it.

Schleicher was calculating, manipulative, and often dishonest. Just as his bantering manner could be interpreted in two ways, his self-confidence could also be taken as frivolity. His staff generally admired him, but there were also many who resented or even hated him. "Estrangement is much too mild" to describe what had happened to their friendship, Defense Minister Wilhelm Groener wrote Schleicher in late 1932. "Fury and rage boil in me." The longtime French ambassador to Germany, André François-Poncet, said that Schleicher was "feared rather than liked."

In almost every photograph, Schleicher's expression seems to hover somewhere between a sarcastic smile and a sneer. François-Poncet remembered Schleicher as physically "unprepossessing," with his shaved head, a face "not merely pale but ashen," his "sharp eyes, glittering from a face covered with an unsavory fat, and his tenuous, barely distinguishable lips." In conversation, he was "direct, brutal, bantering, caustic, and often witty . . . His intelligence was lively and brisk rather than substantial and deep."

Schleicher was born in 1882 in Brandenburg. He served as a staff officer during the war, becoming a protégé of Wilhelm Groener. In 1928, Groener became defense minister and named Schleicher chief of the "Ministerial Office," which made Schleicher, in effect, Groener's deputy. Schleicher's job was to be the army's political representative, its designated lobbyist.

The job perfectly suited Schleicher's outlook and his talents. He had an extensive network among politicians in all camps. Above all, he had the ear of President Hindenburg; Hindenburg's state secretary, Otto Meissner; and the president's son, Oskar von Hindenburg—Schleicher and the young Hindenburg were the same age and had served together in the same regiment. This gave Schleicher an unparalleled level of influence. Under the constitution, it was the Reich president who appointed chancellors. For the last five years of the Weimar Republic, Hindenburg acted largely on Schleicher's advice.

With this kind of power, it mattered what Schleicher thought about politics. As early as 1924, he explained his goals to Vincenz Müller, and they changed little in the following years. Schleicher wanted to strengthen the authority of the central government versus the state governments, and of the executive branch and the army versus the legislature. He wanted to stabilize Weimar's crisis-racked economy, not least so that the country could pay for larger armed forces. Yet by the standards of Prussian officers, Schleicher was a progressive thinker. The government, he said, had to resist pressure from business to turn back social innovations, such as the eight-hour workday and health and unemployment insurance. This was a "core question" for social peace and, in turn, for the strengthening of the state.

Finally, Germany had to free itself from the "chains" of the Treaty of Versailles. Schleicher's approach to foreign affairs was characteristically devious. Germany had to get the Allies accustomed to negotiating on equal terms. Then it should move to lift the French occupation of the Rhineland and win back Germany's sovereignty bit by bit—by guile and stealth, not by confrontation. In an unbuttoned moment in 1933,

Schleicher told a group of journalists that he had always thought signing the Treaty of Versailles had been the right thing to do. It had given Germany "a ten-year pause for recovery." "You have to keep the enemy beyond the borders," he explained, "so that internally you can gradually build up again."

At first Schleicher was willing to work with the Social Democrats if doing so could get him where he wanted. But in the mid-1920s, he grew increasingly disenchanted with Germany's political left. He explained later that he thought the Social Democrats had had a "great mission" at the end of the war, to develop a "nationalist Social Democracy." Success would have made the Nazis "superfluous." But in opposing defense spending, the Social Democrats had failed to recognize their mission. Schleicher began to think about how he could exclude them from any share of political power.

This change in Schleicher's thinking opened a fateful chapter of history.

In December 1926, the *Manchester Guardian* broke a story about the secret armed forces, the "Black Reichswehr," that Germany was maintaining in defiance of the Versailles Treaty. The news outraged the Social Democrats, and they withdrew their support from the administration of Chancellor Wilhelm Marx of the Center Party. Schleicher began to imagine a right-wing coalition that could govern without majority support from the Reichstag—in other words, without the Social Democrats. According to the constitution, this was impossible. Schleicher had an idea for getting around the constitution, and Otto Meissner, as Hindenburg's state secretary, the president's most important legal adviser, had the same idea. The constitution gave the Reich president the power to dissolve the Reichstag and call another election. During the time between the dissolution and the election, the chancellor and cabinet could rule without parliamentary interference. This power could be used as a club to intimidate the opposition, and perhaps to keep a minority right-wing administration in office indefinitely.

There was another angle to this strategy. Article 48 of the Weimar Constitution gave the Reich president the authority to rule through executive order if "public security and order" were "seriously disturbed or endangered." In such a case, the constitution expressly authorized the president to make use of the army and to suspend all basic individual rights and freedoms.

The Reichstag could vote to overturn any such order, but the order would stand if there were no majority against it or if the Reichstag had been dissolved pending an election. So an administration with only minority Reichstag support could keep going with the help of the Reich president and Article 48. Such an administration would soon come to be called a "presidential" cabinet, as opposed to a "parliamentary" cabinet. Article 48 of Weimar's democratic constitution was thus a kind of trapdoor through which Germany could fall into dictatorship.

The election of 1928 added a further edge to Schleicher's thinking. The Social Democrats campaigned on the slogan "Meals for children, not a battle cruiser." When they won this election, and Hindenburg asked the party's leader, Hermann Müller, to become chancellor, Schleicher knew that a Müller administration would not bring in the kind of military budget he wanted. He was also skeptical of its competence in economic management. The last straw for Schleicher was the Social Democrats' refusal, true to their campaign promise, to vote funds to build a battle cruiser, even against Chancellor Müller's own wishes. Schleicher began to consider alternatives.

The one he favored was to commission Heinrich Brüning, the conservative leader of the Center Party, to form a new administration. Brüning would lead an "administration of personalities"—for Schleicher, as for President Hindenburg and State Secretary Meissner, this was code for a right-wing presidential cabinet armed with executive orders under Article 48. Such an administration, Schleicher thought, could repair the state's finances and arrange a satisfactory revision of Germany's reparation payments.

Because Brüning was a war veteran, an officer with a good record from the trenches, Schleicher reasoned he could win Hindenburg's sympathy despite being Catholic. Brüning had a doctorate in economics and a reputation as a financial expert. He was a nationalist who stood on the right wing of his party, but his social ideas were moderate, and he might be able to draw support from the Social Democrats. If he had to rule with executive orders, he would not have to rely on military support alone. He would have a following in the country as well.

This last point was a critical one for Schleicher. "You can't rule with bayonets" was one of his most characteristic and often-repeated sayings. He knew that in a modern, industrial society, even a military dictatorship could not rely on repression forever and needed popular support. This was a lesson that many Germans, even on the right, had drawn from the First World War. They had seen how home front morale broke down in the war's last two years, and how this had become a burden for the German army.

In a different way, and with a different emphasis, both Erich Ludendorff and Adolf Hitler had drawn the same lesson. It was a modern lesson, a lesson of total war. It would shape Germany's future through to the end of the Second World War.

THERE IS A folk belief that the Wall Street crash of October 1929 brought on the Great Depression, and that the Depression boosted Hitler and doomed German democracy. In fact, the Depression, diminishing support for the Weimar Republic, and Nazi political success were all more complex, and all began before the crash. A pattern of events in 1928 and 1929—the death of Stresemann and the rise of Hugenberg, growing rural discontent, the Comintern's pronouncement of the "third period," the frustration of business and the army with the constraints of the republic, and the first Nazi successes in local and state elections—showed that Germany was turning decisively away from integration into the postwar world community, which also meant that it was turning away from democracy. Similarly, what happened to the German economy in the late 1920s was an economic perfect storm. Several unrelated economic and financial trends that had been developing well before 1929 converged.

The worldwide drop in food prices that fueled the Landvolk's protests was one of these. Large sections of eastern Germany—Silesia, Pomerania, West and East Prussia—along with the north and west, especially Schleswig-Holstein and Lower Saxony, were predominantly rural and were suffering greatly by the mid-1920s. The farmers of Schleswig-Holstein were the hardest hit by these trends, and not coincidentally, their province was one of the first in which voters turned strongly against the Republic. By 1932, in some areas of Schleswig-Holstein, 80 percent of voters were choosing the Nazis.

Then there was "rationalization"—we would call it "automation" today—the increased use of technology and more efficient management to improve the productivity of industry. The improvements, as they usually do, came at the expense of employment. Although rationalization was concentrated in only a few industries, those industries were important ones, and the job losses were severe. The mining workforce in the industrial Ruhr region dropped by 33 percent between 1922 and 1928. Similar patterns held in metal fabrication and the automobile industry.

It is partly for this reason that in mid-1928 there were already 1.3 million unemployed Germans. A year later, it was 1.5 million. Paying for their unemployment insurance drove the government into the search either for more revenue or for cuts elsewhere in the budget. The Müller administration could not agree on who should bear the costs, and conflict on this issue dogged the administration's last year.

But above all it was questions of finance that led to crisis in Germany.

It was the bull market on Wall Street in 1928, not the crash a year later, that drove Germany into recession. Germany depended heavily on foreign loans, most of them short-term, to meet its reparation payments and keep up consumer spending. The sensational profits to be earned in New York sucked in capital from all over the world and left Germany short.

This was the situation that greeted the new chancellor upon his assumption of office.

IT WAS HEINRICH Brüning's fate that his time as chancellor, from the spring of 1930 to the early summer of 1932, coincided with the worst of the Great Depression. Opponents called him "the hunger chancellor." A dour, ascetic man and a lifelong bachelor, Brüning tended to look funereal in photographs and had nothing remotely resembling the common touch. The distinguished diplomatic historian Zara Steiner writes that Brüning "lacked the flair and the charisma so badly needed at a time of extreme atomization and politicization," and adds a telling point from her own experience as one of Brüning's students: "Even allowing for his age and post-war disillusionment, those who attended Brüning's post-1945 seminars at Harvard . . . will recall his inability to engage and excite his listeners."

Brüning had served at the front as a lieutenant in a machine-gun company, and his political views were largely a product of the war. He hated the revolution of 1918, seeing it as a cause rather than a product of defeat. He also hated the peace settlement and believed that a German politician's highest duty was to get out from under it. As a Catholic, Brüning had been stung by incessant Protestant attacks on German Catholics' patriotism and loyalty. To compensate, he strove to be more nationalist than the Protestant right.

He was always on his strongest ground with foreign statesmen, among whom he generally commanded great respect. François-Poncet wrote that Brüning "inspired confidence and sympathy" with his "air of modesty and integrity, of intelligence and kindliness." His calm dignity made him an effective advocate for his country. "With such a man governing the Reich," said François-Poncet, "surely anyone would readily believe it worth his while to attempt to resolve the Franco-German problem."

He had more trouble with his own people. With his doctorate in economics, today we would call Brüning a policy wonk. As chancellor, he was always trying to bring reasoned arguments to people who would never be reasonable, who in fact had no interest at all in facts or logic. Brüning's problem was that he was too reasonable to grasp such unreason. On one occasion, he decided to take a trip through the poor and mostly rural regions of eastern Germany, in an effort to counter Nazi agitation there. In Breslau, he was met by a crowd of forty thousand people, many of whom threw stones at his motorcade. For Brüning, this only confirmed that "the more absurd and radical were the claims and promises" made by demagogues like the Nazis, "the greater was the success." Although he had represented an eastern district in the Reichstag for six years, "I still could not have imagined how great was the difference between the east and the west with respect to political maturity."

On another occasion he tried to get through to the notoriously stubborn Alfred Hugenberg. Their meeting lasted for hours as Brüning patiently explained his policies. "From the beginning," Brüning recalled, "I deployed whatever I had at my disposal in the way of benevolence, courtesy, warmth, and utmost openness." He was generous enough to tell Hugenberg that Germany needed a strong and conservative Protestant party (Hugenberg's) next to Brüning's Catholic one. After hours of this, Hugenberg abruptly looked at his watch, stood up, and coldly told Brüning he was "more convinced than ever" that he "must fight you and the whole system."

Yet Brüning was one of the few politicians of real stature that Weimar Germany produced, and despite Hugenberg and the Breslau crowds, many Germans, including political opponents, admired and respected him. In the late fall of 1931, Otto Braun, the Social Democratic prime minister of Prussia, offered to resign if Brüning would replace him. Even Hitler felt the effects of Brüning's competence and natural authority when the two met in 1930. Hitler's associate Gregor Strasser said later that Hitler "was so strongly taken by the appearance and behavior of the Reich chancellor that he was only able to free himself from a feeling of inferiority toward Brüning by forming a hate complex against him."

Schleicher was already starting to plan for Brüning's chancellorship in the summer of 1929. He wanted to wait only for the Reichstag to pass legislation ratifying the Young Plan for restructuring Germany's reparation payments, because he thought Chancellor Hermann Müller the best man to get this legislation through.

At a dinner in late December 1929, Schleicher and State Secretary Otto Meissner approached Brüning about their plans to make him chancellor. They explained their ideas about governing with executive orders through Article 48. Brüning would always be able to count on Hindenburg's signature, they promised, and if the Reichstag overturned the orders, Hindenburg would grant a dissolution. Brüning pointed out a flaw in the theory: the cycle of dissolutions and elections couldn't go on repeatedly. Any other solution, such as simply dissolving the Reichstag without calling an election, would violate the constitution and amount to a coup d'état. Schleicher reassured Brüning that he had obtained favorable legal opinions, but he worried that Brüning did not seem keen on the venture and that he, Schleicher, might have to take on the chancellorship himself.

On March 12, 1930, the Reichstag approved the Young Plan. With this hurdle cleared, a long-simmering disagreement between the German

People's Party and the Social Democrats, the ideological bookends of Müller's coalition, over funding unemployment insurance came to a boil. The positions were unsurprising: the People's Party wanted payouts to be cut, the Social Democrats wanted contributions from employers to be raised. The dutiful Heinrich Brüning worked out a compromise, even though he knew that if the compromise failed he would become chancellor. The cabinet approved Brüning's solution, but the Social Democratic caucus voted it down, all but putting their own chancellor out of office. The Müller coalition fell apart. On March 30, Hindenburg swore in Brüning as the eleventh chancellor of the Republic.

It was traditional for the head of a new German administration to give a "Government's Declaration" upon taking office, and Brüning's declaration showed how closely he was following Schleicher's script. His administration, he said, was not "tied to any coalition." He promised that he would not ignore the views of the Reichstag in shaping policy, but he hinted ominously that his administration would be "the last attempt to carry out a solution with this Reichstag." No one could take responsibility for delaying the "vital tasks": "The hour demands fast action." This was code for the threat that if the Reichstag didn't play along, a more radical, unparliamentary solution was on the way.

Brüning duly introduced legislation to stabilize the budget through severe spending cuts and tax increases. On July 16, the Reichstag rejected Brüning's budget. Hindenburg issued two executive orders to do what the legislation would have done. The Reichstag rejected these on July 18. But true to the plan of the presidential cabinet, Hindenburg had also given Brüning a dissolution order. Brüning "sent the Reichstag home," as the saying went, that same day. Until the election, there would be no Reichstag to interfere with Brüning's plans. The budget measures were passed through two new executive orders that Hindenburg issued on July 26. An election was called for September 14.

The Reichstag election of 1930 raised a question to which no one knew either the answer or the consequences that might follow: What if the Nazis did well?

The Nazis' poor result in the election of 1928 did not give the full picture of their standing with the German people. For an imaginative or prescient observer, signs of present and future success were there to be seen. In May 1928, the Nazis came from nowhere to win 7.5 percent of the vote in local elections in the state of Oldenburg. (Three years later, they would become the largest party there.) In Thuringia in 1929, the Nazis won 11.3 percent of the vote and joined the governing coalition, with one of their leading members, Wilhelm Frick, becoming interior minister. In Baden the same year, they managed 7 percent. In 1930, they formed a governing coalition with the German Nationals in the state of Braunschweig.

The Nazis were reaping the rewards of considerable patient grassroots organizing, under the capable management of Gregor Strasser, the head of the party's political organization. They also benefited from the growing hardship and discontent in rural areas, voter volatility within the middle-class Protestant camp, and growing disenchantment with the German Nationals, who were increasingly seen as too hierarchical, elitist, and wedded to the past.

At the end of June 1930, under the terms of the Treaty of Locarno, the French had pulled the last of their occupation troops out of the Rhineland. Germans celebrated what historian Hermann Graml has called "the still thoroughly deceptive feeling of finally being free of all chains and of being able to move freely in the international field." No one in Germany bothered to express gratitude to the French for keeping to their agreement to evacuate the Rhineland early. Instead, there was an upsurge in aggressive nationalism. Violence erupted against those deemed to have "collaborated" with the French. Theodor Duesterberg, the deputy leader of the right-wing veterans' organization the Steel Helmet, demanded the return of West Prussia and Upper Silesia, territories lost to Poland after the war, along with Eupen-Malmedy from Belgium and Alsace-Lorraine from France. It was one thing for a far-right activist to say such things, but quite another for this kind of rhetoric to spread into the chancellor's cabinet. Brüning's minister for the occupied territories, Gottfried Treviranus, a former German National, appeared at a demonstration in his old naval uniform and spoke of the "brothers" in Eupen-Malmedy and in the Saarland, also former German territory under French administration. He went on to describe the "unhealed wounds" of Germany's eastern border, which demanded the "unity and commitment of the entire German people."

It was fitting that the summer of 1930 witnessed a sad coda to the era of cooperation between Gustav Stresemann and Aristide Briand. The previous fall, just before Stresemann's death, Briand had introduced an idea for what he called a "European Union" in a speech at the League of Nations. Briand's idea was to form an association of European states that would foster political and economic integration. As politicians usually do, Briand had a range of motives. He understood that however much goodwill there was between him and Stresemann, neither man would be around for long, and sooner or later, Germany's size and population would once again make it a threat to France. Perhaps the best move for French security was to draw Germany's fangs by integrating the country more completely into a European community. He also had his eye on the United States and the Soviet Union, powers that only a united Europe could equal in economic, political, and military strength. Yet Briand also had an idealistic streak. His postwar career had been dedicated largely to preventing a repeat of the horrors of the Western Front. Like Stresemann, he sought a peaceful Europe.

By the time Briand could follow up on his idea, Stresemann was gone, the much more conservative Brüning was in, and the patriotic hysteria surrounding the Rhineland evacuation was moving France and Germany ever farther from the spirit of Locarno. Nonetheless, in May 1930, the French government submitted a lengthy memorandum on Briand's idea to all the European governments that were League of Nations members. The plan called for a general pact confirming common European values and desire for peace. There would be a European legislature representing the various governments, a standing political committee like the Council of the League of Nations, and a secretariat for routine work. The union should concern itself at first with political and security questions, rather than economic affairs, but the plan anticipated that economic integration would follow improved security. The long-range goal was the creation of a common market for goods and capital. "It is the hour of decision," the memorandum proclaimed, "in which Europe must take its fate into its own hands." To be "united, and to live and thrive," was the urgent task.

It truly was the hour of decision. In the summer of 1930 two roads opened up before Germany, France, and Europe in general. One led to peace and political and economic integration, something that would have looked very much like the Europe of the 1950s. The other led to nationalist self-assertion and competition, to putting one's own country first. Under the conditions of the 1930s the second road brought with it serious risks of war.

Brüning and his foreign minister, Julius Curtius (from Stresemann's party, but no Stresemann), unhesitatingly picked the second road.

In a cabinet meeting on July 8, Brüning said that Briand's intention was to "stabilize the present European situation"—by which he meant France's temporary advantage over Germany. This was something that Brüning could never accept, given his deep resentment of the Treaty of Versailles, the borders it had drawn, and the reparations it had imposed. In response to the French proposal, said Brüning, Germany must set out its "preconditions for a just and lasting European order, in which Germany must have sufficient natural living space." Curtius agreed, telling the cabinet that the German government's response to the French would amount to "a first-class funeral for Briand's action." This response was delivered in Paris on July 15. Although most European countries had responded enthusiastically to Briand's idea, the Germans received effective cover from the British. The British government, more concerned with its empire and with broader global affairs, was just as unenthusiastic as the Germans about Briand's scheme for a European Union.

And so Europe lurched toward a very different future. With the upsurge in nationalism and the recent successes of the Nazis in state elections, there were enough warning signs for Brüning to put off an election until things were calmer. Yet he charged into an election in the fall of 1930 and has been heavily criticized for it ever since. Some of his loyal supporters, such as Hans Luther, himself a former chancellor and, in 1930, the head of Germany's central bank, later claimed that Brüning had no idea how the election would turn out and that the results came like a "thunderbolt." Brüning himself wrote in 1944 that he had expected the Nazis to do even better than they did—but this might have been an effort to look more perceptive in retrospect than he had really been at the time. In his memoirs, published after his death in 1970, he wrote that he had expected the Depression to last four years and he wanted a mandate to take tough measures.

Schleicher, the co-architect of Brüning's strategy, was also unconcerned. He saw the Nazis as nothing more alarming than a right-wing
counterpart to the Social Democrats. A few years later, he explained
his thinking to Vincenz Müller. "My tactics toward Hitler were basically just the same as our tactics in 1918/19 in the Army High Command
toward the revolution," he said. In 1918, this had meant "bringing the
SPD into the state, fighting the radical parts, and preventing disturbances
from them." The difference was that unlike the Social Democrats, the
Nazis were nationalist and militarist. From Schleicher's standpoint, this
was a significant plus. As a soldier, he had his eye on the Nazis' Stormtroopers. "I believed," he told Müller, "that especially in the Stormtroopers
there were many good elements, in which the army absolutely had an
interest for obtaining reserves." For Schleicher, a Nazi electoral success
was something to be welcomed, not feared.

For the next two and a half years, German politics would revolve
around Schleicher's efforts to apply this strategy, to "bring the Nazis into
the state." Schleicher thought that Hitler and the Nazis could be the ideal
foot soldiers in his campaign to remake Germany along more authoritarian lines, to form the necessary mass base that Schleicher thought
even an authoritarian state needed. Yet this made for a delicate dance.
Schleicher was not so foolish that he wanted the Nazis to have any real
power. His strategy always ran simultaneously on two tracks: trying to
find a way to use the Nazis, if they could be used, but preparing to fight
them if they could not be. It probably never occurred to him that he
might be outmaneuvered in his own devious game.

4

The Hunger Chancellor

A dark night in a poor and dismal section of north Berlin. Near the corner of Wilkestrasse and Schönholzer Weg, in working-class Reinickendorf East, the streetlights are few and far between. This is the area called "seven bridges." The overpass for the North Railway can be dimly made out in the gloom. To the west, an iron railing marks the Felseneck garden colony and the wretched huts of the people who live there—mostly the unemployed, the poorest of the poor, those whom "automation and the dying breath of the crisis drove from their workplaces," in the words of the Communist newspaper Die Rote Fahne *(The Red Flag).*

A man named Johann Banuscher and his sister-in-law hurry along the Wilkestrasse, their footsteps loud in the silence of the night. They are stopped suddenly in front of Banuscher's home in the Felseneck colony by a menacing band of eight or ten men. The men are dressed in civilian clothes because of a ban on uniforms, but they are unmistakably Nazi Stormtroopers. The men surround Banuscher. Someone says, "That's him, we have him now." Someone else: "That's one of the Commies. He lives here—he's the one." A third: "Have you checked the proof?" Hermann Schuhr, the Stormtroopers' leader, asks, "Are you Klemke?" Someone pulls off Banuscher's coat to see if he is wearing the corduroy pants they are expecting. The Nazis are taking off their belts, readying them for use as weapons. But Banuscher can prove who he is. The dangerous moment passes as quickly as it came on. "Away, let's go," Schuhr tells his men.

Fritz Klemke, a smooth-faced young man very similar in dress and appearance to Johann Banuscher, was involved in a brawl with some Stormtroopers at the employment office in Reinickendorf ten days before. And just yesterday, there had been another fight, between Communists and Nazis in the nearby Winterstrasse. This time, criminal charges are pending. The Nazis are out for revenge. It is the early morning of January 16, 1932.

They come back two days later.

On the evening of January 18, several units of Stormtroopers from north Berlin, perhaps two hundred men in all, meet for a social evening in a restaurant called the Bergschloss in the Waidmannslust district. As the evening draws to a close, their commander, Werner Schulze, stands to speak to his men. "We're going to do one more little thing today," he says. He orders them to march directly to Felseneck. "If we meet any Commies, bump 'em off and get out of there."

Felseneck is one of the 236 garden colonies in the district of Reinickendorf. In normal times, these colonies provide city dwellers with a bit of space to relax and work on their rosebushes on a Sunday afternoon. January 1932 is not a normal time. Now the unemployed live here, shivering through the winter in tiny shacks, some made of wood, some only of paper.

Remarkably, Schulze's men march to Felseneck with a police escort. Even more remarkably, the police escort melts away as the Stormtroopers approach the colony. The Nazis assume an attack formation, known as a "firing line."

This time, they find the man they are looking for. One witness, an eighteen-year-old Stormtrooper named Heinrich Villwock, later describes how a small group of Nazis beat Fritz Klemke to the ground with metal bars. Suddenly, a tall man with eyeglasses appears, his coat collar turned up to hide his face, and shoves the others aside. He pulls out a pistol and shoots the unconscious Klemke in the back. The bullet pierces Klemke's heart, and he dies on the spot.

The Nazis do not get away unscathed. As a running battle rages along the dark streets near the colony, someone from the Communist Combat League Against Fascism stabs a Stormtrooper named Ernst Schwartz to

death. Schwartz—at fifty-eight, very old to be a Stormtrooper—made his
living as an art teacher.

This winter of 1932 is the trough of the Great Depression in Germany.
This is what Depression politics looks like.

IN THE SMALL hours of September 15, 1930, Hitler returned to the
Bürgerbräukeller in Munich from which, almost seven years before, he
had tried to launch a coup against the Republic. Now the Nazis were holding a raucous Election Night party. The results had been coming in since
10:00 p.m. By midnight, they knew they had won a great victory. After
midnight, Hitler arrived to speak to his followers.

He chose his words carefully. He wanted to celebrate the victory, but
he knew how easily his unruly troops could be inspired to violence. On
this occasion, violent illegality was not what Hitler wanted. The Nazi
Party, he insisted, would reach its goals in a "totally legal way." But since
other parties would now try to "subvert" Nazi unity, Nazis had "to stand
behind the leadership, united as one man."

There was a clear warning in his words, but he was also confident.
"Time is now working for us," he told his followers. "The hour will come
in which we will finally have power."

Not even the Nazis had expected to do so well. Ernst Hanfstaengl,
who was about to become the party's foreign press chief, claimed that
Hitler had told him he would be satisfied with winning forty seats in the
Reichstag. According to Rudolf Hess, Hitler had expected sixty to sev-
enty seats. In fact, the Nazis won 107 seats with 18.3 percent of the vote,
compared to 12 seats and 2.6 percent in 1928. In sixty years of German
national elections, no party had ever risen so far so quickly. Nazi gains
had come largely at the expense of the Protestant middle-class parties:
Hugenberg's German Nationals, whose vote share fell by half again even
from their poor 1928 showing; the post-Stresemann German People's
Party; and the rightward-lurching former Democratic Party, now campaigning as the State Party.

The gloom of German liberals was correspondingly great. The liberal
aristocrat Count Harry Kessler thought it was a "black day for Germany."
The impression abroad must be "catastrophic," he said, the "foreign policy

and financial repercussions devastating." With a 577-member Reichstag containing 107 Nazis, 49 "Hugenbergers" (German Nationals under Hugenberg), and more than 70 Communists, "thus about two hundred and twenty deputies who radically reject the present German state," Germany faced a crisis that only an alliance of "all the forces that approve or at least can tolerate the republic" could overcome. At the same time, however, Kessler thought it "no bad testimony for the German voter" that it was the firmly ideological parties—the Nazis, the Communists, and the Center—that had succeeded, and not the parties that merely represented economic interests. Diarist and novelist Thea Sternheim thought that "most people from a Jewish background are fully disoriented," while the Berlin society reporter Bella Fromm was already thinking about emigrating. British ambassador Horace Rumbold spoke to a senior Prussian official who said he thought the Nazis' campaign funds had been supplied by the Soviets.

For many liberals, the election outcome cast the viability of democracy itself into question. For how could democracy work if it depended on such voters? It was "monstrous," said the liberal newspaper the *Berliner Tageblatt*, that "six million four hundred thousand voters in this highly civilized country" had backed "the commonest, hollowest and crudest charlatanism." A State Party press release lamented that "radicalism has defeated reason," but the party hoped that German voters would "find the path out of confusion back to the constructive center."

When the new Reichstag opened in October, Bella Fromm recorded how the Nazis had celebrated by vandalizing Jewish-owned businesses in Berlin. The party bosses, she wrote, had given a "confused explanation," defending the Nazi violence as a response to Communist "provocation." This defense was "shameless enough," she thought, but "what dismays me more is the exceedingly cautious reaction of conservative papers who were themselves the first to toss the discreet hint about the 'provocation' to the brown [the Nazis' symbolic color] ruffians."

It wasn't just German liberals who were worried. The election outcome brought on a financial crisis, as nervous foreign investors pulled deposits out of German banks. In one month, 800 million Reichsmarks (about 190 million dollars at the 1930 exchange rate, 2.8 billion dollars today) of foreign capital fled Germany. German securities fell sharply on foreign markets, and the Reichsbank lost half its gold reserves and was forced to raise interest rates to 5 percent (compared to 2 percent in New York and 3 percent in London). Because prices were falling, this put the real cost of borrowing money up to 12 percent—a disastrous thing to do when there was already a downturn. Germany's economy slid deeper into depression.

From France, Aristide Briand surveyed the wreckage of what he and Stresemann had tried to do. His reaction to the news of Hitler's success was similar to his reaction to Stresemann's death the year before: he called himself "the first victim of the Nazis."

Why had the Nazis done so well? What were they offering voters, and what did voters see in them?

ONE OF THE challenges of understanding what the Nazi movement was all about comes from a basic fact of politics. The Nazis were politicians: like all politicians, including fascists in other countries, they moved into the political space that was available to them, and their programs evolved to fit the supporters they attracted. This means that the Nazis' ideology and goals were always deliberately vague and always changing. Hitler announced the "Twenty-Five Points" of the Nazi program with much fanfare in 1920, and sternly declared them unchangeable. He then ignored them, and they bore little relation to what he did once he reached power.

Yet the Twenty-Five Points were important for understanding the attraction of Nazism in its early stages.

Some of them were nationalist boilerplate. The party demanded the "union of all Germans in a greater Germany" on the basis of "the right of national self-determination." This meant union with Austria and the Sudeten region of Czechoslovakia, and the recovery of other "lost" territories in Poland, France, and Belgium. It called for revocation of the Treaties of Versailles and St. Germain (the latter was the peace treaty between the Allies and Austria) and the recovery of Germany's overseas colonies, also taken by the victors in the peace settlement.

Other points took a different direction, expressing the anticapitalism, anti-elitism, and social welfare orientation that were at the core of early

Nazi ideology. The party sought to outlaw war profiteering and called for the nationalization of large business enterprises and department stores, profit sharing in big business, "generous old age insurance," better educational opportunities for poor children (coupled with tight state control of the curriculum), "legislation providing for compulsory gymnastics and sports," and "support for all organizations engaged in the physical training of youth."

The concern for the well-being of humble people slid easily into the third main theme of the manifesto, which was hatred for those defined as being outside the nation. Point 7 demanded that "the state make it its primary duty to provide a livelihood for its citizens. If it should prove impossible to feed the entire population, the members of foreign nations (noncitizens) are to be expelled from Germany." Point 8 continued from this to an expression of hatred for immigrants and a demand for deportations: "Any further immigration of non-Germans is to be prevented. We demand that all non-Germans who entered Germany after August 2, 1914, be forced to leave the Reich without delay."

It was primarily Jewish immigration that the Nazis were concerned about. In the wake of the Great War, perhaps eighty thousand Jews, mostly from the former Russian Empire, had fled to Germany. The refugee flow had abated by 1922, but the Weimar Republic was never able to get firm control of its eastern border, which remained a critical political issue. The "Eastern Jews" (*Ostjuden*), as they were called, were culturally very different from the long-settled and assimilated German Jews. Even the 1923 *Baedeker Guide to Berlin* noted their presence in delicately coded language. The "brilliance of the imperial court has disappeared," the guide lamented, while "the large influx of foreigners, mainly from Eastern Europe, is readily noticed." The refugees were fuel to an antisemitism that had already been exacerbated by the bitterness of war and revolution.

Unsurprisingly, therefore, antisemitism was prominent in the Nazi program. Point 4 articulated a kind of racist syllogism. "Only a people's comrade (*Volksgenosse*) can be a citizen. Only a person of German blood, irrespective of religious denomination, can be a people's comrade. No Jew, therefore, can be a people's comrade." For the Nazis, being Jewish had little to do with religion. Someone they defined as Jewish could not change his or her status through conversion. German Jews, no matter how long their families had lived in Germany, no matter how assimilated they might be, no matter if they had converted to Christianity, no matter if they had served and bled in the trenches of the Great War, could not be citizens of a Nazi Reich. The program went on to spell out a few other implications of this dictum. "Noncitizens shall be able to live in Germany as guests only," read Point 5, "and must be placed under alien legislation." Only citizens could hold public offices. All citizens were "to possess equal rights and obligations," but, of course, this equality would kick in only after the Nazis had excluded from the nation anyone they thought did not fit. In practice, once in power, they would add a few other categories of people who did not enjoy equal rights, including political opponents, the physically and mentally handicapped, habitual criminals, Jehovah's Witnesses, the Sinti and Roma, and eventually gay men.

It was highly revealing which point was developed at the greatest length, several times longer than any of the others. Point 23 combined Hitler's antisemitism with his obsession with media and propaganda. It read:

We demand legal warfare against intentional political lies and their dissemination through the press. To facilitate the creation of a German press, we demand:

a) That all editors of, and contributors to, newspapers that appear in the German language be people's comrades.
b) That no non-German newspaper may appear without the express permission of the government. Such papers may not be printed in the German language.
c) That non-Germans shall be forbidden by law to hold any financial share in a German newspaper, or to influence it in any way.

We demand that the penalty for violating such a law shall be the closing of the newspapers involved, and the immediate expulsion of the non-Germans involved.

Newspapers which violate the general good are to be banned. We demand legal warfare against those tendencies in art and literature which exert an undermining influence on our national life, and the suppression of cultural events which violate this demand.

There would be no free press in a Reich ruled by the Nazis. It was clear enough that the Nazis would equate any dissent with the activity of "non-Germans," and therefore a violation of "the general good."

These points covered a lot of ground, some of it obscure and quirky. (Point 19, for instance, opposed the use of Roman law, hardly a burning concern for most Germans.) It is one thing for a political organization to make claims and promises, but quite another for voters to respond. Which points resonated with German voters?

It is important to remember which social groups were likely to vote for the Nazis. By 1930, the pattern was well established: as we have seen, the Nazis took over the Protestant middle-class camp. They made some slight inroads in the Catholic camp, and a bit more into the socialist camp, but still far less than among Protestants. So, the Nazi electorate was essentially a coalition of Protestants from rural areas, particularly in the north and east of the country, with Protestant urban middle classes. Catholics and workers, for the most part, stayed in their traditional camps.

German Protestants had theological and political reasons to dislike the Weimar Republic. They were inclined to take a pessimistic view of human nature and felt that only an authoritarian state could have the strength to correct human sinfulness. Such a state was God's instrument, which meant that subversion or revolution amounted to working against God. Before 1918, the Prussian kings had been the heads of the Prussian Union, the mainline Protestant Church formed in 1817 from a merger of the Lutheran and Reformed (Calvinist) Churches. And ever since 1517, when the German monk Martin Luther stood up to the wrath of the Roman Catholic Church, it had been natural for German Protestants to be highly nationalistic. "The church is politically neutral," said the minister, later bishop Otto Dibelius, "but"—he seemed oblivious to the contradiction—"it votes German National."

The Weimar Republic concentrated into one package everything Protestants didn't like. Before 1918, Protestants had seen a strong monarchy as both a guarantor of moral social life and as a national institution that stood above politics. Weimar cast them adrift in a secular, democratic state where political parties held power—which meant that politics, with all its compromises and corruption, dominated national life and the old moral certainties were gone. Even worse, this new state was the product of a revolution, with a constitution designed by liberals and socialists, and in which the indispensable political party was the Catholic Center. Because of its electoral weight and its place in the ideological middle ground, the Center Party was essential to any Weimar coalition, and was a part of every administration in Prussia and at the national level until 1932. Protestants envied and resented this Catholic political success, and some, such as Gustav Stresemann, wanted to balance it by assembling the various conservative and liberal parties into a Protestant alternative. Given their outlook, it was inevitable that German Protestants would see the way the war ended, and the revolution that accompanied its end, as treason. The Social Democrats, said one Protestant mission director, had not only "made this unnecessary and unbelievably stupid revolution," but they had "betrayed our country solely in order to bring their party to power."

The new republic was modern, secular, urban, and materialistic—all qualities disagreeable to Protestants. "The alliance between materialistic enlightenment and democracy," said a Protestant professor of theology in 1925, "is usually the typical symptom of the decline of civilized peoples." The Republic wasn't merely too Catholic, it was also too Jewish. The nationalist right always hammered home the point that the main author of the 1919 constitution was the Jewish law professor Hugo Preuss. A poem that circulated in Berlin after the end of the war claimed that Germans were now "nothing more than Jews' slaves." Otto Dibelius boasted that he had always considered himself an antisemite. "One cannot fail to recognize," he said, "that in all of the corrosive manifestations of modern civilizations, Judaism played a leading role." As we have seen, the "Jewish Question" was the ultimate code that expressed Germans' attitudes to nationalism and democracy.

Faced with this despised Republic, Protestants worked out a strategy of resistance. The idea was to create a "People's Church" (*Volkskirche*), an attempt to build a Protestant community and to mobilize Protestants for the mass politics of the twentieth century. The People's Church would be a way of defending Protestant Christianity and German values (which Protestants saw as the same thing) in a godless state. For many Protestants, the idea was very close to the idea of a "People's Community" (*Volksgemeinschaft*), the Nazis' term for the national unity they sought.

Richard Karwehl, a pastor from Osnabrück and a friend of the prominent theologian Karl Barth, provides an illuminating example of Weimar Protestant thinking. Karwehl was an anti-Nazi and an astute critic of Nazi ideology, but he was also no lover of the Weimar Republic, and could understand why the Nazis appealed to Protestants. He thought that with the Nazis, Protestants could build "a people's church in the truest sense of the word." God, he said, had placed individual Germans within "our people" and on the soil of "our fatherland." The Nazis, he felt, had rediscovered that the individual belonged to a community. By contrast, the Republic was all about "an individualistic rationalism, far from reality," and "literary intellectuals unconnected in the ether." In the Nazi "movement," there was an "elementary outrage" against "what is unnatural, against certain manifestations of decay and degeneration in modern culture."

Even in what Karwehl didn't like about Nazism—chiefly its racism— we see that German Protestants could be anti-Nazis because they believed *not* in democracy, tolerance, and pluralism, but in another absolute ideology that simply ran counter to the absolutism of the Nazis. This was a crucial element in the outlook of Protestants who opposed the Nazis. Even years later, facing a trial for treason in the Nazis' People's Supreme Court, the Protestant resistance fighter Count Helmuth James von Moltke agreed enthusiastically when the judge, Roland Freisler, told him, "Christianity and National Socialism have one thing in common, Count von Moltke, and only one: we both demand the whole person." After the war, the pastor and resistance hero Martin Niemöller would say that Christ "claimed a totalitarian regime for the world." Karwehl thought that Nazism could never overcome liberalism because the two ideologies were fundamentally *alike*. Nazism sought only to replace liberalism's "arrogance of the individual" with the "arrogance of the race." Neither ideology put God first, and this was the crucial contrast between them and Protestant Christianity.

Yet certainly many (ultimately, perhaps most) Protestants went farther than Karwehl. At a 1931 meeting of the Lutheran group the Inner

Mission, speaker after speaker waxed enthusiastic about the Nazis, to "storms of applause." A Nazi adviser told the gathering that while the Nazi Party was "still looking for its position" in matters of religion, "in the center stands Christ, His person, His word, and His work . . . Get off the fence! Take the fight to Bolshevism! The evangelical church, from its essence and its history, stands the closest to Germandom!"

Protestant hostility to Weimar democracy would prove crucial to the Republic's fate. It wasn't that the Catholic Church was so much more enthusiastic about the Republic. There were plenty of right-wing and nationalistic German Catholics, in keeping with a general pattern in that era of Catholic authoritarianism across Europe—in Italy and Spain, for instance, or in the Action Française of Charles Maurras. German Catholics, though, had a solid political home in the Center Party, and since the Center Party as an institution was committed to the Republic, this limited the threat from antidemocratic Catholics. The Protestant working classes similarly had a political home in the Social Democratic Party or, especially if they were unemployed, the Communists (in which case they had probably left the Church anyway). In Weimar, however, rural and middle-class Protestants were politically homeless—homeless, but looking. And the idea of popular mobilization that lay behind the People's Church fit perfectly with new kinds of political organization that would eventually deliver these politically homeless Protestants to the Nazis.

One thing that the First World War had changed forever was the deference that most people paid to political elites, those who in Germany were called *Honoratioren*, or "notables." "Notables," in prewar Germany, formed a cozy elite of aristocratic and upper-middle-class men. But the war had called forth a nationalism that was popular and egalitarian. The old notables had led the country to disaster. Very few Germans now hankered for the return of the monarchy or the other prewar elites. The day after the war ended, the conservative newspaper the *Kreuzzeitung* replaced its old motto "Forward with God for King and Fatherland" with "For the German People." In Weimar, the people were everywhere.

There is plenty of evidence that the middle classes of the Weimar Republic wanted an egalitarian politics that dealt with social problems but was still nationalist. One German National voter who switched to the Nazis explained that the older parties lacked "the right attitude toward the people—the willingness to help." Populist political movements almost always combine social reform with nationalism.

Perhaps the middle classes could have found what they were looking for in the Social Democrats. But in Weimar Germany a firm social line separated the working and middle classes. Middle-class people might want social reform and social welfare, but the Bolshevik Revolution in Russia was a terrifying warning of where socialism might lead, and no middle-class person wanted to feel a part of the working class. Such a person was never going to vote Social Democrat, and certainly not Communist. In any case, most middle-class people felt, like Schleicher, that the Social Democrats were nowhere near nationalist enough. Here, too, Germany fit the European pattern. Across Europe, fascism developed only in advanced democracies where the socialist left had become successful enough to frighten the middle classes. Fascism was in part a defensive reaction against the left by those who most feared it.

Religious lines were just as tightly drawn. No Protestant was going to vote for the Center Party or its Bavarian sister party. The Protestant political home would have to be found in the Protestant voting camp. For a time in the early 1920s, that meant the German Nationals, which grew to be the second-largest party in 1924. Yet the German Nationals were too hierarchical and tied to old elites and big business to capture a populist electorate for long. In the later 1920s, as we have seen, the middle-class Protestant constituency migrated to rural protest movements and to economic splinter parties such as the Small Business Party. But these splinter parties could never build enough support to bring real change on the national level.

The Nazis, most of whose leaders came from humble backgrounds, could make a strong case for their social agenda. They certainly made pitches to special interests. The Twenty-Five Points, for instance, particularly favored peasants and small shopkeepers. Yet the Nazis always covered these appeals with talk of the *Volksgemeinschaft*, the "People's Community," a concept that drew on the "myth of 1914" and eventually became their political property. Nazis promised to build a Germany in which all would have their place and all would be equal as well as prosperous—all, at least, who were neither Jewish nor unrepentant Marxists.

It is the Nazis' nationalism that requires a closer look. *Globalization* was not a word anyone used in the 1920s or '30s, but people were very familiar with its reality.

More than anything else, the Nazis were a nationalist protest movement against globalization.

THE PASSAGE MAKES startling reading today. It seems to leap from that time to ours:

"The German people have no interest," Hitler wrote, in "a German financial group or a German shipyard establishing a so-called subsidiary shipyard in Shanghai to build ships for China with Chinese workers and foreign steel." The German company would profit from this arrangement, but the German people would "be deprived of many times that sum through lost sales." The more that capitalist interests shaped the economy and shaped politics, the more these kinds of foreign subsidiaries would be established and Germans' jobs sent abroad. "Today some can still smile about these future developments," but "in thirty years people will moan about their results in Europe."

Hitler wrote these words in 1928 in his unpublished sequel to *Mein Kampf.* In doing so, he touched on an issue of central importance for the Weimar Republic.

The political mobilization of the late 1920s, especially among those Protestant groups who would become the Nazi base, was mostly about Germany's vulnerable position in the world economy and financial system. It was anger at trade agreements that motivated the protests of the Landvolk. These agreements had reduced tariffs on food imports at just the time when world food prices were dropping because of huge new supplies from Canada, the United States, and Argentina. Hitler's breakthrough to social respectability was his involvement in Alfred Hugenberg's campaign against the Young Plan. Hugenberg advocated the adoption of a "Freedom Law" that would make it a criminal offense for German officials to participate in the collection of reparations.

In many ways, Weimar Germany was a victim of international forces no German could control. It was the wealth and power of Britain and the United States that had created a world economic system based on free trade and the gold standard. It was their wealth and power that had won the First World War and continued to define the world in which Germany had to operate. Bernhard von Bülow, the state secretary at the Foreign Office during Heinrich Brüning's administration, put it this way: "The Anglo-Saxons in alliance with the French want to make themselves lords of the 'lower' peoples of the earth, and also bring the Germans under their yoke."

Germans who wanted to break with the world economy often focused in particular on the symbolism of the international gold standard—what Nazi activist Gregor Strasser called "the demon gold."

In its simplest terms, the gold standard stipulated that a country's central bank could not issue currency that was not backed by its own gold reserves, and had to be ready at any time to exchange gold for cash at a fixed price. In all countries that adopted the gold standard—and by the time of the First World War, that was most countries—the relationship between currency and gold was fixed by law. There were also rules regarding how much currency could be issued relative to gold reserves. The Bank of England, for instance, had to ensure that any issue of currency over £15.5 million was fully covered by gold in its vaults. The U.S. Federal Reserve operated under a different system, specifying that 40 percent of U.S. currency had to be backed by gold on hand. After 1924, the Reichsbank adopted the same 40 percent requirement. Since each currency's relation to gold was fixed, it automatically followed that its value was also fixed against other currencies. This made international trade and payments easy and predictable, kept inflation down, and forced fiscal discipline on governments, which could not cover their debts by inflating their currencies. If they did, they would be quickly punished by gold reserves flowing out of their central banks as a result of arbitrage on international markets. Being on the gold standard was a badge of honor and respectability for a government, an indication that it accepted the rules of economic orthodoxy and could play in the world's big leagues.

But it was more than that. The gold standard was also a way of imposing liberal democracy and peace on the world: its check on government spending limited military spending just as much as any other kind. In the post–Great War world, the system of liberal capitalism embodied in the gold standard was a way of ensuring that aggressive militarism could not rise again. It was, most of all, a way of keeping Germany tied down and harmless.

This function of restraining Germany financially became even clearer as Germany's reparation payments were increasingly tied to the workings of the gold standard. By 1930, a dense web of international financial arrangements had grown around the reparations system, further limiting Germany's freedom of action. These arrangements included a new world institution, the Bank for International Settlements in Basel, Switzerland, as well as the Dawes and Young Plans and the various agreements and loans related to them. Obviously, the reparation payments themselves cut into a fragile national budget. Under the 1924 Dawes Plan, Germany's payments were to rise to 5 percent of the country's gross domestic product in 1929. To make the payments and keep its fiscal house in order, the German government borrowed large amounts of money from international lenders—six hundred million dollars per year between 1924 and 1928 (or 8.8 billion dollars in today's terms), about half of which went to reparations.

What made Germany particularly vulnerable was that about one-third of this money was in the form of short-term loans, which could be, and were, easily called. Limiting Germans' freedom of action still more was the fact that Germany could not amend the law governing the Reichsbank (which, among other things, kept Germany on the gold standard) without international agreement. In a 1930 speech, Hans Luther, the president of the Reichsbank, went so far as to call Germany's debt burden and the resulting dependence on foreign countries "an invisible occupation." For all its loaded nationalistic rhetoric, Luther's statement was in fact perfectly correct.

Millions of Germans suffered from rage and frustration triggered by their country's powerlessness in a world they had not made, one that seemed to be operating against their interests. Nearly all Germans wanted a way out of this "invisible occupation," but some remedies were more radical than others. Moderates saw the task as one of international lobbying. State secretary Bernhard von Bülow thought the answer was to "enlighten" the "enemy peoples." Brüning stressed that under his administration, the path to achieving "national freedom" would be—in a faint echo of Stresemann—"the way of peace."

The more radical remedies involved an appeal to autarky, the idea that a country can cut itself off completely from the world economy and rely on its own resources, with no imports, exports, or foreign investment. Germany was not an obvious candidate for such a policy. The orthodox view was spelled out by the Reichsbank's Hans Luther. There was no way around the fact, he explained, that the German people "could not feed themselves from their own soil," and so they had to sell industrial products abroad in order to pay for food imports. If this was true, then, as Luther said, Germany's political and economic leadership had to be trusted "beyond the German border posts."

Yet this conclusion assumed that the German people had to accept the world economy as it was. What if that assumption were wrong? Whether they were for or against autarky, it was clear to all Germans that following it as a national economic policy would have to involve a very different kind of politics.

In the early 1930s, the far-right journalist Ferdinand Fried (pen name of Friedrich Zimmermann), who eventually ended up in the Nazi Party and the SS, made autarky his special subject. Fried wrote that for autarky to work, agriculture, industry, and finance would have to be nationalized, resulting in a dictatorship. Because Germany would lose its overseas markets, it would have to replace them by gaining control of eastern and southeastern Europe and forming there a tightly organized "Federation of States." This federation would also depend on securing raw materials from the Soviet Union. The liberal economist Emil Lederer, who opposed autarky, nonetheless agreed with Fried about its political implications. Putting autarky at the center of an economic program, he said, meant promoting the "perpetuation of war."

Autarky was central to the Nazis' political campaigns, and the theme of freeing Germany from its dependence on a hostile world clearly struck a chord with voters. The canny party propagandist Joseph Goebbels wrote in 1932 that a nation that couldn't manage to get control over the "necessary space, natural forces and natural resources for its material life" would inevitably "fall into dependence on foreign countries and lose its freedom." The outcome of the First World War and the nature of the postwar world had proven this clearly, he claimed. "Thus a thick wall around Germany?" he asked. "Certainly we want to build a wall, a protective wall."

One of the political speeches that most resonated with Germans in the early 1930s also dealt with this theme. It came from Goebbels's bitter internal rival, Gregor Strasser.

Strasser was a Nazi leader who didn't quite seem to fit the Nazi mold. To be sure, he was a big man with a shaved head and a booming voice, and he was always ready to mix it up with political opponents. But Strasser liked to socialize with artists and writers, and he relaxed by reading Homer and other classical authors. He was sensitive and friendly, and was the only leading Nazi who enjoyed wide personal respect beyond the party's supporters. The British ambassador called him "the ablest" of the Nazi leaders. The skeptical American reporter H. R. Knickerbocker thought Strasser had the stuff to be chancellor, while the gloomy historian Oswald Spengler said that, next to businessman Hugo Stinnes, Strasser was "the cleverest fellow" he had ever met. Even the Social Democratic politician Wilhelm Hoegner called Strasser "the most trusty and deserving" of the Nazi leaders.

Strasser was born in 1892 to a middle-class Bavarian family. He would have liked to be a physician, but the family's resources would not cover the long period of training, so he decided to become a pharmacist instead. The outbreak of war in 1914 interrupted his education. He joined an artillery regiment and served with distinction throughout the war. In contrast to Hitler, but typically for soldiers of the First World War, he was promoted rapidly, reaching the rank of lieutenant in early 1916. His battalion commander wrote that Strasser "especially distinguished himself by his personal élan, energy, faithfulness to duty, and ability." The commander added that Strasser became "a close congenial colleague whose intelligent advice I listened to willingly and whose cheerful disposition often took us through difficult moments."

Still, Strasser came away from the war with physical wounds from which he would never entirely recover and an inability to settle back into peacetime civilian life. He joined a Free Corps and, in 1922, the Nazi Party. The contrast between August 1914 and November 1918 defined his political views. The war had changed everything beyond recognition: "Any attempt to restore the old 'quiet and order' of July 31, 1914," he said, would be "partially stupid, partially criminal, in any case useless and reactionary." On August 1, 1914, a revolution had broken out that would "bring forth a new world." By contrast, in Strasser's mind, the revolution of November 1918 was nothing but a revolt "born out of cowardice, depravity, incompetence and treason," which Nazis could only hate just as they hated its supporters and their state.

From 1928 to 1932, Strasser headed up the Nazis' party organization and was generally considered to be Hitler's right-hand man; his high administrative competence was often cited as a large factor in the Nazis' electoral successes. He was also a member of the Nazis' Reichstag caucus, and speeches such as the one he gave there on May 10, 1932, help explain why even political opponents (Wilhelm Hoegner, for example) did not despise him.

The speech became, and remains, famous for one line, in which Strasser spoke of the "anti-capitalist yearning" that "today, consciously or unconsciously, has gripped perhaps 95 percent of our people." In Strasser's view, this anticapitalist yearning amounted to the "protest of the people against a degenerate economy." The people demanded that the state "break with the demons of gold, the world economy, [and] materialism, with thinking in export statistics and Reichsbank discount rates."

The Nazis, he argued, wanted to save the rural economy, stop the flood of rural dwellers into the cities, and raise domestic earnings "hand in hand with the affirmation of a closed economic area." Strasser conveyed his message with some coded antisemitism—comparatively subtle by Nazi standards, but unmistakable nonetheless. Leaders of the financial sector were worried, he said, about the "coming autarkic outlook," which would mean that the "easy *rebbach* of international high finance was over." *Rebbach* is a Yiddish word, meaning to "make a killing," in the sense of a profit. There was little doubt what kind of financier— "one reads their names"—Strasser was referring to.

Aside from international finance, Germans felt vulnerable to other hostile outside forces. Germany had a long and winding new border with Poland. Territories that had been German before the First World War (parts of Silesia and West Prussia) had been given to Poland in the peace settlement. These lost territories caused widespread anger among Germans. Gottfried Treviranus, minister for the occupied territories in

Brüning's cabinet, spoke of how "we remember in the depths of our souls" the "unhealed wounds in our eastern flank." It was common to talk of Germany's "bleeding border."

It wasn't just that most Germans wanted these territories back. The border itself was also a threat. Throughout its existence, the Weimar Republic never had the military or police manpower to control the border effectively. This was partly a matter of national security: at a time when the German Army numbered only one hundred thousand men, Poland was a potential threat, and many German policy makers worried about it. Bernhard von Bülow, for instance, wrote in 1930 that "the present border regime with Poland amounts to a constant, very serious threat to East Prussia." But it was also a matter of immigration and refugee control.

The end of the Great War led to a refugee crisis the likes of which the world had never seen before. Particularly in eastern Europe, the former Russian Empire, and the Near East, about 9.5 million people were uprooted by violence or famine, or found themselves on the wrong side of a newly drawn border. Germany's position at the heart of the European continent inevitably made it a crossroads for refugees. Between 1918 and 1922, around a million and a half refugees found their way to Germany. More than one million of them were Germans from former German territories in France and Poland. Hundreds of thousands were Russians fleeing the Bolshevik Revolution, and about eighty thousand were Jews escaping antisemitic violence farther east. This refugee crisis was one of the reasons the United States clamped down on immigration between 1921 and 1924, leaving the problem all the more bottled up in Europe.

The instability of borders and the diversity of borderlands often provokes hypernationalism as a response. Weimar Germany was no exception. A conspicuous number of prominent Nazis—including Hitler himself, of course—came from borderland regions, particularly Silesia and other territories lost to Poland, or from the German diasporas in the former Habsburg Empire and the Baltic region.

There was yet another reason for Germans to worry about their country's vulnerability: one of their major political parties took its orders from a foreign power. Germany had the largest and most successful

Communist Party outside the Soviet Union. The Communists were above all the party of the unemployed, whose ranks had swollen in Germany since the mid-1920s, first due to workplace automation and then due to the Depression. In those days, all world Communist Parties slavishly followed directives from Moscow, which meant that Communists everywhere became in practice little more than instruments of Stalin's foreign policy. In 1928, Stalin worried that an improvement in Franco-German relations would isolate him, and he calculated that weakening the German Social Democrats would help keep France and Germany apart. The result was the Comintern's pronouncement that Social Democrats were "Social Fascists" and that Communists should fight them the same way they fought the Nazis. Because Germany's Communist Party was so large (360,000 members by the end of 1932, with its vote totals rising at every election), Stalin's German auxiliaries could, and did, frustrate efforts at forming a united left that might have kept the Nazis from power.

Nazi ideology was an answer to every dimension of Germany's vulnerability to the world. Some of this the Nazis spelled out clearly at the time, and it contributed to their popularity. Some of it they only hinted at, or they did not explain the full implications of what they planned to do.

Their commitment to withdrawing from the world economy, from trade deals, and from all the financial arrangements that were part of the gold standard, was explicit. As early as the Twenty-Five Points, the Nazis had been clear that noncitizens, including refugees and all Jews, could not count on remaining in Germany after a Nazi takeover or on having any political or civil rights. Even before 1933, the Nazis' paramilitary forces were deploying themselves covertly for defense of the eastern border. The Nazis left no doubt at all that they would ban the Communist Party and that all Communist activists would be subject to arrest, or worse.

Since the early 1920s, Hitler had talked about the need for Germany to claim *Lebensraum*, or "living space," in the east. As people such as journalist Ferdinand Fried had recognized, if autarky were going to work, it would be necessary for Germany to expand the territory it controlled. Hitler agreed completely. He thought that Germany's security was endangered by "market fluctuations," and that "commercial treaties afforded no guarantee for their actual observance." In fact, he said, countries that depended on foreign trade were militarily weak. Germany's own trade had to be carried on sea-lanes dominated by Britain.

"The only remedy," said Hitler, "and one which might seem to us visionary, lay in the acquisition of greater living space." This "living space" could be found only in Europe, and only in one direction: east, toward the Soviet Union, with its Ukrainian black earth.

In his public pronouncements before he came to power, Hitler left the full implications of this idea in soft focus. But unlike Fried, he was not thinking of a federation of central and eastern European states under German control. Hitler's entire program was fundamentally directed to making Germany economically self-sufficient by conquering the Soviet Union. For that, a great war would be necessary, and so the German people had to learn the lessons of the last war. These lessons had been spelled out most clearly by President Hindenburg's former chief of staff, Erich Ludendorff, in a series of books and articles between 1919 and 1935. Germany would have to mobilize its population much more effectively than before to fight a total war. A greater military and industrial effort would have to be squeezed from the people. There could be no breakdown in morale, no dissent from a rebellious left, and—this point was central for both Ludendorff and Hitler—no betrayal by alien Jews within. Iron control by the government was essential for the conduct of a total war, and the population would have to be strengthened physically as well: a total war could not be fought by the mentally or physically handicapped any more than by political dissidents. Germany's propaganda would have to be more effective, both for its own people and for the world. Hitler accepted Ludendorff's recipe completely.

Though Nazism was a revolution against globalization, it was also, paradoxically, part of a global revolution. Hitler and the Nazis drew on influences from around the world.

Arguably the strongest of their international influences came from Turkey. The military commander Mustafa Kemal, who made his reputation by defeating the British and French at Gallipoli and then, as Kemal Atatürk, become the first president of a refounded Turkey after the war, was a cult figure in Germany in the 1920s and '30s. Hitler called Atatürk his "shining star." At the Beer Hall Putsch trial in 1924, he said that Atatürk had carried out the greatest recent revolution, while the second greatest was Mussolini's. Much later, in 1938, and with unusual modesty, Hitler said that Atatürk was the great teacher. His first student had been Mussolini and his second student Hitler himself.

The Nazis admired Atatürk's success in throwing off the Treaty of Sèvres, which the Allies had imposed on the Ottoman Empire after the end of the First World War. What the Turks called the War of Independence resulted in a new and more favorable treaty, the 1923 Treaty of Lausanne, and the creation of the modern Turkish Republic with Atatürk at its head. It is not hard to see where the Nazis saw parallels to their situation, especially because Atatürk's regime considered the Turkish signatories of the Treaty of Sèvres to be traitors and stripped them of their citizenship.

The Nazis also knew and approved of the 1915 Armenian genocide, in which the Ottoman government had killed somewhere between 750,000 and 1.5 million Armenians. They also approved of the expulsion of Greeks from Turkey under the terms of the Treaty of Lausanne. These instances of ethnic cleansing, so the Nazis thought, had been necessary steps on the way to creating the strong and successful Turkey they admired.

Another influence at an early and decisive moment came from Russia. Between 1920 and 1923, Hitler got to know a number of White Russian émigrés in Munich, and worked closely with a group called Aufbau (Reconstruction). Aufbau was a deeply antisemitic group made up largely of Russian émigrés and a few Nazis. It wanted to overthrow both the Weimar Republic and the Soviet Union. Some of the émigrés were Germans from the newly independent Baltic states. Others were Russians, including Lieutenant Piotr Shabelskii-Bork. Shabelskii-Bork brought the infamous *Protocols of the Elders of Zion* to Germany. This was an antisemitic, conspiratorial forgery created by the Russian secret police before the First World War. In the 1920s, it inspired activists from Hitler to Henry Ford. These émigrés got to Hitler at a point when his antisemitism was still developing. They likely convinced him of the scale of their imagined international Jewish conspiracy, and that the Soviet Union was a "Jewish dictatorship" and a product of that conspiracy.

Russian influences were also at work on the young Joseph Goebbels, who in 1923 wrote that he had the "deepest reverence" for "Holy Russia." This had something to do with his reading of Dostoevsky. But he also called himself "a German Communist."

Throughout his political career, Hitler had a strong admiration for Benito Mussolini and the Fascist regime he had established in Italy in 1922. Hitler began to emulate aspects of Mussolini's style, particularly the cult of the leader that surrounded him. Hitler's followers took the cue, and this is when they began to celebrate Hitler as the *Führer*, or "leader," a translation of Mussolini's title *Duce*. The Nazis also imitated the Italian Fascists' colored shirts and straight-armed salute. Giuseppe Renzetti, Mussolini's friend and agent in Germany, reported in 1932 that Hitler "idolized" Mussolini and desperately wanted to meet him. This was probably more because Hitler admired the dictator's success than because of the ideological affinity between them.

There were extensive contacts between the Italian Fascists and the Nazis before 1933, most of them running through Renzetti, an extroverted former army officer with a German-Jewish wife who soon got to know everyone in Berlin political society. Not surprisingly, Renzetti particularly favored the right. He nurtured connections to Schleicher and Hugenberg, and to most of the leading Nazis, including Hitler, Goebbels, and Göring. Mussolini wanted to see a government of the united right in Germany, on the theory that such a government's efforts to break the Treaty of Versailles would keep France fully occupied and leave space for Italian expansion. Renzetti made it his mission to pursue this goal, and he worked tirelessly behind the scenes to bring the various strands of the German right together.

Renzetti eventually became convinced that only Hitler could be the leader of a united-right government, and in November 1931 he persuaded Mussolini that the Italian Fascists should help Hitler gain power. After that, Renzetti's role changed: he became almost one of the Nazis, advising the leaders and working as a kind of lobbyist trying to convince the other right-wing groups, such as the German Nationals and the Steel Helmet, that they should fall in line. Hitler himself saw Renzetti as a friend, and Goebbels wrote later that Renzetti had contributed so much to the Nazis' rise to power that "he could practically be considered an old Nazi."

Hitler thought from the beginning that Italy could be enrolled as an ally in his quest for living space, and he was willing to pay a high political price for Mussolini's support. The price involved a region called South Tyrol, a former territory of Austria that had been ceded to Italy in 1918, although most of its inhabitants were German speaking (and still are). Since German nationalists hoped one day to unite their country with Austria, it followed that they considered South Tyrol to be German territory as well. Hitler, eager to appease Mussolini, was willing to leave South Tyrol to Italy, but he also knew that nationalists of all stripes (and, opportunistically, the Social Democrats) would make political hay out of his seeming betrayal of a German interest to a foreign power.

During the 1928 election campaign, Social Democratic and nationalist papers alike spread stories that Hitler had taken campaign funds from Mussolini in return for his renouncing of German claims to South Tyrol. Hitler responded with a libel action. The case went to court in May 1929, with appeals and sequels dragging on until 1932. Time and again, judges sympathetic to Hitler minimized the evidence against him and found in his favor. Still, that evidence was considerable, and clearly worried and angered Hitler. During the first trial, a Berlin newspaper reported that when evidence of his collusion with Mussolini arose, "Hitler did not know how to respond, except to complain with great agitation about a 'Jewish press gang' that had united in an 'international conspiracy' against him." At the retrial, a witness named Werner Abel testified that right before the Beer Hall Putsch, he had served as a middleman between Hitler and an Italian officer at the embassy in Berlin, one Captain Migliorati. Migliorati had promised Hitler money in return for Hitler's renunciation of South Tyrol, and, said Abel, Hitler had agreed.

Migliorati later denied having offered Hitler money, and Abel himself was certainly a shady character: a far-right activist who had swung over to the left, with several previous convictions for crimes of dishonesty. In 1932, another Nazi-friendly court convicted Abel of perjury, But Hitler *had* met with Italians in 1923, and he even gave an interview to the Italian paper *Corriere d'Italiano* renouncing claims to South Tyrol.

The interview was printed on October 16, 1923, the very day after Abel claimed Hitler had made his deal with Migliorati.

Support for the Nazis in Germany fit patterns that stretched across much of Europe in the interwar years. The success of fascist parties in drawing significant popular support, even if they didn't come to power, closely tracks two different maps of postwar Europe: the map of those countries defeated in the war and the map of those countries threatened by a Communist Revolution. Hungary, for instance, had been on the losing side of the war, and experienced a Communist revolution and short-lived Communist regime in 1919. Thereafter, it was ruled by a military dictator, Admiral Miklós Horthy. Horthy was not himself a fascist, but Hungary's fascist Arrow Cross movement drew strong support, and its leader, Ferenc Szálasi, eventually succeeded Horthy. Italy was on the winning side of the war, but the Italians felt that the other Allied Powers had cheated them of the spoils; many spoke of their country's "mutilated victory." Italy, too, had a strong Communist movement. Germany, of course, makes it onto both maps, with its defeat in the First World War, its strong Communist Party, and repeated postwar Communist uprisings.

Nazism, therefore, was not just a particularly savage nation-specific reaction to globalization. It was an international reaction, strongly shaped by international influences. Historians used to think that Nazism was an expression of some uniquely German flaw, perhaps traceable to Martin Luther, or the Thirty Years' War. But Hitler's movement was a response to a distinctive crisis of the 1920s and early 1930s, which affected much of the globe. For all their nationalism, the National Socialists were far from purely German.

AFTER THE ELECTION of 1930, the next turning point in Heinrich Brüning's chancellorship came in March 1931.

Brüning had a clear strategy to confront the Depression. Bypassing the deadlocked Reichstag with executive orders signed by President Hindenburg, he raised taxes and cut spending on unemployment insurance and government salaries. This deflationary policy, as economists call it, was the economic orthodoxy of the time. If revenue and spending could be brought into balance, it was believed, the economy would recover by itself.

Yet Brüning thought that Germany's finances could never truly recover until the burden of reparations was lifted. In 1930, he hoped to pressure the British and French into concessions on reparations by running up a trade surplus. He thought this would raise employment in export industries. Germany, in fact, reached a considerable trade surplus with both countries, but only because high tariffs artificially depressed imports. Germany not only suffered the highest unemployment rate in Europe, but also began to confront malnutrition, as the tariffs had put the cost of meat and produce increasingly out of reach of the less well off.

In December 1930, Brüning met with the U.S. ambassador, Frederic M. Sackett, to urge the United States to intervene in the reparations question. This was the only way, said Brüning, to prevent a longer and more severe political as well as economic crisis. When Sackett passed along Brüning's message, President Herbert Hoover was impressed enough to send Undersecretary of State Joseph P. Cotton to Europe to look into the question—but Cotton died the day he was supposed to depart.

Despite a few, faint signs of economic upturn in early 1931, the German government's budget was still in crisis. The deficit stood at 430 million Reichsmarks (about 100 million dollars in 1930, the equivalent of about 1.5 billion dollars today) for the first quarter of 1931. The government financed some of this with short-term borrowing, but it was unable to secure a longer-term loan. One bank the government approached replied that it was worried about the uncertain reparations situation. If Germany defaulted on reparations payments, all other creditors would be in jeopardy. Germany's economic distress was also making an already tense domestic political situation worse. At a cabinet meeting on May 30, Interior Minister Joseph Wirth warned that political violence was on the rise, and he did not think he could long guarantee order.

Into this bleak picture came one remarkable ray of hope: in February 1931, the French government announced it would participate in a large loan to Germany. This dramatic shift in policy came at the urging of the tireless Aristide Briand. It was the latest installment in his campaign for Franco-German reconciliation.

Briand's effort could have been a turning point in Germany's economic and political fortunes. But there were larger strategic questions at work behind both Briand's offer and Brüning's response. Briand was, as always, looking for ways to manage the potential German danger to France, and to create an economically stronger Europe that could compete with the United States. Brüning's broader strategy forced him to avoid policies that would have made the Depression more bearable for ordinary Germans.

Talks about a French loan had actually begun the previous July, at the time of the Rhineland evacuation and the surge in nationalist passions in Germany. The French agenda was clear. As the talks went on, Prime Minister André Tardieu said that long-term credits would be linked to Germany's promises to respect its eastern borders and limit the development of armaments. The French asked that the Germans refrain from building two battleships that were then in the planning stage—then known as the battle cruisers B and C, later as the ships *Admiral Scheer* and *Admiral Graf Spee*—and also that the German government clamp down on demonstrations by the radical right. It was also very important to the French that the Germans keep making payments according to the Young Plan.

This points squarely to Brüning's problems with the French loan offer. His goal was not to reduce or delay reparations payments. It was to end them permanently. The Depression had given him an opportunity to make the case that Germany was simply unable to continue with the Young Plan. If the Allies nonetheless forced Germany to continue making payments, the result would be financial and political chaos that would have dangerous and unforeseeable consequences in their countries as well. Brüning, therefore, was working against time. What if the terrible conditions improved and he lost his strongest argument? The French loan might put him in this position, as there was a real chance it would boost German economic growth. The loan had to be avoided. But how?

Brüning was nothing if not clever, and his solution to this problem was effective without damaging him politically where it counted—with Hindenburg and Schleicher. On March 21, 1931, his cabinet announced plans for a customs union with Austria. This would arguably amount to

a breach of the Treaties of Versailles and St. Germain, both of which pro-
hibited union between Germany and Austria. Britain and especially
France saw in this idea the renewal of German expansionism, not just to
Austria but toward all of southeastern Europe. The idea had not been
Brüning's. It was thought up by the German Foreign Office, which, under
Stresemann's successor as foreign minister, Julius Curtius, and secretary
of state, Bernhard von Bülow, was moving more and more to the right.
Curtius was the scheme's public champion. Brüning himself stayed in
the background.

There was an outcry in France, and by the end of March the idea of
the French loan was dead. Briand was in the midst of an election campaign for the French presidency, and the outrage over Germany's Austrian gambit destroyed his chances. On May 13, he suffered a rout at the
hands of the right-wing candidate, Paul Doumer.

Brüning was too intelligent not to realize that the customs union plan
would damage Franco-German relations and bring about the collapse of
the French loan. Therefore, it had to be what he wanted to happen. It
would have been politically difficult for him to decline the loan, but
the Austrian customs union could earn him points with nationalists
without hurting his strategy of exploiting the Depression to get out of
reparations. At the same time, he kept his distance from the Austrian
idea, so that his reputation with the French and British would not be
irretrievably harmed.

Two other things are clear about this episode. First, it shows once
again how financial arrangements in interwar Europe were really about
security and, in particular, keeping Germany in line. So long as Germany was constrained by reparations and the gold standard, it could
not threaten its neighbors. It would be another story if Germany were
free of these obstacles. Second, Brüning could afford to be cavalier about
the Depression because he was a presidential chancellor, accountable
only to Hindenburg. A parliamentary chancellor, beholden to a Reichstag majority, would have found it much more difficult to turn down life-
saving economic aid. This was precisely why Schleicher and his circle
had wanted a presidential chancellor. Once again, as Stresemann had
seen so clearly, the foreign and domestic policies in the Weimar Republic were woven together particularly tightly.

On June 6, Brüning compounded Germany's economic problems. Forced to introduce another executive order calling for more austerity, he tried to make the medicine politically palatable by including inflammatory language, saying that the German people had reached "the limits of the privations" that could be imposed on them by the "tribute payments" of reparations. The international community took this as a threat to halt payments unilaterally.

There had already been rumors of such a default, and the nervousness in financial markets caused gold reserves once again to flow out of Germany. The great fear was that Germany would soon repudiate private international debts along with the reparations, precisely because an official statement *denied* any such notions. No one believed such official statements in the 1930s any more than they do today.

That very day, Brüning was in Britain to meet with Prime Minister Ramsay MacDonald and other British officials at Chequers, the prime minister's official country house. No German chancellor had met with a British prime minister since the war. Although the British took Brüning sternly to task for his choice of language on reparations, the chancellor in the end made his usual favorable impression on them. He argued that the Allies had to let Germany out of reparations before the world economy was ruined and Germany went either Nazi or Communist. He treated his listeners to an avalanche of figures showing that the German government had done all it could do with tax increases and expenditure cuts. MacDonald was sympathetic, as was Montagu Norman, the governor of the Bank of England. Later, Norman told MacDonald that after Brüning had been so frank, no one could blame the Germans for unilaterally refusing to go on paying reparations.

At Chequers, Brüning had succeeded in turning MacDonald into a lobbyist on Germany's behalf, and the British prime minister wrote to President Hoover setting out the chancellor's arguments. American officials were already well aware of the political as well as economic stakes at play. Secretary of State Henry Stimson promised he would do all he could to save the "Germany of Dr. Brüning" from the "other Germany." Ambassador Sackett and his British counterpart, Sir Horace Rumbold, also believed it was necessary to prop up Brüning to keep the Nazis out, and they pressed this view on their governments. Officials in Hoover's own administration had been advocating the idea as well. On June 20, the president announced the "Hoover Moratorium," halting all reparation and war debt payments for a year. To cover himself domestically, he asked President Hindenburg to send him a telegram formally requesting the moratorium. A year later, the moratorium was made permanent. By then, Brüning was no longer in office to savor his triumph.

The ending of reparations was a considerable diplomatic success for Brüning, but his government's Austrian initiative and its threats to stop reparation payments stimulated a flight from the German Reichsmark that spread into the massive world financial crisis of 1931. First, a major bank failed in Austria. When the Austrian government imposed limits on withdrawals, financial panic spread to Germany, where another major bank failed. The dangerous draining of the Reichsbank's gold reserves continued despite the announcement of the Hoover Moratorium, not least because, for several weeks, the French refused to accept Hoover's terms. Loans based on worthless assets spread the financial contagion to Britain, and by September, the crisis had grown so severe that even the British government felt forced to abandon the gold standard.

It was the 1931 crisis that turned a severe but still manageable economic downturn into the Great Depression of legend. In every major country, the economic indicators tumbled further downward. By early 1932, unemployment in Germany had reached an extraordinary six million people, or 40 percent of the insured workforce. Brüning's government kept cutting back unemployment insurance payments, and after these benefits ran out, workers were left at the mercy of spotty municipal relief services. Millions of Germans were literally going hungry. Illnesses related to malnutrition reappeared as they had under the naval blockade in 1917 and 1918. Political radicalism grew apace.

Brüning did not have to take the actions that metastasized the Depression in 1931. He and his ministers were well informed about other options, including John Maynard Keynes's advocacy of public works and government-created credit to combat the Depression. Brüning and Keynes met and talked about economic policy when the economist traveled to Germany to give a lecture. Brüning thought Keynes simply did not understand the German situation.

More important, Brüning's administration did not feel it was politically free to adopt Keynes's ideas. The hyperinflation of 1922 and 1923 had left psychological scars among the German people. Any stimulus effort might lead to inflation and would therefore spark huge public resistance. There were also cultural factors at work. Some of Brüning's ministers, and even Brüning himself, thought that the degree of industrialization and urbanization that Germany had reached by 1928 was artificial and could not be sustained. Better, they thought, to solve the Depression by moving urban workers to rural areas.

Adopting Keynes's ideas for combating the Depression would have required expanding the reach of government. Where could the money for such an expansion have come from? This is the critical issue. German domestic law and international agreements prohibited the Reichsbank from creating credit or "printing money." In 1931, the German government was all but unable to borrow money. Behind these economic factors lay political realities. One major reason the German government could not borrow was that Brüning had decided to put a nationalist agenda ahead of economic expansion. He could have had the French loan if his government had yielded to French demands regarding battleship construction and not pursued the Austrian customs union. To appease the nationalist right, and particularly Hindenburg, Brüning would not make this compromise. He sought the end of reparations at the cost of unprecedented unemployment. His ill-timed nationalist rhetoric stimulated the catastrophic 1931 bank crisis.

The gold standard had been the ultimate symbol of a peaceful, liberal capitalist world order, and the 1931 crisis brought it down. Britain's abandonment of gold and its subsequent devaluation of the pound hurt German exports. Unemployment and bankruptcies rose to new heights. To appease French anger over the Hoover Moratorium, Brüning was forced in the end to promise that Germany would not spend more on defense as long as the moratorium lasted. Conforming to the international system was once again clearly at odds with German nationalist goals. Integration grew ever less appealing, and economic nationalism more so. The damage to German democracy was severe.

Brüning himself felt he had to underplay his triumph in attaining the Hoover Moratorium. His goal remained the permanent elimination of reparations. To celebrate the moratorium would have been to invite parties such as the Social Democrats to advocate more spending to combat the Depression. This in turn would have worked against Brüning's strategy.

Yet Brüning's triumph also drew a surprisingly cool response from his real backers. Soon afterward, he began to get the feeling that Schleicher's attitude toward him had changed. Schleicher told Brüning how excited Hindenburg's son, Oskar, had been at Brüning's success, but Schleicher had replied coolly to Oskar, "Not so fast. The worst is yet to come."

As BRÜNING WRESTLED with the world financial situation, there was another kind of Depression politics going on in Germany's cities.

"Berlin needs its sensation like a fish needs water," ran a blunt sentence in a book with a blunt title: *Struggle for Berlin*. "This city lives on sensation, and any political propaganda that does not recognize that will fail to achieve its purpose." The author of the book was a rising star in the Nazi Party, the thirty-six-year-old Joseph Goebbels, whom Hitler had sent to Berlin in 1926 to be the Nazi Party boss (Gauleiter) in the capital city.

Promoting the Nazis in Berlin was a difficult job. Berlin was a working-class city, a bastion of the Social Democrats and the Communists. It had also been a home for migrants, including refugees escaping persecution, ever since Louis XIV expelled the Protestant Huguenots from France in the late seventeenth century. The Huguenots had left their mark on Berlin in many ways: in the city's distinctive dialect, with its many borrowings from French; in one of its signature dishes, a meatball called a *Boulette*; and in one of its greatest writers, the nineteenth-century novelist Theodor Fontane. Other waves of migrants had followed. The Prussian king Friedrich II (the "Great") brought Dutch engineers to drain the marshlands. They gave the name "orange" to many places in and around Berlin, such as the village of Oranienburg. Starting in the 1880s, Jews came to Berlin fleeing violence in the Russian Empire, a flow that crested after 1918. There was a popular saying that "all real Berliners come from Silesia," and certainly by German standards, Berlin's ethnic and religious mixture was highly diverse. Berlin was Germany's intellectual and cultural capital, its financial capital, its media capital. For a party with its base in the Protestant countryside, Berlin was as far from natural ground as there could be.

When Goebbels arrived in the capital, the Nazis had few followers, and hardly anyone took them seriously.. He admitted that his debut speech to Berlin's local Nazis attracted no attention, save from "A Jew-paper, which in later years would always condemn me." And all this paper said was that "a certain Herr Göbels [sic]" had "dished up the familiar phrases."

If Berlin was not a natural Nazi city, Goebbels, like his bitter rival Gregor Strasser, was not a typical Nazi. Before going into politics, he had earned a doctorate in literature, studying under Jewish professors. He had a lively intelligence and a gift that is particularly rare among political fanatics: he could step outside his own fanaticism and imagine how Nazi views looked to someone who did not share them. His keen appreciation for writers and artists opposed to Nazism filled his diary: German-Jewish writers such as Maximilian Harden, liberal political opponents like Theodor Heuss, filmmakers such as Fritz Lang. This mental flexibility made him an effective salesman.

Not that Goebbels liked Berlin's lively media environment. "Daily the rotation machines spew out the Jewish poison into the Reich's capital city in the form of millions of copies of newspapers," he wrote. Still, he knew how to use the media, and he understood intuitively that all publicity was good publicity. It didn't matter if liberal or left-wing papers fiercely criticized his party. "The main thing is, they're talking about us," he wrote over and over in his diary. But Goebbels also had another tool to promote the Nazi Party, one that was much darker.

In the Weimar Republic, all the political parties had their own paramilitary forces. The Nazis had their SA—the letters stood for *Sturmabteilung*, or "Storm Section," also known as the Stormtroopers or Brownshirts. The Communists had the Red Front Fighters' League, until it was outlawed in 1929 and replaced by the Combat League Against Fascism. The three main democratic parties had the Reich Banner Black-Red-Gold, named for the colors of the Weimar Republic's new flag (the black, red, and gold bars had been the emblem of German democracy since 1848, while the Bismarckian empire, the German National Party, and the Nazis shared the colors of German nationalism, black, white, and red). Later, Social Democrats who found the Reich Banner too moderate formed a new group called the Iron Front, in close emulation of the Brownshirts. The German Nationals had the veterans' organization the Steel Helmet, which by the 1930s was open to anyone interested, veteran or not—except Jews, even if they had served at the front.

All of these forces had the same role: to win control of territory. They were to keep their party's meetings and rallies from being disrupted and make sure their activists could campaign. Less officially, they fought one another in street battles that made Berlin and other German cities look more like Al Capone's Chicago than like their counterparts elsewhere in Europe.

Certain Berlin neighborhoods—Neukölln, Friedrichshain, Wedding, parts of Charlottenburg—were home to the poorest workers and, correspondingly, were bastions of the Communist Party. After Goebbels's arrival, the Nazi strategy was to take the fight to the Communists. The Brownshirts would find themselves a tavern in a working-class area and guarantee the owner a generous minimum level of monthly beer consumption. All the owner had to do was let an SA detachment, a "Storm," use his tavern as its headquarters. The tavern would then become known as a "Storm Tavern." The Brownshirts would use it as a base from which to go out, usually at night, looking for Communists to attack. Often there would be ferocious battles between the two sides, sometimes involving the other parties' paramilitary groups. By the early 1930s, the conditions in Berlin and other major German cities came close to a state of civil war.

This strategy did several things at once. Bit by bit, the Nazis got control of Berlin's tougher neighborhoods. This made it easier for them to campaign, put up posters, and hold rallies. But the real payoff was in media coverage.

Goebbels knew that the Stormtroopers' violence was a magnet for the press, and although the Nazis provoked most of the violence, they always presented their own actions as defensive. Their propaganda played constantly on the theme of the violent, vengeful Communists always in hot pursuit of the brown-shirted boys. The attack on the Felseneck colony and the murder of Fritz Klemke was an example. Nazi propaganda spun this case as a Communist ambush of innocent Stormtroopers—and much of the middle-class press, the police, the prosecutors, and, ultimately, the criminal court accepted this story.

This propaganda often scaled the heights of absurdity—but it also worked. Law-abiding middle-class Germans increasingly came to conclude that, rough as they might be, the Brownshirts were good-hearted, patriotic boys, the only ones with the guts to stop the Communists.

The Nazis brought something else to German politics. Even their supposedly legal and constitutional representatives, the Nazi deputies in state parliaments and the Reichstag, made a point of conducting themselves with the coarse brutality of the Stormtroopers. Brawls involving Nazi parliamentarians were common. Indeed, Nazis made a point of violating every principle of parliamentary courtesy. During a Reichstag debate in May 1932, a Nazi deputy interrupted a Communist speech by calling out, "Your stupidity is priceless." The presiding officer called the deputy to order, and the Communist caucus leader, Ernst Torgler, shouted, "You have to hold your trap." Another Nazi deputy responded by yelling at Torgler, "You will be a Cossack general in Russia!"

Even Nazis who had not served in the First World War, such as Goebbels, had no scruples about criticizing those who had. In the Reichstag in February 1932, Goebbels caused outrage by referring to the Social Democrats as the "party of deserters." Deputies from all parties rose to condemn him. Ernst Lemmer, a State Party deputy, noted that Goebbels "and a great portion of his caucus colleagues" had not served, while many Social Democrats had. The bluntest and most colorful response came from Kurt Schumacher, a Social Democrat from West Prussia, who would go on to fame as the Social Democrats' brave and charismatic leader in the first years after the Second World War. Schumacher, too, had served and been wounded in the war. It was pointless, he said, to lodge a formal protest against Goebbels's conduct. "The whole National Socialist agitation," he continued, "is a constant appeal to the inner swine in human beings. If we recognize anything at all about National Socialism, it is the fact that it has succeeded for the first time in German politics in completely mobilizing human stupidity." Witheringly, he concluded that the Nazis could "do what they like, they can never match the level of our contempt for them."

In the steadily worsening civil war of 1931 and 1932, it became increasingly clear that the government of the Weimar Republic could not maintain order. Just like Brüning's pursuit of nationalist political goals at the expense of economic well-being, this inability to keep the peace corroded the democratic state's legitimacy in the eyes of many of its citizens. The growing pervasiveness of violence also prepared people to accept the state violence the Nazis would later direct.

Yet this didn't mean the Nazis were close to power, or even that they had a very good chance of getting there in 1931 or 1932. From the failure of the 1923 Beer Hall Putsch, Hitler had learned the lesson that the Nazis could never seize power against the opposition of the army and police, and through 1931 and 1932, the doors of the establishment seemed to stay firmly closed to Hitler's movement. Perhaps the Nazis could win an electoral majority. But if not, then what?

Alfred Hugenberg had been the first conservative to try to make use of Hitler in the 1929 campaign against the Young Plan. He tried again through much of 1931, getting the Nazis to join the German Nationals and the Steel Helmet in a petition and plebiscite campaign to force early elections in Prussia. This effort also failed. In October, the joint forces of the nationalist right arranged a meeting at the spa town of Bad Harzburg in the state of Braunschweig, which was governed by a German National–Nazi coalition, ensuring that the meeting's participants would be safe from the police. In addition to the Nazis and the German Nationals, the Steel Helmet, some members of the German People's Party, the Pan-German League, and other right-wing lobby groups went to Bad Harzburg for two days of talks and a parade. The idea was to show that these elements had come together in a truly unified and effective bloc. But this was Hugenberg's dream, not Hitler's. Hitler and the Nazis wanted to make as much use as they could of the publicity and legitimacy they got by working with Hugenberg without in fact conceding anything. Just before the meeting, President Hindenburg had received Hitler and Hermann Göring for the first time—which suggested that associating with the German Nationals really did grant Hitler's movement a veneer of respectability.

Still, the Nazis were anything but obliging. At the parade, Hitler pointedly left the reviewing stand after his Stormtroopers had passed, ignoring the other groups. Goebbels wrote a blunt editorial affirming that the point of working with the German Nationals was purely tactical, since the only way to come to power legally was in a coalition. His private thoughts about Bad Harzburg were even more scathing. He especially disliked the German Nationals' Reichstag caucus leader, Ernst Oberfohren, who "pisses and puffs himself up." "Oh, what better people are we savages!" he continued. "I have to puke." Coalition or no coalition, when the Nazis themselves finally got power, the goal would be to "kick out the reactionaries as fast as possible. We alone will be the lords of Germany."

But to be lords of Germany, the Nazis needed others to act: voters to support them, conservatives to offer an alliance, Hindenburg to open the gates of power. The year 1932 would be dominated by the question of which of these it might be—if any.

5

State of Emergency

They are called "Litfass columns." In the middle of the nineteenth century, a Berlin printer named Ernst Litfass came up with the idea. A true Prussian, Litfass wanted order even in the posting of handbills. They shouldn't be just anywhere. The Litfass column is tall and squat; its broad, rounded surfaces provide space for advertising posters, most of the time for plays, concerts, "Evenings at the Scala," Overstolz cigarettes. In the endless political season of 1932, however, the posters are political.

In this year, politics has become "mass," but not yet very electronic. Politicians are beginning to use radio, but few are good at it yet. They haven't learned that you can't yell into a radio microphone the way you can yell at a rally. Joseph Goebbels is experimenting with spreading the Nazi Party's message through film and phonograph records, but these are new as well. Newspapers and rallies may reach those who are already converted, but for the masses, you need posters. "Our war will mainly be conducted with posters and speeches," Goebbels explains to Hitler early in 1932.

A lot of the posters look remarkably similar. A lantern-jawed, muscular worker, shirtless, breaks the chains that bind his wrists. "Enough!" reads the text. This is a Nazi poster, one of the many drawn by "Mjölnir," Joseph Goebbels's friend Hans Herbert Schweitzer. Another shirtless, lantern-jawed, muscular worker is armed with a sword. He is using it to strike back at the three-headed snake labelled "Nazi dictatorship." This poster is from the Bavarian People's Party, the Catholic Center Party's sister organization. A third half-naked muscular worker, his face mostly hidden but clearly in agony, is bound, Christ-like, to the arms of the Nazis' emblem. "The Worker in the Empire of the Swastika!" reads the text. This is from the Social Democrats. The liberal State Party distinguishes itself by having its muscular men appear wholly, not partially, naked. The German People's Party at least gives them a loincloth.

When women appear, they have all their clothes on. A beautiful young woman in a demure dress, hair neatly tied back and eyes shining with idealism, raises her right arm and looks toward a future of "Unity, Progress, and National Community" with the State Party. Two resolute women in sprightly white blouses, one smiling into the future, one looking somberly at the viewer, announce that "we women" are voting National Socialist.

The Center Party evokes its usual paranoia. For decades, its symbol has been a castle tower, like the rook in a chess set. This is how the Center sees itself in the larger German Protestant world. In this poster, the Center's lonely tower is besieged by threatening crowds waving Communist and Nazi banners. Huge letters on the tower's walls proclaim Heinrich Brüning "The Last Bulwark of Law and Order!"

Sometimes the leader alone is the argument. The Communists present Ernst Thälmann before a stirring backdrop of red flags. With a faint, pensive smile, Thälmann urges us to "Fight Against Hunger and War!" He conveys a certain revolutionary optimism. The Nazis are much bleaker. A charcoal sketch shows countless unemployed workers, gaunt, hungry, grim-faced. The message is just as blunt. "Our Last Hope: Hitler."

In 1932, these hungry workers aren't the only ones who think this.

KURT VON SCHLEICHER put the point with his usual cynical humor: "We'll make the Nazis believers in the state only when we let them at the trough."

Schleicher understood that the government could not fight the country's largest political group forever—even with the army. Germany's army commanders dreaded a civil war more than almost anything else.

"They can only pray and wish that this cup might pass from them," a senior official would write in late 1932. To strengthen the army, the national government, and Germany's international clout, Schleicher preferred to seek a parliamentary majority from the right. The traditional conservatives, such as the German Nationals, could not get him near that majority. Maybe the Nazis could.

Chancellor Brüning also understood that a government needed a solid base of support, but he drew a different conclusion from Schleicher's. Brüning was a pious Catholic and deeply conservative. "In cultural matters," he wrote in his memoirs, "a gulf separated me from the Social Democrats." Politics, however, was different. "Like Stresemann and many others, I had grudgingly come to the conviction that when it was about saving the fatherland in an extreme emergency, without relying on a brutal exercise of power, one could depend much more on the Social Democratic Party" than on the far right.

In the months following the election of 1930, Brüning had in fact been relying on the Social Democrats. Any of the executive orders with which he tried to combat the Depression could have been overturned by a majority vote in the Reichstag. But in what they called a policy of "toleration," the Social Democrats supported Brüning's government again and again. His policies were causing catastrophic unemployment and pain for the working classes, but the Social Democrats understood that however difficult Brüning might be, Hitler would be infinitely worse—and it was becoming clear that the most likely alternative to Brüning was Hitler. Toleration was a painful policy nonetheless. It angered and disillusioned many of the Social Democrats' core supporters.

In a strange way, it hurt Brüning, too. His strategy of tacit reliance on the Social Democrats increasingly frustrated Schleicher and Hindenburg. In 1931, Schleicher began to worry that his conservative chancellor might be a bit too left-leaning. He wanted to move Brüning to the right or, if that didn't work, replace him with someone who could arrange a coalition with Nazis and the German Nationals.

Alert observers could see the dangers of such a policy. The journalist Konrad Heiden talked to politicians in the state of Thuringia who had formed a coalition with the Nazis in 1930. They tried to reassure him that this arrangement could never lead to a Nazi coup there. Heiden found their assurances marked by a trust that "reminds you that mistrust is a political virtue. And that virtues are rare."

Schleicher did not fully grasp the dangers of working with the Nazis. One reason for this lay in his understanding of which voters supported them, and why. He thought the Nazis had an unstable base of support that would fly apart under the pressures of governing, or even of sustained opposition. He also thought that a large segment of Nazi supporters were actually Communists, and if the Nazi Party fell apart, these voters would make the Communists too strong to be stopped. He suspected that "Moscow" had long since recognized the Communist sympathies of many Nazis and was covertly supporting them.

The other reason was that Schleicher fundamentally underestimated Hitler, as did countless other German and world statesmen before 1939. Meeting with Hitler personally, as Schleicher did twice in October 1931, did nothing to change his views. After the first of these meetings, Schleicher wrote privately that Hitler was "an interesting man with an outstanding gift as a speaker." His only reservation about that Nazi leader was that he could get carried away with his own plans. "One must then pull him back by the coattails to a basis of fact."

By the summer of 1931, Chancellor Brüning's stock was falling with several key constituencies. One was big business. Prominent industrialists urged him to break more radically with the Weimar system of industrial wage arbitration, to "remove the chains from the economy" and let it operate freely according to the "eternally valid economic laws." Naturally, this meant wages would fall, and equally naturally, such a policy would put an end to Brüning's informal collaboration with the Social Democrats. Long-term collaboration with the left would lead to Germany's "bleeding to death," in the words of one senior business executive with ties to the German People's Party. These business circles were considering various political scenarios: if Hugenberg and Hitler would not work with Brüning's government, then the options were a dictatorship or a coalition of the Nazis and the German Nationals.

More important for Brüning's political survival, his dependence on the parliamentary left was becoming an increasing annoyance for Schleicher and for Hindenburg as well. Schleicher increasingly found even the now-marginalized Social Democrats a hindrance to the plans he had in mind. Hindenburg had his own reasons.

The Reich president's biggest concern was, as always, the mainte-nance of his own reputation. Throughout his career, Hindenburg had proven to be a virtuoso at seizing credit for successes (the victory at Tan-nenberg early in the First World War) and thrusting onto someone else the responsibility for failures (defeat in 1918, the Kaiser's abdication, the signing of the Armistice, the Treaty of Versailles). By 1931, it was beginning to weigh on Hindenburg that it was *his* executive orders that Brüning was using to carry out his harsh deflationary policy, and so Hindenburg could not avoid sharing responsibility for the consequences. A restructured right-wing parliamentary majority governing without the need of executive orders would lift this burden from him.

Hindenburg also yearned for national unity—as he understood it. His definition of national unity extended no further than that the fractious political right, especially the Nazis and the German Nationals, should come together to work with him. Hindenburg had no interest in working with the Social Democrats. He disliked knowing that his chancellor's agenda was subject to the acquiescence of a party that he, Hindenburg, despised, and he did not consider the Social Democrats a legitimate part of the nation he wanted to unite.

Hindenburg was also getting pressure from the representatives of big agriculture. In July 1931, in a letter to Hindenburg, the Reichslandbund (Reich Land League), the biggest agricultural lobby group, demanded "a complete break with the forces of international Marxism" (that is, the Social Democrats). Because Hindenburg was himself a Prussian aristo-crat and estate owner, groups such as the Reichslandbund had a strong influence on him.

Another major factor in everyone's political calculations was the government of the state of Prussia. Prussia accounted for three-fifths of Germany's territory and population, which meant that its government was almost a second national government. For almost the whole dura-tion of the Weimar Republic, Prussia was governed by a stable coalition of the Social Democrats, the German Democratic Party, and the Center Party, with the Social Democrats Otto Braun as prime minister and Carl

Severing as interior minister. Braun and Severing were able and far-sighted politicians who enjoyed the respect of leaders from across the political spectrum. Gustav Stresemann expressed a typical view when he referred to them as "truly statesmanlike figures" with whom he could gladly work. But their left-leaning administration made Prussia a thorn in the side of the political right.

In an effort to win German National backing for Brüning's administration and thus take a step toward a consolidated right, Hindenburg met with Alfred Hugenberg in the fall of 1931. Hugenberg made it clear that the price of his support would be the disbanding of the Braun-Severing administration's coalition with the Center Party in Prussia. Chancellor Brüning, the national leader of the Center Party, could have brought this about, but the issue opened up the problem of the complex interdependency of the Prussian and Reich governments in the early 1930s. Brüning could only avoid having the Reichstag overturn Hindenburg's executive orders, and thus avoid a vote of no confidence in his own administration, through the support of the Social Democrats. If Brüning were to terminate the coalition in Prussia, the Social Democrats in the Reichstag would likely retaliate by bringing him down. Brüning's only hope, then, would be to seek a majority on the far right, from the German Nationals and the Nazis. This was of course precisely what Hindenburg wanted, but Brüning did not, and in any case, there was no prospect in 1931 of the far right backing him or, in all likelihood, uniting itself.

One of Schleicher's main concerns was the security of Germany's eastern border with Poland, which was also Prussia's border. The army and the police did not have sufficient resources for border security, so Schleicher had to rely on paramilitary groups such as the Steel Helmet or even the SA. By September, Carl Severing was complaining that, on border security, the Reich defense ministry dealt more closely with these right-wing paramilitary groups than with the Prussian interior ministry. Understandably, the Prussian government opposed having its border defended by the armed groups of its fiercest political opponents. Schleicher thought the Braun-Severing administration's unwillingness to play along made it a national security threat.

By September, both Schleicher and Hindenburg were telling Brüning to restructure his cabinet to move it to the right. It was clear to Brüning that their confidence in him was failing, and relations only deteriorated further. Brüning suggested that Hindenburg meet with Hitler. The president was outraged—he objected not to Hitler's politics but, rather, to his military rank, social station, and probably national origins. "I really cannot be made to converse with this Austrian private," Hindenburg told Brüning. He was being asked to sacrifice too much of his "personal feelings and convictions." Brüning said he had never previously heard "this tone of voice" from Hindenburg.

In fact, there was a lively conspiracy under way around the president: not only Schleicher but also the president's son, Oskar (who, because of his influence on his father and his lack of intellect, was known to sardonic political insiders as "the son not foreseen in the constitution"), and State Secretary Otto Meissner were working to influence Hindenburg against Brüning. They were growing closer to the Nazis as well. Oskar von Hindenburg became friends with Hermann Göring, and another member of Hindenburg's entourage leaked secrets to the Nazis.

With his military way of thinking, Brüning saw himself as Hindenburg's subaltern and did what he was told—to an extent. He reformed his cabinet to shift it to the right. He himself took over the foreign ministry. Gottfried Treviranus, a former German National who had left the party over objections to Hugenberg's extremism, became transport minister. General Wilhelm Groener added the interior ministry to the defense portfolio he already held. Yet Hugenberg and the main body of the German Nationals, to say nothing of the Nazis, remained in opposition. Brüning was still dependent on the Social Democrats in the Reichstag, and correspondingly, the situation in Prussia was, from the standpoint of the right, unsolved. Schleicher and Hindenburg found their frustration growing.

Brüning's misplaced loyalty therefore did him little good. Ironically, it was his tireless efforts to get Hindenburg reelected that precipitated the end of his chancellorship.

HINDENBURG'S SEVEN-YEAR PRESIDENTIAL term was due to run out in the spring of 1932, and if he wanted another term, his legendary stature would ensure his reelection. But if he did not run again, Hitler would be the likely winner. With the steadily worsening Depression and the Nazis' surging popularity, it was unlikely that anyone but Hindenburg could beat Hitler.

Hindenburg himself was reluctant to run again. He would turn eighty-five in October. He worried about what use the Nationalist and Nazi opposition would make of "the events of 1918"—that is, his pushing the Kaiser into exile. "It will be worse this time," he told Brüning.

To make things easier on the old field marshal, Brüning tried to get all the party leaders to agree to extend Hindenburg's term without an election. As a constitutional change, this would require a two-thirds vote in the Reichstag, for which the support of the Nazis and the German Nationals would be necessary. Predictably, Hitler and Hugenberg refused, and Brüning had accomplished nothing more than handing Hitler the chance to pose as the guardian of the constitution. Hindenburg's next objection was that he would not run as the candidate of the center-left. He wanted right-wing support. He also wanted to win an outright majority in the first round and not have to go through a runoff. Yet even the Steel Helmet, of which Hindenburg was honorary leader, refused to endorse his reelection. It was only in mid-February, when the smaller, right-wing veterans' group the Kyffhäuser League endorsed him, that Hindenburg grudgingly agreed to stand again.

Three main candidates ran against him. Theodor Duesterberg, one of the leaders of the Steel Helmet, became the joint candidate of the Steel Helmet and the German Nationals. The Communists put up their leader, Ernst Thälmann. The political center and center left predictably lined up behind Hindenburg. On February 22, Joseph Goebbels announced that Adolf Hitler would run on behalf of the Nazis. The one problem was that Hitler was still not a German citizen. Four days later, the government of the state of Braunschweig, where the Nazis governed in coalition with the German Nationals, named Hitler its Berlin representative. This automatically made him a Braunschweig civil servant and German citizen, and thus eligible for the presidency. After this, Hitler's irreverent friend Ernst Hanfstaengl delightedly addressed Hitler as "Mr. Government Counselor," teasing the Führer with his new formal title from the hated Weimar state.

Hindenburg barely campaigned. He limited himself to one speech

A liberal prince:
Prince Max von Baden, looking
typically unimpressed.

Regime change: Revolutionary soldiers drive through Berlin's Brandenburg Gate,
November 1918.

The spirit of Locarno: German foreign minister Gustav Stresemann (left) meets with British foreign secretary Austen Chamberlain (center), and French foreign minister Aristide Briand.

A man from another time: Reich president Paul von Hindenburg, the venerated field marshal who was first elected in 1925 at the age of seventy-seven.

Blood May: Barricades on the mean streets of Neukölln, May 1929.

He "lacked the flair and the charisma so badly needed at a time of extreme atomization and politicization": Chancellor Heinrich Brüning, the Catholic conservative who held office from March 1930 until May 1932.

"Don't believe him, he's telling the truth": A tense Adolf Hitler under cross-examination by Hans Litten at the Eden Dance Palace trial, May 8, 1931.

"The main thing is, they're talking about us": The Nazi Party's propaganda director Joseph Goebbels in full flight, around 1930.

"An anticapitalist yearning": Gregor Strasser, one of the Nazis' leading political strategists and most effective spokesmen, around 1930.

"Germany's autarky": The satirical magazine *Simplicissimus* ties political violence to economic policy, as Social Democrats of the Iron Front (left) confront Nazi Stormtroopers (right). The caption reads, "What progress since 1914! Germans have now made themselves completely independent of foreign countries in the conduct of war."

"Our war will be conducted with posters": Voters contemplate campaign advertising, 1930.

Order even in the posting of handbills: Litfass columns like this one, displaying advertisements and campaign posters, dotted the streetscape in most large German cities.

"The worker in the Reich of the Swastika": A 1932 Social Democratic election poster by the artist Karl Geiss exemplifies the high standards of German graphic art.

A "social general": Kurt von Schleicher, a master of backstairs intrigue, finally felt forced to take the chancellor's office for himself. Here he delivers his government's declaration over the radio on December 15, 1932.

"We have hired him": Adolf Hitler and his vice-chancellor, Franz von Papen, on the second day of their administration, January 31, 1933.

Diplomacy: Hitler's future foreign minister Joachim von Ribbentrop (left) and French ambassador André François-Poncet attend a concert with their wives.

"A signal of merciless danger": Hitler speaks at Berlin's Sportpalast shortly after becoming chancellor.

The last night of German democracy: The Reichstag burns, February 27, 1933.

Symbolic performance of a partnership: Hindenburg and Hitler at the "Day of German Labor," May 1, 1933.

"His manners require constant instruction": The right-wing political activist Edgar Julius Jung in the 1920s, around the time he called democracy "the rule of inferiors."

Architect of resistance from within: Fritz Günther von Tschirschky, von Papen's intelligence adviser, in 1934.

over the radio on March 10, three days before the first-round vote. His dutiful chancellor did the work for him, appearing at rallies and giving speeches all over the country. On March 13, with 49.6 percent of the vote, Hindenburg missed a first-round victory by a hair. Hitler was well back with 30.1 percent, while Thälmann earned 13.2 percent and Duesterberg 6.8 percent.

An electoral truce over Easter meant that campaigning for the second round was packed into five short days, April 4–9. Duesterberg dropped out while Thälmann remained, but clearly the election was a duel between Hitler and Hindenburg. To accentuate his youthful, modern image, Hitler campaigned by plane with the slogan "Hitler over Germany." His words were spread with films and phonograph records as well. It was, as the historian Heinrich August Winkler writes, the "most modern and technically perfect" election campaign Germany had yet seen.

To no avail—this time, Hindenburg won 53 percent of the vote to Hitler's 36.8 percent, with Thälmann running a distant third. Brüning considered the election a referendum on his chancellorship, from which he had emerged vindicated. The nature of the campaign justified his view. In campaigning against Hindenburg, the Nazis had been faced with a serious tactical problem: they had to overcome the veneration for the field marshal commonly felt among the middle-class conservatives the Nazis were trying to attract. Goebbels's solution was rhetorically not to run against Hindenburg at all, but against the "bourgeois-social democratic system." The "system," here as always, was Nazi code for the democracy of Weimar. Yet here, even as late as the spring of 1932, the system had won.

For precisely this reason, however, the victory brought Hindenburg no satisfaction. The patterns of support in the 1925 election had been completely reversed. An analysis of voting data shows that the best statistical predictor of a vote for Hitler in 1932 was a vote for Hindenburg in 1925. Now Hindenburg had behind him the democratic center and left, but not the right, exactly the situation he had feared. When Prussian prime minister Otto Braun congratulated him on his victory, Hindenburg replied bluntly that he did not feel bound to his supporters. As a routine courtesy, Brüning offered Hindenburg his administration's resignation, not expecting the offer to be accepted. Hindenburg growled that he might soon come back to the idea.

With childish ingratitude, Hindenburg blamed Brüning for the electoral outcome. He blamed Brüning, not Hitler or Hugenberg, for the fact that he had had to campaign at all, and that the election had gone through two rounds. His grievances piled up. One of Brüning's ideas to combat the Depression had been to settle unemployed workers on bankrupt farming estates in the Prussian east. This was a very unpopular idea with the aristocratic landowners whom Hindenburg knew from the time he spent at his East Prussian estate of Neudeck. Hindenburg's neighbors denounced his chancellor as an "agrarian Bolshevik."

And then there was the SA ban, perhaps the most fateful political development of the spring of 1932.

NO RATIONAL AND well-informed person could doubt that a large share of responsibility for the steadily worsening political violence in Germany's towns and cities lay with the SA, the Nazi Stormtroopers. During the presidential elections in March and April 1932, the SA had assembled *Alarmbereitschaften*, or "emergency squads," which looked like they were intended to stage a coup in the event of Hitler's victory. It only made sense, therefore, to think about banning the Brownshirts. Yet this did not fit Schleicher's desire to use the Nazis, and especially the SA, for his own purposes. Although his opinion fluctuated in response to events, in April 1932 he thought that a ban would make the Nazis look like martyrs, would have a bad effect on the upcoming state elections, and would bring Hindenburg negative publicity. He wanted to give Hitler an ultimatum to reform the SA to make it harmless, with a ban to follow if he did not comply. Yet Brüning and Wilhelm Groener preferred an outright ban. Hindenburg feared this would cause still more division between himself and the right, thereby frustrating one of his main political goals. Brüning and Groener threatened to resign if Hindenburg didn't agree, and the president grudgingly relented.

Schleicher was stunned. It was his first significant political defeat, something he seemed to have thought could never happen. Groener told a friend that Schleicher had suffered "almost a nervous breakdown" over the issue. The wily general was now out for revenge.

Some of the stress Schleicher was under showed in a private meeting with Brüning on the evening of May 2. Brüning, in his calm, rational, and personally insensitive manner, tried to convince Schleicher that he couldn't go on operating from behind the scenes. He should have the courage to step out front and be chancellor, and Brüning offered him this possibility—if Schleicher would use his influence with Hindenburg to let Brüning remain a few months more in office. Brüning noted that this conversation had had an impact on Schleicher's "reason," but "emotionally had brought him close to rage," a result that would have been unsurprising to anyone more socially adept than Brüning. Brüning knew that Schleicher suffered from liver disease. "The general sat alternating between ash gray and yellow, tired, almost sick," he recalled. "After a few minutes, he looked at me with the shining eyes of a man in a fever. Anyone who knew him, who had for years studied the features of this face, would know: now it is over."

Schleicher exploited his military connections and clout with Hindenburg to sabotage both the SA ban and Wilhelm Groener. Typically, he did this from behind the scenes. He called all the military district commanders and asked them to complain to Hindenburg about Groener and the ban. He got Kurt von Hammerstein-Equord, the commander in chief of the army, to give Hindenburg a file on the Reich Banner, the paramilitary formation associated with the Social Democrats and other democratic parties. The point of the file was that many sides were to blame for political violence. The accusations that could be made against the SA could also be made against the Reich Banner, so why ban only the SA? In fact, the "file" contained only clippings from right-wing newspapers and a polemical commentary on a Reich Banner training manual, and was hardly the last word in domestic intelligence. Groener had long since discounted it. Still, it had the desired effect: an annoyed Hindenburg called for an investigation of the Reich Banner.

Schleicher's rage over the ban drove him to a still more dangerous and politically fateful step. He shed his last reservations about the Nazis and opened negotiations with Hitler.

The Nazis were keen to negotiate with Schleicher, for they knew where power really lay. Wilhelm Frick, an early Nazi activist and eventually Hitler's interior minister, made the point bluntly in 1932 to Schleicher's biographer Rudolf Fischer: "He [Schleicher] alone has at least 100,000 men behind him," referring to the army. Everyone knew how much influence Schleicher had with Hindenburg. The failure of the Beer Hall Putsch had taught Hitler that the Nazis could come to power only with Hindenburg and the army and never against them. Together, Schleicher and the Nazis began plotting. They had a list of the things they all wanted: the repeal of the SA ban, the fall of Brüning and Groener, and the end of the Braun-Severing administration in Prussia.

It is easy to see how these points of agreement could emerge from Schleicher's wounded feelings and desire for revenge against Brüning and Groener. Yet they also fit with his longer-term strategy of establishing a workable right-wing government. They were disastrous for German democracy, and in the following two months, they all came to pass.

On a late-April car journey with Wilhelm Groener, "in glorious weather along the Rhine," Brüning and his minister had the time for a longer and more personal conversation than usual. As the miles ticked by, Brüning's last illusions fell one by one. Groener knew that Schleicher had been scheming against him. He was badly shaken. Groener recounted how he had discovered Schleicher, furthered his career, and "loved him like a son."

Brüning asked the general to tell him about his experiences in the wartime high command. Groener talked about Hindenburg. He had had "strong doubts" about Hindenburg's character, he said, since the summer of 1919. Friedrich Ebert's government had been ready to refuse to sign the Treaty of Versailles if Hindenburg attested that the army could still defend Germany. Hindenburg told Groener that "you know as well as I" that there could be no possibility of military resistance, but had left Groener to give this advice to Ebert, so that Hindenburg could escape responsibility. Hindenburg had repaid this by leaving Groener to face public criticism undefended for fourteen years. After this conversation,

Brüning recognized that "a policy that was built on a personality like Hindenburg would *have* to fail once again."

Even as Brüning and Groener drove along the Rhine, Schleicher was working to overthrow Brüning's administration.

Through April and May an active conspiracy developed, involving on the one hand Hitler, Goebbels, Hermann Göring, Gregor Strasser, and Count Wolff Heinrich von Helldorff, the Berlin SA commander, and on the other hand, Schleicher, eventually joined by Meissner and Oskar von Hindenburg. The conspirators agreed on the importance of toppling Groener and Brüning, and between them worked out the personnel and the policies of the cabinet that would replace them. They also wanted to get rid of the Braun-Severing administration in Prussia, which was limping along as a "caretaker" government after losing its majority in the state elections of April 24, in which the Nazis had taken 36.3 percent of the vote.

The Schleicher-Nazi negotiations revealed the pressures under which both sides felt they were working. For Schleicher, it was urgent to get a right-wing bloc of support behind the administration and move away from Brüning's center-left orientation—all the more so after Schleicher's stinging defeat with the SA ban. Goebbels, always a realist when it came to political tactics, recognized that the Nazis' electoral momentum could be fragile and that they needed to obtain results soon. "We stand before a difficult decision," he wrote on April 27. Only with the Center Party could they form a coalition and get at least a share of power. Yet working the Center was an unpalatable prospect. Even so, "we have to get power," Goebbels wrote. Otherwise, the Nazis would simply win themselves "to death" in elections.

On April 28, Hitler and Schleicher met directly, remarkably enough accompanied by Hammerstein-Equord, who was an anti-Nazi but wanted to see the repeal of the SA ban and the fall of Groener. That night, Helldorff called Goebbels to tell him that the meeting had gone well and that they had all agreed on what to do. "Brüning is supposed to fall even this week," Goebbels wrote on May 9, as "the old man [Hindenburg] is withdrawing his confidence."

May 9 also marked the start of a four-day Reichstag session that would feature a debate on the SA ban, a furious Nazi attack on Groener, and a motion of no confidence in Brüning's government brought by the Nazis, the German Nationals, and the Communists. Schleicher secretly fed Göring damaging information about Groener. Groener, who was ill, defended himself weakly in a performance that even sympathetic observers thought would mark the end of his political career. But Brüning spoke effectively, and his government won the confidence vote. Afterward, Schleicher pressured Groener into resigning by claiming that the defense minister had lost the confidence of the army's commanders.

"When the mantle falls, so falls the Duke," wrote Goebbels on May 12—a reference to Schiller's play *A Republican Tragedy.*

Brüning was the duke, and by May 24, Goebbels knew that Hindenburg would sack the chancellor that coming weekend.

The following Sunday, May 29, Brüning went for his final interview with Hindenburg. He noticed Schleicher's coat and hat in the anteroom. Hindenburg put on his glasses, took a document from his desk, and read aloud: Brüning's administration would not be permitted any more executive orders or changes in personnel.

"If I understand this statement which you have just read to me correctly, Herr Reich President, you would like the resignation of the entire cabinet."

"Yes," said Hindenburg. "The administration must go, because it is unpopular." Hindenburg obviously did not care what the outcome of the presidential election and the recent confidence vote had shown about the popularity of Brüning and his administration. He just wanted the resignations as soon as possible. He told Brüning, "My conscience compels me to break with you." Still, he wanted Brüning to stay on as foreign minister. Brüning replied coldly, "Herr Reich President, I have a conscience, too." He declined any further office.

On Tuesday, May 31, Goebbels recorded in his diary, "The bomb burst yesterday. At 12:00 Brüning submitted the resignation of the entire cabinet to the old man." He added a telling note: "With that, the System has fallen."

FRANZ VON PAPEN was not an obvious choice to succeed Brüning as chancellor of the German Reich.

Papen was born in 1879 in Westphalia into an aristocratic family. His father, a friend of Kaiser Wilhelm II, had served in the Franco-Prussian War, and like Hindenburg, he had been present at the proclamation of the German Empire at Versailles in 1871. As a younger son, Papen would not inherit his father's estate and had to find a profession. He chose the army. He was educated at military academies and, in 1898, commissioned as a second lieutenant in a cavalry regiment. Papen's excellent horsemanship led him to a number of racing victories and also to his enduring nickname, which political opponents would later use against him: the "gentleman jockey." Later, undergoing training at the War Academy to serve on the Prussian General Staff, one of his fellow students was Kurt von Schleicher.

In January 1914, he was posted as military attaché to the German embassy in Washington, DC, where he got to know the young assistant secretary of the navy, Franklin D. Roosevelt, and a rising young military officer named Douglas MacArthur, among many others. When war broke out that summer, Papen ran an intelligence and sabotage operation from a base in New York City, trying to prevent Canadian soldiers from reaching Europe; luring Irish American and German American workers away from the armaments industry; and frustrating American arms production for the Allies by buying up essential supplies. This work came to an end in 1915, when American intelligence officers managed to steal documents from a member of Papen's staff during a ride on a New York subway train. The documents were leaked to the press, and Papen was declared persona non grata at the end of the year.

In a display of incompetence that would surprise no German of the early 1930s, Papen mistakenly assumed that his safe passage home extended to his luggage. It did not, and many confidential documents revealing the names of German agents in the United States fell into the hands of British intelligence. The British published a selection of the documents, and Papen became, in this undesired way, a worldwide celebrity.

Papen redeemed himself by serving with distinction in the Kaiser's army. In 1917, he was sent as a staff officer to the German troops in Turkey, where he met Mustafa Kemal, the future Kemal Atatürk, and was given the rank of major-general in the Ottoman Army. When the war ended, the German commander in Turkey, Liman von Sanders, permitted the formation of a revolutionary soldiers' council among the interned German soldiers, on the model of developments in Germany. Papen rebelled against the revolutionary council and thus against von Sanders's orders. When he made it back to Germany and reported to Hindenburg, the field marshal approved of his actions and did not allow Papen to be prosecuted for breach of discipline.

Papen left the army and went into politics. As a devout Catholic, he joined the Center Party and, in 1921, was elected to the Prussian parliament. Ideologically, the German Nationals would have suited him better, but they were too Protestant—proof again of the power of Germany's political confessions. In his first parliamentary term, he spoke often, and later in the decade, he was occasionally considered for various high offices. Though he became a majority shareholder of *Germania*, the Center's main newspaper, Papen gradually isolated himself within his own party. He frequently broke party discipline and even supported Hindenburg against the Center's Wilhelm Marx in the 1925 presidential election—which once again stored up credit with the old field marshal. Until 1932, however, he remained more a well-connected insider than a publicly prominent figure.

Papen was every inch the aristocrat—smooth, urbane, and always elegantly tailored. He had a worldly air and a reputation for light and amusing conversation, including in fluent French. In every possible respect, he was the opposite of the earnest and uncharismatic Brüning. No one considered Papen very bright, and he had nothing like the reputation for policy expertise of Brüning in finance or Stresemann in diplomacy. Papen himself wrote that he was "thoroughly conscious of the limits of my knowledge." The wonderfully malicious French ambassador André François-Poncet wrote that Papen "enjoyed the peculiarity of being taken seriously by neither his friends nor his enemies."

This, then, was the man whom Hindenburg commissioned as chancellor on June 1, 1932, replacing Heinrich Brüning. Just as in the change-over from Müller to Brüning in 1930, Schleicher had probably had Papen in mind for months as Brüning's successor, although Papen claimed he knew nothing of these plans until a phone call from Schleicher on May 26 summoned him to Berlin from his Saarland estate. More plausible is Papen's account of how much Schleicher had already arranged. He had picked out Papen's cabinet—"you will certainly like it"—and had dis-cussed Papen's appointment with Hindenburg. He told Papen about his negotiations with the Nazis over repealing the SA ban. The Nazis, he said, had promised in return to support Papen's administration.

Papen's inadequacies did not worry Schleicher. They were the point. Schleicher intended Papen to be his puppet. Schleicher arranged for himself to rise to defense minister in the new administration and imagined he would be the real power in the cabinet. When a friend com-plained to Schleicher that "Papen is not a head!" Schleicher replied, "He doesn't have to be. He is a hat."

Papen's government marked a dramatic lurch away from democratic constitutionality and the rule of law. His cabinet was far more right-wing and socially elite than Brüning's. With seven aristocrats and only three middle-class members, it soon acquired the nickname "the cabinet of barons." Before 1918, this cabinet's elite profile would have passed without comment. But by 1932 the culture had changed and Germans expected a more socially inclusive administration. Under the terms of the deal Schleicher had worked out with the Nazis, the SA ban was lifted and a Reichstag election was called for July 31. Predictably, the level of politi-cal violence shot upward, and just as predictably, Papen's response was authoritarian. In August, he issued two executive orders creating "Spe-cial Courts" for political violence, stripping defendants of most of their procedural rights, including that of appeal, and instituting death sentences for those convicted of homicide. In language that already sounded Nazi, a Berlin prosecutor explained that the Special Courts were sup-posed to "obliterate elements hostile to the state."

Brüning had been a "presidential" chancellor, governing by executive orders, which was already a step away from parliamentary democracy. Yet, right up to the end, he had had a de facto parliamentary majority behind him. His administration was more democratic in practice than it was in theory—exactly why Hindenburg and Schleicher had wanted to get rid of it. Papen's government was entirely different. Brüning had relied on executive orders to cope with parliamentary stalemate. Papen and Schleicher wanted to use executive orders to end parliamentary gov-ernment altogether. The sharp-eyed diarist Count Harry Kessler saw the point immediately. Brüning's dismissal meant not only "the end, for the moment, of the parliamentary republic," but also an "essential escalation of the world crisis." Sardonically, he noted that the Berlin stock exchange had reacted with a steep rise in values, "probably in anticipation of the blessings of the Third Reich."

The Social Democrats would not "tolerate" Papen as they had his predecessor, and the Center Party was enraged by Papen's betrayal of Brüning. The new administration would have to depend on the far right, the Nationalists and the Nazis. This of course was the whole idea: it was Schleicher's strategy to assemble a new right-wing majority. He was as unconcerned by signs that the Nazis would achieve a huge gain in the coming elections as he was by Papen's lack of gravitas. That, too, was all in the plan. Of course, the plan depended on Nazi good faith—and as Konrad Heiden had observed, mistrust was a rare political virtue.

Yet another lurch away from democracy was coming. Schleicher had long been developing a plan for a coup d'état against Prussia's democratic government. It was another part of his arrangement with the Nazis. One of Papen's functions in Schleicher's eyes was to serve as the front man for the coup.

Schleicher's thinking was subtle, however, and revealed once again his two-track strategy with the Nazis: to use them while containing them. Schleicher thought the Nazis' claim on power could be satisfied with control of Prussia. Central to this strategy, however, was that the Nazis would get a Prussia without its fifty-thousand-strong police force, itself a major power factor in the Reich. If the Nazis were going to have Prussia, Schleicher wanted the police under the control of the central government.

Schleicher prepared his coup carefully. He enlisted the aid of a young official in the Prussian interior ministry named Rudolf Diels. Diels, a handsome and highly intelligent ladies' man, had been brought to the ministry to strengthen its democratic forces when the officials took him for a liberal. But Diels was mostly interested in his own career, and his shrewd political instincts told him that the nationalist right was now a better bet. He started conspiring along with Schleicher, Papen, and, by the summer of 1932, the Nazis. The conspirators assigned Diels the crucial task of digging up "information" concerning supposed illicit ties between the Prussian government and the Communists. The information was meant for Hindenburg. The president had insisted that he would move against the Prussian government only if he were shown evidence of treason that would support a case in the Supreme Constitutional Court.

Diels got the evidence, such as it was, in a particularly tricky way. His superior, Wilhelm Abegg, head of the Prussian interior ministry's police division, arranged to meet secretly with two Communist politicians—to encourage them to tone down their violence, not to conspire against the state. Diels volunteered to sit in on the meeting, promising Abegg to be a sympathetic witness. Afterward, he gave Papen a distorted account of the meeting, falsely implicating Abegg in conspiracy and treason.

Schleicher had cynically calculated that ending the SA ban would cause political violence to rise, for which the Prussian government could be blamed. On July 17, in Altona, a suburb of Hamburg, violence erupted between Nazis and Communists. Fifteen people were killed and more than sixty wounded. The event became known as "Bloody Sunday." Although Hamburg was a city-state within the German Reich, Altona lay across the border in the Prussian province of Schleswig-Holstein, and so the Prussian government was responsible for order there.

On July 20, after thorough consultation and planning with the Nazis, Papen struck. Under an executive order signed by Hindenburg, relying on the emergency powers in Article 48 of the Constitution, he removed the Braun-Severing administration from office. Papen himself became the "Reich commissar" and therefore head of the Prussian government. The new acting Prussian interior minister, in control of the all-important police, was Franz Bracht, the former mayor of Essen and a member of the Center Party. Goebbels had known of his appointment in advance.

Papen's administration gave different versions of its reasons for the coup. A written official statement emphasized the political violence the Prussian government allegedly could not control. Subordinate points mentioned that senior Prussian officials had lost the "inner independence" to combat communism, and complained of Carl Severing's "unrestrained sharp attacks" on the Reich government. Yet, in a radio address to the nation on the evening of July 20, Papen himself put it differently. The point he stressed was that when "high-level functionaries of the Prussian state offer their hand to leaders of the Communist Party to make possible the concealment of illegal plans for terrorist activities . . . then the authority of the state is undermined from above in a way that is untenable for the security of the Reich." Papen repeatedly mentioned communism but never addressed the threat from the extreme right.

The "Papen coup," as it became known, was a decisive nail in the coffin of German democracy and a spectacular legal abuse, roughly comparable to an American president simultaneously removing the governors of New York and California from office and taking over their jobs personally. The Braun-Severing administration was the last important democratic government Germany had. With its dissolution, a major obstacle to dictatorship was gone.

The Prussian ministers, exhausted by years of political battles, did little to fight back. There were no mass protests. Instead, the Braun-Severing administration took Papen to court. In the autumn, it won a partial victory, but by then it did not matter very much.

Young Rudolf Diels's fortunes continued to rise. Less than a year after the Papen coup, the Nazis made him chief of the Prussian secret police. This was the organization that grew into the Gestapo.

ON JULY 31, the Nazis won their most stunning electoral victory yet. With 37.3 percent of the vote and 230 Reichstag seats, they were now by a wide margin Germany's largest party. The Social Democrats, with 21.5 percent and 133 seats, came in a distant second. This outcome would prove to be the Nazis' best performance in a wholly free election. It was an unsurprising product of the dramatically worsening economic situation since 1931 and of growing German anger at uncontrollable global forces, filtered through the "confessional" structure of German politics. Once again, the strongest Nazi support came from Protestant rural areas such as Schleswig-Holstein.

The night of the election, Nazi Stormtroopers launched a wave of violence that swept across much of northern and eastern Germany. It started in Königsberg with six murders and attempted murders of local officials or Communist politicians, along with a dozen arson attacks, including on the local Social Democratic headquarters and a liberal newspaper office. In the days that followed, the Stormtroopers' violence spread across East Prussia and into Silesia. The climax came on the night of August 9–10, in the Silesian village of Potempa. In the small hours, a group of Stormtroopers broke into the house shared by a thirty-five-year-old Polish worker named Konrad Pietrzuch, his younger brother Alfons, and their mother, Maria. The Stormtroopers savagely beat Konrad in front of his mother and then shot him dead. They beat Alfons into unconsciousness.

The Stormtroopers probably did not know that just as they committed their crime, Papen's draconian executive orders providing for expedited trials and quick death sentences for politically motivated homicide had just gone into effect. On August 11, nine of the Nazis were arrested for Pietrzuch's murder. And on August 22, the newly formed Special Court in the town of Beuthen sentenced five of them to death.

The Nazi leaders responded to these sentences (certainly not to the underlying crime) with venom. They blamed Papen's administration. In a telegram to the five condemned men, Hitler called the sentences "a most outrageous blood verdict." "From now on," he continued, "your freedom is a question of honor for all of us, and to fight against the government which has made possible such a verdict is our duty." In an article in the Nazi paper the *Völkischer Beobachter*, Hitler issued an unmistakable threat against Papen, who had "engraved his name with the blood of national warriors on German history." Göring also sent the men a telegram of support, and the SA commander Ernst Röhm visited them in prison. This sequence of events—the Nazis' brutality and their leaders' defiance in the face of it—came as a shock not only to many in the German public and media who were otherwise sympathetic to the Nazis, but also to the administration and the army. It seemed that the Nazis were once again leaving the path of "legality." The army started drawing up plans for the suppression of Hitler's party, and Papen's cabinet began thinking hard about its strategy.

With the election and its violent aftermath, the endgame of the Weimar Republic had begun. Over the next five months, from August 1932 to January 1933, German politics would take the form of a duel between Schleicher and Hitler. Papen stood first on one side and then the other. The point of the duel was to capture the favor of Hindenburg.

The Nazi leaders had a plan for how they would get and hold power, the details of which were worked out largely by Wilhelm Frick, a lawyer and early Nazi activist who had served briefly as interior minister in the state of Thuringia. Other Nazi leaders such as Göring, Goebbels, and Strasser—to say nothing of Hitler—also played a part. They knew that their main threat to the establishment came from the fact that they could deploy the SA in a civil war. Ultimately, only President Hindenburg could appoint a chancellor; so the Nazis' strategy was directed to him as well. They planned to threaten or intimidate Hindenburg into naming Hitler chancellor. Under Article 43 of the Weimar constitution, the president could be impeached through a two-thirds majority vote in the Reichstag, which would then have to be confirmed by a national referendum. Alternatively, under Article 59, one hundred Reichstag deputies could propose and a two-thirds majority could confirm that the president be prosecuted for illegal actions in office.

Hindenburg's practice with executive orders since 1930 and the Prussian coup offered plausible targets for a hostile Reichstag majority—and the developing political crisis promised to bring still more. Heinrich Brüning remembered years later that Gregor Strasser, with whom he had become friends in 1932, told him that "immediately after the Reichstag elections of July 1932, the National Socialists intended to bring an application under Article 59" for an "indictment of the Reich president" and one "for Hindenburg's removal from office according to Article 43." The Nazis would allege, said Strasser, that Hindenburg had acted illegally in ordering the Prussian coup.

Hindenburg, Papen, and Schleicher had two choices. They could find a way to involve the Nazis in governing—by bringing them into the cabinet or at least arranging that their parliamentary caucus "tolerate" Papen's administration. Or they could dissolve the Reichstag again, probably while also delaying a new election, which would be unconstitutional and would risk civil war if the Nazis responded with more SA violence. In 1932, more and more German politicians and lawyers were beginning to talk about this second option. It was based on the assumption that the deadlock between Reichstag and administration rendered the proper functioning of the state impossible and amounted to a governmental state of emergency, or *Staatsnotstand*. The specter of the state of emergency and the response of dissolving the Reichstag and postponing elections, with the risk of violence and civil war, hovered over all the events of the second half of the year, especially after Königsberg and Potempa.

The point was clear to all the main players: with their high-handed treatment of Brüning and the Social Democrats, Schleicher and Papen had painted themselves into a corner. They could now find support only on the far right. Yet the traditional conservatives, the German Nationals, did not have the strength to support an administration on their own. The Nazis certainly offered the chance of such support, but at a price few in the mainstream wanted to pay. And the Communists loomed. In July, they had reached a new high of 14.5 percent of the vote, more than the Center Party.

The intransigence of Germany's political parties, especially the right-wingers, and several years of miscalculation by Hindenburg, Schleicher, Brüning, and Papen, had thrown German politics into a full-blown crisis. The Nazis knew they could not come to power against the establishment. But neither could the establishment go on without the Nazis.

Schleicher met with Hitler again on August 6. Hitler had worked out his plans with Goebbels the day before. He would demand the chancellorship for himself and cabinet posts for four other leading Nazis: Wilhelm Frick as interior minister, Hermann Göring as minister of air transport, Gregor Strasser as minister of labor, and Goebbels as minister of "people's education." Since Hitler now led the largest party, he was in a position to make such demands, and it seems that Schleicher agreed, with the qualification that Frick be the state secretary in the Reich Chancellery. Yet, when Schleicher presented the plan to Hindenburg, the old field marshal was furious. He found the very idea of having as his chancellor the man he called "the Bohemian private" an outrage. He was insulted that Schleicher would even suggest it. Hindenburg's dignity was sensitive, and he was no less peevish with Schleicher than he had been with Brüning in earlier days. This exchange sparked a deterioration in Schleicher's relationship with Hindenburg.

On August 10, Papen's cabinet wrestled inconclusively with its dilemma. Papen put a brave face on things, saying that his government had been formed to create a synthesis of the political right, and the election had justified the strategy. Now the question was how the state should "enlist" the "right-wing movement." Was there a "middle way" between maintaining a presidential cabinet and the Nazis' desire to take over power?

Schleicher spoke next and told the cabinet bluntly that there were two choices. The present cabinet could keep going, in the hope that its policies would bring economic recovery and eventually popularity. Yet Papen's administration could count on Reichstag support only from the German Nationals, who held fewer than 10 percent of the seats, and excluding the Nazis from power altogether meant risking civil war. The Nazis might seek a way out by forming a coalition with the Center, which would yield a parliamentary majority. Alternatively, Papen could negotiate to bring several Nazis into the cabinet. But, Schleicher warned his colleagues, "in the interest of his movement" Hitler would insist on "the highest post."

Justice minister Franz Gürtner was equally blunt: the present cabinet could not remain in office unchanged without breaching the constitution, and he would have to advise the Reich president accordingly. What Gürtner meant was that to stay in office, Papen's administration would have to opt for the state of emergency, breaching the constitution and becoming an unambiguous dictatorship. Gürtner also said that the idea that the Nazis could be brought into the cabinet without giving them the leadership was a "pipe dream." He added that the Nazis' idea of the state was "strongly based on the instinct for revenge," particularly against Jews and "Marxists," a remarkable statement from a man who would go on to serve as Hitler's minister of justice for eight years.

In an uncanny echo of the cabinet's deliberations, Goebbels recorded an almost identical analysis in his diary on August 12. "The old man is reluctant," he wrote. "Doesn't want Hitler as Chancellor." Yet that was not negotiable. "If Schleicher doesn't hold up, threaten with the Center. That will mean his and Papen's head. The Commies or us, that is the question."

The moment of decision came on August 13. Hindenburg summoned Hitler to an audience. The Nazis were doing their level best to intimidate Hindenburg and Papen with the threat of civil war. Goebbels wrote in his diary that "Papen is getting weak." The Brownshirts had been ostentatiously mobilized in large numbers around Berlin. "Makes the gentlemen very nervous," wrote Goebbels. "That's the point of the exercise."

He noted nervously that Papen, Schleicher, and Meissner all wanted Hitler in the government, "Papen even strongly," but Hindenburg had "doubts." "Terrible, that one cannot talk the whole complex through with Hindenburg because of his age." On August 13, Hitler would meet with Schleicher, Papen, and then finally Hindenburg. "Then comes the decision. Will the fruit of ten years' work now be ripe?" Goebbels wondered.

At 3:00 that afternoon, Papen's state secretary, Erwin Planck, telephoned Hitler, who knew by this time that Schleicher and Papen wanted to fob him off with the vice-chancellorship. "Has the decision been made already?" Hitler asked Planck. "If so, there is no point in my coming." "Well, the Reich president wants to speak to you," Planck replied. This raised, said Goebbels, "short, vague hope." Hitler went to his appointment with Hindenburg.

Hindenburg opened the conversation in a friendly tone. He was ready, he explained, to ask Hitler and the National Socialists to participate in the administration, and would welcome their collaboration. Was Hitler willing to be a part of Papen's government? No, said Hitler. As he had explained to Papen earlier, this was out of the question. The importance of the National Socialist movement entitled him to the chancellorship.

Hindenburg's response was firm. He explained that he could not "before God, [my] conscience and the fatherland" turn the government over to one party, still less a party that was "biased against those who thought differently." He also worried about "great disturbances" at home and opinion abroad.

Hitler repeated that any other solution was impossible for him.

"So you will go into opposition, then?" Hindenburg asked.

"I have no other option," said Hitler.

Hindenburg asked Hitler to conduct his opposition "chivalrously" and patriotically. "I have had no doubts about your patriotism," he said, but he would take firm action against any acts of terror and violence by the SA. "We are old comrades," said Hindenburg, the field marshal rather absurdly trying to strike a bond with the private over their war service, "and want to remain so. So, I would like to hold out my hand to you in a comradely spirit." This took considerable self-discipline for Hindenburg.

He had nothing but contempt for the "Bohemian private," and was even less happy that he had had to shake hands with Hitler's associate, the openly gay Ernst Röhm.

Hitler was furious. Afterward, in the corridor outside Hindenburg's office, his rage led him to blurt out an element of the Nazis' strategy. He told Papen and Meissner that either he would come to power or Hindenburg would be overthrown, pointing to the plan to threaten Hindenburg with impeachment or prosecution. Tellingly, this threat appears in Otto Meissner's summary of the conversation but not in the one prepared by Hitler's side. Hitler added that the Nazis' opposition to Papen's administration would be fierce, and he warned that he could take no responsibility for the consequences.

Hitler thought that Schleicher had promised him the chancellorship at their meeting on August 6 and had now double-crossed him. Even Papen was irritated that Schleicher had been talking to Hitler behind Papen's back. These grudges would simmer through the autumn.

PAPEN'S GOVERNMENT WRESTLED with the problem of how to handle the crisis for two more weeks, but it was Schleicher and his staff from the defense ministry who worked out the strategy—with significant assistance from the constitutional law professor Carl Schmitt, who would later go on to be so prominent in Nazi Germany that he was dubbed the Nazis' "crown jurist." On August 30, at a meeting at Hindenburg's Neudeck estate, the president, Meissner, Papen, Schleicher, and interior minister Baron Wilhelm von Gayl agreed to pursue the state of emergency. Since Hindenburg did not want to be seen to break the law, they massaged the point for him. Schmitt had given the government a legal opinion that the president's duty to preserve the German people from harm in Article 42 of the constitution overrode the mandated time to an election in Article 24. Hindenburg accepted this. He authorized the dissolution of the Reichstag and the postponement of an election beyond sixty days. The ministers thought there were signs the economy was improving. The more the economy recovered, the more Nazi support would fade. They would simply run out the clock on the Nazis.

Or at least, that was the plan. But not for the first time, and not for the last, Papen's incompetence got in the way. The new Reichstag session opened on August 30, with the key ministers in Neudeck. They airily assumed it would adjourn while more coalition negotiations went on— and it did, though not before electing Hermann Göring as its new speaker. Göring let slip another indication of the Nazis' strategy. The newly elected Reichstag had a "large nationalist majority, capable of work," he said. The situation in no way met "the legal requirements of a state of emergency." It is very likely that Göring and the Nazis knew what Hindenburg and his ministers were discussing in Neudeck, and were now issuing a warning that relying on the state of emergency could be just the legal justification the opposition needed to move for Hindenburg's impeachment.

The Reichstag met again two weeks later, on September 12. The Communists proposed a motion of no confidence in Papen's administration. There was a recess while the other parties met and ultimately agreed to support it. Papen had assumed he would have a chance to give his government's declaration before anything like this happened, and he was so unprepared for a confidence vote he had not even brought Hindenburg's dissolution order with him. He had to have it rushed over from his office. When the assembly reconvened, Göring called for a vote on the Communist motion. The wasp-tongued André François-Poncet described what happened next: "Papen, bobbing up in his seat and brandishing a paper in his hand, requested the floor. Göring was aware of the Chancellor's agitation and plainly understood that the paper Papen was waving was a decree of dissolution. But he pretended he did not see, he looked in the other direction; obstinately he turned his back upon the Chancellor while pressing for an immediate vote." François-Poncet saw Papen approach Göring and place the dissolution order on a corner of his desk.

The result of the vote, 512 to 42, was a humiliating defeat for Papen— in fact, the worst parliamentary defeat any German administration had ever suffered. Papen drew support only from the German Nationals and the German People's Party, both of them drastically reduced in strength as their voters had fled to the Nazis. Only after the vote was taken did Göring seem to notice Papen's dissolution order. He read it to the house and dismissed it as worthless, "since it was countersigned by a ministry legally deposed."

Schleicher sought to convince Hindenburg to stick with the plan of dissolving the Reichstag and delaying an election. But the scale of Papen's defeat was too severe to serve as a basis for the state of emergency. Hindenburg now refused to postpone an election, and another vote was duly scheduled for November 6.

After two rounds of the presidential election, the state elections of late April, and the Reichstag election of July 31, this would be the fifth major campaign of the year in Germany. Fatigue was setting in. Voter turnout would drop from 84 percent of the electorate in July to 80.5 percent in November. The parties' campaign coffers were severely strained.

Anger and fear were still running high. Enraged at the rejection they had experienced in August, the Nazis now campaigned without mercy against Papen, Hindenburg, and the German Nationals. After all, they were competing for the same voters. "We are now going over to the attack," said an order from Goebbels's propaganda department. The point was to show that Papen's cabinet was a "feudal clique." The Nazi Stormtroopers diverted some of their violence from the Communists to the German Nationals. In October, in a debate with the German National Reichstag deputy Otto Schmidt-Hannover, Goebbels growled, "In Berlin we have laid twenty-six SA men in their graves. Where are the martyrs for your party?"

Schleicher's staff was drafting plans for civil war, even for a preemptive strike on the Nazis. Some rough notes from a meeting reveal Schleicher's thinking about Hitler's party—as always, open to different possibilities. "Will you play along?" Schleicher wrote. "If not, there will be a fight."

In this atmosphere, the election outcome was an anticlimax and changed nothing in the political deadlock. The Nazis remained the largest party, but their share of the vote dropped from 37 percent to 33 percent. Some of their support had bled back to the German Nationals, staying within the Protestant middle-class camp.

Yet political changes were coming nonetheless.

Papen had begun to grate on Schleicher's nerves. The "gentleman jockey" enjoyed occupying a prestigious office, but he had little enthusiasm for work. On one occasion, as his cabinet wrestled with critical issues of constitutional procedure and the threat of civil war, Papen arrived two hours late for the meeting in formal dress, with a carnation in his buttonhole. "You can take care of these little details yourself," he airily told his ministers, and left for the horse races at Hoppegarten.

Schleicher had probably expected this kind of thing from Papen. After all, he had wanted a chancellor who would do what he was told and be content as a puppet. The problem was that having tasted power, Papen was starting to exercise it. "What do you say," Schleicher wrote ruefully to a friend, "little Franz has discovered himself." In Schleicher's view, Papen had missed the chance to bring the Nazis into the government, the one crucial political task Schleicher had wanted him to execute. By November, many mainstream figures thought all they had to do was wait for the Nazis to disintegrate further, but for Schleicher, this made winning over the Nazis all the more urgent. If they fell apart, he worried, their support would go over to the Communists, who might then be unstoppable. Schleicher thought the election results of November 6, with Nazi losses and still more Communist gains (the Communists won nearly 17 percent of the vote, making them the third-largest party and now well ahead of the Center), showed that this was already happening.

Perhaps most important, Schleicher had heard that the key Nazi official Gregor Strasser opposed Hitler's policy of holding out for the chancellorship, and might be willing to "throw himself personally into the breach" if nothing came of Hitler's plans.

These issues came to a head on December 1. That evening, Hindenburg summoned Papen and Schleicher to meet with him; his son, Oskar; and Otto Meissner. Hindenburg began the meeting by asking Papen what they should do. The chancellor told him that Hitler had refused all possible parliamentary coalitions and that the only way of bringing him into the government was to make him a presidential chancellor. On August 13, Hindenburg had found this too dangerous a step to take, and the "demagogy and lack of moderation" the Nazis had shown since then had "certainly not increased confidence in Hitler's statesmanlike capabilities"—a reference to the Potempa murder and its aftermath. If there was to be no deal with the Nazis, then the only thing to do was to accept the state of emergency. Papen suggested that his administration remain in office without the Reichstag being summoned again. A new constitution could then be drafted and put to the people in a referendum or to a specially summoned national assembly. This meant violating the present constitution, but Papen assured Hindenburg there was a good precedent: no less a figure than Prince Otto von Bismarck, the architect of German unification, had acted similarly in the 1860s.

Then Schleicher spoke up. To Papen's astonishment, Schleicher said he saw a way to spare Hindenburg the need to break his oath to preserve the constitution. Schleicher said that if Hindenburg made him chancellor he could put together a majority in the new Reichstag by splitting the Nazis. Gregor Strasser would join his cabinet and bring with him sixty Nazi deputies. With their help, Schleicher could assemble a "union axis" that would extend through the centrist parties to the Social Democrats. Such a coalition could then tackle a solution to the Depression and the unemployment crisis.

Schleicher's suggestion astonished Papen. He replied that he doubted Schleicher would be able to split a party so focused on its leader, but he conceded that Schleicher knew the leading Nazis better than he did. His stronger objection was that Schleicher's plan involved a move back to a parliamentary system, whereas Papen had thought Hindenburg's plan was to create a more powerful and independent executive.

Hindenburg had listened to all this silently and seriously. Papen speculated that the Reich president was facing "the most difficult decision of his long life." Hindenburg did not discuss or debate any of the points with Papen or Schleicher; he simply stood up and said, "My decision is for Herr von Papen's solution." He asked Papen to begin right away forming a cabinet that could carry out his plans.

Now it was Schleicher's turn to be astonished. Papen recalled later that, for several weeks, he had felt that Schleicher's usual friendliness had grown markedly cooler. Now, as Papen tried to explain to Schleicher that they had to protect the president, Schleicher looked at him with uncomprehending disapproval. Drawing on the kind of religious reference that came so easily to these men, Schleicher told Papen, "Little monk, you are taking a hard path"—words of warning that had been given to Martin Luther when he took on the Catholic Church.

Now the rivalry and the grievances between Schleicher and Papen came into the open. Schleicher was determined to get rid of Papen and to do the job himself. The very next day, he came to a cabinet meeting armed with heavier ammunition: a report on the so-called Planspiel Ott, a war game that Lieutenant Colonel Eugen Ott had conducted at the defense ministry. The scenario was a civil war in which the Nazis and the Communists staged a joint uprising. The gist of Ott's report was that, faced with such an uprising *and* a foreign attack, the army would not be able to preserve order and defend the country. Schleicher conceded that the scenario was an extreme case, but now at least part of Ott's scenario did not seem so far-fetched: the Nazis and Communists had in fact worked together during an illegal transit strike in Berlin in the first days of November. For those such as Schleicher, who worried about both civil war and the crypto-Communists among the Nazis, this strike came as a warning signal. The impact of Ott's report on the cabinet was strong: Papen himself reportedly wept as he listened to it. Some cabinet members felt that Papen had lied to them about the army's ability to handle a state of emergency. They also began to think that Schleicher might be right. Perhaps he could indeed assemble a larger coalition and bring the Nazis "into the state" without completely alienating the moderate left.

Papen reported to Hindenburg what Ott had said. He explained that the president had to make a decision: he could keep Papen in office, in which case Papen wanted a new defense minister—understandably, he didn't think he could work with Schleicher any longer—or he could call on Schleicher to be chancellor.

"The Field Marshal had listened wordlessly to my explanation," Papen remembered years later. Finally, he stood up and, in a shaky voice, said, "You will think me a scoundrel, my dear Papen, if I change my mind now. But I am too old to take on the responsibility for a civil war at the end of my life. So in God's name we must let Herr von Schleicher try his luck." As they shook hands, Papen saw "two fat tears" run down Hindenburg's cheeks.

General Kurt von Schleicher now stepped out fully from his long years in the political back room. On December 3, at the age of fifty, he was sworn in as chancellor of the German Reich. He would try his luck at a broad coalition, his last, desperate effort to bring political stability on right-wing terms without civil war. He had used Ott's war game with powerful effect against Papen. He would soon see its effects rebound on him.

6

The Bohemian Private and the Gentleman Jockey

Fifteen-year-old Melita Maschmann is drawn to the Nazis out of a desire to rebel against her parents. One day, at the end of January, the family's dressmaker comes to the Maschmanns' Berlin home to alter a dress for Melita. The dressmaker limps and has a hunchback. She wears a swastika under the lapel of her coat. Melita's mother thinks it is presumptuous for working-class people to have opinions about politics, but the dressmaker tells Melita that things are changing. The day is coming, she says, when servants will no longer have to eat at the kitchen table, like inferiors.

That evening, Melita's parents take her and her twin brother, Hans-Hermann, into the center of Berlin to see a parade. "Some of the uncanny feel of that night remains with me even today," she will remember many years later. "The crashing tread of the feet, the somber pomp of the red and black flags, the flickering light from the torches on the faces and the songs with melodies that were at once aggressive and sentimental."

Melita realizes that some of the young people marching are not much older than she is. She envies them, and yearns for their sense of purpose. Being a child forces her to live a life with no stakes, a life that doesn't matter. The boys and girls in the marching columns in front of her matter. Melita notices they carry banners bearing the names of their dead.

She is not blind to the violence of the moment. She sees how suddenly one of the marchers breaks ranks to strike a spectator standing only a few feet away from her. She assumes the spectator made some kind of hostile remark. She sees him cry out and fall, with blood streaming down his face. Melita's parents pull her away, but the image haunts her for days.

Yet she finds her horror is also mixed with an "intoxicating joy." The young people marching with their torches sing of how they are ready to die for the cause. This is something far beyond Melita's daily grind of "clothing or food or school essays." She feels overcome "with a burning desire to belong to these people," for whom it is "a matter of life and death."

Many other Germans share Melita's sense of exaltation on this night. Joseph Goebbels waits for the torchlight procession at the Kaiserhof Hotel. "It begins at about 7 o'clock," he notes, and it goes on until after midnight. He has trouble finding words strong enough. "Endless," he writes, "a million people on the march . . . Awakening! Spontaneous explosion of the people. Indescribable."

Others are considerably more jaundiced. The conservative intellectual Edgar Julius Jung and the editor Rudolf Pechel watch the procession together with distaste. Finally, Jung turns to Pechel and says, "Isn't it terrible how alone we are in this German people, whom we love so much." The pithiest reaction comes from the great impressionist painter Max Liebermann, as he watches the marchers from the window of his apartment on the grand boulevard Unter den Linden: "I just can't eat as much as I would like to puke."

It is January 30, 1933.

That morning, Reich president Paul von Hindenburg has sworn in Adolf Hitler as chancellor of the German Reich. Now Hitler's followers celebrate with a torchlight procession through the center of Berlin. The Nazis' paramilitary formations, the SA and the more elite, black-uniformed SS (Schutzstaffel, or "Protection Squads"), are prominent. Yet Hitler's new administration is a coalition, and representatives of the other right-wing groups, such as the Steel Helmet, march and celebrate as well.

Hitler's movement has always been driven by the gap between two German myths: the unity of August 1914 and the betrayal of November 1918. For the Nazis, January 1933 is August. As the torch bearers file past Hitler's Chancellery window, Hermann Göring tells a radio audience that the mood can "only be compared with that of 1914." The Nazis' newspaper, *the Völkischer Beobachter, finds that "our memory drifts back to the inspiring days of August 1914. Then, as today, the signs of a people rising up." Nazis such as Goebbels and Robert Ley go so far as to say that their "revolution" really began in August 1914.*

This is a crucial element of the meaning of the event. Since 1929, Brüning, Schleicher, Papen, and Hindenburg have all been looking for a way to bring unity to Germany's fractured political right. They have been trying to find a way to recruit the Nazis to support the establishment. President Hindenburg in particular has needed a lot of persuasion to make Hitler his chancellor. Now Hindenburg stands at the window of the Old Chancellery and is serenaded by Nazi Stormtroopers. An SA band honors him by playing a march called "The Old Dessauer," the traditional salute of Prussian soldiers to their field marshal. They sing patriotic songs such as "The Watch on the Rhine." This is the national integration Hindenburg has been looking for. The mood of January 30 reassures Hindenburg that he has done the right thing by bringing Hitler to the chancellorship. A few weeks later, he writes to his daughter, "Patriotic upsurge very gratifying. God preserve our unity."

KURT VON SCHLEICHER came into office in December 1932 with a plan for solving the political crisis into which Germany had fallen that autumn.

Schleicher's plan revolved around the idea of a "cross front" (*Querfront*). The cross front was a political coalition that would unite seemingly deadly adversaries, from the Social Democrats and labor unions to the "Strasser wing" of the Nazis. It began as an idea for job creation promoted by a conservative politician named Günther Gereke. Gereke's plan called for publicly financed public works and infrastructure projects, which might employ about half a million people—conventional now, but original thinking in 1931 and 1932.

The cross-front concept was avidly discussed in the German press, and in late November, Schleicher's deputy, Ferdinand von Bredow, wrote Schleicher two acerbic memos about what he called representatives of the cross front who had been to see him to urge their case. Bredow did not think much of them. The visitors had told Bredow that they would willingly support Schleicher as chancellor, but not Papen. Among them was a Nazi activist named Reinhold Cordemann, who was friends with Strasser, Schleicher, and Gereke. Cordemann said that he was unhappy with the course of Hitler's negotiations with the Papen cabinet and Hindenburg. He thought that an "extraordinarily strong current" in the Nazi Party would regret it if the party returned to "unfruitful opposition," and in the event that Hitler "failed," the administration should try to win over the Nazi Party for work on "national tasks." Perhaps not all in the party would comply, but Cordemann thought "a considerable portion" would.

This is how Schleicher thought he could improve on Papen: the cross-front people would support him where they would not support Papen, and this would enable Schleicher to escape from Papen's trap of being supported by only 10 percent of the Reichstag. Then he would have succeeded in bringing the Nazis "into the state" and prevented a civil war.

The centerpiece of the strategy was therefore Gregor Strasser. During 1932, Strasser had been growing increasingly unhappy with Hitler's all-or-nothing approach to political power. He was on his way to becoming more of a free-thinking national conservative—more like Schleicher than like his fellow Nazis. The brutality of the Altona and Potempa killings, to say nothing of Hitler's defense of the Potempa murderers, had sickened Strasser, leading him increasingly to reject the Nazis' cult of violence. In the summer of 1932, he met Schleicher for the first time, at the home of another cross-front advocate, the journalist Hans Zehrer. Zehrer wanted to bring together not only Schleicher and Strasser but also Strasser and the labor unions. The cross-front supporters who visited Bredow in November told him that Strasser was ready to "throw himself into the breach."

On November 28, Schleicher saw André François-Poncet at a dinner given by Otto Meissner. The two men were on friendly terms, and François-Poncet reported to Paris the next day that Schleicher had spoken "very freely to me about the political situation." Schleicher said that he had asked Strasser, "Hitler's most intelligent lieutenant," if he would accept the position of interior minister in a Schleicher cabinet. Strasser replied that he would like to get Hitler's permission to do so, but if Hitler refused, Schleicher continued, "it is possible that he [Strasser] will cross over." This would "throw a new disorder" into the ranks of the Nazi Party, said Schleicher, which would be "of great importance for the future." If Strasser agreed to join him, Schleicher felt he would be "obliged" to take over the chancellery and form a cabinet. Indeed, he told François-Poncet that "most of the people I have seen" had reacted positively to the idea of his chancellorship. The Social Democrats had warned Schleicher that they could not refrain from fighting him, but he had asked if they might do so with restraint, and "they have not refused this." He also related that the labor unions, "serious and positive people," had been very friendly to him.

Schleicher was therefore confident that he would be able to find a parliamentary majority stretching ideologically from Strasser to the Social Democrats. He told a cabinet meeting on December 7 that "if the Center, the Bavarian People's Party, the so-called Technical Working Community [a loose grouping of smaller centrist parties] and the National Socialists come together in the most important points, a majority will come into being even without the German Nationals."

Schleicher being Schleicher, he was working on several possibilities at once. He was not completely blind to the dangers that working with the Nazis presented; nor was Strasser the only egg in his basket. On December 1, Schleicher sent the trusty Eugen Ott, architect of the war game, to the town of Weimar, where Hitler was campaigning in local elections. Ott's mission was to offer Hitler the position of vice-chancellor and to see if the Nazis would tolerate a Schleicher administration. Hitler resolutely refused both suggestions. Ott then delivered a warning: "Should you collaborate with the Communists, as in the Berlin transit strike, then I guarantee you, Herr Hitler, that you will be standing before the machine guns of the army."

That Schleicher would send Ott on this mission seems at first glance strange. Schleicher and Hitler had met just a week before, on November 23, and Schleicher had asked Hitler a series of questions. Would Hitler be willing to join a "differently composed and perhaps differently led" cabinet? The answer was no. Would he allow other members of his party to join a cabinet he did not lead? Again, a firm no. Would he fight a cabinet led by Schleicher? To this, Hitler answered yes, though he courteously added that he would "very much regret this necessary fight." Schleicher therefore knew Hitler's position and could hardly expect different answers a week later. In all likelihood, the real point of Ott's mission was to deliver to Hitler the threat about "machine guns."

The reality was that in this tense political deadlock, both Schleicher and Hitler were under enormous pressure. Each had weapons he could bring to bear, and each could feel that time was running out. Around the beginning of December, Schleicher told an associate, "If Hitler thinks about it too long, I'll just dissolve the Reichstag. Hitler doesn't have the money for another election campaign." This was Schleicher's threat. Hitler could threaten civil war, which presumably Ott's visit to Weimar was meant to neutralize. Hitler also had to worry that his movement was losing momentum and, if it did not come to power soon, might dissolve completely. Paradoxically, as we have seen, this was Schleicher's worry as well: if the Nazis fell apart because they had gained no access to power, the only winners would be the Communists.

Soon after accepting the chancellorship, Schleicher delivered the traditional government's declaration, a speech that demonstrated his rhetorical and political skill. He had hesitated to take on this office, he said. It was not just that he did not want to succeed his friend Papen, whom (along with Brüning) he praised extravagantly. He was also aware that having the defense minister as chancellor could awaken fears of a military dictatorship and drag the army into politics. Only the idea that the drastic nature of this step might have a "cooling" effect on "certain troublemakers," and thereby avoid any need to deploy the army in domestic conflicts, had overcome his doubts. He asked his "national comrades" to see him not as "only the soldier" but as a "social general," the "nonpartisan custodian" of the interests of all classes of society, and even that only for a short interval. He had "come to bring peace, not the sword."

Schleicher understood that not everyone would find his "social general" identity plausible—he could imagine many of his listeners reacting with "a doubtful or even a mocking shrug." He insisted that there had been "nothing more social than the [prewar] army of general conscription, in which poor and rich, officers and men" had served and, in the war, had proven their "comradeship and feeling of belonging together."

Schleicher's program, he said, consisted of a single point: "create jobs." Here, too, he struck a conciliatory tone. "I am heretical enough," he said, "that I am a follower neither of capitalism nor of socialism. For me, concepts like 'private or planned economy' have lost their terror." He thought "with the economy one should do that which is reasonable in the given moment and, in all probability, will lead to the best results for the people and the country" rather than "smash heads for the sake of a dogma." The speech concluded with a subtle warning to "parties, groups and associations." They were not ends in themselves and would lose their justification if they refused "to work with the state." His government would follow the advice of the venerable military commander Helmuth von Moltke the Elder: "First ponder, then dare."

Schleicher did take some important steps away from Papen's authoritarianism, including repealing Papen's draconian executive orders on political offenses. But the cross front failed almost immediately. Schleicher could attract neither Hitler nor Strasser to his government. On December 5, both the Nazis and the Social Democrats announced that they would not "tolerate" his administration. The Social Democrats said they would bring a no-confidence motion as soon as the Reichstag met, although they probably hoped the motion would not succeed, as they feared being passed by the Communists in a subsequent election. The Communists also said they would bring a no-confidence motion, but unlike the Social Democrats, they really wanted to do so. The Reichstag in fact met for a few days in early December, but then adjourned after some minor legislative moves and without any confidence votes.

Hitler once again categorically refused to permit Strasser to join a Schleicher cabinet. In Hitler's view, he himself would be chancellor or there would be no Nazis in power at all. Strasser feared Hitler's all-or-nothing policy was cutting off the last possible road to power. In early December, Strasser became increasingly marginalized with the Nazi leadership, as the other leaders stuck with Hitler's approach. A note in Goebbels's diary described Strasser's face "looking increasingly stony" as a meeting went against him. On December 8, he resigned his party office and withdrew for a vacation in Italy. He sent a letter to Hitler explaining his move in Schleicher-like terms—he thought it was a mistake not to build a broad front of "constructive people" and integrate them "into the state." Hitler was well aware that the popular Strasser had thrown the party into a crisis. "Hitler very pale," Goebbels recorded. "A fight, if it must be." Hitler and his paladins assumed that Strasser's resignation was the first step in a "palace revolution."

This crisis came at a bad moment for Hitler, following the decline in Nazi votes in the November Reichstag election and again in the state election in Thuringia in early December. His hold on the movement was on the line. In this situation, Hitler did what he did best: he called together the party's most important leaders and delivered a two-hour critique of Strasser's policy coupled with an emotional appeal for loyalty. Hitler's histrionic skills held the party together, and over the next weeks, he would consolidate his hold on his followers once again. It turned out that Schleicher and Strasser had exaggerated Strasser's support within the Nazi Party—at least if it came to a showdown with Hitler. The numbers who would follow him at the cost of breaking with Hitler turned out to be negligible. For his part, Strasser, as he would later tell his brother, could no longer stomach his increasing marginalization within the party leadership. "I did not feel like being placed after Göring, Goebbels, Röhm," he said. He saw such subordination as "a snub, as a humiliation of my person, which I have not deserved."

What is more puzzling is that Strasser didn't even try to fight—he turned out to lack the drive to challenge Hitler, and he merely withdrew from political activity, although he retained his Reichstag seat until March 1933. There are several possible reasons for this. He seems not have grasped the strategic importance at that moment of control over the National Socialist Party. In the preceding years, he had made wide contacts beyond the party, and he probably thought these were more important. Soon after his resignation, he wrote to a friend that he wanted "to promote the coming together of all constructive-minded people, no matter where they come from, on the basis of new ideas." He added that "I am convinced that the time of agitation and of parties is fast disappearing and that the immediate future calls for men who are prepared to come into government with courage and a sense of responsibility." Yet, although Strasser had always shown more independence from Hitler than the other members of the inner circle, in the final analysis he could not summon the will for the ultimate break with his Führer.

Well into January, Schleicher still seemed to hope vaguely for some political solution involving Strasser, and Strasser still seemed to think vaguely about joining Schleicher's government—especially after he returned to Berlin at the end of December, following his Italian vacation. But by quitting his party offices, Strasser had given up his political base and his best chance of influence. This meant that a solution to Germany's constitutional deadlock was as far from sight as ever. Hindenburg remained determined not to have Hitler as his chancellor. Who, then, could do the job, and where could that person find majority support? Was the only solution a "fighting cabinet" (*Kampfkabinett*) that would have to rely on the army and would probably face civil war? What would happen to the powerful Nazi movement, which, even after surviving Strasser's defection, confronted the seemingly unsolvable problem of how it could come to power? On Christmas Eve, Goebbels wrote in his diary that 1932 had been "just one run of bad luck."

THERE WAS PROBABLY only one man in Germany who could square the political circle by finding a way to put Hitler in power. That man was Franz von Papen.

In the course of 1932, Papen had come to enjoy being chancellor, and as the year came to a close, he was nursing a bitter grudge against his former friend Schleicher. "Papen caustic about Schleicher," Goebbels wrote in January. "Wants to overthrow him and get rid of him altogether."

On December 16, Papen had given a speech at the Herrenklub, or "Gentlemen's Club," a gathering spot for Germany's business, political, and professional elites. Afterward, he spoke to Kurt von Schröder, a banker from Cologne. Schröder had once been a supporter of Gustav Stresemann's German People's Party, but after Stresemann's death, he had drifted toward the Nazis. He was one of the cofounders of a group called the Freundeskreis der Wirtschaft (Friends of the Economy), whose goal was to raise funds for the Nazis from the business community. Papen recalled that Schröder had said it must be possible to find a way to work with the Nazis. Papen said that both he and Schleicher had tried and failed at this, but that he would be willing to try again. Schröder's recollection gave Papen the active role: "When I saw von Papen, he said,

'I think we can perhaps now have a meeting together to clear these different points which have kept us apart.'"

Schröder arranged for Papen and Hitler to meet secretly at his house in Cologne on January 4, 1933. Hitler was on his way to campaign in the local elections in the nearby state of Lippe-Detmold, and he used this journey as cover. Goebbels, and even some of Hitler's traveling entourage, learned of the meeting only after it had happened. Yet news of the meeting had been leaked to Schleicher, and a photographer captured a startled Papen getting out of a taxi in front of Schröder's house. The story was in all the papers the next day.

The talk didn't start well. "Hitler poured his bitterest anger over me" about the Potempa case, Papen remembered. Papen told Hitler it was a waste of time to talk about that. He had come because he heard Hitler wanted to take up contact with the government again and talk about the near future. A few days later, Hitler told Goebbels what had happened at the meeting. Papen, he reported, "still has the ear of the old man" (Hindenburg) and had a strong desire to overthrow Schleicher. Papen and Hitler had thus worked out an "arrangement." "Either the chancellorship or ministries of power: defense and interior," was the way Goebbels recorded it, adding, "We're listening." This new conspiracy—Papen and the Nazis against Schleicher—had good contacts with Hindenburg's inner circle and possessed an item of crucial inside information: Hindenburg had refused Schleicher an order to dissolve the Reichstag to prevent a vote of no confidence against him. This meant, with a Reichstag session pending, Schleicher was trapped and his time was running out. "He's going south," Goebbels noted gleefully.

The key to this alliance was Papen's close relationship with Hindenburg. If anyone could sell Hindenburg on the idea of making Hitler chancellor, it was Papen. Through January, Papen and Hitler negotiated and fenced with each other. Each wanted the chancellorship for himself. Who would give way? In the end, would Hindenburg really agree to a Hitler government? And how would Schleicher respond? It was assumed he had the army behind him. How far would he be willing to go to keep Hitler or Papen from power?

Schleicher did not seem to have grasped the gravity of his situation. He knew he couldn't face the Reichstag without a secure coalition, and as early as January 6, he told Otto Braun, the Social Democratic prime minister of Prussia, that Hindenburg would not grant him a dissolution with elections delayed beyond the mandated sixty-day period. (The Supreme Court had partially restored Braun to his position, with limited powers, a few months after the Papen coup.) Yet, at other times, Schleicher was more optimistic. At a cabinet meeting on January 16, he was confident that Hindenburg would give him a dissolution and would delay the subsequent elections, and that Hitler did not even want to be chancellor anymore. Schleicher seems to have assumed that Hindenburg would come around, even though this was exactly the violation of the constitution that in December Schleicher had argued could lead to civil war—the very argument that had won him Papen's job. The point had been crucial for Hindenburg, who had hardly forgotten it in the intervening weeks.

Schleicher was still talking to Strasser, and raved about him to François-Poncet, telling the French ambassador that Strasser was the only man of stature among the Nazis. In early January, clearly not knowing that Strasser had been defanged within the Nazi Party, Schleicher was still confident that Strasser would follow him and that Strasser would refuse, along with his "friends," to vote against Schleicher's government in the Reichstag. He even thought that Strasser would campaign against Hitler in the event of a dissolution. Schleicher also retained his usual condescension toward Papen. When François-Poncet asked Schleicher about Papen's January 4 meeting with Hitler, Schleicher seemed to think only that Papen had made a mistake in trying to win Hitler over to the support of Schleicher's government. Papen had hurt himself, Schleicher continued, "especially in the mind of Field Marshal von Hindenburg, whom [Papen's] approach has shocked." Schleicher said he would treat his friend's mistake indulgently: "I will say to him: My little Franz, you have been foolish!" Coming away from the conversation, François-Poncet thought that Schleicher seemed cheerful, confident, and, "in spite of his pallor," healthy.

It would soon become clear just how much Schleicher had misjudged his situation.

Ultimately, everything depended on Hindenburg, and in January, Schleicher faced trouble from this direction as well. Schleicher wanted to revive Brüning's policy of settling unemployed workers on bankrupt agricultural estates in the Prussian east, an idea that was still extremely unpopular with the aristocrats who owned those estates. In January 1933, Hindenburg's neighbors were once again bringing him complaints about this policy. A scandal also emerged about the abuse of funds for the Eastern Aid program for Prussian farmers, as it was discovered that landowners were using funds that had been allocated to make their farms more competitive to pay for a more comfortable lifestyle. Scandals over corruption involving eastern estates also moved close to Hindenburg personally. The *Tägliche Rundschau* (Daily Review), a newspaper that was generally thought to be Schleicher's mouthpiece, reported that the title to Hindenburg's estate at Neudeck had been registered in the name of his son, Oskar, in order to avoid inheritance tax. This was hardly a credit to Hindenburg, who was so concerned about his image. Appearing where it did, the story looked like an effort by Schleicher to put pressure on Hindenburg. Hindenburg must have felt that he was being forced to choose between Schleicher on the one hand, and his image and his aristocratic neighbors on the other. This could only mean that for Hindenburg, Schleicher was looking increasingly dispensable.

Yet time and time again in that month of January 1933, Hindenburg told his advisers that he would never turn the government over to Hitler, just as he had sworn in August and November of the preceding year. Since the summer of 1931, Hindenburg had consistently sought a right-wing majority government, which would have to involve Hitler and the Nazis in some way. This prospect had been as much on offer in August and November as it was in January. But in 1932 Hindenburg would not create a right-wing government at the price of having Hitler lead it. Suddenly, in January 1933, this changed. What was different?

One difference was the state election in Lippe-Detmold, held on January 15. Lippe-Detmold was tiny, with a total population of 173,000. Under normal circumstances, its local election would not have mattered much for national politics. But in this case, the Nazis saw a chance for a psychologically important change in momentum, following their loss of votes at the November Reichstag elections and the Thuringian state elections that followed, and the defection of Strasser. For Lippe-Detmold, they pulled out all the stops and campaigned intensely. The gambit worked: the Nazis won 43 percent of the vote against 39 percent for the Social Democrats and just under 8 percent for the German Nationals. As little as it mattered in real political terms, the outcome gave the Nazis a propaganda boost when they desperately needed it, and delivered a major blow to Schleicher's strategy. The always astute and well-informed André François-Poncet reported to Paris that the Lippe-Detmold elections had put a final end to whatever threat Strasser posed to Nazi Party unity. "Strasser is in reality the vanquished of January 15," he wrote. The election had caused Schleicher to abandon the idea of offering Strasser the posts of vice-chancellor and Prussian prime minister. Erwin Planck, the state secretary in Schleicher's chancellery, told François-Poncet that the administration had lost any hope that Strasser could bring a large contingent of Nazis along with him and that, under these circumstances, they preferred to see Strasser remain as a divisive influence within the Nazi Party.

Yet the bigger factor in shifting the political fortunes of Hitler and Schleicher was the Nazi strategy of threatening Hindenburg with impeachment or prosecution. This became particularly clear in the dramatic events of the last week of January, as negotiations between Hitler, Papen, and Hindenburg's advisers Otto Meissner and Oskar von Hindenburg, mediated by Hitler's future foreign minister Joachim von Ribbentrop, took a tense and unpredictable path.

Ribbentrop had served in the First World War, but when wounds rendered him unfit for further front service, he was sent to Turkey, where he got to know Franz von Papen. This connection would prove valuable in August 1932, just after Hindenburg rebuffed Hitler's hopes of being chancellor. Papen contacted his old friend Ribbentrop to serve as an intermediary with Hitler. Ribbentrop had Nazi friends as well, and it was at this time (much later than most of the other leading Nazis) that he joined the party. Ribbentrop traveled to Berchtesgaden to meet Hitler, who, he later recalled, "impressed me very strongly." Ribbentrop became convinced that only "[Hitler] and his party could save Germany from Communism." At the time, of course, in light of Hitler's resentments and Hindenburg's stubbornness, little could happen.

But by January, things were different. Hitler's associate Heinrich Himmler and the businessman Wilhelm Keppler asked Ribbentrop if he could help arrange another meeting between Hitler and Papen. Ribbentrop offered his house, and late in the evening of Sunday, January 22, Papen met there with Hitler, Wilhelm Frick, Hermann Göring, Otto Meissner, and Oskar von Hindenburg. Hitler began by taking Oskar aside for two hours for a private talk, after which he and Papen spoke. To the young Hindenburg, Hitler simply seems to have delivered his usual ponderous monologue about his political plans, to which Oskar replied simply that he was not a politician. There was not much meeting of the minds between them: Hitler told Goebbels a few days later that the young Hindenburg was "the personification of stupidity." Papen told Hitler that he would now press the Reich president to make Hitler chancellor, but he was far from sure the old field marshal would accept the idea. Oskar von Hindenburg and Otto Meissner shared a taxi back to the center of Berlin. After a long silence, Oskar said that if Papen had accepted the idea of being vice-chancellor under Hitler there was probably no way around it, but he still didn't like the idea.

Nor, in fact, did President Hindenburg. When Papen met with him the next day, Hindenburg once again firmly refused to name Hitler chancellor. It was not that Hindenburg wanted to stay with Schleicher—relations between the field marshal and the general were now chilly indeed. Later that day, Schleicher also came to see Hindenburg. Schleicher's staff had prepared a brief outlining three options for "an active executive policy against the Reichstag." The first was for Hindenburg to declare a state of emergency, dissolving the Reichstag and postponing new elections. The second was simply to force an adjournment of the Reichstag, summoning it again if and when the representatives could agree on "a positive majority and positive work." The third option was the most novel. It was based on the idea that there was a gap in the Weimar constitution: the constitution provided for votes of no-confidence but did not oblige those who took such a step to propose an administration that could win a majority. The framers of the constitution had not foreseen the possibility of a Reichstag deadlocked by a "negative" majority, such as the Nazis and the Communists, who in 1933 controlled a slim majority of seats but could agree on little beyond declaring an amnesty for their imprisoned activists. So, if this negative majority were to vote no confidence in Schleicher, it would arguably be constitutionally proper for Hindenburg to ask Schleicher's cabinet to continue in office indefinitely as a "caretaker" administration, until a majority in the Reichstag came up with its own alternative administration.

Schleicher's right-hand man, Eugen Ott, advised the chancellor to press for the state of emergency, and when he met with Hindenburg, this is what Schleicher did. He did not present the "caretaker government" scenario. Since this was the most plausible and constitutionally acceptable plan for him to stay in power, his motives for failing to push it are unclear. At a dinner in Berlin for journalists earlier in the month, on January 13, Schleicher pointed out that in this scenario, the negative majority could still vote down the cabinet's executive orders and damage the economy, which would leave the administration facing the other options after all. Still, there may well have been more to it than this. Many people who talked to Schleicher during his chancellorship came away with the feeling that he was exhausted and overstressed and simply did not want to be chancellor much longer. A reporter noted in the middle of January that Schleicher looked pale, and had grown "considerably thinner in the face than he was before." In his usual sardonic way, Schleicher said of himself, "too bad I have no propensity for megalomania." He approached the denouement of late January with fatalism, even relief.

On January 23, Hindenburg told Schleicher that he would consider granting a dissolution of the Reichstag but not a delay of elections. Such a step, said Hindenburg, "would be interpreted by all sides as a breach of the constitution," and before it could be taken, Hindenburg would need assurances from all party leaders that they recognized the state of emergency and would not accuse him of illegal action. According to Papen, Hindenburg also made a telling point: "On December 2, you predicted a civil war if I were to follow Papen's suggestion. The army and the police, you thought, were not in a position to fight internal unrest." In the last seven weeks, the internal divisions had only grown sharper and the Nazis and the Communists still more radical, while the army and police forces were no larger. "If a civil war was to be expected then—how much more will that be so today?"

As late as January 26, Hindenburg seems to have remained adamantly opposed to naming Hitler chancellor. On that day, the army commander in chief Kurt von Hammerstein-Equord was growing increasingly concerned about rumors that Papen and Hugenberg might form a new administration. Such a cabinet would have almost the entire population against it, and for the army, this would be "worrying in the highest degree." Hammerstein-Equord took this concern straight to Hindenburg. The president "forbade with the greatest sensitivity any political influence" on him, Hammerstein-Equord recorded two years later, "but then, seemingly to calm me, said he would never think of making the Austrian private defense minister or chancellor." Hindenburg's response about Hitler obviously did not follow from Hammerstein-Equord's concern about Papen. It might be that Hindenburg, who really *did* want Papen to return to the chancellery, did not want to admit this outright. Or his comment might have been a slip revealing his recent conversations with Papen. In any case, the old man's rejection of Hitler still seemed to be clear. At around the same time, Hindenburg is said to have told an aristocratic friend privately that Hitler was at best qualified to be his postal minister.

Yet Hindenburg's views were changing. On January 25, Ribbentrop met with Oskar von Hindenburg, after which Ribbentrop's wife, Annelies, recorded that the idea of a coalition with Hitler as chancellor "does not appear quite hopeless." Negotiations went on, and three days later there was a breakthrough. On the morning of January 28, Papen met again with Hindenburg, and this time the old man relented. Ribbentrop went to see Papen, "who received me with the question: 'Where is Hitler?' I told him that he had probably left, but could perhaps be contacted in Weimar. Papen said he had to be got back without delay, because . . . after a long talk with Hindenburg he, Papen, considered Hitler's chancellorship possible."

On that same day, Hindenburg summoned the veteran conservative politician Elard von Oldenburg-Januschau and the incoming defense minister, Werner von Blomberg, to get their views on the looming constitutional crisis. Both told the Reich president that a Hitler government was the only solution. The message was reinforced in a meeting between Hindenburg; his son, Oskar; Papen; and Meissner. Hindenburg's advisers told the old man that "no other constitutional solution appeared possible other than to form a government under Hitler's leadership with as strong as possible a counterweight against a National Socialist predominance." Finally and grudgingly, Hindenburg agreed.

Why Hindenburg should suddenly change his mind in this way is one of the most important questions in the story of Hitler's rise to power. Something crucial had happened between January 26 and January 28. Then and later, some have speculated about the Eastern Aid scandals and Hindenburg's possible tax evasion, or pressure from his East Prussian neighbors. But the answer seems to have more to do with his fear of impeachment and prosecution.

In the last week of January, Hindenburg came under an enormous media assault regarding the legality of a state of emergency. François-Poncet reported on January 24 that "the prospect of an open dictatorship, with the suppression of all parliamentary life," had alarmed the "liberal, Catholic and socialist press." On the same day, the Social Democratic paper the *Hamburger Echo* wrote that "The proclamation of a state of emergency has no foundation in the constitution." Anyone who attempted such a thing would be violating the constitution, the paper went on, and might perhaps "know how such a game begins, but not how it will end." The next day, the Social Democrats' national leadership released a statement saying, in no uncertain terms, that a declaration of a state of emergency would be a coup d'état leading to "a lawless condition against which all resistance would be permissible and necessary." On January 26, Monsignor Ludwig Kaas, leader of the Center Party, wrote to Schleicher, with a copy to Hindenburg, along similar lines, and the letter was published three days later in the Catholic paper *Germania*. The Prussian prime minister Otto Braun took a different approach. In a letter to Schleicher published in *Germania* on January 29, Braun argued that attempting to alter the constitution with violence was the definition of high treason under Section 81 of the Criminal Code. Declaring a state of emergency would amount to such an action. This meant that calling on the president to dissolve the Reichstag and postpone elections was an incitement to high treason, itself punishable by up to ten years in a penitentiary.

There seems little doubt that these messages, and others like them, reached their target. When Hindenburg and Schleicher met on January 23, it was clear that Hindenburg's main worry about permitting a state of emergency was his own legal exposure. Heinrich Brüning remembered years later that Erwin Planck, the state secretary in the Reich Chancellery, had visited him in late January and complained of the "difficulties for the government that arose from Hindenburg's fear of an indictment." Brüning said he had been "assured"—he did not say by whom—that this was one of the reasons for Hindenburg's eventual agreement to make Hitler chancellor.

From today's perspective, it seems astonishing that democratic politicians of all stripes strongly favored a Hitler administration over a state of emergency. In part, this was because of their fear of a civil war in which the Nazis or the Communists might emerge victorious. In part, it says something about the ingrained fetish for constitutional legality that had become characteristic of Social Democratic thinking—and had been fiercely criticized for its shortsightedness even by some Social Democratic intellectuals.

On January 27, the Reichstag Council of Elders—the senior members from all parties who decided on matters of procedure—agreed to end the adjournment and hold a Reichstag session on January 31. Now the figurative clock was ticking, as the Reichstag was certain to vote no confidence in Schleicher as soon as it met.

On the morning of January 28, Schleicher met his cabinet and explained that it was pointless to appear before the Reichstag without a dissolution order, which Hindenburg would not grant. Schleicher told his colleagues that he feared the worst: "The difficulties would perhaps not be so great if the Herr Reich President were prepared to name Hitler as Reich chancellor." Yet, as far as Schleicher knew, Hindenburg still refused to do this. So, the only alternative was another presidential cabinet, to which Papen and German National leader Hugenberg would probably belong. Such a cabinet was likely to provoke "a state and a presidential crisis." Schleicher's ministers agreed strongly with him on that assessment, and the cabinet resolved that if Hindenburg did not grant a dissolution order, all members would resign.

Schleicher left the cabinet meeting to report to Hindenburg. He told Hindenburg that there were three possibilities: a parliamentary cabinet led by Hitler with a Reichstag majority (although Schleicher was not sure Hitler would be able to find a majority); a presidential cabinet led by Hitler;

or keeping the present administration, the last possible only with a dissolution order. A cabinet based only on the German Nationals—this meant a Papen or Hugenberg cabinet—would lead to a crisis.

Hindenburg was firm. A dissolution was "something that in the present situation I cannot do," he told Schleicher. "I recognize with gratitude that you have tried to win over the National Socialists and create a Reichstag majority. But unfortunately, it did not work out, and so other possibilities have to be attempted." Hindenburg accepted the resignation of Schleicher's cabinet. The last act of Schleicher and his ministers was to approve funding for a massive job creation program. In the following six months, two million unemployed Germans found work again, but it was Hitler who reaped the credit for this, not Schleicher.

Soon after Schleicher's resignation, Hindenburg summoned Papen and officially asked him to "examine the possibility of the formation of a government under Hitler." Still, no one quite knew what would happen. Goebbels was in Rostock on January 28 when he heard the news about Schleicher's resignation. He heard also that Hindenburg had commissioned Papen to talk to the parties about what should happen next. Goebbels, too, thought that if Papen became chancellor again "there will be revolution." He also had a shrewd idea about the nature of Hindenburg's relations with his chancellors. "The old man with his well-known lack of loyalty let [Schleicher] go . . . But you can't begrudge it for Schl." Now, he wrote, the tug of war between the parties would begin, and "the old man is unpredictable." It might be for the best, Goebbels thought, if Hindenburg turned to Papen: "Because then the situation would become so threatening that without us nothing could be done."

In the course of Sunday, January 29, most of the details were ironed out. Hitler and Papen met that morning. Hitler insisted that there would have to be new elections right away, followed by the passage of an "Enabling Law" that would give his government sweeping powers. Hindenburg did not want new elections and had to be persuaded by Hitler's promise that the next elections would be the last ones. That afternoon, Ribbentrop and Göring went to see Papen, who told them that "all obstacles are removed and that Hindenburg expects Hitler tomorrow at 11 a.m."

At the Kaiserhof Hotel on January 29, Göring told Goebbels that the cabinet would be "Hitler chancellor, Papen vice, Frick Reich Interior, Göring Prussian Interior, Hugenberg crises." (By "crises," Goebbels meant the economic and agriculture ministries.) The Reichstag would be dissolved for an election—"the last time," as they had assured Hindenburg. Yet Goebbels wasn't sure: "One doesn't dare to believe it. Is Papen honest? Who knows?"

Hitler and his entourage heard rumors that Schleicher and his associates at the defense ministry were plotting a military coup. (Some of the officers had indeed discussed this possibility, but Schleicher firmly rejected it.) The Nazi brass sat up at the Kaiserhof Hotel until five in the morning on January 30, waiting for news and ready for anything. Nothing had happened. Then Hitler had to go to the president's office for his swearing in.

Even at this stage, the deal almost fell apart. Just before 11:00 a.m., the members of the new cabinet gathered in Meissner's office. Hugenberg had just learned about the plan to call a new election, and he refused to join the cabinet on these terms. A furious bargaining session followed. Only after Meissner irritably told the politicians that they couldn't keep Hindenburg waiting, and Hitler solemnly promised Hugenberg that whatever happened in the election, the composition of the cabinet would remain the same, did Hugenberg relent.

"It has happened," Goebbels recorded. "We are sitting in the Wilhelmstrasse. Hitler is Reich chancellor. Like a fairy tale!" Always purposeful, he quickly added, "Straight to work. Reichstag will be dissolved. In 4 weeks election."

After all the catastrophes of Nazi rule, it has often been argued that Hindenburg had no choice but to appoint Hitler. Testifying at Nuremberg after the war, Hitler's finance minister, Count Lutz Schwerin von Krosigk, said that "no one, not even the strongest opponent of Hitler, has yet told me what possibility there was in 1933 other than calling on the leader of the strongest party, since the parliament could not itself produce an administration." Meissner quoted these words approvingly in his memoirs, but this claim obscures how much responsibility conservative politicians such as Krosigk and Meissner themselves bore for what happened. Hermann Müller's government in 1928–30 had had a stable majority. Heinrich Brüning had won a confidence vote in the Reichstag just days before Hindenburg sacked him. There was no need to call an election in 1932. The crisis and the deadlock of 1932 and early 1933, to which Hitler appeared as the only solution, was manufactured by a political right wing that wanted to exclude more than half the population from political representation and refused even the mildest compromise. To this end, a succession of conservative politicians (Hugenberg, Brüning, Schleicher, Papen, and Hindenburg) courted the Nazis as the only way to retain power on terms congenial to them. Hitler's regime was the result.

Not that Hitler's position on January 30 was overwhelming in its strength. Initially, only three of the eleven ministers were Nazis: in addition to Hitler, there was Wilhelm Frick as interior minister and Hermann Göring as minister without portfolio. The Steel Helmet was represented by Franz Seldte, as minister of labor. The rest were figures of the establishment right: men such as Vice-Chancellor Papen, Foreign Minister Konstantin von Neurath, and Alfred Hugenberg, who held five different economic portfolios. Neurath, along with Finance Minister Schwerin von Krosigk, Transport Minister Paul von Eltz-Rübenach, and Justice Minister Franz Gürtner (whose appointment was delayed a few days to create the impression that the office was being held for a Center Party representative) were holdovers from Schleicher's and Papen's cabinets, which seemed to promise stability and continuity. Most Germans believed that the presence of these conservatives in the cabinet, the authority of Hindenburg and, in the last resort, the army would surely keep Hitler on the straight and narrow. Papen, as usual, was fatuously confident. "We have hired him," he told one friend. "In a few months, we will have pushed him so far into the corner that he will squeak."

Not everyone was so complacent. Shrewd observers could see the dangers. After reporting all the reassuring things he had been told by conservative insiders, André François-Poncet advised his government that "the formation of the Hitler-Papen-Hugenberg Cabinet is nonetheless a hazardous experiment for Germany and for Europe." He saw clearly the nature of the establishment-Nazi relationship, and its risks. "It was precisely one of the intentions of those who prepared and provoked the crisis to preserve what remains, and is still considerable, of Nazi strength. It remains to be seen whether, in saving it, the means of action will not have been placed in hands which will be tempted to abuse it, and which will no longer give it up." The former Reich chief prosecutor, Ludwig Ebermayer, had similar concerns. "Even if it only lasts half a year," he told his son, "a lot of damage can be done, especially in foreign policy." Turning grimmer, he added, "But it will last longer. This is no cabinet like any other, one that will just resign someday."

There was one major point that Hitler's minders seem to have overlooked. As a result of Papen's 1932 coup against the Prussian government, the key Prussian ministries were part of the Reich government. Hitler arranged for Hermann Göring to be named Prussian interior minister. This put him, and the Nazis, in control of the Prussian state police, a major power factor. As we have seen, one of Schleicher's motives for pushing Papen toward the coup was to keep the Prussian police out of Nazi hands. His successors were not so careful.

For the Nazis, gaining the chancellorship was hardly an end in itself. It was only the first step toward wider power. "The first stage! Keep fighting," Goebbels wrote in his diary. He then named the conservative ministers around Hitler. "These are blemishes. Must be rubbed out."

Göring's police, and the Nazi desire to "rub out" the "blemishes," would set the terms for the coming months of German history.

7

Coordination

"Because the Reichstag has burned, I have been arrested. I don't even know that it has burned." These are the words of Lina Haag, a Communist Party activist since her teenage years. She even met her husband in the Communist Party's youth group.

At the door of her apartment on this Tuesday afternoon she sees two trench coats, two gray hats. Gradually, she notices a "brutal" mouth and a yellow-tinged face; she hears a "cold and unpleasant" voice. The officers are in a hurry. "They see that lunch is on the stove, that I have a child, that I can't just drop everything," Haag will later recall. They don't care. The officers leave her daughter with the neighbor, then take her coat from the hook and throw it at her. "Move it, move it!" they say. She recognizes that they have to prove their "reliability" to the new masters. They have to fill the jails. "The 'unbloodiest' revolution of all time needs its victims," as she says.

It is February 28, 1933. The night before, the Reichstag went up in flames.

"As we go down the stairs," she continues, "I hear doors closing throughout the building, very softly and carefully, but I hear them." Once on the street, she is suddenly very cold. She feels eyes on her back. She is being watched from every window. "I don't see it," she writes, "but I know it."

They take her to the prison at Gotteszell and put her in solitary confinement.

They have already arrested her husband. Alfred Haag is a Communist deputy in the Württemberg state parliament, at age twenty-eight, the youngest of all the deputies. Lina tried to get him to go abroad, but he refused. "Leave my workers?" he asked. "Now?" The Stormtroopers came for him at 5:00 a.m., only days after Hitler entered the chancellery. "They rip open the chests, throw the clothes around, turn the drawers over, rummage through the desk," Lina remembers. They weren't looking for anything in particular. They were interested only in vandalism.

As the Stormtroopers prepared to take Alfred away, Lina said to him, "But you're a deputy!" One of the Stormtroopers laughed derisively. "Deputy, did you hear that?" he said to his friends. Then he yelled at the Haags, "You are commies! Your gang of filth is now going to be cleaned out!"

Lina watched from the window as the Stormtroopers led Alfred through the streets. She saw them start to beat him. She had to pull her daughter away from the window so the little girl couldn't see what was happening to her father.

Lina is kept in prison until the Christmas Amnesty. Alfred is not so lucky. Political prisoners have networks of information, and Lina hears many things. She hears that the Gestapo killed an old friend of hers by pressing him against a red-hot stove. She hears about Alfred as well. He has been taken to the Oberer Kuhberg concentration camp, where he conducts himself with the same courage he showed before his arrest. When he refuses to salute a swastika flag, the guards beat him savagely. On another occasion, the guards make him crawl up a hill on all fours, calling out, "I am a scumbag, I lied to the workers and betrayed them!" His face is unrecognizable from the blood.

A few weeks after Lina Haag's arrest, a squad of Stormtroopers breaks down Maria Jankowski's front door. Jankowski is a Social Democratic borough councilor for the Berlin district of Köpenick. The Stormtroopers bring her to their Köpenick headquarters. There in the courtyard, they force her to undress and lie down on a wooden pallet. They cover her with the black-red-gold flag of the Republic and then, for two hours, beat her with whips, clubs, and crowbars. While they beat her, they ask for the names of socialist and Communist workers, and force her to describe the flag as "black-red-shit." They ask her, "Did you steal shoes from unemployed workers? Did you prepare a boycott list of Nazi businesses?" Whenever she cries out in pain, one of her tormentors presses her face into a bundle of old rags.

"After I had received at least a hundred blows," she will recall later, "I fell off the pallet. They yanked me back up again and hit me so hard in the face that I fell into a corner." They make her sing the "Deutschlandlied"— the song with the line "Deutschland über alles" (Germany above all else)—the official national anthem since 1922, but the anthem of German nationalism for much longer.

The Stormtroopers force Jankowski to sign a declaration that she will leave the Social Democratic Party, never be politically active again, and report to a Nazi office every Thursday. Then, as she will tell it later, suddenly "the treatment of me changed." She is given a glass of water and her clothes. The Brownshirt commander orders one of his men to "Escort the lady out," and courteously wishes her "good evening." They leave her on the street. A passerby takes her to a hospital. She barely survives, and will struggle with the after-effects of her beating for the rest of her life. Shortly thereafter, she arranges for the facts of her "arrest" to be spread to news outlets abroad. The Nazis prosecute her for the "spreading of false atrocity stories."

This is what the Nazis call the "national rising." In August 1932, there was still widespread outrage about the brutal Potempa murder. Now, in the spring of 1933, the Stormtroopers face hardly any legal restraints.

As Lina Haag writes, "It is better to look away. It is not good to see so much in this more beautiful, happier Germany."

SOON ENOUGH, IT began to become clear what it meant to have Hitler as chancellor and Hermann Göring in charge of the Prussian police. From the beginning of February, there came a steady drumbeat of legal and police measures aimed at anyone who might be a Nazi opponent: Communists, Social Democrats, liberals, pacifists, intellectuals and journalists, artists, human rights activists—and their press. On February 4, Hindenburg signed a decree giving the police wide powers to break up political meetings, ban associations, and shut down media outlets. Social Democratic and Communist newspapers began feeling the effects immediately. On February 14, a small army of Berlin police officers searched the Communists' Reichstag offices, and ten days later, the police shut down the Communist Party's Berlin headquarters. On February 17, Göring ordered all Prussian police officers to use their firearms against "enemies of the state." On February 22, a further decree allowed members of the "Patriotic Associations"—this meant the SA, SS, and Steel Helmet—to be enrolled as auxiliary police officers.

Yet it was the Reichstag fire of February 27 that changed the situation beyond recognition.

Most of the importance of the fire rests in the Nazis' response to it. Hitler's government claimed that the fire in the plenary chamber of Germany's parliament, six days before the country was to vote in yet another general election, was an act of terrorist arson, the opening act of a Communist uprising. The following morning, seizing the emergency, the cabinet passed and Hindenburg signed an executive order known formally as the Decree of the Reich President for the Protection of People and State, and informally as the Reichstag Fire Decree. This decree tore the heart out of the democratic constitution of the Weimar Republic, cancelling at a stroke freedom of speech and assembly, the confidentiality of post and telegraphic communication, and freedom from arbitrary searches, arrest, and detention. The second paragraph of the decree allowed the central government to remove any state government from office—as in the Prussian coup of the previous year, an effective way to eliminate opposition. Even as the Reichstag burned, the government cracked down on its opponents, arresting thousands of people across the country. The Reichstag Fire Decree became the legal foundation for Hitler's twelve-year dictatorship. Some scholars have called it the constitution of Hitler's Reich.

Because the Reichstag fire worked out so well for Hitler's regime, it seemed obvious to most non-Nazis at the time, and many people later, that the Nazis themselves must have set it. But since 1933, the origins of the fire have remained controversial, and historians still debate the question.

The major complication came from the one individual who was arrested at the scene of the crime, a twenty-four-year-old Dutch journeyman stonemason named Marinus van der Lubbe. Van der Lubbe appeared to have broken into a second-floor window of the Reichstag building at around 9:10 p.m., armed with matches and fire lighters (naphthalene-covered balls of sawdust, commonly used in those days to light domestic stoves). For about fifteen minutes, van der Lubbe raced around inside the darkened and mostly empty Reichstag, setting a number of fires. Most of them soon fizzled out, as his equipment could do little damage to the heavy oak furniture and paneling. At 9:25, the police found and arrested him inside the building. He was naked to the waist and sweating profusely.

Van der Lubbe claimed fiercely that he and he alone had set all the fires in the Reichstag, including the devastating blaze in the main chamber. He maintained this claim through months of often brutal interrogations, through his trial, and up to his execution by the Nazis in early 1934. Hardly anyone believed him at the time, although shrewder Nazis began to see the virtues of van der Lubbe's story as they suffered under a barrage of skillful foreign propaganda claiming that a squad of Nazis had set the fire. If there had been only one culprit, then that culprit was van der Lubbe and the Nazis were off the hook. Conveniently enough, van der Lubbe was a former member of the Dutch Communist Party.

However, from the evidence now available, it appears all but impossible that van der Lubbe could have set the fire by himself. This point has been established by a number of independent investigations by scientists who study the effects of fire on buildings. This scientific evidence is supported by other factors. Van der Lubbe himself was a highly implausible perpetrator. As a result of a workplace injury, he was approximately 80 percent blind, and at the time of the fire, the darkness inside the Reichstag building was near absolute. Van der Lubbe had never been in the building before and did not even seem to understand what the chamber was—he called it "the church." The police and expert examiners found physical evidence in the Reichstag building inconsistent with van der Lubbe's sole-culprit status: soot in the air vents that could have come only from burning kerosene or gasoline, and the remains of a torch. Neither van der Lubbe nor anyone else claimed that he had had any accelerant or a torch with him. Some police and firefighters thought they had found traces of kerosene or gasoline in the building, although this evidence is less clear. More important is that van der Lubbe himself could give no coherent or convincing account of how he might have set the massive fire in the chamber—he thought it had spontaneously exploded into flames as he ran through the chamber carrying a burning cloth. Indeed, he testified to seeing major fires he could not have set spring up in the chamber.

If van der Lubbe did not act alone, then he was almost certainly the fall guy in someone else's plot. But whose? The specific identity of his fellow perpetrators is a question to which we may never have a certain answer. But under the conditions of February 1933, it is difficult to imagine that anyone but the Nazis could have moved multiple culprits in and out of the Reichstag without leaving traces that the police might find—or at least would want to find. Apart from this commonsense argument, there is some specific evidence pointing to a particular group of Nazi Stormtroopers. At the Nuremberg trials after the war, two men who were Nazi secret police officials in 1933, Rudolf Diels and Hans Bernd Gisevius, identified a former Stormtrooper named Hans Georg Gewehr as the main culprit in the fire. Gewehr denied the allegation, but in 1933, he had been known as the Stormtroopers' incendiary expert. He told inconsistent and highly implausible stories about where he was on the night of the fire, and on at least one later occasion, he is said to have boasted of his involvement.

The question of who set the Reichstag fire is more than just an interesting historical parlor game. It points to two broader points about the Nazis. The first is how much they relied on the Stormtroopers and their violence to get and hold power. The Reichstag fit smoothly into a chain of events since the late 1920s in which the Stormtroopers committed an act of violence and then sought to shift responsibility to the Communists, and usually followed this up by committing more violence. The attack on the Felseneck cottage colony in January 1932 was just one example among many. The Reichstag fire is most likely another. And whether or not the fire was set by SA men, in the days and weeks after the fire, there were no more limits on SA violence. This violence, and the fear it inspired, was a crucial element in deterring opposition and consolidating support for the new regime, and it was something the Nazis had thought about long before they were in power. In August 1932, just after the meeting between Hitler and Hindenburg, Brüning's former state secretary Hermann Pünder heard from Erwin Planck, Papen's state secretary, that if Hitler had become chancellor, the Nazis had planned to deploy the SA at the Reichstag to drive out "the Marxists." "Furthermore," he wrote, "according to Count Helldorff [the Berlin SA commander] the SA would have been 'let go' for a few days, whereby probably about 5,000 Marxist opponents recorded on lists were to be 'rendered harmless.'" Pünder wondered if this information could be correct. "I certainly wouldn't put anything past many Nazis," he wrote. What he described is what came to pass after the Reichstag fire.

The second point involves how carefully, and how strategically, the Nazis thought about getting and consolidating power. The historian Irene Strenge has described this as their "legal path to power." As we have seen, the Nazis had to overcome Hindenburg's refusal to give Hitler the chancellorship. For this, the most effective weapon was the threat of impeachment or prosecution—and it worked. Then the political left and other determined opponents had to be driven from any vestige of power and rendered incapable of effective opposition. The Reichstag fire, the Nazification of the police, and the deployment of the Stormtroopers all served this purpose. The Nazis had been thinking about the use of the SA to consolidate power since at least 1931. They were assisted by a series of executive orders issued in the first weeks of the Nazi regime that were designed to make it impossible for political opposition to operate by shutting down liberal and left-wing media outlets and allowing the police to break up political meetings and rallies. These executive orders, along with the Reichstag Fire Decree, were largely drafted by Wilhelm Frick, based on a careful consideration of Weimar precedents. Finally, there was the passage of an "Enabling Law" by which the Reichstag would delegate all its lawmaking powers to Hitler's government. This, too, was an element that had long featured in Nazi planning. Goebbels referred to it in his diary in August 1932, and Hitler repeatedly mentioned it as one of his requirements in his negotiations with Hindenburg.

The Nazis' plan for power, though certainly rough and ready, didn't always work well. Sometimes the Nazis' execution of their plan was incompetent, and sometimes the plan's strategic objectives were crowded out by the barbarity at the heart of the movement. Yet, as ruthless people intent on power, they had devoted a good deal of thought to how they were actually going to get it.

In November 1931, a Nazi politician in the state of Hesse leaked some documents to the Frankfurt police. The documents included a draft proclamation to follow a Nazi counter-coup against an imagined Communist coup d'état. The plans demonstrated the centrality of the trauma of the revolution of 1918 for Nazis, as this revolution served them as a model for the future—with the difference that, this time, the right would strike back against the left. The "holders of power in the Reich and the federal states have fallen away through the events of recent days (weeks)," read the text, which meant that "as in Nov. 1918," a new legal situation had been created. It was the SA or other paramilitary formations that now had power, according to the scenario; this gave their leadership "the right and the duty for the salvation of the people to take up and exercise the abandoned state power." The urgent task was to enforce public safety and control the food supply. "Only the most severe discipline of the population and the ruthless crackdown of the armed powers makes the accomplishment of these tasks appear possible. To this end, all orders of the SA or other paramilitary force were to be obeyed on pain of death." Drumhead courts would be established to try offenses against these regulations. All Germans over the age of sixteen would be subject to compulsory labor, or they would have no right to food. Jews were expressly excluded from both the duty to work and the right to rations.

The author of these leaked documents was a young Nazi lawyer and activist from Hesse named Werner Best, who would go on to be a senior Gestapo officer and the deputy of the infamous SS official Reinhard Heydrich. The documents themselves became known as the "Boxheim Documents" after the farm at which Best presented them to several Hessian Nazi leaders. Because these documents clearly contradicted Hitler's pious talk of "legality," they came as an embarrassment to the party leadership. Goebbels's newspaper, *Der Angriff,* claimed that they were Best's purely private plan for defeating "a hypothetical bloody takeover by the Commies." Yet, at the same time, and underscoring the fact that the Nazis always sought to paint the Communists as the aggressors and themselves as defenders, Goebbels's paper also reported that Best was responding to "a plan drafted according to the most precise orders from Moscow for the violent seizure of power in Germany."

There is considerable evidence that the Boxheim Documents represented more than just Werner Best's passing fancy. In early September 1931, Best reported to the Nazis' national leadership about his plan. Shortly afterward, Goebbels recorded in his diary a conversation with Hitler about "SA questions." "What to do," Goebbels wrote, "when the KPD [Communist Party of Germany] strikes. Concrete plan of action. I will be the police commissioner for the entire east. . . . [SA commander Count Wolf Heinrich von] Helldorff my military leader. We will work well together." This of course sounds very similar to Best's scenario. Six months later, in the spring of 1932, the Berlin police discovered SA plans for mobilization in the event of an "emergency." The anticipated emergency was a coup or counter-coup by democratic or left-wing forces. On January 29, 1933, the night before Hitler came to power, when there were rumors of a military coup, Goebbels wrote in his diary that Helldorff and the Berlin police official Walther Wecke were working together on countermeasures. On February 1, Goebbels recorded that he had "Discussed the terror of the reds with Hitler. For now, still no countermeasures. First let it flare up." "First let it flare up" was a concise summary of a basic Nazi strategic principle.

In the early weeks of Hitler's government, such a flare-up seemed to be precisely what the Nazis were preparing for. The new secret police chief, Rudolf Diels, wrote that the Nazi leaders were waiting hopefully for a Communist uprising, "like a tiger that waited for its prey to appear before tearing it to pieces." Diels recalled that his boss, Prussian interior minister Hermann Göring, believed that the Communist Party would have to "come out of its lair" if the Nazis moved to outlaw it.

Yet the Communist uprising refused to come. Germany's Communists were hobbled both by Soviet leader Joseph Stalin's refusal to let them rebel and by their ideology, which told them that Hitler's arrival in power was a sign that capitalism was going to fail very soon and bring them to victory. There is some evidence that the Nazi leaders themselves understood the weak position of German communism. In a cabinet meeting in early February, Hitler wondered aloud if it were "psychologically correct" to minimize the Communist threat during the election campaign by banning the party.

Eventually, the Reichstag fire gave the Nazis what they had needed and planned for: the appearance of an attempted Communist coup, against which they could deploy the SA.

The Nazis' strategy, therefore, relied on a pattern of shifting the appearance of aggression to the Communists in order to provide an alibi for their own violence. This required a healthy dose of dishonesty and media manipulation—Goebbels's main stock in trade.

Goebbels offered a good example of his standard narrative of Communist violence and Nazi response when he testified as a witness at Marinus van der Lubbe's trial in November 1933. His story started with the murder of a Nazi Stormtrooper named Horst Wessel in 1930, which for Goebbels had been a targeted assassination of a Nazi activist who was too good at recruiting workers away from the Communists. In fact, the killing had arisen out of a dispute over rent between Wessel and his landlady. Goebbels's story continued with the case of the Nazi attack on the Felseneck cottage colony in early 1932, which he claimed had been a premeditated Communist ambush when in reality it was a military-style assault by about 150 Stormtroopers, who attacked the colony with the goal of killing the Communist Fritz Klemke. The last event in Goebbels's narrative sequence was the Reichstag fire.

Whatever Goebbels's knowledge of and involvement in the Reichstag fire might have been, there can be little doubt that his propaganda blaming it on the Communists was an act of calculated dishonesty. Nothing in Goebbels's diary suggests that the Nazis truly thought van der Lubbe was acting on behalf of the Communist Party. Nor did any of the evidence collected by the police—as opposed to evidence that the police themselves fabricated—support such a suspicion. As there were no opinion polls in Nazi Germany, we cannot know with certainty whether many Germans accepted the Nazis' version of the story, but all available evidence suggests that those who were already supporters of the Nazis believed them and those who were opponents did not. A woman from Braunschweig, writing to her daughter in Holland in early March, noted with approval that a Social Democratic editor had been arrested because he had told the foreign press that the Nazis might have set fire to the Reichstag. "One need not be surprised any longer," she continued, "that such false news about the National Socialists is always being spread by the foreign press." She added that no foreigner could possibly understand "how Hitler is loved, celebrated and revered by the German people." Looking back years later, Heinrich Brüning thought that "the Reichstag fire and the news about its alleged perpetrators had such an effect that the broad public no longer got upset about the government's acts of violence." The people "were as though stunned."

GOEBBELS THOUGHT CAREFULLY about how to persuade people, but unlike Hitler or Ludendorff, he was not much interested in other kinds of political propaganda. His model was commercial advertising, and he understood the prevailing idea that advertising should aim to influence the consumer with simple, partly subliminal messages, endlessly repeated. Catchy and memorable slogans were essential. Goebbels was a quick study: his managing and selling of Hitler's image matched or exceeded the sophistication of the best commercial advertising of the time. Germany's advertising professionals were partly dismayed (at the thought of lost business) but also impressed when Hitler put Goebbels at the head of the new "Ministry of Public Enlightenment and Propaganda"—here was a government committing itself to advertising on a scale they had never envisioned, a strong endorsement of their work. They proudly claimed Goebbels as one of their own.

The cynical dishonesty of the Nazis' propaganda received a significant boost from the cult of irrationality that drove their followers: the contempt for, indeed the revolution against, Enlightenment standards of rationality. To many people in the 1920s and '30s, it was beginning to seem that such a revolution against reason might be a chronic ailment of democracy.

The last three decades of the nineteenth century saw two important and related developments. The first was that mass electoral politics emerged in most European countries. In 1871, there had been just two major European countries in which all adult men had the right to vote in national elections: Germany and France. Even in relatively democratic

Britain, the vote was still tied to the tax rolls, excluding a large proportion of working-class men. By 1914, however, after round upon round of reform, most major European countries had something close to "manhood suffrage," and votes for women were clearly on the way.

The second development was that the hatreds, prejudices, and superstitions that civilized Europeans thought belonged to the distant medieval past had reemerged. Many Europeans thought that this second development was connected to the first. At the turn of the twentieth century, an epidemic of "ritual murder" allegations spread across central and eastern Europe. This was the notion that Jews murdered Christian children to use their blood for baking Passover matzoh. Even in cosmopolitan France, the framing of Captain Alfred Dreyfus on charges of treason in 1894, and the scandal that followed, revealed a new and vitriolic kind of antisemitism. In 1903, Erich Sello, the most prominent of Berlin's trial lawyers and a cultivated writer of books and periodical articles, wrote despairingly of "how desperately thin . . . is the veneer of culture that covers the age-old swamp of moral and intellectual barbarity." Classes of the population "which counted themselves with pride among the cultivated" could "no longer hold the horrors of the witch persecutions for a popular plague which for us is only a sinister legend from the past, and whose return in our golden age of enlightenment and tolerance is no longer to be feared."

European thinkers began to concern themselves with the rise of such irrationality and particularly its effects on politics. The French sociologist Gustav Le Bon became famous and influential with his theories on crowd behavior, as did the German philosopher Friedrich Nietzsche with his withering dissection of conventional morality, and the Austrian psychoanalyst Sigmund Freud with his claim that the sex drive, not rational thought, lay at the root of human motivation. The fascination with irrationality began to crop up everywhere, even in disciplines such as the law, which had once sought to be a paradigm of dispassionate logic.

The experience of the Great War gave an added boost to the embrace of irrationality. Nothing about the war made much sense. What was the point of walking slowly into machine-gun fire? In no country did the casualties stand in any proportion to what might have been gained. In all countries, people were exposed to four years of propaganda emphasizing gut-level hatreds and exaltation.

Hitler pulled all this together—the deliberate dishonesty, the concern with public irrationality, and yet also the desire to revel in this irrationality. The Nazis' emphasis on race as the key to history, and racial thinking as the answer to all problems, grew out of both prewar irrationality and wartime violence. Nazi racial thinking was consciously anti-intellectual; "thinking with the blood" was its watchword. Elsewhere in Europe, this kind of racial ideology was beginning to come under attack. It was in the 1930s in France that the concept of "racism" as something negative arose. Opposition in Britain to the kind of racism practiced in Germany was stronger still. Often these critiques had their own ambiguity. Julian Huxley, a British biologist who supported eugenics, thought the Nazis were hurting the cause. But his takedown of Nazi racial doctrines could hardly have been more scathing: "Our German neighbors," he wrote, liked to imagine themselves as "fair, long-headed, tall and virile." Huxley proposed a composite picture "from the most prominent exponents of this view. Let him be as blond as Hitler, as dolichocephalic [having a long, narrow skull] as [Alfred] Rosenberg [who had a round face], as tall as Goebbels [who stood five feet five inches], as slender as Göring [who was notoriously portly]. . . . How much would this resemble the German ideal?"

The rejection of rationality often went hand in hand with a rejection of the liberal, capitalist West that was so central to the Nazi movement, and to the Weimar far right in general. During the First World War, the novelist Thomas Mann had glorified German "culture" and contrasted it to the liberal capitalist "civilization" of Britain and France, which he denigrated. He changed his mind later, but others didn't. The nationalist conservative writer Edgar Julius Jung wrote with contempt that the Treaty of Versailles and the League of Nations were "the symbols of the victory of 1789"—in other words, of the democratic and liberal values of the French Revolution. The Weimar Republic was similarly a "belated breakthrough by the Enlightenment into the middle of Europe." The Germans, said Jung, should oppose the Enlightenment with "tradition, blood and historical spirit."

Contemporary observers were keenly aware of how the Nazis profited from their appeal to irrationality. One of the most astute observers was the young Peter Drucker, who later became famous in the United States as an expert on business management. In the 1930s, he was a journalist and law student in Germany. Drucker was born into a Viennese Jewish family, well connected in the Austrian intellectual elite. The famous economists Joseph Schumpeter, Friedrich Hayek, and Ludwig von Mises were family friends, while the distinguished legal scholar Hans Kelsen was his uncle.

Drucker intuitively grasped some elements of Nazism that historians were still trying to work out decades later. He thought that Nazi and fascist doctrines had evolved in a general climate of loss of belief—not only in capitalism but in socialism as well. Since there were no positive answers to any social problems, Nazism could only be *against* everything, even against inconsistent things: it was antiliberal and anticonservative, antireligious and anti-atheist, anticapitalist and antisocialist, and most of all antisemitic. In a particularly sharp observation, he noted that Nazism had succeeded not because people believed its messages, but in spite of the fact that they did not. Nazi successes, he pointed out, had been "witnessed by a hostile press, a hostile radio, a hostile cinema, a hostile church, and a hostile government which untiringly pointed out the Nazi lies, the Nazi inconsistency, the unattainability of their promises, and the dangers and folly of their course." Clearly, he concluded, "nobody would have been a Nazi if rational belief in the Nazi promises had been a prerequisite."

The best explanation of Nazism that Drucker had ever encountered came from a Nazi agitator "whom, many years ago, I heard proclaim to a wildly cheering peasants' meeting: 'We don't want lower bread prices, we don't want higher bread prices, we don't want unchanged bread prices—we want National-Socialist bread prices.'" Since their logically inconsistent rage and hatred could never deliver any satisfactory social progress, the Nazis' only recourse was to this kind of irrationality: Nazism could only "accomplish its task through a miracle." Higher bread prices, lower bread prices, and unchanged bread prices "have all failed. The only hope lies in a kind of bread price which is none of these, which nobody has ever seen before, and which belies the evidence of one's reason."

The result was that it was often those Germans who had fought the hardest for the poor and underprivileged who were the most disillusioned about the democratic capacity of ordinary people. When the Nazis achieved their first breakthrough in 1930, Prussian prime minister Otto Braun protested that it was not the idea of democracy that had failed. The failure lay rather with "a considerable portion of the German people," who had not proven equal to the "responsibility which suddenly lay on their shoulders." Early in 1933, the veteran Social Democratic lawyer and politician Wolfgang Heine wrote to his friend Carl Severing, "It seems to me that the working class was also not yet ripe for this democratic will." Severing replied that it "went without saying" that he agreed. The Weimar Constitution was not to blame for the results, he continued. The problem was "the politically uneducated people, who did not know the correct things to do with the rights that had been conferred on them." The revolutionary socialist Ernst Toller struck the same note in the gloomy autobiography he finished after going into exile in 1933: "The people are tired of reason, tired of thought and reflection. They ask, what has reason done in the last few years, what good have insights and knowledge done us."

The sharp-eyed political reporter Konrad Heiden was also frustrated by his own inability to make his readers grasp the Nazis' contempt for truth and to counter their lies effectively. On one occasion, he admired the rhetorical skill with which Hitler drew a picture of "the Jew, who goes [to a mountain resort] to lose his fat." In fact, even though he had "brand-spanking new yellow boots" and a "beautiful backpack, in which truly mostly nothing at all is ever stored," this person would never hike in the mountains. He would stop where the trains stop, and gladly limit himself to the hotel bar. "These are truly not our working classes," Hitler continued. He drew a contrast to the thin, overworked, impoverished "Germans" who had to make do with gear from 1913 or 1914. Commenting on this performance, Heiden lamented that "it would be senseless to refute it; senseless to refer to the fact that fat Aryans in new yellow boots also do not gladly remove themselves from the vicinity of the mountain railway." It would be senseless, Heiden continued, because "the refutation would be heard, perhaps believed, and definitely forgotten again." Yet Hitler's image, drawn with "dazzling masterstrokes," would "stick indissolubly. Once you have heard it, you will never forget it."

In a 1932 book on the Nazi movement titled *Hitler's Path* (*Hitlers Weg*), the future West German president Theodor Heuss paid a similar depressed tribute to the Nazi leader's propagandistic skill. Heuss noticed that the passages on propaganda in *Mein Kampf* were "better and more precisely written" than the rest of the book. "Here," said Heuss, "speaks a man who understands something of the matter."

In a direct and material sense, the Great Depression had made life difficult for reporters such as Heiden and for that section of the German press that was committed both to a rational investigation of social reality and democratic or centrist politics. The Weimar Republic was famous for, among other things, its great liberal newspapers the *Frankfurter Zeitung*, the *Vossische Zeitung*, and the *Berliner Tageblatt*. Yet these papers failed along with the centrist democratic constituency that had sustained them. The *Frankfurter Zeitung*, for instance, had sold on average 110,000 copies per day in 1918, but by 1932, the daily sales had fallen by half. The fate of the other two papers was similar. The loss of hundreds of thousands of marks per year obviously could not be sustained. The *Frankfurter Zeitung* was "saved" by an infusion of financing from industrial circles, in particular from the huge chemical conglomerate IG Farben.

This financing had a predictable impact on the paper's reporting. In 1930, the novelist Joseph Roth, whose day job was writing for the paper, reported on the pollution caused by the Leuna chemical factory in Merseburg. A member of IG Farben's board wrote to Roth's editor to complain that "you have simply not succeeded in removing from the reporting staff" those "elements" who, with "all means, even sordid ones, vent their resentment against big business." The *Frankfurter Zeitung* also relegated Konrad Heiden to the "illustrated" and "women's" supplements—by the standards of the day, a serious demotion for a male journalist.

In fact, it was in the press and in the administration of justice (two areas where the rational evaluation of evidence is supposed to be paramount) that the Nazi contempt for truth and reason showed up most clearly. We have seen how revealingly detailed Nazi plans for the press were even in the party's 1920 program. As soon as they came to power, the Nazis started shutting down oppositional newspapers. Critical, left-leaning journalists were likely to find themselves in prison or in concentration camps. Such was the fate of Carl von Ossietzky, the pacifist and editor of the weekly journal *The World Stage*, and of the investigative reporter Egon Erwin Kisch, who had once been a fixture at the "Café Megalomania." Journalists who were not imprisoned were quickly brought into line, receiving daily guidelines on what they were supposed to write and how they were supposed to write it. By the middle of 1933, all German newspapers carried essentially the same content. Foreign correspondents could still tell the truth to an audience outside Germany, but even they were threatened, hassled, and occasionally arrested. Their cables were often blocked. When one of the best of these journalists, the American correspondent Edgar Ansel Mowrer, was finally forced out of the country, a Gestapo officer asked him when he might return. "When I can come back with about two million of my countrymen" was Mowrer's defiant response. The Gestapo man, who got the point, insisted that such a thing was impossible. "Not for the Führer," said Mowrer. "The Führer can bring anything about."

Soon after becoming chancellor, Hitler met with representatives of the Nazi press and told them he expected them to educate "the entire German press in the idea of service to the Volk as the highest principle." The press should be a "true reflection of German life and spirit," he went on, but this mission "had frequently been subordinated to other interests by a major part of the press today." He would "bring [his] feelings to bear" on "the type of journalism which abused its freedom" to engage in "anti-national agitation." By 1934, Goebbels could express his satisfaction that the press responded to events "correctly" even without being told what to do. Yet, typically, he wrote in his diary that "any man who still has a residue of honor will be very careful not to become a journalist."

Similarly, judges, lawyers, and the law were among the things Hitler most despised, and his regime was one long assault on the rationality, predictability, and integrity of the law. The most prominent legal case in the first year of Hitler's regime was the Reichstag fire trial, in which not only Marinus van der Lubbe but also three Bulgarian and one German Communist activist faced charges of high treason. The judges of the

Reich Supreme Court showed a modicum of courage in acquitting the four Communists, against whom the evidence was either nonexistent or conspicuously and laughably fabricated by the police. Hitler was so enraged by these acquittals that he ordered the creation of a new court, the People's Supreme Court (*Volksgerichtshof*), specially for political offenses. Throughout the Third Reich, judges were subject to direct criticism and sometimes dismissal for rendering verdicts that displeased the Führer. The whole idea of law as a clear and predictable scheme of rights and duties was upended in Hitler's regime. Nazi jurists, among them the notorious Carl Schmitt, who had once been counsel to Papen's and Schleicher's governments, tied themselves in knots explaining how law was whatever the Führer said it was. They spoke of a new legal concept, "Führer Power," in place of older ideas about constitutional legitimacy. Although the Nazis talked about bringing in entirely new versions of Germany's major laws, particularly its criminal and civil codes, they never followed through. The fact was that even their own law, reduced to binding codes, would have been too much an infringement on Hitler's arbitrary power.

AFTER HITLER'S ASCENSION to the chancellorship, the Nazis still had to win what they frankly called the last election, on March 5, 1933. After another campaign marked by severe violence, and in which it became ever more difficult for opposition parties to operate at all, the Nazis secured 43 percent of the vote. Their German National partners received 8 percent, giving their coalition a bare majority in the Reichstag. Yet Hitler had expected more. Martin Sommerfeldt, Göring's press secretary, claimed he heard Hitler tell Göring on Election Night, "So long as the old man is still alive, we won't be able to get rid of that gang." The "old man" was of course Hindenburg. The "gang" meant Papen, Hugenberg, and the German Nationals.

Hitler wanted the Reichstag to pass an "Enabling Act" to give all its lawmaking powers to his administration for four years. As a constitutional amendment, such a law would require a two-thirds majority. Hitler would have to threaten or cajole other parties to vote with him.

The new Reichstag session opened with the so-called Day of Potsdam.

Potsdam, a small city southwest of Berlin, had long been home to the kings of Prussia and was the spiritual home of conservative Prussian patriotism. Since 1929, establishment conservatives had been looking for a way to tie Hitler's movement to their agenda. The Day of Potsdam was designed as a demonstration of this supposed "national unity." The day began with separate Catholic and Protestant services. The ceremonial opening of the Reichstag itself took place in Potsdam's Garrison Church, sacred ground for Prussian conservative patriotism, where, among others, Prussia's two greatest kings, Friedrich Wilhelm I and his son Friedrich II, "the Great," were buried.

The idea of national unity had long been caught up with the legend of the "spirit of 1914," and 1914 hung conspicuously over everything that happened on the Day of Potsdam. At the Lutheran service, the local church leader Dr. Otto Dibelius told his listeners that in August 1914 the "call through the masses had been: One Reich, One People, One God," a call that today remained a "yearning." His closing words were "hundreds of thousands of brothers and sisters still groan under foreign slavery. It has always been the fate of the German people to have to fight anew for their freedom."

The services were followed by the official Reichstag opening, and the day closed with a military parade, which featured not only the Potsdam army garrison but also police units, the Nazis' SA and SS, even their "League of German Girls." In his speech, Hitler, in morning dress, went out of his way to praise Hindenburg and to call for national unity. Hindenburg appeared in his field marshal's uniform and ostentatiously saluted Kaiser Wilhelm's son, who was in attendance—a gesture of support for the return of the monarchy.

The Day of Potsdam also pointed to the limitations of unity on Hindenburg's and Hitler's terms. Hitler avoided the church service, instead visiting the graves of SA men. The Social Democrats avoided the services as well, and none of the Communist members could risk showing their faces—by this time, they had either been arrested or had fled abroad. Even Dibelius had pointedly asserted that "state office must not be mixed with personal despotism," and his invocation of "One Reich, One People, One God" was significantly at variance with the Nazi slogan, which changed the last element to "One Leader." What the Day of Potsdam really illustrated was a national unity on right-wing terms that excluded a third of the country, and about which even the other groups had obvious reservations.

Two days later, the Reichstag met for real business. Because the chamber where the members usually deliberated had been destroyed by the fire, they gathered instead at the nearby Kroll Opera House. Hitler wore a brown SA uniform, and the Nazis' enforcers were present in large numbers.

Before the session began, the Social Democratic deputies had to decide whether they could risk attending it. Plausible rumors were circulating that the Nazis planned such violence against them that "we would be lucky if half of our caucus members came away with their lives," in the memorable account of Wilhelm Hoegner, a Social Democratic deputy from Bavaria. When the Social Democrats bravely decided to appear, they found that "the wide square in front of the Kroll Opera House was crowded with dark masses of people," Hoegner remembered. The Social Democratic and Center Party deputies "were received with wild choruses: 'We want the Enabling Act!' Youths with swastikas on their chests eyed us insolently, blocked our way, in fact made us run the gauntlet, calling us names like 'Center pig,' 'Marxist sow.' The Kroll Opera House was crawling with armed SA and SS men." When the deputies got inside, they heard that Carl Severing had been arrested, and they also learned about the arrest and beating of Maria Jankowski. "When we Social Democrats had taken our seats on the extreme left, SA and SS men lined up at the exits and along the walls behind us in a semicircle. Their expressions boded no good."

If the "spirit of 1914," the myth of unity, had hovered over Potsdam, in the Kroll Opera House it was the countermyth of disunity, of the "stab in the back," that was front and center. Hitler opened the debate with a long speech. All the promises, he thundered, that had been "made by the men of November 1918" had turned out to be "if not acts of intentional deception, then no less damnable illusions." It was pluralism and diversity itself, "the completely opposite approaches of individuals to the concepts of state, society, religion, morality, family, and economy" that had destroyed "any possible community life." The only alternative was "the creation of a real *Volksgemeinschaft*," rising above the interests and

conflicts of all classes and sections of society. His government, therefore, wanted a "clear decision" on the one question before it this day,
the passage of the Enabling Act. Hitler was "offering the parties of the
Reichstag the possibility of a peaceful development out of which a future
understanding can emerge." Yet a rejection would not faze his government. He concluded ominously, "May you, Gentlemen, now choose for
yourselves between peace or war!"

This day was the only occasion on which Hitler participated in an
actual parliamentary debate. The Social Democrats' leader, Otto Wels,
rose to speak against him. Under the conditions of the day, with the SA
and SS men threatening the Social Democratic deputies and with many
left-wing members already imprisoned and subject to beatings, torture,
and even murder, Wels's speech was as courageous as it was eloquent and
moving. "It is clear that the opponents are after our honor," he said. But
this would only "one day rebound" on the Nazis, "for it is not our honor
which is being destroyed in the worldwide tragedy." "Freedom and life
they can take from us," he continued, "but not honor." With the Nazi
bullyboys laughing in mockery and calling out abuse and threats,
Wels, looking straight at Hitler, concluded, "No Enabling Act can give
you the power to destroy ideas which are eternal and indestructible. . . .
We hail those who are persecuted and in despair. We hail our friends in
the Reich. Their steadfastness and loyalty are worthy of acclaim. The
courage of their convictions, their unbroken faith are the guarantees of
a brighter future."

The Social Democrats had given the text of Wels's speech to the press
ahead of time, and Hitler had gotten a copy. He now returned to the ros-
trum. Nothing could bring out Hitler's rage like an effective challenge.
Wels had gotten to him.

"You're late in coming, but you've come," Hitler began, sarcastically
quoting a line from Schiller's play *Wallenstein*, a favorite of Weimar politicians from Stresemann to Hindenburg. The Social Democrats could
have opposed the "lie" of German war guilt, they could have opposed
reparations, they could have led an uprising against the Treaty of
Versailles. They had not done so. If Wels talked of persecution, "I think
there are few of us here present who were not forced to pay in prison for

the persecution you practiced." When the Social Democratic delegates cried out in protest, Göring, presiding over the session, told them, "Stop talking and listen to this for once." Hitler complained about what he called Social Democratic media lies, growing steadily angrier and more intemperate. At the end, he told the Social Democrats that he did not want them to vote for his Enabling Act. "Germany will be liberated, but not by you!" He sat down to "thunderous cries of 'Heil!'"

When the vote was held later that day, all parties save the Social Democrats voted for Hitler's law. The Center, anchor of the Republic for fourteen years, and the two old liberal parties, the German People's Party of Stresemann and the former German Democratic Party, abandoned their principles in the face of Nazi success and intimidation.

Heinrich Brüning claimed after the war that he and several German National Reichstag members had made a last-minute effort to fend off the worst of the Enabling Act. The plan was to introduce an amendment to the legislation that would limit its duration to six months and restore the civil liberties taken away in the Reichstag Fire Decree. On the Day of Potsdam, just before the ceremony in the Garrison Church, the German National caucus leader Ernst Oberfohren had spoken to Brüning about this, and the next day, Oberfohren's friend Otto Schmidt-Hannover invited Brüning to an evening meeting with Alfred Hugenberg. "Hugenberg was unusually sensible," Brüning recalled years later, and they agreed on the form of an amendment.

But there was a revolt in the German National Reichstag caucus, led by extreme right-wing members who wanted to support the Nazis. Brüning did not know this until the Enabling Act reached its second reading. "Behind every row of seats there stood an SS man," Brüning remembered. "So Schmidt-Hannover could only whisper to me in passing" that the previous night's meeting had been betrayed, he himself was being pursued, and there would be no amendment.

The real significance of the Enabling Act was not that the Reichstag had given Hitler's government its lawmaking powers for four years, it was that in getting this authorization, Hitler had made himself independent of President Hindenburg as well. At a stroke, one of the main guarantees on which conservatives had counted to restrain Hitler was gone. In the course of the next four months, most other guarantees of liberty and the rule of law would be swept away in a remarkably fast and relentless process of consolidating power.

The Nazis called it *Gleichschaltung*, or "coordination," a term borrowed from electronics, meaning that all the switches are on the same circuit. Amid a genuine upsurge of popular enthusiasm for their government, the Nazis attacked the federal system, rapidly "coordinating" the governments of the individual states so that no possible opposition could come from places like perennially contrary Bavaria. Every kind of professional organization was taken over and Nazified. Radio stations and newspapers were to be "coordinated" under the oversight of Joseph Goebbels's new Ministry of Public Enlightenment and Propaganda.

In April came the "Law for the Restoration of the Professional Civil Service." This allowed the regime to dismiss from public service anyone whose political record did not "offer sufficient guarantee" that he would "at all times wholeheartedly stand up for the national state," or who was "non-Aryan." This law cast a particularly broad net because, in Germany, such groups as university professors and private lawyers also fell under its terms.

One by one, the political parties—even the German Nationals—were either outlawed or wound themselves up. In July, Hitler's government issued a decree declaring the Nazis the sole political party in Germany.

A week after the passage of the Enabling Act, Hitler's government made its first move against Germany's Jewish community. It declared a boycott of Jewish businesses and professional offices. On April 1, SA men planted themselves in front of all such businesses they could identify, and warned Germans, "Defend yourselves, don't buy from Jews." Yet the boycott turned out to be a flop. Many Germans defied the Stormtroopers and pushed their way into the shops they always visited. This lack of respect for the boycott became an embarrassment for the government, and Goebbels called it off. It turned out that discrimination that was more hidden from public view, as with the Civil Service Law, was more effective.

Already in March, the Nazis had announced with great fanfare the creation of their first concentration camp, borrowing the term from the Boer War and the Russian Civil War. The camp was at Dachau, near Munich. Others quickly followed, one in a converted brewery in Oranienburg, north of Berlin, others in former penitentiaries in Sonnenburg and Brandenburg, or in converted fortresses such as Oberer Kuhberg. The first wave of victims consisted largely of political opponents of the Nazis: liberal, left-wing, or pacifist politicians, activists, journalists, writers, and lawyers. Among them were some who have figured in this story, like Hans Litten, Egon Erwin Kisch, Carl von Ossietzky, Max Fürst, and Lina Haag. Litten and Ossietzky would die. In nearly all cases, the tortures and beatings were beyond description.

TWELVE YEARS LATER, on April 27, 1945, as the Soviet Red Army closed in on his Berlin bunker, Hitler chatted about old times with his loyal propaganda minister, Joseph Goebbels, and an SS general named Wilhelm Mohnke. The great city of Berlin was almost entirely in rubble, most of Germany was occupied by foreign troops, and millions of Germans had died in Hitler's war. Seemingly without irony, Mohnke commented, "We haven't quite done what we wanted to do in 1933, my Führer!" Hitler seemed to agree, and he gave a surprising reason: he had come to power a year and a half too soon. The old system had not yet sufficiently discredited itself, he said. Coming to power when he did, with Hindenburg still alive, he had had to make deals with the conservative establishment. "I had to wriggle from one compromise to another," Hitler complained. He had been forced to appoint many officials who were not reliable, which explained why there had been frequent leaks of information. Hitler also said that he had planned to bring "ruthlessly to account" people such as Hammerstein, Schleicher, and indeed "the whole clique around this vermin." But after eighteen months in office he had grown milder, and in any case, the great upswing in Germany's economic and political fortunes was under way. "You regret it afterwards," Hitler said, "that you are so kind."

Hitler's assessment of his early days in office (if not of his "kindness") wasn't entirely wrong. In his first eighteen months as chancellor, the establishment conservatives had been the source of his greatest worries. Only they had enough control of the real levers of power (political, economic, and military) to have put him in office. And only they could remove him.

They, and Hitler, knew this.

8

"We Have to Get Rid of Him"

For Fritz Günther von Tschirschky, the first sign that something is up comes with a phone call at 3:30 in the morning. A man's voice says he is calling from a Steel Helmet group. He wants to know if Tschirschky and Vice-Chancellor von Papen are at home. Tschirschky asks him if he is crazy. Two more calls follow. Now alarmed, Tschirschky calls Papen's press secretary, Herbert von Bose. They agree to meet at the vice-chancellor's office in the Palais Borsig, so named because it was built for the nineteenth-century railroad millionaire Albert Borsig. By 7:15, they are there. When Tschirschky tells Bose about the phone calls, Bose turns pale and says, "Now it's over." Tschirschky doesn't fully understand, but he calls Papen and convinces him to come to the vice-chancellery, too.

Tschirschky is a handsome young man with a sardonic glint in his intelligent eyes. Thirty-four years old, he comes from a prominent Silesian aristocratic family. One uncle was the German ambassador in Vienna before the First World War, another is currently serving as the Dutch ambassador in Berlin. Tschirschky is one of a number of bright young men who have been recruited to serve in Vice-Chancellor von Papen's office. He is designated Papen's "adjutant." Actually, his job is to run an informal political intelligence service.

Starting at 8:00, they receive a series of increasingly impatient phone calls from the office of Hermann Göring, who, since the previous spring, has replaced Papen as Prussian prime minister. Will Papen come to a meeting with Göring? Finally, Göring himself calls. Papen, now very agitated, takes Tschirschky with him to Göring's office. Göring tells Papen that the SA is attempting a coup d'état. Hitler has gone to Munich to lead the crackdown there. Göring is in charge in Berlin. Papen complains that, as vice-chancellor, he should be leading things. A state of emergency should be declared and the army called out. Göring brushes all objections aside. He sends Papen out again and orders Tschirschky to take the vice-chancellery staff to Papen's house and stay there until the situation is cleared up—for their own safety.

While Papen is with Göring, Tschirschky waits in the hall. He sees Heinrich Himmler, the head of Hitler's elite guard, the SS, emerge from Göring's office and go to a telephone. "Now it can start," Himmler says into the phone.

It is June 30, 1934. The events of the next twenty-four hours will come to be known as "the Night of the Long Knives."

When Papen and Tschirschky return to the Palais Borsig, they find it filled with black-uniformed SS men. A man who appears to be a plainclothes police officer tells Tschirschky he is under arrest. A moment of dark comedy follows. As Tschirschky is leaving the building with this officer, another man in plainclothes arrives and tries to arrest Tschirschky as well. "I'm sorry," Tschirschky politely tells the second officer, "but I've already been arrested by this gentleman here." The two apparent secret police officers carry on a ferocious argument with each other. The first, however, is accompanied by several SS men with machine pistols, and he wins the argument. He takes Tschirschky to the Gestapo headquarters at Prinz-Albrecht-Strasse 8. The cells in the basement are full, and Tschirschky, like many other recent arrivals, must spend hours sitting on a bench in the corridor. He will learn only much later that Papen has been taken under guard to his villa on Lennéstrasse and put under house arrest.

It is men from Hitler's own bodyguard, the "Leibstandarte SS Adolf Hitler," who have seized control of the Palais Borsig. The squad is commanded by a senior Gestapo official, Anton Dunckern, a friend of Himmler's. There are also plainclothes officers of the SD, the intelligence service that is a part of the SS, under the command of the Berlin SD chief

Herman Behrends. The SS men cut off all telephone connections to the outside world and then post armed guards at all the office doors.

Papen's staff take this assault with a careful show of calm. "We're all getting busted today," Herbert von Bose tells his colleagues with phlegmatic gallows humor. Another man warns the staff against armed resistance and says the only thing to do is "keep a stiff upper lip (Haltung bewahren)." When Bose learns that the orders for the raid have come from Heinrich Himmler personally, he notes drily, "That's not a good sign." His stoic composure is a performance to reassure his colleagues. He understands perfectly well what is happening. In case "worse comes to worst," Bose gives his colleagues some things for his family: his briefcase, his signet ring, a few banknotes.

It is just after this that two plainclothes men, Gestapo or SD officers, call Bose into one of the offices and close the door. A few seconds later comes the sound of ten shots, and then, after a pause, an eleventh. As the men leave the room, Papen's staff can hear one of them say, "Well, that's taken care of." They leave Bose as he fell, with pools and spatters of blood all over the room. It is about 11:40 a.m.

It will never be possible, even for German police after the war, to identify Bose's killers.

Meanwhile, at 12:30 p.m., Kurt von Schleicher is at his house in Neubabelsberg, west of Berlin. Two men are standing at his front door arguing with Marie Güntel, his cook, and demanding to see the former chancellor. Güntel tells them Schleicher has gone for a walk. One of the men shows Güntel some kind of identification document, but she doesn't pay much attention to it. He also threatens her with consequences if she is lying. "I'll have a look," she says, and goes to find Schleicher. The man with the ID simply follows her.

Schleicher is at his desk in his study. His wife, Elisabeth, sits nearby, listening to the radio. Later that day, Güntel will tell the police what happens next. The "gentleman with the ID" asks if the man at the desk is General von Schleicher. "Jawohl," Schleicher replies. The gentleman with the ID immediately opens fire, not just on Kurt but on Elisabeth von Schleicher as well. Güntel screams and runs out of the room. Later, a doctor pronounces Kurt von Schleicher dead at the scene, with seven gunshot wounds. Elisabeth is rushed to the hospital but dies soon after. The official story is that

Schleicher was shot while resisting arrest and his wife was caught in the crossfire. Supposedly, Schleicher had been conspiring against Hitler's government along with the SA commander Ernst Röhm and the French ambassador André François-Poncet. But two weeks later, when Hitler gives a major speech about these events to the Reichstag, he seems to drop the story that Schleicher was "shot while resisting arrest."

Hitler says simply that he had Schleicher shot.

A year later, Marie Güntel will drown under mysterious circumstances. Her family believes it is a case of "witness removal."

That afternoon, Tschirschky is surprised to see guards open a cell door opposite him and bring out Edgar Julius Jung to relieve himself. Jung is just a few years older than Tschirschky, balding, with wire-framed glasses and a serious, intense stare. Although Jung is not formally part of Papen's staff—he works on contract as a speechwriter—in some ways, he is the center of the group. He has already been in custody since June 25. Tschirschky is sure he can read Jung's glance: the speechwriter is thinking, "Well, if Tschirschky is down here already, it's all over." The next time the guards bring Jung out, Tschirschky is ready. He manages to follow Jung into the restroom and stands next to him. "Don't be worried," Tschirschky tells Jung, "that you're seeing us down here, too. Up above there is a revolution. We have been taken into protective custody, but nothing will happen." It seems to Tschirschky that Jung looks relieved. He admits later that, in this moment, he was not trying to be honest; he was trying to comfort his friend.

This is the last time Tschirschky will ever see Jung. Jung is taken away later that night. The next day, his body is found in a roadside ditch north of Berlin.

Jung's interrogators had really only wanted to know one thing: Did he write the speech?

EDGAR JULIUS JUNG was no angel. In Weimar's turbulent early days, he was a radical nationalist activist in his native Bavarian Palatinate. In 1924, he led an assassination squad that murdered a Rhineland separatist whom Jung considered a traitor. Jung moved to the center of what became known as the "young conservative" movement with a 1927 book on democracy titled *The Rule of Inferiors* (*Die Herrschaft der Minderwertigen*). He was fiercely ambitious and not especially likable. Even his commanding officer at an air force training station in the First World War wrote that Jung's "manners require constant instruction." The much more extroverted and sociable Tschirschky called him "not entirely easy to handle," while some suspected that Jung's real problem with Hitler was that Hitler was chancellor and Jung wasn't.

Like other young conservatives, Jung hated the Weimar Republic, its parliamentary democratic system, and its political parties. He believed that world history had taken a wrong turn when the French Revolution of 1789 introduced the principles of liberty and equality into political life. Jung wanted a return to a form of medieval society structured by guilds and by the values of Christianity. He believed that this would mean a return to nature and God. Jung sought a meritocratic hierarchical society in which great individuals would rise to leadership on the basis of education and natural talent. The "masses" would have no involvement in politics. Needless to say, Jung assumed he was one of the leaders of this natural hierarchy. Paradoxically, for all the misty medievalism of his ideas, Jung became popular with Ruhr industrialists who liked his elitism and hostility to democracy. The steel magnate Paul Reusch became Jung's patron.

But when Hitler came to power, Jung experienced a sudden conversion. He didn't find the Nazis much different from the Weimar Republic. To Jung, they were just another secular expression of uneducated mass opinion. He had nothing but contempt for their violence, their lawlessness, their dishonesty, their anti-intellectualism, their disdain for the principles of Christianity. He said that he regretted writing his famous book. On one occasion, he told a Social Democratic journalist, "Now I'd like to throw my arms around every Social Democrat." Most remarkable was a line in a letter he wrote in February 1933 to his friend Rudolf Pechel, the editor of a highbrow conservative journal called the *Deutsche Rundschau* (the German Review). "We are partly responsible for this guy coming to power," said Jung. "We have to get rid of him."

In fact, Jung's views had been evolving since about 1929, in some very forward-looking ways. He became a convinced advocate of federalism as a solution to the problems of minority rights in European countries.

Even more remarkably, the burning nationalist of 1924 had begun to envision a new kind of federal Europe, a way to bring peace and stability to the continent—not so different from the hopes of the French foreign minister Aristide Briand, although Jung seems to have imagined Europe as a federation of federations and not as one political union.

Jung's aggressive personality remained, as did traces of his older views. In part, he disliked the Nazis because he thought that, as a mass movement, they were too liberal and too democratic. He thought that Christianity should be the organizing principle for German and European politics. He opposed the Nazis' violent antisemitism, but his own views were far from enlightened—he thought German Jews were responsible for their own oppression. As someone who was supported financially by steel magnates, he was always careful to advocate their interests in his political writings. Yet Jung was fearless, strident, and often witheringly sarcastic in his criticisms of the Nazis. In July 1933, he and his Catholic friend Edmund Forschbach attended a meeting of Catholic academics at the Benedictine abbey at Maria Laach, where they heard the legal scholar Carl Schmitt praise the Nazis for their "totalitarian" approach and for the way they had gotten rid of parliamentary democracy and political parties. Jung spoke up and suggested that if all parties were to be abolished, then why not abolish the Nazi Party as well? Surely in a country that was now without parties, the Nazis served no more purpose. A Nazi official was heard to say, "This guy belongs in Dachau."

Where Jung actually ended up was in the circle around Franz von Papen.

As chancellor, Papen had been popular with Germany's major industrialists, some of whom were worried about Hitler's radicalism. One of these was Nikolaus von Ballestrem, a friend of Fritz Günther von Tschirschky's from Silesia. Although also a young man, Ballestrem was as well connected as he was wealthy. A Catholic active in the Center Party and, like Papen, a major shareholder in the Center Party's newspaper, *Germania*, he was friends with both Papen and Brüning. He decided to use these advantages to create a resistance cell planted inside the government itself.

Ballestrem suggested to Tschirschky that they assemble a team of "clear-eyed, brave young men" to work in Papen's office and use Papen's seemingly strong position as the base for anti-Nazi resistance. Another young Papen protégé, the lawyer Wilhelm von Ketteler, arranged for Tschirschky to meet Papen and carefully sound him out. Tschirschky found that Papen had "no line of his own and no actual goal"; he simply assumed that the Nazis would eventually tone down their violence and that he and Hindenburg would continue to exert a moderating influence. Tschirschky was more impressed with Papen's "clear-eyed and brave" wife, Martha, who called Hitler "Dodo" and, throughout the Third Reich, even in Hitler's presence, conspicuously avoided giving the Hitler salute. Tschirschky left the conversation with Papen feeling he had encountered only incomprehension and mistrust.

Ketteler and Tschirschky didn't give up; they simply changed their tactics. Tschirschky arranged for Papen to speak at a rally in Breslau. The rally went well, and Papen was pleased. On the train back to Berlin, Tschirschky told Papen about the intelligence work he had done the year before in Papen's administration, and sold the vice-chancellor on the idea of having a man he could trust to do the same things in his present office. They agreed that that man would be Tschirschky himself. This was the beginning of the new office. Tschirschky took up his job at the end of March 1933.

Over time, the office expanded and changed. At first, Tschirschky worked out of Papen's office as prime minister of Prussia. When Papen lost this position in April 1933, Tschirschky recognized that this might leave Papen completely without an independent power base. He knew the Reich finance minister Count Lutz Schwerin von Krosigk and managed to negotiate an arrangement to fund and create "the Office of the Deputy Chancellor" in the Palais Borsig. Gradually, Tschirschky and Ketteler recruited other key personnel, most of them young law graduates.

The core of the group was formed by Jung, Bose, Ketteler, and Tschirschky. Herbert von Bose, the former intelligence officer and Papen's press secretary, who, at forty, was the oldest of the group, became the informal leader. Jung didn't have a fixed position in Papen's entourage and kept up his residence in Munich, but he was the clear intellectual leader and the most uncompromising in his determination to fight the

Nazis. Ketteler worked for Bose in the press office, and Tschirschky took the title of "adjutant" to Papen to cover his real functions.

None of these men had a high opinion of Papen, and they kept him utterly in the dark about what they were up to. Edgar Jung put it this way: "Papen was Hitler's doorman, now he'll be mine." On another occasion, Jung explained Papen's feeble excuses for helping Hitler into power with the words "This asshole really believes that." Bose, playing on Papen's connection to horses, referred to him contemptuously as a "vain thoroughbred" who could only think with blinders on. The most balanced was Tschirschky, who admitted that after "the many depressing experiences" with Papen, it was hard to be objective about him. He found Papen a mixture of a "young cavalry officer," a "diplomat and aristocrat of the old school," and a "believing Catholic." He lacked the qualities to make use of his position, when not forced to act by circumstances or by other people. Papen was so convinced of his own good intentions that he was oblivious to "the damage he often caused through his egotistical, superficial actions." "For us," said Tschirschky, "he served only as a smoke screen."

Though Papen was oblivious to what his young staff members were up to, the Nazis and their secret police were not. They were suspicious of Papen's people from the beginning, and soon the Gestapo was shadowing them and tapping their phones. In April 1933, Kurt Daluege, a Nazi of long standing whom Göring had put in charge of all Prussian police, got hold of a document claiming the Nazis had set the Reichstag fire. Daluege did not know where the document had come from, but he suspected it was a product of Papen's office. One day, standing in the garden of the Reich Chancellery, the Nazi ideologist Alfred Rosenberg complained to Hitler of a press leak from Papen's office. Hitler gestured in the direction of the Palais Borsig and said, "Yes, that's where it all comes from, someday I'll have the whole office cleared out." It didn't help that Jung and Tschirschky were indiscreet about their views. Jung kept up his prolific writing for various press outlets and began to come under increasing criticism in Nazi media.

At first, Papen's staff concentrated on trying to help people who were suffering from the brutality of the Nazis' early months in power. Their work could run to freeing prisoners of the SA or Gestapo, warning vulnerable people of an impending arrest, and arranging money and papers to enable them to emigrate. Political and religious differences from before 1933 played no role in their willingness to help. These conservative men did what they could for Communists, Social Democrats, and labor leaders, and for Protestants, Catholics, and Jews. As Goebbels noted repeatedly in his diary, their office became known as the "Democratic Complaints Office."

Another form of resistance involved trying to counteract the process of *Gleichschaltung*, or "coordination." Edgar Jung sought to persuade several Reichstag deputies to vote against the Enabling Act. Jung had come to realize the danger of "totalitarianism" now facing Germany and to intensify his desire to act against it. Papen's staff succeeded in influencing Hindenburg to appoint Nazi skeptic Werner von Fritsch commander in chief of the army instead of the Nazi-friendly Walter von Reichenau. They also provided information on conditions in Germany to the foreign press, particularly British, French, and American outlets.

By the summer of 1933, however, the group was beginning to move toward the most active and dangerous kind of resistance—efforts to undermine Hitler and his regime and eventually replace it altogether. The first step in this strategy was a resourceful idea of Jung's. Hitler had destroyed the democratic system by having his party compete successfully within that system until he was strong enough to bring it down. Jung's idea was to get inside Hitler's system and repeat the trick. The vice-chancellery group planned to use the parliamentary "elections" Hitler would hold on November 12, for which voters would be offered only one slate of Nazi-approved candidates. Jung and his coconspirators saw this as a way to secure positions for their own people within the system, so that they would be ready when the day came for a coup d'état. Jung also thought that once these independent people were in the Reichstag and able to act, Hitler would be forced to acknowledge them as a "loyal opposition."

The vice-chancellery group put together a list of approximately eighty candidates and sent it to Interior Minister Wilhelm Frick. Frick selected a dozen from this list to receive the party's endorsement. Jung himself wanted to be on the list, but Frick knew better than to select him. Jung's friend Edmund Forschbach made it, however.

Jung and the others were also active in building a diverse network of potential resistance activists. Jung reached out to the dissident Nazi Otto Strasser, brother of Gregor, and the liberal politician Theodor Heuss. The vice-chancellery group established connections with former chancellor Heinrich Brüning, German Nationals such as Otto Schmidt-Hannover and Leipzig mayor Carl Goerdeler, leading Social Democrats like Otto Braun and Carl Severing, leaders of the Steel Helmet such as Theodor Duesterberg, and Church figures such as Catholic cardinal Clemens von Galen and the Protestant minister Otto Dibelius, who had given the sermon on the Day of Potsdam but had since moved into opposition. Otto Strasser remembered that when he and Jung met in early 1934, Jung told him of "increasing tensions in Hitler's cabinet, of differences between the army and the SA, of friction between the SA and SS . . . and of a growing repugnance among the population against the worsening terror." Jung, he said, "gave me to understand" that "influential circles would not look on these things forever without taking action." Working within the system but building a broad network, these men pioneered the approach that would later be used in the "Operation Valkyrie" attempt on Hitler's life in July 1944. Some of the people were in fact the same: Carl Goerdeler would go on to be the leader of the civilian side of the Valkyrie resistance, and it is likely that Jung made contact with the Social Democrat Julius Leber, who would also be at the center of Valkyrie.

Because so many of the main figures died suddenly and young, without leaving accounts behind, it is not always easy to retrace their steps. Yet it seems that in the fall of 1933, Jung and Bose made contact with Schleicher and with Schleicher's former defense ministry associate Ferdinand von Bredow, to recruit them to their resistance circle. There is clear evidence of a meeting, on December 4, 1933, between Jung, Schleicher, and Bredow in the house of Schleicher's friend Arno von Moyzischewitz. On April 16, 1934, Schleicher wrote to Moyzischewitz about a memo from Jung he had just read: "It was interesting, especially since I had chatted with the author about all these problems a little while ago. A pity that this man did not cross my path in the Papen era. Perhaps much would have been different. Fate!" Fate indeed, and Bredow would soon share Schleicher's. He, too, was murdered on June 30, 1934.

By early 1934, the vice-chancellery group had moved beyond trying to mitigate conditions in Hitler's Germany and were looking for a way to remove Hitler from power. Jung contemplated an assassination. "He should just be blown away," Jung told his friend Leopold Ziegler. But Ziegler warned Jung that a murderer would stand no chance of ever becoming chancellor himself, and this was enough to persuade Jung to take a more moderate line.

The more refined plan was for Papen to give Hindenburg a negative report on conditions in Germany. He would emphasize the threat from the radicalism of the SA, to which the army, naturally at the center of Hindenburg's concerns, would have to respond. Hindenburg would use his presidential powers to declare martial law, summon Hitler and Göring to Neudeck, and tell them that the army was disbanding the SA. The constitution would be suspended while Hindenburg took over power as supreme commander of the army. A transitional government, or "Directory," would be formed, under the control of establishment conservatives: the army commanders Fritsch and Gerd von Rundstedt, flanked by Papen, Brüning, and Goerdeler. Hitler and Göring would be present only to deter other Nazis from resisting. Here again, Jung favored killing Hitler right away, but the others talked him out of it. After a period of martial law sufficient for Hitler's gauleiters and police chiefs to be neutralized, there would be a national assembly to draft a new constitution.

These thoughts and plans evolved against a background of political trouble for the regime in the early months of 1934. Over a year into Hitler's rule, things were not going well for the Nazis. The wave of real and spontaneous enthusiasm that had greeted Hitler's consolidation of power was gone. Germans were thoroughly tired of the lawless brutality of the Stormtroopers. Workers were frustrated by the destruction of free trade unions, and economic conditions had not yet improved enough to head off discontent. Goebbels's censorship had drained the press and much of the entertainment sector of any vitality or originality. The Nazis were demonstrating, at best, a cold disregard for and, at worst, serious repression of the rights and traditions of religious communities of all kinds. In May, Goebbels felt forced to launch a major propaganda campaign against "grumblers and fault-finders" precisely because there were so many of them.

The Nazi leadership also had to worry about specific political threats. The relationship between the party leadership and its Stormtroopers had always been complicated and often antagonistic. By early 1934, many in the SA were grumbling about what they saw as the regime's backsliding into mainstream conformity, and some called for a "second revolution" or a "National Socialist," not just a "nationalist," revolution. Because the SA by then counted over three million members, its discontent could develop into a serious problem for the regime. But the pressures from the conservative right were much more alarming. The army high command was growing increasingly worried about the SA and putting more and more pressure on Hitler to bring the Stormtroopers to heel.

Meanwhile, President von Hindenburg was now eighty-six years old, and in the spring of 1934, his always robust health finally began to fail. What would happen when he was gone? Many conservatives wanted to take the opportunity of Hindenburg's death to restore the monarchy, which would at least put a permanent check on Hitler's power and possibly lead to his removal. And, of course, the Nazis knew about the subversion being practiced from within Papen's own office.

Amid such tension and discontent, the men in Papen's office hoped that one gesture of defiance could spark a revolution. Their plan was to get Papen to give a speech containing a frank and devastating critique of the regime. They would ensure that the speech was widely disseminated, broadcast on the radio and available everywhere in print. It would spark a surge of approval for Papen's daring and further criticism of the regime. With this wind at his back, Papen would go to Hindenburg, deliver his report, and get Hindenburg to declare martial law.

Edgar Jung would write the speech. As a first step, Jung drafted a memo in April on basic principles of German and European policy and circulated it widely among his friends and associates. Even Papen approved of its contents. Jung's memo is one of the first programmatic statements of an opposition group in Nazi Germany. We have seen that the Nazis fundamentally represented a protest against European and global integration. It is entirely consistent that the main theme of Jung's memo was the need for openness and closer ties to other countries.

Jung began by proclaiming that the century of "the rule of the white race" over the rest of the world, which had been based on European industry, was now over. With the industrialization and liberation of colonized peoples now well under way, Europe would have to rethink its economic organization. To be able to afford raw materials from abroad, it would have to keep on exporting its most competitive products beyond Europe, but Europeans would have to reorient the bulk of their exports to each others' markets. It followed that they would have to build up a common economic zone. Economic spaces are natural units, Jung said, but state borders are often artificial: the second should not limit the first. In the twentieth century, autarky was a utopian dream. Here Jung proved particularly farsighted. After the Second World War, when European countries did in fact lose or give up their overseas empires, their response was to replace the lost colonial markets by turning to one another and forming the European Economic Community, the forerunner to today's European Union. Jung also thought that an integrated federal Europe would make "wars of extermination" impossible, and here, too, he anticipated the thinking of the 1950s and, indirectly, the slaughter of the 1940s.

Jung argued that the Germans had to reject the "fascist system" for several reasons: it was too Italian and, thus, by analogy to the influence of the Roman Catholic Church, threatened an "ultramontanism fascist style." For all Jung's forward thinking, he could not entirely overcome a German Protestant's traditional suspicion of Catholics. Over the long term, said Jung, fascism could not satisfy a cultivated, reading and thinking people such as the Germans. It lacked controls, such as freedom of the press, to prevent corruption. And, again, Jung would not have been Jung if he had not added that it "guarantees no political elite, without which no people can develop its positive energies."

Perhaps most remarkably, Jung wrote that Germany needed a foreign policy that could create "European justice" and overcome national divisions. This meant in turn that Germans needed to be open to other countries in matters of culture and intellect. The Nazis were unable to do this because of their "racial and national exclusivity." The "decisive precondition," Jung concluded, for breaking through the "hostile ring that surrounds us, is to give up the voluntary intellectual isolation into which we have maneuvered ourselves through an intolerant ideology."

After the memo, the next step was the speech. Papen would be the keynote speaker at the meeting of the Marburg University League on June 17. His staff decided this would be the great occasion. Naturally, they told Papen nothing about their plans, but they made arrangements to ensure that he could not back out of what they wanted him to say. The Germania printing house produced a thousand copies of the speech ahead of time, and Papen's staff gave them to the press. At the very last minute on the evening of June 16, they submitted a summary of the speech to Goebbels's propaganda ministry, so that it could not be cancelled for lack of official authorization. The staff did not let Papen see the text until he was on the train to Marburg. Tschirschky, who traveled with him, later told the story.

"As I came back to the compartment after leaving for a while," Tschirschky remembered, "I noticed that Herr von Papen was in the middle of marking up the manuscript of the speech." Tschirschky asked him what he was doing. Papen said he had to make some changes because some parts of the speech "could cost him his head." Tschirschky told him that "he could not make any more changes, since hundreds of copies of the speech in its present form had been given to the domestic and foreign press." After a "ferocious argument," Papen grudgingly conceded that "under these circumstances he could probably not avoid giving the speech in its present form."

Papen faced an audience of about six hundred in the main lecture hall of Marburg University. Many local dignitaries were present, along with students and faculty. Jung listened to the speech on the radio with his friend Heinrich Schnee, a former colonial official. Jung was worried that Papen would not deliver the speech as he had written it; there were a few places where he feared Papen would cut the text. Yet "as the first such place came," Schnee remembered, "he was happily excited and cried out, leaning forward and repeatedly banging his hand on the table: 'He brought it, he brought it!'" In his excitement, Jung did not stop to consider that he was listening to his own death sentence.

Papen's (or Jung's) real message was covered by a smoke screen of elaborate, careful courtesies toward Hitler and the regime. Papen stressed his "inner commitment" to Adolf Hitler, "the unknown soldier of the World War," who had "conquered the hearts of his national comrades." Yet, Papen continued, some said that he had a duty to observe developments "more sharply than most other Germans," and he would not attempt to escape his duty.

Now, said Papen, "the enthusiasm has gone flat," and it was becoming clear that "a purification process of this extent also produces slag." Slag was appearing in "all areas of our life, in the material and the mental."

The speech moved subtly from an evocation of anti-Weimar conservative ideas to a critique of Nazi practice. Papen started with religion. There was controversy now, he said, about whether the new Reich would be "Christian" or "lose itself in half-religious materialism." It would be better if the state did not try to bring about a "violent Reformation," because political interference in religious matters "forces those affected to reject on religious grounds the claim of totality which is unnatural in this area." As a Catholic, said Papen, he could understand "that a religious conviction based on freedom of conscience rejects letting itself be commanded by politics in its innermost beliefs."

The religious question led him into what were really ideas about European community versus national isolation. "In those circles that hope for a new, racially specific religious union"—here he was referring to the paganism that some Nazis, such as the party's chief "philosopher," Alfred Rosenberg, preferred to Christianity—"one should ask how they imagine the German mission in Europe, if we voluntarily exclude ourselves from the ranks of the Christian peoples." This led into the praise of common European values and culture that had appeared in Jung's memo.

There was no point in denying, Papen continued, that a gap had opened up between the hopes of the revolution and its actual practice. Jung's elitism again appeared in explaining the reason for this gap. The "spiritual transformation" of the "German revolution" had been inspired by the "aristocratic principle of nature," but this had coincided with a "social breakthrough" that was closer to Marxism—by which Papen/Jung really meant that it was driven by the lower classes whom they wanted to exclude from politics. This led to a complaint about the Nazis' anti-intellectualism: "A limited or primitive intellect does not justify a struggle against intellectuality." Germans who complained about doctrinaire Nazis, said Papen, were usually really talking about those who "would like to deprive world-renowned scientists of their living because they are not party members."

Papen then delivered a fierce critique of Nazi ideas about freedom and legality, cleverly framed in terms that might make it acceptable to many conservative opponents of Weimar. Some Nazis thought that genuine humanitarianism was "liberal," when in fact it was a product of the Christian culture of antiquity. Nazis thought that freedom was a liberal concept when, really, it was an ancient German one. The same went for equality before the law, which was not liberal but, rather, the precondition of every just verdict: "These people suppress the foundation of the state, which always, not just in liberal eras, is justice." The Nazis' attacks were directed against "the security and freedom" of private life, which Germans had won in centuries of struggle.

Freedom was a basic need of human nature, Papen continued. There were limits to how much military discipline could be imposed on an entire people, and "it would be reprehensible to believe that a people could be united with terror." All terror was "the product of a bad conscience." Real education could be based only on morality, and "patriotism, dedication, and willingness to sacrifice" existed only when individuals were taught that these goods were "divine commands."

Then Papen turned his fire once again on the regime, particularly Goebbels and his dumbed-down propaganda. One could not underestimate the intelligence of the people, he said. The German people knew their situation was serious. They only laughed at "clumsy attempts to deceive them through false whitewashing." Loud propaganda could never win their trust because "a disenfranchised people has no trust to give."

The speech concluded in a pan-European tone. Germans were "a people among peoples in the middle of Europe," said Papen. If they neglected their cultural inheritance and the three thousand years of European history they would miss the chances the twentieth century offered.

The audience had followed Papen's words with, as the vice-chancellor later recalled, "skeptical, astonished, almost unbelieving expressions." The "thunderous applause" with which they greeted his conclusion showed that he had struck a chord. Tschirschky remembered that dozens of Papen's listeners excitedly surrounded him when he was finished, to "congratulate him on his candor." On the other hand, two SA men who were present demonstratively left the room.

Papen's staff had been neither naïve nor wrong about how Nazi leaders would react to their challenge. Goebbels immediately blocked any dissemination of the speech, by print or radio. The same day Papen was at Marburg, Hitler returned from his first foreign visit as chancellor, to Benito Mussolini in Italy. The visit had not gone well. Mussolini had made no secret of the mild contempt in which he held this raw newcomer to the dictatorial ranks. Hitler was already in a foul mood, and news of Papen's speech threw him into a fury. He spoke that day to a meeting of gauleiters in the small town of Gera, in the state of Thuringia. Although he didn't mention Papen by name, the target of his remarks was clear enough: "In the coming years and decades," he thundered, the victory of National Socialism would deepen, "and all the little dwarves who fancy that they will be able to do anything to stop it will be swept away by the force of this common idea." The dwarves were forgetting that, "no matter what fault they believe they have found," there was nothing better to put in place of the Nazis' system. "It is ridiculous when such a little worm tries to fight such a powerful renewal of the people. Ridiculous, when such a little dwarf fancies himself capable of obstructing the gigantic renewal of the people with a few empty phrases." As Edmund Forschbach noted, Hitler's audience probably had no idea of the identity of the "worm" and the "dwarf," but it roared approval nonetheless.

That night, the Gestapo raided the Germania printing house and confiscated the remaining copies of the speech. Hitler sent his press secretary, Walther Funk, to the Reich president with the message that Hitler, Papen, and Hindenburg could not continue to work together. In the face of this swift reaction, the plans of the vice-chancellery group were already starting to unravel. Their problem was that in Papen and Hindenburg, they had bet on two utterly unreliable actors. Papen's speech was a hit, and suddenly the vice-chancellor could revel in the approval of crowds wherever he went. A more decisive and courageous man might have been able to use the surge in political capital to lever Hitler out of power. But Papen was not that man.

Hitler handled Papen cleverly. When Papen complained about Goebbels's suppression of his speech, Hitler privately assured him that he understood Papen's outrage. Hitler would not accept Papen's threatened resignation from the cabinet. He won Papen over with his usual acting skill, performing the role of faithful comrade, and by appealing to Papen's sense of soldierly duty. Of course, Hitler also told Papen that such sensitive matters should be discussed only internally, and he still refused to allow full publication of Papen's speech.

If the plans of the vice-chancellery staff were going to work, it was vital that Papen get immediately to Hindenburg. Yet Hitler convinced Papen to delay a visit to Hindenburg's Neudeck estate. Papen's staff were beside themselves with frustration, but their boss had knuckled under, and even ordered that his staff not disseminate the speech any further. Papen then left Berlin for a few days, not to travel east to see Hindenburg, but to go north, to Kiel and Hamburg and then to a family gathering in Westphalia. Strikingly, Papen, who seldom admitted in retrospect any political mistakes, acknowledged that he had made one in not seizing the moment in June 1934.

But even if Papen had gotten to meet with Hindenburg, it would likely not have made any difference. A persistent myth has circulated among conservatives sympathetic to Hindenburg that he was growing disenchanted with Hitler in 1934. In his memoirs, Papen writes of his last meeting with Hindenburg in May. He claims that Hindenburg left him with the words "It is going terribly, Papen. Try to put things in order." Yet Papen's memoirs are frequently dishonest, and these supposed words of Hindenburg's are almost certainly invented. They are inconsistent with much else that Hindenburg said and with the general line of his conduct. Hindenburg's fundamental political goal had been to bring about a unified government of the right with mass support. Hitler had given him this, and Hindenburg was never anything but highly satisfied with his last chancellor. On June 18, Walther Funk reported to Hindenburg on Papen's speech and on the measures that Goebbels had taken to suppress it. Hindenburg approved the measures and was utterly devoid of sympathy for Papen. "If Papen can't maintain discipline," said Hindenburg, "then he will have to take the consequences." Hitler himself visited Hindenburg three days later and found, according to Alfred Rosenberg, that never had "the old man been so friendly." There was even worse news for the conspirators, had they known it. On June 26, Werner von Fritsch, the commander in chief of the army, briefed Hindenburg about the problems with the SA. Fritsch and Hindenburg agreed that whatever happened, the army should stay out of it, and the SA should be handled by the police and the SS. This was consistent with their desire never to deploy the army in domestic affairs, but it fatally undercut the plans of the vice-chancellery group.

No one who was well informed about politics thought Papen could actually have written the Marburg speech. Even the Nazis understood that Papen was not up to that level of thinking or eloquence. "Who wrote it for him?" Goebbels wondered in his diary.

They didn't have to look far. Insiders knew that for most of the past year, Edgar Jung had done Papen's thinking for him. The ideas and the tone of Papen's speech sounded strikingly like Jung's writing. On June 20, Alfred Rosenberg dropped a big hint in this direction. He wrote an editorial in the *Völkischer Beobachter* on "reactionaries" with the revealing title "On the Meaning and Interpretation of the German Revolution," a clear reference to Jung—it echoed the title of his most recent book. In private conversation, Hitler showed that he had the same idea. Jung himself was eager for credit and was indiscreet about his authorship of the speech.

For a period of almost two weeks, German politics seemed eerily suspended. The chargé d'affaires at the French embassy in Berlin cabled home on June 27 that in the past week the Reich government had gone through a crisis "the repercussions of which are still being felt and the full gravity of which it is still impossible to determine." Some kind of violent discharge was almost certainly coming, but for the moment, politicians went about their work as if everything were normal. Goebbels and Hitler were almost certainly preparing a strike against Papen's office. On June 22, Goebbels had talked about the "Papen question" with Funk. "The Führer has to intervene there," Goebbels wrote. "Papen is committing sabotage. Even pulls the army in. I brief the Führer also."

In these tense days, Papen and Goebbels circled each other in an almost surreal performance. On June 21, Reichsbank president Hjalmar Schacht gave a lecture at the propaganda ministry before an invited audience consisting largely of foreign journalists and diplomats. At the end of the lecture, an American reporter addressed a question directly to Goebbels: "Herr Minister, is it correct that because of the Marburg speech, your relationship with Herr Vice-Chancellor von Papen is now extremely tense?"

Goebbels immediately called Papen up to the front of the room. Papen obeyed. Goebbels took a few steps toward Papen, held out his arms, and embraced him. "My dear Herr von Papen," said Goebbels, "did you hear that? The two of us are supposed to have a tense relationship with one another. The two of us, of all people, who are the best of friends!" Papen was seemingly so moved he couldn't speak; he could only nod his head. Few who were present—apparently Papen excepted—thought this was anything other than a performance for the foreign press.

Three days later, on Sunday, June 24, both Papen and Goebbels attended the Hamburg derby. All credible accounts recorded that there was a striking difference between the enthusiastic applause and cheers for Papen and the coldness with which the crowd responded to Goebbels. The French chargé d'affaires noted this as one of the signs that "a large part of the public, especially among the well-to-do classes," had come down on the vice-chancellor's side. This was intolerable to Goebbels, who could never accept that a rival might draw more support from a crowd. In a revealing glimpse of the Nazi attitude toward reality, Goebbels wrote in his diary that the public had been "sharply against Papen. . . . Embarrassing scenes. At the end together with Papen. Public totally for me. I go among the people. These ovations! Poor Gentlemen's Club, if it ever comes to a flap."

That same evening, the former member of Brüning's cabinet Gottfried Treviranus and the British journalist John Wheeler Bennett met Jung at the Hotel Kaiserhof. They warned him that British intelligence had learned of his impending arrest and urged him to get out of the country that night. Jung protested that he stood under the protection of Papen and the army. By one account, he then agreed to go to Switzerland, but that evening he let slip word of his plans to a woman who was an SD agent.

The next day, the Gestapo arrested Jung and searched his apartment. They found evidence that he had written Papen's Marburg speech in the form of correspondence between Jung and Papen arguing about the fee Papen should pay for it. When he learned of Jung's arrest, Papen flew back from Westphalia to press for his release, but neither Hitler nor Göring would see him. Hitler remarked scornfully to Rosenberg that Papen was trying to see him "because of his Dr. Jung"—and Hitler made it clear that Jung's arrest had come directly on his own orders. Gestapo chief Heinrich Himmler told Papen that some incriminating documents had been found tying Jung to a circle of "Austrian legitimists," advocates of a return to the monarchy. This had to be cleared up, but Himmler promised that Jung would be released in a few days.

THE "NIGHT OF the Long Knives" of June 30, 1934, was Hitler's answer to the bind he had fallen into, trapped between the conservative establishment on one side and the radical Stormtroopers on the other. The conservatives, particularly in the army high command, were both the primary target and the audience for the whole affair. Röhm and his SA were little more than collateral damage.

The SA men had been talking for a long time about becoming the nucleus of a new German "people's army," replacing the professionals with their aristocratic officers. This talk alarmed the army high command, and in early 1934, the generals were putting increasing pressure on Hitler to neutralize Röhm. Yet the threat of a coup from Röhm was a fabrication. There was never any prospect of such a thing. In fact, to allay any such concerns, Röhm had ostentatiously sent the SA on leave for the month of July. The idea of an imminent coup was a story that some of the beneficiaries of the murders, particularly in the army high command, constructed to excuse their complicity in what happened next.

Röhm had summoned the SA commanders to a meeting at Bad Wiessee, near Munich, prior to the start of the planned month of leave. On June 30, Hitler traveled there in person to oversee their arrest. Röhm himself was shot the next day. Around the country, particularly in Berlin, other SA men were arrested and as many as ninety were killed.

Hitler also took the opportunity to settle scores with people against whom he bore grudges, including Kurt von Schleicher. Hitler remembered Schleicher's insulting comment about him ("It's just a pity that he's crazy"), and he resented Schleicher's efforts to lure Gregor Strasser into his administration in 1932. Hitler also believed that Schleicher had contemplated a military coup against him in January 1933. Not surprisingly, Strasser was also caught up in the purge. Tschirschky saw what happened to Strasser as he was being held in the Gestapo's cellars. Just after he had spoken to Jung in the restroom and returned to his bench in the corridor, Tschirschky saw "a tall, burly man, chained and accompanied by three men armed with machine pistols." Tschirschky immediately recognized the man as Strasser. The guards led Strasser into another corridor, where there were cells for solitary confinement. "I heard the order 'guard the doors!' and the door from our area to this corridor was closed. Five shots were fired. Immediately after the shots, the *Hauptsturmführer* [captain] came through the door with the pistol in his hand, saying, 'The swine has been taken care of.'"

Hindenburg was highly pleased with Hitler's conduct on June 30. He sent his chancellor a telegram, praising Hitler's "decisive intervention" and the "brave deployment of your own person," through which Hitler had "nipped all treasonous machinations in the bud" and "saved the German people from great danger." On July 6, Hitler told Goebbels about his meeting with the Reich president. "Hindenburg was awesome [*knorke*]," Goebbels noted. "The old gentleman has stature."

The troublemakers in the SA had been a minor worry for Hitler, but not a threat to his rule in 1934. He was worried about the army, and striking against the SA could reassure the leaders of what was, after all, the ultimate source of power. Hindenburg was just as important. In the early summer of 1934, everyone in politics knew that Hindenburg, aware that he had little time left, had drafted a "political testament." Few knew anything about its contents, but at all costs Hitler wanted to head off any suggestion from Hindenburg that the monarchy should be restored upon the president's death. Neutralizing the SA could, and did, reassure Hindenburg about Hitler's fitness to assume the presidency in addition to retaining his post as chancellor. Fabricating a complex story that Schleicher, Papen's staff, the SA command, and Ambassador François-Poncet were all conspiring against the government gave Hitler the pretext to strike simultaneously at his more dangerous enemies in the conservative establishment. François-Poncet, predictably stung by the allegations of his role in this conspiracy, was typically scathing about the evidence Hitler offered and the Nazi method of solving the problem. "Fragile clues, coincidences, gratuitous assumptions were presented as if they were proof of facts," he reported home in a cable. This was the same method, he continued, that the Nazis had used to implicate the Communist defendants in the Reichstag fire trial. But since then, he wrote, "the method has been perfected." In 1933, the Nazis had made the mistake of putting the Reichstag fire case in front of judges, who recognized the inadequacy of the evidence. This time, the judges had been cut out of the process and had nothing more to say. "The precaution was taken of keeping the accused away from [the judges] and killing them at once," François-Poncet acidly noted.

Yet the Nazi spin worked. In large part because of the genuine unpopularity of the SA, the Night of the Long Knives restored a good deal of the regime's popularity within Germany—and the conservative resistance was shattered.

The army, like Hindenburg, was pleased with the outcome. Courageous drivers of resistance such as Jung and Bose were dead. Tschirschky went into exile in Great Britain. Ketteler was given a diplomatic posting in Austria but was murdered, almost certainly by the Gestapo or the SS, when the Nazis annexed that country in March 1938.

Papen's story after June 30 is particularly disgraceful, a "moral low point" in the words of his biographer. With his staff murdered or under arrest, Papen groveled for Hitler's favor. On July 3, he sent Hitler a letter, thanking him for his "soldierly decisiveness" in "saving the fatherland from an enormous danger." No one, Papen insisted, had followed Hitler with a "warmer heart" along this path—"for the nation so necessary, for you so painful"—than had Papen himself. Hitler released Papen from house arrest and let him live, partly through the influence of Hindenburg, although Papen's days as vice-chancellor were over. He was posted to Vienna as German ambassador and then, when that job disappeared, to Turkey, where he served through the Second World War. The International Military Tribunal in Nuremberg acquitted Papen of war crimes in 1946.

If this were not craven enough, in his memoirs, published in 1952, Papen claimed all credit for the brave resistance his staff had carried on without his knowledge. He particularly minimized the role of Edgar Jung, whom he criticized for his vanity in taking credit for the Marburg speech. Rising to the heights of solipsism, Papen insisted that the murders of Jung and Bose were really aimed at him.

FIELD MARSHAL AND Reich president Paul von Hindenburg died of kidney failure on August 2, 1934. Hitler immediately took over the powers of the presidency. He then explained that no one could ever replace Hindenburg, and therefore the office of the president itself would be abolished. Hitler assumed the formal title of "Führer and Reich Chancellor." All members of the armed forces and all civil servants were obliged to swear an oath of loyalty to him personally.

Hitler's hold on dictatorial rule was now complete, and all efforts to control or "tame" him had decisively failed. Effective political opposition always requires an institutional basis. By the late summer of 1934, none remained. The political parties, the labor unions, the Reichstag, the cabinet, the federal states, and the SA had all been brought into line. Only the army remained as a possible source of resistance, and so long as Hitler tore up the Treaty of Versailles and expanded the armed forces, the soldiers and their officers were content. From August 1934, the switches were set for war—a war to overcome the global economic dominance of Great Britain and the United States and to make Germany an economic superpower by seizing a massive land empire in eastern Europe.

Yet the sacrifices of Jung and Bose were not altogether in vain. Their example helped to inspire the next round of resistance, which began in 1938 within similar circles (the military and conservative civilian politicians) and, in time, would lead to the Valkyrie plot.

The words of one of the Valkyrie leaders apply equally to Jung, Bose, and their friends. In June 1944, after the Allied invasion of Normandy, Count Claus von Stauffenberg wanted to know if it still made any sense to try to overthrow Hitler. He sent this question to his colleague and coconspirator Henning von Tresckow. Tresckow's answer was clear: The coup they had planned must happen, he said, "at any cost. Even if it is to fail, the coup must nevertheless be attempted." The practical effects did not matter. What mattered was that "the members of the German resistance movement dared to take the decisive step, before the world and before history, at the risk of their lives. Everything else is irrelevant."

As with Stauffenberg and Tresckow, so with Jung and Bose. They were flawed heroes, to be sure, holding many of the prejudices of their class, their background, and their era. Still, they risked and lost their lives to get rid of Hitler, something very few people would dare, and in so doing, they expiated the responsibility they felt for bringing him to power. In a dark time, their courage offered their country a moral foundation for a better future.

JOURNALISTS OFTEN TRY to reduce complex political developments to simple formulas: they speak of "change elections" or "protest votes." No simple formula can explain why democracy failed in Weimar Germany and Hitler and the Nazis came to power. The Nazi movement was rooted in the experiences of the First World War and the multiple crises of interwar Europe. Analogous movements arose across Europe in these years, particularly in countries on the losing side of the war (and in Italy, which felt as if it had lost). Yet, although the Nazis were typical of their time, hardly anyone, even in 1932, could have foreseen the position of power that Hitler would occupy after the death of Hindenburg. Fewer still desired such an outcome. Miscalculations and shortsightedness are as much a part of this story as are rage and hatred.

The Nazis would have been unthinkable without the First World War, and here, right at the beginning of the story, we see something else: the trauma of defeat left millions of Germans believing a particular narrative about the war not because it was demonstrably true, but because it was emotionally necessary. The nation had been gloriously unified in the sunshine of August 1914, or so most Germans thought. Yet, in the cold rain of November 1918, betrayal and cowardice at home—the "stab in the back"—had brought defeat on the battlefield. Neither part of this narrative was accurate, but the constant contrast between August and November allowed the Nazis to promise that they would bring back the unity of August once they had defeated the treason of November. What a nation believes about its past is at least as important as what that past actually was.

In reality, Germany had been defeated by the overwhelming economic power of Great Britain, the United States, and France. In the years after the war, the question for Germans was whether they would accommodate themselves to the Western global order or rebel against it. Everyone understood that the outward and inward faces of Germany were as connected as the two sides of a coin: A Germany integrated into the world and at peace with its neighbors would also be a democratic Germany. A Germany that rebelled against the world would have to be a dictatorship of unprecedented ruthlessness.

After five years of political and economic crisis culminating in hyperinflation and Hitler's Beer Hall Putsch in November 1923, the new democracy of the Weimar Republic began to stabilize—and as it did so, Germany returned as an indispensable player in the international community. This could not have happened without the courage and skill of statesmen such as Gustav Stresemann. Yet Stresemann never forgot about the reactionary nationalists at home, the "glaciers" he had to overcome in order to secure Germany's place in a peaceful world.

It was the very success of Germany's democratic recovery that drove the antidemocratic nationalists into increasingly desperate and furious resistance. Big business wanted to weaken the unions and abolish the state-mandated wage arbitration system. The army wanted more money for weapons. Farmers wanted an end to the imports and trade deals that they thought were driving German agriculture into collective bankruptcy. Their grievances all had a common root: Germany's place in a world defined by defeat in the First World War and by British and American economic power. And they pointed to a common solution: driving Germany's largest political party, the Social Democrats—antimilitarist and internationally oriented, guardian of democracy, workers, and cities—from any share of power. In practice this meant putting an end to the democracy the Social Democrats had created, and finding an alternative political base among the farmers, soldiers, and business executives.

The Weimar Republic seethed with other resentments and hatreds: the German people were bitterly divided along every conceivable line. Rural people disliked the big cities for breaking with traditions of religion and sexual identity and morality. A postwar tide of refugees, particularly from eastern Europe, alarmed millions of Germans. German Catholics and Protestants had distrusted one another since the Reformation. The stresses of war and revolution had exacerbated antisemitism in both Christian groupings. Eventually, these different grievances coalesced, especially among the numerically dominant Protestants: Weimar was too Jewish, too Catholic, too modern, too urban—all in all, too morally degenerate. But this cultural code always expressed grievances about something beyond itself. Antisemitism did not spell the end of German democracy or the coming of Hitler, but it did provide a language with which antidemocrats could criticize the democratic global order they detested.

Few members of Weimar's insurgent groups wanted a lawless and barbaric dictatorship ruled over by someone like Hitler. They simply wanted the fastest and easiest solutions to their own particular problems, and they were deeply unwilling to compromise with their opponents. When the Nazis proved to be the most skillful politicians at capturing the resentments of the disaffected, particularly of rural Protestants, the political equation shifted. After 1929, there was no viable antidemocratic coalition that did not include Hitler and the Nazis.

This fact handed the business leaders and military commanders a serious problem. Democracy was not working for them precisely because their interests could not attract the support of a majority, even a large plurality, of voters. Hitler's movement, on the other hand, could provide substantial support for crushing the labor movement and for rebuilding the armed forces. But at what cost? Gradually, Germany's conservative political elites decided they had no choice but to find a way to work with Hitler—to use him and his movement. Otherwise they would have to give up too much of their own self-interest.

The Night of the Long Knives was the denouement of the establishment's flirtation with Hitler. One after another, the conservatives found themselves outmaneuvered and sidelined—from Hugenberg to Brüning, to Papen and Schleicher, to Jung and Bose. In no small part, they had been betrayed by Hindenburg, as the Reich president strove for his overarching goal of building a government of the nationalist right, while preserving at all costs his image as the great commander and the bringer of unity. In the end, Hindenburg himself was captured by the man he had once dismissed as "the Bohemian private." He went to his grave serene in the belief that his good name had been secured by Hitler's success in overcoming the political divisions of the early 1930s. The final irony, of course, is that his appointment of Hitler definitively and permanently ruined the reputation Hindenburg had always been so careful to guard.

Thinking about the end of Weimar democracy in this way—as the result of a large protest movement colliding with complex patterns of elite self-interest, in a culture increasingly prone to aggressive mythmaking and irrationality—strips away the exotic and foreign look of swastika banners and goose-stepping Stormtroopers. Suddenly, the whole thing looks close and familiar. Alongside the viciousness of much of German politics in the Weimar years was an incongruous innocence: few people could imagine the worst possibilities. A civilized nation could not possibly vote for Hitler, some had thought. When he became chancellor nonetheless, millions expected his time in office to be short and ineffectual. Germany was a notoriously law-abiding as well as cultured land. How could a German government systematically brutalize its own people? German Jews were highly assimilated and patriotic. Many refused to leave their homeland, even as things got worse and worse. "I am German and am waiting for the Germans to come back; they have gone to ground somewhere," Victor Klemperer wrote in his diary— he was the son of a rabbi and a veteran of the First World War who chose to stay, and miraculously survived.

Few Germans in 1933 could imagine Treblinka or Auschwitz, the mass shootings of Babi Yar or the death marches of the last months of the Second World War. It is hard to blame them for not foreseeing the unthinkable. Yet their innocence failed them, and they were catastrophically wrong about their future. We who come later have one advantage over them: we have their example before us.

NOTES

A NOTE ON SOURCES AND FURTHER READING

The literature on the rise of the Nazis and the downfall of Weimar democracy is vast. In a short book like this, meant for a general audience, I have not been able in the text or notes to take account of more than a small part of it. In addition to the works mentioned in the citations below, I would like to acknowledge some other works that have informed my thinking (if sometimes in respectful dissent). This list makes no pretense of being comprehensive, but I encourage interested readers to turn to these works for more information and different perspectives.

Several important surveys of the Weimar Republic form the starting point for all thinking about the subject—although they certainly express a range of very different viewpoints. These include Detlev Peukert, *The Weimar Republic: The Crisis of Classical Modernity* (New York: Hill and Wang, 1989); Hans Mommsen, *The Rise and Fall of Weimar Democracy* (Chapel Hill: University of North Carolina Press, 1998); the excellent narrative history by Heinrich August Winkler, *Weimar 1918–1933: Die Geschichte der ersten deutschen Demokratie* (Munich: C. H. Beck, 1993); and the latest edition of a classic, Eberhard Kolb, *Die Weimarer Republik*, 8. Auflage (Munich: Oldenbourg Verlag, 2013) (an earlier edition is available in English: Eberhard Kolb, *The Weimar Republic*, 2nd edition [New York: Routledge, 2004]). Among the most recent thoughtful summaries is Eric D. Weitz, *Weimar Germany: Promise and Tragedy*, 2nd expanded edition (Princeton: Princeton University Press, 2013).

On the Revolution of 1918 and the Republic's early years: Joachim Petzold, *Die Dolchstoßlegende: Eine Geschichtsfälschung im Dienst des deutschen Imperialismus und Militärismus* (East Berlin: Akademie-Verlag, 1963); Richard Bessel, *Germany After the First World War* (Oxford: Oxford University Press, 1993); Mark Jones, *Founding Weimar: Violence and the German Revolution of 1918–1919* (Cambridge: Cambridge

University Press, 2016); Thomas Weber, *Wie Hitler zum Nazi wurde: Vom unpolitischen Soldaten zum Autor von* Mein Kampf (Berlin: Ullstein, 2016).

Some of the most interesting and important recent work has examined, in different ways, matters of gender and sexuality in Weimar (and later): Julia Sneeringer, *Winning Women's Votes: Propaganda and Politics in Weimar Germany* (Chapel Hill: University of North Carolina Press, 2002); Wendy Lower, *Hitler's Furies: German Women in the Nazi Killing Fields* (Boston: Houghton Mifflin Harcourt, 2013); Robert Beachy, *Gay Berlin: Birthplace of a Modern Identity* (New York: Alfred A. Knopf, 2014); Laurie Marhoefer, *Sex and the Weimar Republic: German Homosexual Emancipation and the Rise of the Nazis* (Toronto: University of Toronto Press, 2015).

Susan Pedersen, *The Guardians: The League of Nations and the Crisis of Empire* (New York: Oxford University Press, 2015), has some brilliant and original things to say about Germany's arrival in the League. I also benefited from a much older book, Henry Ashby Turner, *Stresemann and the Politics of the Weimar Republic* (Princeton: Princeton University Press, 1965).

Several thought-provoking books examine foreign influences and the way the future looked to Weimar Germans: Mary Nolan, *Visions of Modernity: American Business and the Modernization of Germany* (New York: Oxford University Press, 1994); Rüdiger Graf, *Die Zukunft der Weimarer Republik: Krisen und Zukunftsaneignungen in Deutschland 1918–1933* (Munich: Oldenbourg Verlag, 2008); James Q. Whitman, *Hitler's American Model: The United States and the Making of Nazi Race Law* (Princeton: Princeton University Press, 2017).

On business and the economy there are some further classics: Gerald D. Feldman, *Iron and Steel in the German Inflation, 1916–1923* (Princeton: Princeton University Press, 1977); Henry Ashby Turner, *German Big Business and the Rise of Hitler* (New York: Oxford University Press, 1985); Harold James, *The German Slump: Politics and Economics, 1924–1936* (Oxford: Clarendon Press, 1986); Gerald D. Feldman, *The Great Disorder: Politics, Economics, and Society in the German Inflation, 1914–1924* (New York: Oxford University Press, 1993); Peter Langer, *Macht und Verantwortung: Der Ruhrbaron Paul Reusch* (Essen: Klartext Verlag, 2012).

On politics generally in the Weimar Republic: Richard F. Hamilton, *Who Voted for Hitler?* (Princeton: Princeton University Press, 1982); Thomas Childers, *The Nazi Voter: The Social Foundations of Fascism in Germany 1919–1933* (Chapel Hill: University of North Carolina Press, 1983); Peter Fritzsche, *Rehearsals for Fascism: Populism and Political Mobilization in Weimar Germany* (New York: Oxford University Press, 1990); Donna Harsch, *German Social Democracy and the Rise of Nazism* (Chapel Hill: University of North Carolina Press, 1993); Peter Fritzsche, "Did Weimar Fail?," *Journal of Modern History* 68, no. 3 (1996): 629–56; Larry Eugene Jones, ed., *The German Right in the Weimar Republic: Studies in the History of German Conservatism, Nationalism, and Antisemitism* (New York: Berghahn Books, 2016), along with many enlightening journal articles by Jones, including "'The Greatest Stupidity of My Life': Alfred Hugenberg and the Formation of the Hitler Cabinet, January 1933," *Journal of Contemporary History*, no. 1 (1992): 63–87.

On the Republic's final crisis of the early 1930s, there are a number of old but still valuable classics: Karl Dietrich Bracher, *Die Auflösung der Weimarer Republik. Eine Studie zum Problem des Machtverfalls in der Demokratie* (Düsseldorf: Droste Verlag,

2000); Karl Dietrich Bracher, Wolfgang Sauer, and Gerhard Schulz, *Die nationalsozial-istische Machtergreifung. Studien zur Errichtung des totalitären Herrschaftssystem in Deutschland* (Berlin: Ullstein, 1974); William Sheridan Allen, *The Nazi Seizure of Power: The Experience of a Single German Town, 1930–1935* (Chicago: Quadrangle Books, 1965); Thilo Vogelsang, *Reichswehr, Staat und NSDAP. Beiträge zur deutschen Geschichte 1930–1932* (Stuttgart: Deutsche Verlags-Anstalt, 1962); Thilo Vogelsang, *Kurt von Schleicher: Ein General als Politiker* (Göttingen: Musterschmidt Verlag, 1965); Alex Schildt, *Militär-diktatur mit Massenbasis? Die Querfrontkonzeption der Reichswehrführung um General von Schleicher am Ende der Weimarer Republik* (Frankfurt: Campus, 1981).

A brilliantly researched recent book by the young German historian Rainer Orth has transformed our view of the resistance conducted from Vice-Chancellor von Pap-en's office. See *"Der Amtssitz der Opposition"? Politik und Staatsumbaupläne im Büro des Stellvertreters des Reichskanzlers in den Jahren 1933–1934* (Cologne: Böhlau, 2016). I hope that Orth's important research might soon be translated for those not equipped to read a thousand pages of German.

INTRODUCTION

2   **"a most unpolice-like rendezvous"**: Rudolf Diels, "Die Nacht der langen Messer . . . fand nicht statt," *Der Spiegel*, June 2, 1949, p. 22.

2   **Hitler already seems to know**: Rudolf Diels, *Lucifer Ante Portas: Zwischen Sev-ering und Heydrich* (Zürich: Interverlag, 1949), p. 144, translation from J. Noakes and G. Pridham, *Nazism 1919–1945: A Documentary Reader*, vol. 1: *The Rise to Power* (Exeter: University of Exeter Press, 1998), pp. 140–41.

2   **After describing the extensive damage**: Amtlicher Preussischer Pressedienst bulletin, February 28, 1933, Bundesarchiv Berlin-Lichterfelde R 43 II/294.

2   **It is not yet midnight**: Willi Frischauer, *The Rise and Fall of Hermann Goering* (Boston: Houghton Mifflin, 1951), p. 4.

4   **Prussia had fifty thousand men**: Benjamin Carter Hett, *Burning the Reichstag: An Investigation into the Third Reich's Enduring Mystery* (New York: Oxford University Press, 2014), p. 30.

4   **"We have hired him"**: Papen quoted in Joachim Fest, *Hitler: Eine Biographie* (Berlin: Ullstein Taschenbuch, 1998), p. 528.

5   **The independent Nationalist politician**: Gottfried Reinhold Treviranus, *Das Ende von Weimar: Heinrich Brüning und seine Zeit* (Düsseldorf: Econ Verlag, 1968), p. 366.

5   **Friedrich Stampfer**: Stampfer quoted in ibid.

5   **A young carpenter**: Max Fürst, *Gefilte Fisch: Und wie es weiterging* (Munich: Deutscher Taschenbuch Verlag, 2004), pp. 658–59.

5   **"Heads will roll in the sand"**: Adolf Hitler, "Zeugenaussage vor dem IV. Strafsenat des Reichsgerichts in Leipzig," September 25, 1930, in Christian Hartmann, ed., *Hitler: Reden, Schriften, Anordnungen. Februar 1925 bis Januar 1933*, Bd. 3: *Zwischen den Reichstagswahlen Juli 1928–September 1930*, Teil 3: *Januar 1930–September 1930* (Munich: K. G. Saur, 1995), pp. 434–51.

5   **One well-connected and thoughtful observer**: Erich Ebermayer, *Denn heute gehört uns Deutschland . . . Persönliches und politisches Tagebuch: Von der*

Machtergreifung bis zum 31. Dezember 1935 (Hamburg: Paul Zsolnay Verlag, 1959), p. 17.

6   **The decree expressed Hitler's theory**: "Verordnung des Reichspräsidenten zum Schutz von Volk und Staat," *Reichsgesetzblatt* 17, February 28, 1933.

6   **"First the Reichstag burned"**: Walther Kiaulehn, *Berlin: Schicksal einer Weltstadt* (Munich: C. H. Beck, 1997), p. 567.

8   **"The uncertain Germans"**: Wolf Jobst Siedler, "Glanzvolles Zwischenspiel auf abgeräumter Bühne, die lange Wirkung der kurzen Dauer," in Ruth Glatzer, *Berlin zur Weimarer Zeit: Panorama einer Metropole* (Berlin: Siedler Verlag, 2000), pp. 17–18.

9   **Many distinguished scholars**: See, for instance, Volker Ullrich, *Hitler: Ascent, 1889–1939* (New York: Alfred A. Knopf, 2016), pp. 8–10.

10   **an overwhelming triumph of global liberal capitalism**: On this theme see, among others, Adam Tooze, *The Deluge: The Great War and the Making of Global Order* (London: Penguin Books, 2014); Robert Boyce, *The Great Interwar Crisis and the Collapse of Globalization* (New York: Palgrave Macmillan, 2009).

14   **Defenders of the Republic**: Joachim Fest, *Hitler* (New York: Harcourt, 1974), p. 380.

14   **Hitler was thrilled**: Ibid., p. 381.

14   **"Dictatorship, abolition of the parliament"**: Quoted in Ullrich, *Hitler*, p. 374.

14   **"starts from the recognition"**: Theodor Heuss, *Hitlers Weg: Eine historisch-politische Studie über den Nationalsozialismus* (Stuttgart: Union Deutsche Verlagsgesellschaft, 1932), pp. 100, 160–163.

I. AUGUST AND NOVEMBER

15   **He knows that the revolution . . . "If Ebert"**: Maximilian, Prince of Baden, *The Memoirs of Prince Max of Baden*, trans. W. M. Caulder and C. W. H. Sutton (New York: Charles Scribner's Sons, 1928), p. 351

16   **Prince Max doesn't know**: Wolfram Pyta, *Hindenburg: Herrschaft zwischen Hohenzollern und Hitler* (Munich: Siedler Verlag, 2007), pp. 365–69.

17   **"too late . . . I have lost two sons"**: Prince Max of Baden, *Memoirs*, pp. 357–63.

17   **"So it had all been in vain"**: Adolf Hitler, *Mein Kampf: Eine kritische Edition*, ed. Christian Hartmann et al. (Munich: Institut für Zeitgeschichte, 2016) (hereafter *MK*), Bd. 1, 551–53.

19   **There was a paradox here**: Martin Kitchen, *The Silent Dictatorship: The Politics of the German High Command Under Hindenburg and Ludendorff* (London: Croom Helm, 1976), p. 22. The term *silent dictatorship* is Kitchen's.

19   **Gustav Stresemann**: Anthony McElligott, *Rethinking the Weimar Republic: Authority and Authoritarianism 1916–1936* (London: Bloomsbury, 2014), p. 20.

19   **Even the "Patriotic Auxiliary Service Law"**: Ibid., p. 16.

20   **their membership plummeted**: Ibid., p. 19.

21   **carry the blame**: Joachim Riecker, *Hitlers 9. November. Wie der erste Weltkrieg zum Holocaust führte* (Berlin: Wolf Jobst Siedler, 2009), pp. 28–32.

23   **The breach between**: Ulrich Herbert, *Geschichte Deutschlands im 20. Jahrhundert* (Munich: C. H. Beck, 2014), pp. 181–83.

23   **The revolutionary wing**: Ibid., pp. 187–88.

24 **A few years later**: Frederick F. Blachley and Miriam E. Oatman, "Hugo Preuss Talks on the Weimar Constitution," *Southwestern Political and Social Science Quarterly* 6, no. 3 (December 1925): 252–53.

24 **At the heart of the constitution**: Text of the Weimar Constitution, in Ernst Rudolf Huber, *Dokumente zur deutschen Verfassungsgeschichte*, 3rd ed. (Stuttgart: Verlag W. Kohlhammer, 1991), 4:151–79.

26 **One of the debates**: McElligott, *Rethinking*, pp. 184–85.

26 **In 1925, Preuss's American interviewers**: Blachley and Oatman, "Hugo Preuss," p. 254.

27 **laws must be drafted with the "bad man" in mind**: Oliver Wendell Homes Jr., "The Path of the Law," *Harvard Law Review* 10 (1897): 457.

28 **"a thoroughly shattering"**: Benjamin Carter Hett, *Death in the Tiergarten: Murder and Criminal Justice in the Kaiser's Berlin* (Cambridge, MA: Harvard University Press, 2004), p. 218.

29 **The conservative intellectual**: Roshan Magub, *Edgar Julius Jung, Right-Wing Enemy of the Nazis: A Political Biography* (Rochester, NY: Camden House, 2017), p. 18.

29 **A persistent myth**: Sally Marks, "The Allies, Germany, and the Versailles Treaty, 1918–1921," *Journal of Modern History* 85, no. 3 (September 2013): 632–33.

30 **"The very fact:"** Sebastian Haffner, *Defying Hitler* (Lexington, MA: Plunkett Lake Press, 2014), p. 23.

30 **The future playwright**: Carl Zuckmayer, *A Part of Myself* (New York: Harcourt, 1970), p. 143.

31 **As for the first**: Peter Fritzsche, *Germans into Nazis* (Cambridge, MA: Harvard University Press, 1997), p. 19.

31 **For the second**: Jeffrey Verhey, *The Spirit of 1914: Militarism, Myth, and Mobilization in Germany* (Cambridge: Cambridge University Press, 2004), p. 20.

31 **It was an ideal**: Ibid., p. 217.

31 **In the spring of 1919**: Riecker, *Hitlers 9. November*, p. 63.

31 **In November 1919**: John W. Wheeler-Bennett, *Hindenburg: The Wooden Titan* (London: Macmillan, 1936), pp. 234–39.

32 **The myth of 1914**: Verhey, *Spirit of 1914*, pp. 213 and 219.

32 **Democrats tended to respond**: Ibid., p. 222.

32 **The fundamental problem**: Riecker, *Hitlers 9. November*, p. 58.

33 **The Washington Naval Treaty**: Tooze, *Deluge*, pp. 11–12.

33 **The implications were clearly spelled out**: Erich Ludendorff, *The Nation at War* (London: Hutchinson, 1936).

34 **Ludendorff's former adviser**: Martin Kitchen, "Militarism and the Development of Fascist Ideology: The Political Ideas of Colonel Max Bauer, 1916–18," *Central European History* 8, no. 3 (September 1975): 206.

2. "DON'T BELIEVE HIM, HE'S TELLING THE TRUTH"

35 **The officials are worried . . . not to be brought low**: Benjamin Carter Hett, *Crossing Hitler: The Man Who Put the Nazis on the Witness Stand* (New York: Oxford University Press, 2008), pp. 65–66 and 92.

37   The climax comes . . . "That has nothing to do with this trial": Ibid., pp. 93–98.

37   The shrewdest commentary . . . "Don't believe him": Ibid., p. 102.

38   "here was someone who meant what he said": Ullrich, *Hitler*, p. 97.

38   "At the highpoints": Heiden, quoted in Stefan Aust, *Hitlers erster Feind: Der Kampf des Konrad Heiden* (Reinbek bei Hamburg: Rowohlt, 2016), p. 84.

38   "He wasn't even honest": Ullrich, *Hitler*, p. 7.

38   In "the greatness of the lie . . . lies that were too big": Hitler, *MK*, 1:617.

39   "colossal untruths . . . all great expert liars": Ibid.

39   "From time immemorial . . . Truth to prevail": Ibid.

39   "The mass of the people": Hitler, *MK*, 2:1477.

40   "have the average quality": Adolf Hitler, *Hitler's Second Book: The Unpublished Sequel to* Mein Kampf, ed. Gerhard Weinberg (New York: Enigma Books, 2006), p. 111.

40   "if the German people": Ian Kershaw, *Hitler 1936–1945: Nemesis* (New York: W. W. Norton, 2000) (hereafter *Nemesis*), p. 555.

40   "As soon as some person of interest . . . I have ever met": Ernst Hanfstaengl, *Hitler: The Missing Years* (New York: Arcade Publishing, 1994), p. 266.

41   Hitler could appear quiet: Ian Kershaw, *Hitler 1889–1936: Hubris* (New York: W. W. Norton, 1998) (hereafter *Hubris*), p. 281.

41   Konrad Heiden: Aust, *Hitlers erster Feind*, pp. 141–42.

42   Adolf Hitler was born: Brigitte Hamann, *Hitler's Vienna: A Dictator's Apprenticeship*, trans. Thomas Thornton (New York: Oxford University Press, 1999), p. 7.

42   Right at the beginning . . . in those days: Kershaw, *Hubris*, pp. 3–5.

42   Yet Hitler himself . . . with its cemetery: Robert G. L. Waite, *The Psychopathic God: Adolf Hitler* (New York: Basic Books, 1977), pp. 128–31.

42   Hitler said later: August Kubizek, *The Young Hitler I Knew*, trans. Geoffrey Brooks (London: Greenhill Books, 2006), p. 54.

43   This is another of Hitler's stories: Ullrich, *Hitler*, p. 21.

43   The doctor who treated her: Hamann, *Hitler's Vienna*, pp. 34–35.

44   "I sank down": Hitler, *MK*, 1:453.

44   On October 29: Thomas Weber, *Hitler's First War: Adolf Hitler, the Men of the List Regiment, and the First World War* (Oxford: Oxford University Press, 2010), p. 48.

44   "A feeling of horror" . . . but "it was actually just cowardice": Hitler, *MK*, 1:461–65.

44   "the internal strife was over": Ibid.

45   There is some debate: Weber, *Hitler's First War*, especially chap. 7.

45   "When we weigh up": Ullrich, *Hitler*, p. 59.

45   Mystery also surrounds . . . "Führer" qualities: Ibid.; Weber, *Hitler's First War*, chap. 7.

46   Yet the testimony of Max Amann: Ullrich, *Hitler*, p. 60.

46   The sacrifices of the war . . . "I would take up political work": Hitler, *MK*, 1:553–57.

46   Hitler actually began: Weber, *Hitler's First War*, pp. 250–52.

47   in the spring of 1919: Ibid., pp. 250–51 and 257.

47   How do we square this: Ibid., pp. 350–51; Ullrich, *Hitler*, pp. 79–80.

47   **He illustrated the point . . . "I began to hate them"**: Hitler, *MK*, 1:209 and 1:225.

47   **Many of Hitler's toxic**: Hamann, *Hitler's Vienna*, pp. 202 and 352; Weber, *Hitler's First War*, pp. 250–51.

48   **A committee began investigating**: Weber, *Hitler's First War*, pp. 255–56 and 258–59.

48   **"make men strive for higher things"**: Hitler to Gemlich, September 19, 1919, in Noakes and Pridham, eds., *Nazism*, 1:12–13.

48   **That month, Mayr asked Hitler**: Noakes and Pridham, eds., *Nazism*, 1:13. By the spring of 1920 Hitler was making speeches calling explicitly for the "extermination" of all Jews: see *Hitler: Sämtliche Aufzeichnungen 1905–1924*, ed. Eberhard Jäckel (Stuttgart: Deutsche Verlags-Anstalt, 1980), pp. 119–120. I am grateful to Professor Gerhard Weinberg for this reference.

48   **"the dreamland of the armistice"**: Wolfgang Schivelbusch, *The Culture of Defeat: On National Trauma, Mourning, and Recovery*, trans. Jefferson Chase (New York: Picador, 2001), p. 255n31.

49   **In the course of his work**: Kershaw, *Hubris*, p. 124.

49   **"I started out"**: Hitler, *MK*, 1:579.

49   **By chance, Hitler had discovered**: Kershaw, *Hubris*, p. 125; Ernst Deuerlein, "Hitlers Eintritt in die Politik und die Reichswehr," *Vierteljahrshefte für Zeitgeschichte* 7 (1959): 177–227.

50   **Captain Mayr began to develop**: Kershaw, *Hubris*, p. 126.

50   **Hitler, still in the army**: Ibid., p. 145.

50   **A Munich police report . . . "our goal"**: Reginald H. Phelps, "Hitler als Parteiredner," *Vierteljahrshefte für Zeitgeschichte* 11 (1963): 274–330 and 294–95.

51   **Konrad Heiden was one of the few**: Aust, *Hitlers erster Feind*, pp. 21 and 82–84.

52   **His boyhood friend**: Kubizek, *Young Hitler*, pp. 157 and 174–75.

53   **"Like most basically ignorant people"**: Hanfstaengl, *Hitler: The Missing Years*, p. 133.

53   **"He looked at me"**: Kubizek, *Young Hitler*, p. 182.

53   **He routinely voiced scorn**: Ullrich, *Hitler*, pp. 389–90.

53   **That the exchange rate**: Richard J. Evans, *The Coming of the Third Reich* (New York: Penguin, 2004), p. 105.

54   **"What a tremendous chap"**: Kershaw, *Hubris*, p. 216.

54   **There is a legend**: Ullrich, *Hitler*, p. 173.

55   **There was debate about him**: Jonathan Wright, *Gustav Stresemann: Weimar's Greatest Statesman* (New York: Oxford University Press, 2002), "Introduction."

55   **The British journalist . . . Theodor Heuss . . . the novelist Thomas Mann**: Ibid., p. 2.

55   **Viscount D'Abernon**: Ibid., p. 498.

55   **Stresemann was born**: Ibid., chap. 1.

56   **When he started working**: Ibid., chap. 2.

56   **Throughout his life**: Ibid., chap. 3.

56   **Stresemann began furiously denouncing**: Ibid., pp. 106–7.

56   **and in his brief chancellorship**: Wright, *Stresemann*, p. 494; generally, Zara Steiner, *The Lights That Failed: European International History 1919–1933* (New York: Oxford University Press, 2005), chaps. 7 and 8.

57   **Complex factors**: Wright, *Stresemann*, pp. 323 and 518.

57   **On one occasion**: Ibid., p. 332.

58   **British foreign secretary Austen Chamberlain**: Ibid., p. 499.

58   **After one meeting in 1926**: Ibid., p. 370n196.

58   **Alfred Hugenberg rose from a humble background**: John A. Leopold, *Alfred Hugenberg: The Radical Nationalist Campaign Against the Weimar Republic* (London and New Haven: Yale University Press, 1977), pp. 1–2.

58   **In 1916, Hugenberg purchased**: Ibid., pp. 8–20.

59   **Hugenberg became**: Ibid., pp. 21–23.

59   **He feared his party**: Hugenberg, "Block oder Brei?," in Herbert Michaelis et al., eds., *Ursachen und Folgen vom deutschen Zusammenbruch 1918 und 1945 bis zur staatlichen Neuordnung Deutschlands in der Gegenwart* (Berlin: Dokumenten-Verlag Dr. Herbert Wendler, 1959–1978), 8:350.

59   **Gustav Stresemann understood**: Wright, *Stresemann*, pp. 373–74.

60   **Hitler would tell his own foreign minister**: Ibid., p. 514.

60   **When Hugenberg won . . . By then**: Ibid., pp. 434 and 408.

60   **That July, Stresemann told a French journalist**: Ibid., p. 469.

60   **"Order a coffin for two"**: Ibid., p. 501.

61   **On September 30**: Ibid., p. 482.

61   **"German collapse"**: Ullrich, *Hitler*, pp. 201–2 n70.

61   **"a decrepit industrial sector"**: Ibid., pp. 201–2.

3. BLOOD MAY AND THE CREEPER

62   **The police have been prepared**: Thomas Kurz, *"Blutmai": Sozialdemokraten und Kommunisten im Brennpunkt der Berliner Ereignisse von 1929* (Berlin: Verlag J. H. W. Dietz Nachf., 1988), pp. 13–14.

62   **A young carpenter**: Fürst, *Gefilte Fisch*, p. 567.

62   **In the morning**: Kurz, *"Blutmai,"* pp. 29–30.

62   **Max Fürst and his young wife**: Fürst, *Gefilte Fisch*, pp. 568–69.

63   **Still the situation escalates**: Kurz, *"Blutmai,"* pp. 32–33.

63   **One man does not respond**: Ibid., p. 45.

63   **Some protesters**: Ibid., pp. 36–40.

64   **The same kind of thing**: Bericht über die von dem Ausschuß zur Prüfung der Mai-Vorgänge am 6.6.1929 im Großen Schauspielhaus Versammlung, Landesarchiv Berlin A Pr. Br. Rep. 30 Tit. 95 Nr. 21731, Bl. 110.

64   **Soon, much of the press**: Kurz, *"Blutmai,"* p. 63.

65   **The official report**: Ibid., pp. 42, 47–48.

65   **The dead of Blood May**: Hett, *Crossing Hitler*, p. 55.

66   **The journalist Matheo Quinz**: Matheo Quinz, "The Romanisches Café," in Anton Kaes et al., *The Weimar Republic Sourcebook* (Berkeley and Los Angeles: University of California Press, 1994) (hereafter Kaes et al., *Weimar Republic Sourcebook*), pp. 415–17.

66   **The house would permit only**: David Clay Large, *Berlin* (New York: Basic Books, 2000), p. 191.

66   **The historian Eric Weitz**: Eric D. Weitz, *Weimar Germany,* New and Expanded Edition (Princeton: Princeton University Press, 2013), pp. 77–78.

66   **Markus Wolf, for many years**: Markus Wolf, *Man Without a Face: The Autobiography of Communism's Greatest Spymaster* (New York: PublicAffairs, 1997), p. 25.

67   **There were three "confessionalized" camps**: Jürgen Falter, *Hitlers Wähler* (Munich: C. H. Beck, 1991); Walter Dean Burnham, "Political Immunization and Political Confessionalism: The United States and Weimar Germany," *Journal of Interdisciplinary History* 3, no. 1 (Summer 1972): 1–30.

67   **"We shall have to hold our noses"**: Kershaw, *Hubris*, p. 228.

68   **Until 1932**: Falter, *Hitlers Wähler*, pp. 51–52 and 368–72.

68   **But in 1925**: Wolfram Pyta, *Dorfgemeinschaft und Parteipolitik 1918–1933: Die Verschränkung von Milieu und Parteien in den protestantischen Landgebieten Deutschlands in der Weimarer Republik* (Düsseldorf: Droste Verlag, 1996), p. 37.

69   **This social structure was absent**: Shelley Baranowski, *The Sanctity of Rural Life: Nobility, Protestantism, and Nazism in Weimar Prussia* (New York: Oxford University Press, 1995), pp. 6–8, 20, and 39.

69   **Rural people had understandable reasons**: Ibid., pp. 118–22.

70   **The First World War**: Ibid., p. 102.

70   **"Berlin is not Germany"**: Large, *Berlin*, 164.

70   **the conservative journalist**: Wilhelm Stapel, "The Intellectual and His People," in Kaes et al., *Weimar Republic Sourcebook*, pp. 423–25.

71   **Disapproval of big-city sexual mores**: Baranowski, *Sanctity*, p. 111.

71   **The poet and children's book author**: Weitz, *Weimar*, p. 77.

71   **The journalist Kurt Tucholsky described**: Kurt Tucholsky, "Berlin and the Provinces," in Kaes et al., *Weimar Republic Sourcebook*, pp. 418–20.

71   **Wilhelm Stapel was correct**: Baranowski, *Sanctity*, 129; Hett, *Burning the Reichstag*, pp. 80–81.

72   **a "cultural code"**: Shulamit Volkov, *Germans, Jews and Antisemites: Trials in Emancipation* (New York: Cambridge University Press, 2006), pp. 113–115.

72   **German nationalism**: Ibid.; Hermann Graml, *Antisemitism in the Third Reich*, trans. Tim Kirk (Oxford: Blackwell, 1988), pp. 67–68.

72   ***anti*-antisemitism**: Volkov, *Germans, Jews, and Antisemites*, pp. 118, 129, and 135–39.

73   **Antisemitic outbursts**: Peter Hayes, *Why: Explaining the Holocaust* (New York: W. W. Norton, 2017), pp. 53–56.

73   **The Weimar political structure**: Graml, *Antisemitism*, p. 80.

73   **"international finance spiders"**: Ullrich, *Hitler*, p. 231.

74   **In 1928, the Sixth Congress**: Eva Rosenhaft, *Beating the Fascists: The German Communists and Political Violence* (New York: Cambridge University Press, 1983), p. 30.

75   **One was structural**: Fritzsche, *Germans into Nazis*, p. 79; Wolfram Pyta, *Die Weimarer Republik* (Berlin: Landeszentrale für politische Bildungsarbeit, 2004), p. 156.

75   **On several occasions in the 1920s**: Thomas Mergel, "Das Scheitern des deutschen Tory-Konservatismus: Die Umformung der DNVP zu einer rechtsradikalen Partei 1928–1932," *Historische Zeitschrift* 275, no. 2 (2003): 325–26 and 337.

75   **Paul von Beneckendorff und von Hindenburg**: Wheeler-Bennett, *Wooden Titan*, pp. 3–4.

76   **On August 22, 1914**: Ibid., pp. 26–29.

76   **Hoffmann later commented**: Anna von der Goltz, *Hindenburg: Power, Myth, and the Rise of the Nazis* (Oxford: Oxford University Press, 2009), p. 19.

76   **Hindenburg habitually displayed a solemn expression**: Henry Ashby Turner, *Hitler's Thirty Days to Power: January 1933* (Reading, MA: Addison-Wesley, 1997), p. 4.

76   **Hindenburg embodied German history**: von der Goltz, *Hindenburg*, p. 14.

77   **Hindenburg was devoted to his family**: Pyta, *Hindenburg*, p. 21.

77   **He was a deeply religious Lutheran**: von der Goltz, *Hindenburg*, p. 14.

77   **when a delegation of Social Democrats**: Harry Graf Kessler, *Tagebücher 1918 bis 1937* (Frankfurt: Insel Taschenbuch, 1996), p. 698.

77   **"I myself do not understand"**: Quoted in Pyta, *Hindenburg*, p. 15.

77   **The high command appointed him**: von der Goltz, *Hindenburg*, p. 15.

78   **When he traveled**: Pyta, *Hindenburg*, pp. 18–19.

78   **As a young officer**: Ibid., p. 19.

78   **His writing was precise**: Ibid., pp. 559–60.

78   **The admiral and chief of the naval staff**: Ibid., p. 333.

79   **When Hindenburg decided to run**: von der Goltz, *Hindenburg*, p. 93.

80   **Reich Association of German Industry** : *Ursachen und Folgen*, 8:101–3.

80   **As business leaders well knew**: Harold James, "Economic Reasons for the Collapse of the Weimar Republic," in Ian Kershaw, ed., *Weimar: Why Did Democracy Fail?* (London: Weidenfeld and Nicolson, 1990), p. 40.

81   **"open and frank"**: Vincenz Müller, *Ich fand das wahre Vaterland* (East Berlin: Deutscher Militärverlag, 1963), p. 199.

81   **German humor**: Turner, *Hitler's Thirty Days*, p. 20.

81   **colleagues were not always sure**: Irene Strenge, *Schleicher: Politik im Reichswehrministerium am Ende der Weimarer Republik* (Berlin: Duncker und Humblot, 2006), pp. 12–13.

81   **"Have you really thought that through?"**: Müller, *Wahre Vaterland*, p. 196.

81   **"Yes, it's just a pity"**: Otto Meißner, *Staatssekretär unter Ebert—Hindenburg—Hitler* (Hamburg: Hoffmann und Campe Verlag, 1950), pp. 257–58.

81   **"Estrangement is much too mild"**: Michaelis et al., *Ursachen und Folgen*, Bd. 8, Doc. 1922, p. 711.

81   **"feared rather than liked" . . . "rather than substantial"**: André François-Poncet, *The Fateful Years: Memoirs of a French Ambassador in Berlin, 1931–1938*, trans. Jacques LeClercq (New York: Howard Fertig, 1971), pp. 28–29.

82   **Schleicher was born**: Strenge, *Schleicher*, pp. 11 and 54–55.

82   **As early as 1924**: Müller, *Wahre Vaterland*, pp. 223–24.

82   **free itself from the "chains"**: Ibid., pp. 219 and 224–25.

82   **In an unbuttoned moment**: "Moscow Document," in Henry Ashby Turner, *Hitlers Weg zur Macht: Der Januar 1933*, trans. Enrico Heinemann and Thomas Pfeiffer (Berlin: Ullstein, 1999), p. 184. The full text of this document does not appear in the original English edition of Professor Turner's book.

83   **He explained later**: Ibid., p. 182.

83   **In December 1926**: Strenge, *Schleicher*, pp. 46–51.

84   **The election of 1928**: Ibid., p. 62.

84   **Schleicher knew**: Ibid., p. 60.

85   **"You can't rule"**: Müller, *Wahre Vaterland*, p. 223.

85   **The farmers of Schleswig-Holstein**: McElliigott, *Rethinking*, p. 78.

86   **Then there was "rationalization"**: Weitz, *Weimar*, p. 152; James, "Economic Reasons," p. 31.

86   **1.3 million unemployed**: Theo Balderston, *Economics and Politics in the Weimar Republic* (Cambridge: Cambridge University Press, 2002), p. 79.

86   **It was the bull market**: Liaquat Ahamed, *Lords of Finance: The Bankers Who Broke the World* (New York: Penguin Books, 2009), pp. 324–25.

86   **The distinguished diplomatic historian**: Steiner, *Lights That Failed*, p. 641.

87   **Brüning had served**: Pyta, *Weimar*, p. 99.

87   **"inspired confidence and sympathy"**: François-Poncet, *Fateful Years*, p. 4.

87   **"the more absurd and radical"**: Heinrich Brüning, *Memoiren: 1918–1934* (Stuttgart: Deutsche Verlags-Anstalt, 1970), p. 243.

87   **"From the beginning"**: Ibid., p. 211.

88   **In the late fall**: Ibid., p. 247.

88   **Brüning's competence**: William L. Patch, *Heinrich Brüning and the Dissolution of the Weimar Republic* (New York: Cambridge University Press, 1998), p. 136.

88   **At a dinner**: Strenge, *Schleicher*, p. 63; Treviranus, *Weimar*, p. 115; Brüning, *Memoiren*, pp. 150–51.

89   **His administration**: Strenge, *Schleicher*, p. 67; *Akten der Reichskanzlei: Die Kabinette Brüning I und II (1930–1932)* (hereafter *AdR Brüning*), ed. Tilmann Koops (Boppard am Rhein: Boldt Verlag, 1982); *Verhandlungen des Reichstages*, 427:4727–30.

90   **In May 1928**: Jürgen Falter, *Wahlen und Abstimmungen in der Weimarer Republik* (Munich: C. H. Beck, 1986), pp. 90, 100, and 111.

90   **The Nazis were reaping**: Fritzsche, *Germans*, p. 173.

90   **At the end of June 1930**: Hermann Graml, *Zwischen Stresemann und Hitler: Die Aussenpolitik der Präsidialkabinette Brüning, Papen und Schleicher* (Munich: R. Oldenbourg Verlag, 2001), pp. 48–53.

91   **The previous fall**: Wright, *Stresemann*, p. 476.

91   **By the time Briand could follow up**: Ferdinand Siebert, *Aristide Briand: Ein Staatsmann zwischen Frankreich und Europa* (Erlenbach-Zürich: Eugen Rentsch Verlag, 1973), pp. 545–47.

92   **In a cabinet meeting**: *AdR Brüning*, Bd. 1, Dok. 68.

92   **Although most European countries**: Siebert, *Briand*, p. 553.

92   **Some of his loyal supporters . . . tough measures**: C. Edmund Clingan, *The Lives of Hans Luther, 1879–1962: German Chancellor, Reichsbank President, and Hitler's Ambassador* (Lanham, MD: Lexington Books, 2010), p. 87.

93   **A few years later**: Müller, *Wahre Vaterland*, p. 349.

4. THE HUNGER CHANCELLOR

94   **"automation"**: "Laubenkolonie Felseneck," *Die Rote Fahne*, January 20, 1932.

94   **A man named Johann Banuscher**: Bundesarchiv Berlin-Lichterfelde R 22/66804, *Adam und Genossen*, judgment, December 22, 1932, pp. 23–35.

95   **On the evening of January 18 . . . dies on the spot**: Ibid.

96   **In the small hours**: Adolf Hitler, *Reden, Schriften, Anordnungen 1925–1933* (hereafter Hitler, *Reden*), 3:3, ed. Christian Hartmann (Munich: K. G. Saur, 1995), pp. 418–19.

96   **Ernst Hanfstaengl . . . claimed**: Ernst Hanfstaengl, *Zwischen Weißen und Braunem Haus: Memoiren eines politischen Aussenseiters* (Munich: R. Piper Verlag, 1970), p. 207.

96   **According to Rudolf Hess**: Ullrich, *Hitler*, p. 231.

96   **"black day for Germany"**: Kessler, *Tagebücher*, pp. 677–78.

97   **Thea Sternheim . . . Bella Fromm**: Ullrich, *Hitler*, p. 233; Bella Fromm, *Blood and Banquets: A Social Diary* (New York: Harper and Brothers, 1942), p. 25.

97   **British ambassador Horace Rumbold**: Michaelis et al., *Ursachen und Folgen*, 8:93.

97   **"monstrous"**: Fritzsche, *Germans*, p. 150.

97   **A State Party**: Michaelis et al., *Ursachen und Folgen*, 8:92.

97   **When the new Reichstag opened**: Fromm, *Blood and Banquets*, p. 25.

97   **It wasn't just German liberals**: Balderston, *Economics and Politics*, p. 84; Ahamed, *Lords of Finance*, p. 400; Thomas Ferguson and Peter Temin, "Made in Germany: The German Currency Crisis of July 1931," *MIT Department of Economics Working Paper Series*, February 2001, p. 12.

98   **His reaction to the news**: Siebert, *Briand*, p. 562.

98   **The Nazis were politicians**: Robert Paxton, *The Anatomy of Fascism* (New York: Vintage, 2004), pp. 83–84.

99   **The "brilliance of the imperial court"**: *Berlin and Its Environs*, 6th ed. (Leipzig: Karl Baedeker, 1923), p. 50.

99   **antisemitism was prominent**: Noakes and Pridham, *Nazi Germany*, 1:14–16.

100   **"We demand legal warfare"**: Ibid., 1:15–16.

101   **"The church is politically neutral"**: Karl Wilhelm Dahm, *Pfarrer und Politik* (Cologne: Westdeutscher Verlag, 1965), pp. 104–9. I am particularly grateful to Ky Woltering for these citations on Protestants in Weimar and for his explanation of the German Protestant outlook.

102   **The Social Democrats**: Karl Wilhelm Dahm, "German Protestantism and Politics, 1918–39," *Journal of Contemporary History* 3, no. 1 (January 1968): 33.

102   **"The alliance between"**: R. Seeberg, quoted in ibid., p. 40.

102   **A poem that circulated**: Victoria Barnett, *For the Soul of the People: Protestant Protest Against Hitler* (New York: Oxford University Press, 1992), p. 16.

102   **Otto Dibelius boasted**: Michael Wildt, *Hitler's Volksgemeinschaft and the Dynamics of Racial Exclusion: Violence Against Jews in Provincial Germany 1919–1939*, trans. Bernhard Heise (New York: Berghahn Books, 2012), p. 84.

103   **"a people's church" . . . "in modern culture"**: Richard Karwehl, "Politisches Messiastum," *Zwischen den Zeiten* 9 (1931): 520 and 530–31. I am grateful to Dagmar Herzog for this reference.

103   **Even in what Karwehl didn't like**: Dagmar Herzog, conversation with the author, February 2017.

103   **Even years later**: Joachim Fest, *Plotting Hitler's Death: The Story of the German Resistance* (New York: Metropolitan Books, 2006), p. 316.

103   **the pastor and resistance hero**: Martin Niemöller, speech of December 22,

1946, Microform No. 252, WWII Era Records of the WCC, Yale Divinity School. I am grateful to Ky Woltering for this reference.

103   **Karwehl thought that Nazism**: Karwehl, "Politisches Messiastum," p. 531.

103   **Yet certainly many**: Ibid., pp. 519–20.

104   **politically homeless**: Riecker, *Hitlers 9. November*, p. 115.

104   **The day after the war ended**: Fritzsche, *Germans*, p. 111, and following argument based generally on Fritzsche.

105   **"the right attitude" . . . Populist political movements**: Ibid., pp. 182 and 200; generally, Pyta, *Hindenburg*, pp. 583–84.

105   **Across Europe, fascism developed**: Paxton, *Anatomy of Fascism*, p. 81.

105   **For a time**: Argument based on Fritzsche, *Germans*.

106   **"The German people . . . results in Europe"**: Hitler, *Second Book*, pp. 24–25.

106   **It was anger**: Fritzsche, *Germans*, p. 173.

107   **Bernhard von Bülow**: Hermann Graml, *Bernhard von Bülow und die deutsche Aussenpolitik. Hybris und Augenmass im Auswärtigen Amt* (Munich: Oldenbourg, 2012), pp. 33–34.

107   **In its simplest terms**: Ahamed, *Lords of Finance*, pp. 11–13. The definitive work on the operations of the gold standard in the interwar world is Barry Eichengreen, *Golden Fetters: The Gold Standard and the Great Depression 1919–1939* (New York: Oxford University Press, 1992). I am very grateful to Professor Eichengreen, Professor Benjamin Friedman, and Professor Edmund Clingan for advice on these points.

107   **In the post–Great War world**: Tooze, *Deluge*, pp. 487–88.

108   **Under the 1924 Dawes Plan**: Ahamed, *Lords of Finance*, p. 325.

108   **Limiting Germans' freedom of action**: Clingan, *Luther*, p. 98.

108   **In a 1930 speech, Hans Luther**: Michaelis et al., *Ursachen und Folgen*, 8:118. Luther was quoting the banker Carl Melchior.

108   **State secretary Bernhard von Bülow**: Graml, *Bülow*, pp. 33–34.

108   **Brüning stressed**: Michaelis et al., *Ursachen und Folgen*, 8:109.

109   **The orthodox view**: Ibid., 8:118.

109   **the far-right journalist**: Ibid., 8:5.

109   **The liberal economist**: Ibid., 8:7.

109   **The canny party propagandist Joseph Goebbels**: Ibid., 8:7–8.

110   **Strasser was a Nazi leader**: Peter D. Stachura, *Gregor Strasser and the Rise of Nazism* (London: George Allen and Unwin, 1983), p. 3.

110   **Strasser was born**: Ibid., pp. 12–13.

110   **Still, Strasser came away**: Ibid., p. 14.

111   **The speech became, and remains, famous**: *Verhandlungen des Reichstages*, 446:2511.

111   **The Nazis, he argued, wanted to save the rural economy**: Ibid., 446:2520.

111   **Gottfried Treviranus**: Graml, *Zwischen Stresemann und Hitler*, p. 53.

112   **Bernhard von Bülow**: Graml, *Bülow*, p. 92.

112   **led to a refugee crisis**: Annemarie H. Sammartino, *The Impossible Border: Germany and the East, 1913–1922* (Ithaca, NY: Cornell University Press, 2010), pp. 2 and 120.

112   **This refugee crisis**: Ibid., p. 10.

112   **A conspicuous number**: Hett, *Burning the Reichstag*; Michael Mann, "Were the Perpetrators of Genocide 'Ordinary Men' or 'Real Nazis'?" *Holocaust and Genocide Studies* 14, no. 3 (2001): 331–66.

113   **In 1928**: Rosenhaft, *Beating the Fascists*, p. 30.

113   **Because Germany's Communist Party was so large**: Hermann Weber, *Die Wandlung des deutschen Kommunismus: Die Stalinisierung der KPD in der Weimarer Republik* (Frankfurt: Europäische Verlagsanstalt, 1971), pp. 362–64.

113   **Hitler agreed completely**: Hitler, Hossbach Memorandum, in Noakes and Pridham, *Nazism*, 3:74–75.

114   **These lessons**: Ludendorff, *Nation at War*.

114   **Arguably the strongest**: Stefan Ihrig, *Atatürk in the Nazi Imagination* (Cambridge, MA: Harvard University Press, 2014), p. 223.

115   **The Nazis admired**: Ibid., p. 224.

115   **Between 1920 and 1923 . . . a product of that conspiracy**: Michael Kellogg, *The Russian Roots of Nazism: White Emigrés and the Making of National Socialism, 1917–1945* (Cambridge: Cambridge University Press, 2005), pp. 1–4.

116   **"deepest reverence" . . . "German Communist"**: Peter Longerich, *Goebbels: A Biography*, trans. Alan Bance et al. (New York: Random House, 2015), pp. 26 and 29.

116   **Throughout his political career**: Kershaw, *Hubris*, pp. 180–82.

116   **Giuseppe Renzetti**: Hans Woller, "Machtpolitisches Kalkul oder ideologische Affinität? Zur Frage des Verhältnisses zwischen Mussolini und Hitler," in Wolfgang Benz et al., eds., *Der Nationalsozialismus: Studien zur Ideologie und Herrschaft* (Frankfurt: Fischer Taschenbuch Verlag, 1993), p. 46.

116   **There were extensive contacts**: Ibid., p. 52.

116   **Mussolini wanted to see a government**: Ibid., pp. 52–54.

116   **Renzetti eventually became convinced**: Ibid., pp. 54–60.

117   **The price involved**: Weinberg, Introduction to Hitler, *Second Book*, pp. xiv–xxi.

117   **During the 1928 election campaign . . . Hitler had made his deal with Migliorati**: Douglas G. Morris, *Justice Imperiled: The Anti-Nazi Lawyer Max Hirschberg in Weimar Germany* (Ann Arbor: University of Michigan Press, 2005), pp. 254–72; Allan Cassels, *Mussolini's Early Diplomacy* (Princeton: Princeton University Press, 1970), pp. 171–72.

118   **Support for the Nazis in Germany**: Paxton, *Fascism*, pp. 80–81.

118   **It was an international reaction**: Ihrig, *Atatürk*, p. 228; Kellogg, *Russian Roots*, p. 1.

119   **Yet Brüning thought**: Patch, *Brüning*, p. 151.

119   **In December 1930**: Brüning, *Memoiren*, pp. 222–24.

119   **Despite a few, faint signs of economic upturn**: Ferguson and Temin, "Made in Germany," p. 31.

119   **At a cabinet meeting**: Heinrich August Winkler, *Weimar 1918–1933: Die Geschichte der ersten deutschen Demokratie* (Munich: C. H. Beck, 1993), p. 405.

119   **Into this bleak picture**: Ferguson and Temin, "Made in Germany," pp. 18–19.

120   **As the talks went on**: Graml, *Zwischen Stresemann und Hitler*, pp. 81 and 152–53.

120   **The Depression had given him an opportunity**: Ibid., pp. 77–79.

120   **On March 21, 1931**: Winkler, *Weimar*, pp. 403–5; Brüning, *Memoiren*.

121   **There was an outcry**: Winkler, *Weimar*, p. 406.

121   **Brüning was too intelligent**: This is the clever and persuasive argument Hermann Graml makes in *Zwischen Stresemann und Hitler*, p. 97.

121   **First, it shows once again**: This point is made by Boyce in *Interwar Crisis*, p. 310.

121   **Second, Brüning could afford**: Graml, *Zwischen Stresemann und Hitler*, p. 155.

122   **On June 6**: Ferguson and Temin, "Made in Germany," p. 34; Winkler, *Weimar*, p. 408.

122   **There had already been rumors**: Ferguson and Temin, "Made in Germany," p. 36.

122   **That very day**: Patch, *Brüning*, pp. 160–62.

122   **At Chequers**: Brüning, *Memoiren*, p. 413.

122   **Ambassador Sackett and his British counterpart**: Patch, *Brüning*, p. 156.

122   **Officials in Hoover's own administration**: Winkler, *Weimar*, p. 415.

123   **The ending of reparations**: This is the overall argument of Ferguson and Temin, "Made in Germany."

123   **First, a major bank failed**: Barry Eichengreen, *Hall of Mirrors: The Great Depression, the Great Recession, and the Uses—and Misuses—of History* (New York: Oxford University Press, 2015), pp. 142–43 and 149–51.

123   **He and his ministers**: Patch, *Brüning*, pp. 201 and 219.

123   **More important, Brüning's administration did not feel**: Ibid., pp. 201–4.

124   **Where could the money for such an expansion have come from?**: The whole question of Brüning's response to the Great Depression is a hotly debated issue among specialists. The debate started with the work of Knut Borchardt in the 1970s. Borchardt argued, against the then-still-prevailing Keynesian orthodoxy, that Brüning had had no option but to follow the course he did, because the Weimar economy was "sick" and it was impossible for the government to borrow. Others, such as Ferguson and Temin, have argued that it was Brüning's political choices that made solving the German government's financial problems impossible. My argument follows Ferguson and Temin, "Made in Germany," Edmund Clingan, *Finance from Kaiser to Führer: Budget Politics in Germany 1912-1934* (Westport, CT: Greenwood Press, 2001), and Clingan, *Luther*. See also Knut Borchardt, *Perspectives on Modern German Economic History and Policy*, trans. Peter Lambert (Cambridge: Cambridge University Press, 1991), especially chaps. 9, 10, and 11; Eichengreen, *Golden Fetters* and *Hall of Mirrors*; Boyce, *Interwar Crisis*.

124   **The gold standard**: Tooze, *Deluge*, pp. 502–3.

125   **Soon afterward**: Brüning, *Memoiren*, p. 293.

125   **"Berlin needs its sensation"**: Joseph Goebbels, *Kampf um Berlin: Der Anfang* (Munich: Eher Verlag, 1934), p. 28.

126   **He admitted**: Ibid., p. 21.

126   **"Daily the rotation machines"**: Ibid., p. 27.

127   **By the early 1930s**: The discussion of political violence in Berlin is based in part on Rosenhaft, *Beating the Fascists*; Pamela E. Swett, *Neighbors and Enemies: The Culture of Radicalism in Berlin* (Cambridge: Cambridge University Press, 2004); Hett, *Crossing Hitler*; and Hett, *Burning the Reichstag*.

127   **The attack on the Felseneck colony**: Hett, *Crossing Hitler*, pp. 149–50.

128   **Law-abiding middle-class Germans**: Richard Bessel, "Violence as Propaganda,"

in Thomas Childers, *The Formation of the Nazi Constituency, 1919–1933* (London: Croom Helm, 1986), pp. 131–46.

128   **During a Reichstag debate in May**: *Verhandlungen des Reichstages*, 446:2486.

128   **Goebbels caused outrage**: Michaelis et al., *Ursachen und Folgen*, 8:398.

128   **Ernst Lemmer**: Ibid., 8:399.

128   **The bluntest and most colorful**: Ibid., 8:400.

129   **it became increasingly clear**: Swett, *Neighbors and Enemies*.

129   **In October**: Hermann Beck, *The Fateful Alliance: German Conservatives and Nazis in 1933—the Machtergreifung in a New Light* (New York: Berghahn Books, 2008), pp. 72–73.

130   **Goebbels wrote a blunt editorial**: Beck, *Fateful Alliance*, pp. 72–73.

130   **His private thoughts . . . were even more scathing**: Joseph Goebbels, diary entry October 12, 1931, TB, Teil 1, Vol. 2/II, pp. 122–23.

5. STATE OF EMERGENCY

131   **"Our war"**: Joseph Goebbels, diary entry for March 1, 1932, TB Teil 1, Vol. 2/II, pp. 230–31.

132   **"We'll make the Nazis believers"**: Franz von Papen, *Der Wahrheit eine Gasse* (Munich: Paul List Verlag, 1952), p. 187.

133   **"They can only pray"**: Diary entry of Schwerin von Krosigk, in Karl-Heinz Minuth, ed., *Das Kabinett von Papen* (Boppard am Rhein: Boldt Verlag, 1989) (hereafter *AdR Papen*), vol. 2, doc. 239b, p. 1038.

133   **"In cultural matters"**: Brüning, *Memoiren*, p. 379.

133   **The journalist Konrad Heiden**: Aust, *Hitlers erster Feind*, p. 157.

134   **One reason for this**: Strenge, *Schleicher*, pp. 77–78; Michaelis et al., *Ursachen und Folgen*, 7:537–48.

134   **"an interesting man"**: Strenge, *Schleicher*, p. 81.

134   **"remove the chains"**: Winkler, *Weimar*, 422; *AdR Brüning*, 2:1470–77.

134   **Long-term collaboration**: Winkler, *Weimar*, p. 422.

135   **He disliked knowing**: Patch, *Brüning*, pp. 184–85.

135   **In July 1931**: Winkler, *Weimar*, p. 422.

135   **Another major factor . . . "truly statesmanlike figures"**: Ibid.; Wright, *Stresemann*, p. 341.

136   **One of Schleicher's main concerns**: Patch, *Brüning*, pp. 184–85; Winkler, *Weimar*, p. 425.

136   **It was clear to Brüning**: Brüning, *Memoiren*, p. 386.

137   **In fact, there was a lively conspiracy**: Ibid., pp. 467–68.

137   **He reformed his cabinet**: Strenge, *Schleicher*, pp. 83–84.

138   **Hindenburg himself was reluctant to run**: Wheeler-Bennett, *Wooden Titan*, p. 356.

138   **To make things easier**: Brüning, *Memoiren*, pp. 518–19.

138   **Yet even the Steel Helmet**: Winkler, *Weimar*, p. 445.

138   **Three main candidates**: Ibid.

138   **After this**: Hanfstaengl, *Hitler*, pp. 176 and 196.

138   **Hindenburg barely campaigned**: Winkler, *Weimar*, p. 448.

139   **An electoral truce . . . Germany had yet seen**: Ibid., p. 452.

139   **Brüning considered the election**: Patch, *Brüning*, p. 247; von der Goltz, *Hindenburg*, pp. 153–54.

139   **An analysis of voting data**: Falter, *Hitlers Wähler*, pp. 123–24.

139   **Now Hindenburg**: Patch, *Brüning*, p. 247.

139   **As a routine courtesy**: Winkler, *Weimar*, p. 414.

140   **No rational and well-informed person**: *AdR Brüning* 2: 692; Strenge, *Schleicher*, p. 90; Winkler, *Weimar*, pp. 447–48 and 454.

140   **Schleicher was stunned**: Strenge, *Schleicher*, pp. 89–94.

141   **Some of the stress**: Brüning, *Memoiren*, p. 580.

141   **Schleicher exploited**: Patch, *Brüning*, pp. 251–52.

142   **Wilhelm Frick**: Rudolf Fischer, *Schleicher: Mythos und Wirklichkeit* (Hamburg: Hanseatische Verlagsanstalt, 1932), p. 10.

142   **Everyone knew how much**: Strenge, *Schleicher*, p. 95.

142   **On a late-April car journey**: Brüning, *Memoiren*, p. 547.

142   **Brüning asked the general**: Ibid., pp. 547–52.

143   **Through April and May**: Joseph Goebbels, diary entry for April 24, 1932, TB, Teil 1, Vol. 2/II, p. 265; diary entry for April 25, 1932, TB, Teil 1, Vol. 2/II, p. 268; diary entry for April 26, 1932, TB, Teil 1, Vol. 2/II, p. 268; diary entry for April 27, 1932, TB, Teil 1, Vol. 2/II, p. 269.

143   **"We stand before a difficult decision"**: Joseph Goebbels, diary entry for April 27, 1932, TB, Teil 1, Vol. 2/II, p. 269; diary entry for April 25, 1932, TB, Part 1, Vol. 2/II, p. 268.

143   **On April 28**: Joseph Goebbels, diary entry for April 29, 1932, TB, Teil 1, Vol. 2/II, p. 271.

143   **"Brüning is supposed to fall"**: Joseph Goebbels, diary entry for May 9, 1932, TB, Teil 1, Vol. 2/II, p. 276.

143   **May 9 also marked**: Winkler, *Weimar*, p. 465; Brüning, *Memoiren*, p. 587.

144   **Afterward, Schleicher**: Strenge, *Schleicher*, p. 106.

144   **"When the mantle falls"**: Joseph Goebbels, diary entry for May 12, 1932, TB, Teil 1, Vol. 2/II, p. 279.

144   **and by May 24**: Joseph Goebbels, diary entry for May 25, 1932, TB, Teil 1, Vol. 2/II, p. 288.

144   **The following Sunday**: Brüning, *Memoiren*, p. 600.

144   **"The bomb burst"**: Joseph Goebbels, diary entry for May 25, 1932, and May 31, 1932, TB, Teil 1, Vol. 2/II, pp. 288–93.

145   **Papen was born**: Rainer Orth, *Der "Amtssitz der Opposition?" Politik und Staatsumbaupläne im Büro des Stellvertreters des Reichskanzlers in den Jahren 1933–1934* (Cologne: Böhlau Verlag, 2016), pp. 29–31.

145   **In January 1914**: Ibid., pp. 33–34.

145   **In a display of incompetence**: Ibid., pp. 34–35.

145   **In 1917, he was sent**: Ihrig, *Atatürk*, pp. 103 and 119.

145   **When the war ended**: Orth, *"Amtssitz,"* p. 37.

146   **Papen left the army**: Ibid., pp. 41–42.

146   **"thoroughly conscious"**: Papen, *Wahrheit*, p. 185.

146   **"enjoyed the peculiarity"**: François-Poncet, *Fateful Years*, p. 23.

146   **although Papen claimed**: Papen, *Wahrheit*, pp. 184–85.

147   **"Papen is not a head!"**: Orth, *"Amtssitz,"* p. 55.

147   **With seven aristocrats**: Winkler, *Weimar*, p. 479.

147   **In August, he issued two executive orders**: Hett, *Crossing Hitler*, p. 129.

147   **Brüning had relied**: McElligott, *Rethinking*, p. 193.

147   **The sharp-eyed diarist**: Kessler, *Tagebücher*, pp. 709–10.

148   **The conspirators assigned Diels**: Ott to Friedrich von Papen, December 26, 1949, Institut für Zeitgeschichte ZS 279 Eugen Ott.

149   **Diels got the evidence**: Hett, *Burning the Reichstag*, pp. 31–32.

149   **Goebbels had known**: Joseph Goebbels, diary entry for July 20, 1932, TB, Teil 1, Vol. 2/II, pp. 323–24.

149   **A written official statement**: Huber, *Verfassungsgeschichte*, 4:563.

149   **Yet, in a radio address**: Franz von Papen, radio address, July 20, 1933, Deutsches Historisches Museum/ Deutsches Rundfunkarchiv, Stimmen des 20. Jahrhunderts: Preußen in Weimar, audio compact disc, 2001.

150   **The night of the election**: Hett, *Burning the Reichstag*, p. 82.

151   **The climax**: Daniel Siemens, *Stormtroopers: A New History of Hitler's Brownshirts* (New Haven: Yale University Press, 2017), pp. xiv–xviii.

151   **Papen's draconian executive orders**: Huber, *Verfassungsgeschichte*, 4:574–77.

151   **On August 11**: Siemens, *Stormtroopers*, pp. xiv–xviii.

151   **The Nazi leaders responded**: Ibid., p. xix.

151   **In an article**: Beck, *Fateful Alliance*, p. 81.

151   **Göring also sent the men a telegram**: Siemens, *Stormtroopers*, p. xix.

151   **This sequence of events**: Wolfram Pyta, *Die Weimarer Republik* (Berlin: Landeszentrale für politische Bildungsarbeit, 2004), p. 143.

151   **It seemed**: Strenge, *Schleicher*, p. 138.

151   **The Nazi leaders had a plan**: Irene Strenge, *Machtübernahme 1933: Alles auf legalem Weg?* (Berlin: Duncker und Humblot, 2002), pp. 92 and 98.

152   **Under Article 43**: Huber, *Verfassungsgeschichte*, 4:158 and 4:160.

152   **Heinrich Brüning remembered**: Heinrich Brüning, "Ein Brief," *Deutsche Rundschau* 70, no. 7 (July 1947): 13.

153   **Hitler had worked out his plans**: Joseph Goebbels, diary entry for August 5, 1932, TB, Teil 1, Vol. 2/II, p. 333.

153   **Yet, when Schleicher presented the plan**: AdR Papen, Dok. 99n4, p. 380; Strenge, *Schleicher*, p. 134.

153   **On August 10**: AdR Papen, Dok. 99, pp. 378–86.

154   **"The old man"**: Joseph Goebbels, diary entry for August 12, 1932, TB, Teil 1, Vol. 2/II, p. 338.

154   **"Papen is getting weak"**: Joseph Goebbels, diary entry for August 11, 1932, TB, Teil 1, Vol. 2/II, p. 337.

155   **all wanted Hitler**: Joseph Goebbels, diary entry for August 12, 1932, TB, Teil 1, Vol. 2/II, p. 338.

155   **"Then comes the decision"**: Joseph Goebbels, diary entry for August 13, 1932, TB, Teil 1, Vol. 2/II, p. 339.

155   **At 3:00 that afternoon**: Joseph Goebbels, diary entry for August 14, 1932, TB, Teil 1, Vol. 2/II, p. 340.

155   **Hindenburg opened the conversation**: AdR Papen, Dok. 101, pp. 391–92.

156   **Tellingly, this threat**: Strenge, *Machtübernahme*, p. 78.

156   **Hitler thought**: Strenge, *Schleicher*, p. 135.

156   **with significant assistance**: Ernst Rudolf Huber, "Carl Schmitt in der Reichskrise der Weimarer Republik," in Helmut Quaritsch, ed., *Complexio Oppositorum: Vorträge und Diskussionsbeiträge des 28. Sonderseminars 1986 der Hochschule für Verwaltungswissenschaften Speyer* (Berlin: Duncker und Humblot, 1988), pp. 33–70.

156   **On August 30**: AdR Papen, Dok. 120, pp. 474–79; Strenge, *Schleicher*, p. 143.

157   **Göring let slip**: Strenge, *Machtübernahme*, p. 103.

157   **wasp-tongued André François-Poncet**: François-Poncet, *Fateful Years*, pp. 38–39.

158   **"We are now going over"**: Noakes and Pridham, *Nazism*, 1:106.

158   **In October**: "Versammlung," Bundesarchiv Berlin-Lichterfelde R. 8005 Bd. 60.

158   **"Will you play along?"**: Strenge, *Schleicher*, p. 163.

158   **On one occasion**: Ibid., p. 171.

159   **Schleicher had probably expected**: Ibid., pp. 172–73.

159   **Schleicher had heard**: Ibid., p. 178.

159   **These issues came to a head**: Papen, *Wahrheit*, pp. 243–44.

160   **Then Schleicher spoke up**: Ibid., p. 244. The whole issue of what exactly Schleicher planned to do when he became chancellor is controversial. Henry A. Turner, for instance, rejects the idea that Schleicher aimed to split the Nazis by bringing Strasser into this cabinet (Turner, "The Myth of Chancellor von Schleicher's Querfront Strategy," *Central European History* 41 [2008]: 673–81). Turner points out that the only source for Schleicher laying out his strategy at this December 1 meeting is Papen's memoirs, which were often highly dishonest. In fact, the point is at least implied in the notes taken by Meissner at this meeting (in Huber, *Verfassungsgeschichte*, 4:621) and also in an article in the *Vossische Zeitung*, "Der General," December 11, 1932, probably relying on information from Schleicher, who had good connections to the *Vossische*. The legal historian Ernst Rudolf Huber, who was a student and protégé of Carl Schmitt, remembered in the 1980s how he and Schmitt had been involved in some of the negotiations to put together the cross front (Huber, "Carl Schmitt in der Reichskrise," 47). While certainly Papen's memoirs are often mendacious, in this case his account is credible. As Turner himself argues, the idea that Schleicher wanted to split the Nazis makes him look rather better than worse in the eyes of posterity, and Papen had every interest in making Schleicher look worse. As we will see in the next chapter, Papen's account is consistent with other sources from the same time.

160   **Schleicher's suggestion**: Papen, *Wahrheit*, p. 244.

160   **Hindenburg had listened**: Ibid., pp. 244–45.

160   **he came to a cabinet meeting**: Lutz Graf Schwerin von Krosigk, diary entry, December 2, 1932, AdR Papen, Bd. 2, Dok. 239b, pp. 1036–38.

161   **"The Field Marshal had listened"**: Papen, *Wahrheit*, p. 250.

6. THE BOHEMIAN PRIVATE AND THE GENTLEMAN JOCKEY

162 **Fifteen-year-old Melita**: Melita Maschmann, *Account Rendered: A Dossier on My Former Self* (London: Abelard-Schuman, 1964), pp. 9–12.

163 **Joseph Goebbels waits**: Joseph Goebbels, diary entry for January 31, 1933, TB, Teil 1, Vol. 2/III, p. 120.

163 **The conservative intellectual**: Edmund Forschbach, *Edgar J. Jung. Ein konservativer Revolutionär 30. Juni 1934* (Pfullingen: Verlag Günther Neske, 1984), p. 54.

163 **The pithiest reaction**: Bernd Küster, *Max Liebermann. Ein Maler* (Hamburg: Eller und Richter, 1988), p. 216.

163 **As the torch bearers file past**: Verhey, *Spirit of 1914*, p. 224.

164 **Now Hindenburg stands at the window**: Pyta, *Hindenburg*, p. 808.

165 **Among them**: Stachura, *Strasser*, p. 100.

165 **the administration should try to win over**: Strenge, *Schleicher*, pp. 173 and 178–80. As noted in the previous chapter, historians debate the question of Schleicher's strategy. For a long time, it was taken as a given that he had pursued a "cross front" strategy upon becoming chancellor, of which the central elements were building an alliance with Social Democrats and unionists, including Gregor Strasser in his cabinet, and using Strasser to split the Nazis and bring perhaps sixty Nazi Reichstag deputies into a majority coalition behind Schleicher's administration. Recent scholarship has cast doubt on this interpretation. As we have seen, Henry A. Turner maintained that the evidence this was Schleicher's scheme rested on the unreliable Papen memoirs. But given Papen's hostility to Schleicher, his account is plausible and is in fact supported by still more credible sources, such as Ambassador André François-Poncet's report to Paris of November 29, 1932 (see below). Another element of the revision involves the diaries of Joseph Goebbels. Goebbels published a doctored version of his diaries for this period in 1934, under the title *Vom Kaiserhof zur Reichskanzlei* (*From the Kaiserhof to the Reich Chancellery*). After the end of the Cold War, the originals of Goebbels's diary were discovered in Moscow and were published in a scholarly edition by the Institute of Contemporary History in Munich—in the case of the 1932 entries, in 2006. Goebbels's most recent biographer, Peter Longerich, has argued that while in the *Kaiserhof* version, Goebbels refers explicitly to Schleicher making an offer to Strasser with a view to splitting the Nazis, this element was missing from the undoctored 1932 original text. (Longerich also says that the *Kaiserhof* version of Goebbels's diary is the "single source" for Schleicher's offer, neglecting such sources as Papen's memoir and François-Poncet's report of November 29 as well as his reports from January 1933, discussed in the main text, which indicate that Schleicher in fact made such an offer to Strasser). Longerich argues that by the time the *Kaiserhof* edition was published (January 1934), Strasser was a clear political opponent upon whom Goebbels was free to take vengeance, and he exaggerated the claims about Strasser accordingly. Without any doubt, Goebbels's diaries, in both versions, are, like Papen's memoir, rife with dishonest depictions and must be read critically. But the point about Strasser is not

as clear-cut as Longerich suggests. In fact, diary entries for December 1932 show that Goebbels believed Strasser *would* join Schleicher's government and try to split the Nazi Party. On December 9, writing of the events of the day before, Goebbels notes that Strasser "wants to become a minister. *Schleicher . . . [has] set that in motion*" (emphasis added). And a bit later, in the same entry: Strasser "wants to be in Schleicher's cabinet. He will be heard from soon from there, so he thinks." The next day, Goebbels writes, "Schleicher's coup failed. We are no DNVP and have only one Treviranus"—this last a reference to the splitting of the German Nationals by Gottfried Treviranus in opposition to Hugenberg's leadership. Goebbels clearly meant that the Nazis' only Treviranus was Strasser, who would not be able to lead others out of the party, however much he might want to. In this case, it is likely that the account of Strasser's "treachery" that Goebbels supplied in the *Kaiserhof* edition was more a fleshing-out of the notes he had made at the time than a complete after-the-fact fabrication. Goebbels's original diary entries are, of course, also consistent with Papen's account. All in all, the idea that Schleicher pursued the cross-front strategy and sought to win over Strasser and a number of other Nazis seems the most plausible and consistent with the evidence. See Longerich, *Goebbels*, pp. 194–95; Joseph Goebbels, *Vom Kaiserhof zur Reichskanzlei* (Munich: Franz Eher Nachf., 1938), pp. 196–202; Goebbels, *Die Tagebücher von Joseph Goebbels*, ed. Elke Fröhlich, Teil 1, Bd. 2/III (Munich: K. G. Saur, 2006), entries for December 9 and 10, 1932, pp. 77–79.

165   **The centerpiece of the strategy**: Stachura, *Strasser*, pp. 10 and 96–105.

165   **On November 28**: François-Poncet to Herriot, November 29, 1932, *Documents Diplomatiques Français, 1932–1939*, 1re Serie, Tome II (Paris: Imprimerie Nationale, 1966), p. 89.

166   **He told a cabinet meeting**: Anton Golecki, ed., *Das Kabinett von Schleicher* (Boppard am Rhein: Boldt Verlag, 1986) (hereafter *AdR Schleicher*), Dok. 5.

166   **"Should you collaborate"**: Strenge, *Schleicher*, p. 183.

166   **Schleicher and Hitler had met**: *AdR Papen*, Bd. 2, Dok. 232.

167   **In all likelihood**: Strenge, *Schleicher*, p. 183.

167   **The reality was**: Ibid., p. 182.

167   **Soon after accepting**: *AdR Schleicher*, Dok. 25. The Moltke quote is catchier in German: "Erst wägen, dann wagen."

168   **On December 5**: Strenge, *Schleicher*, p. 201.

168   **A note in Goebbels's diary**: Joseph Goebbels, diary entry for December 9, 1932, TB, Teil 1, Bd. 2/III, pp. 77–78. Text of Strasser's letter in Stachura, *Strasser*, pp. 113–14.

169   **This crisis came**: Kershaw, *Hubris*, pp. 399–400.

169   **For his part**: Stachura, *Strasser*, p. 115.

169   **Soon after his resignation**: Ibid.

169   **Yet, although Strasser**: Ibid., p. 116.

170   **"just one run of bad luck"**: Joseph Goebbels, diary entry for December 24, 1932, TB, Teil 1, Bd. 2/III, p. 89.

170   **"Papen caustic"**: Joseph Goebbels, diary entry for January 10, 1933, TB, Teil 1, Bd. 2/III, pp. 102–3.

170   **Papen recalled**: Papen, *Wahrheit*, pp. 253–54.

170   **Schröder's recollection**: Freiherr von Schröder, Vernehmung, June 18, 1947, Institut für Zeitgeschichte ZS 557.

171   **"Hitler poured his bitterest anger"**: Papen, *Wahrheit*, pp. 255–56.

171   **A few days later**: Joseph Goebbels, diary entry for January 10, 1933, TB, Teil 1, Bd. 2/III, pp. 102–3.

172   **At a cabinet meeting on January 16**: *AdR Schleicher*, Dok. 56, cabinet meeting January 16.

172   **Schleicher was still talking to Strasser**: François-Poncet to Paul-Boncour, January 7, 1933, *Documents Diplomatiques Français*, 1re Serie, Tome 2, pp. 375–76.

173   **One difference was**: Kershaw, *Hubris*, p. 415.

174   **The always astute and well-informed**: François-Poncet to Paul-Boncour, January 25, 1933, *Documents Diplomatiques Français*, 1re Serie, Tome 2, pp. 528–29.

174   **Ribbentrop had served**: Joachim von Ribbentrop, *The Ribbentrop Memoirs* (London: Weidenfeld and Nicolson, 1954), pp. 1–15.

174   **in August 1932**: Ibid., p. 21.

175   **To the young Hindenburg**: Turner, *Hitler's Thirty Days*, pp. 114–15.

175   **Papen told Hitler**: Ribbentrop, *Memoirs*, p. 23; Papen, *Wahrheit*, p. 265.

175   **After a long silence**: Turner, *Hitler's Thirty Days*, p. 116.

175   **When Papen met with him**: Ribbentrop, *Memoirs*, p. 23.

175   **Schleicher's staff had prepared**: *AdR Schleicher*, Dok. 56, Anlage 2.

176   **At a dinner**: "Moscow Document," in Turner, *Hitlers Weg zur Macht*, p. 185.

176   **Still, there may well have been more to it**: Turner, *Hitler's Thirty Days*, pp. 128–30; "Moscow Document," in Turner, *Hitlers Weg zur Macht*, p. 179.

176   **On January 23**: Huber, *Verfassungsgeschichte*, 4: 651.

176   **According to Papen**: Papen, *Wahrheit*, p. 266.

176   **As late as January 26**: Huber, *Verfassungsgeschichte*, 4: 655. Hans Mommsen writes that Hammerstein told Hindenburg that, from the army's standpoint a Hitler government, if necessary, was preferable to a Papen-Hugenberg cabinet, to which Hindenburg reacted by rejecting the idea of making the "Austrian private" chancellor. Mommsen's supposition is certainly logical, but Hammerstein's record of the meeting contradicts it. Furthermore, while the English edition of Mommsen's book does not have source notes, the source note supporting this point in the German edition directs the reader to a work that squarely contradicts it: Thilo Vogelsang, *Reichswehr, Staat und NSDAP: Beiträge zur deutschen Geschichte 1930–1932* (Stuttgart: Deutsche Verlags-Anstalt, 1962), pp. 378–79, which gives the view that Hammerstein "expressed warnings" to Hindenburg about Hitler. Hammerstein's record of the meeting was written in 1935, at a time when he would have been under no pressure to distort his narrative to conceal support for Hitler. See Mommsen, *The Rise and Fall of Weimar Democracy* (Chapel Hill: University of North Carolina Press, 1998), pp. 522–23; Mommsen, *Aufstieg und Untergang der Republik von Weimar 1918–1933* (Berlin: Ullstein, 2009), p. 631, 687n44.

177   **At around the same time**: Turner, *Hitler's Thirty Days*, p. 117.

177   **On January 25 . . . On the morning of January 28**: Ribbentrop, *Memoirs*, pp. 24–25; Papen, *Wahrheit*, p. 269.

177   **On that same day**: Otto Meissner, *Staatssekretär unter Ebert, Hindenburg, Hitler* (Hamburg: Hoffmann und Campe Verlag, 1950), p. 266.

178   **François-Poncet reported on January 24**: François-Poncet to Paul-Boncour, January 24, 1933, *Documents Diplomatiques Français*, 1re Serie, Tome 2, pp. 504–5.

178   **the Social Democratic paper**: Strenge, *Machtübernahme*, pp. 108–9.

178   **Monsignor Ludwig Kaas . . . The Prussian prime minister**: Huber, *Verfassungsgeschichte*, 4: 649–50.

179   **Heinrich Brüning remembered**: Brüning, "Ein Brief," p. 15.

179   **and had been fiercely criticized**: Pyta, *Weimar*, p. 151.

179   **On the morning of January 28**: *AdR Schleicher*, Dok. 71.

179   **Schleicher left the cabinet meeting**: Ibid., Dok. 72.

180   **The last act**: Turner, *Hitler's Thirty Days*, p. 133.

180   **Soon after Schleicher's resignation**: Papen, *Wahrheit*, p. 69.

180   **Still, no one quite knew**: Joseph Goebbels, diary entry for January 29, 1933, TB, Teil 1, Bd. 2/III, p. 118.

180   **In the course of Sunday**: Ribbentrop, *Memoirs*, p. 26.

180   **At the Kaiserhof Hotel**: Joseph Goebbels, diary entry for January 30, 1933, TB, Teil 1, Bd. 2/III, p. 119.

181   **Hitler and his entourage**: Ibid.

181   **Even at this stage**: Meissner, *Staatssekretär*, p. 270.

181   **"It has happened"**: Joseph Goebbels, diary entry for January 31, 1933, TB, Teil 1, Bd. 2/III, pp. 120–21.

182   **"We have hired him"**: Fest, *Hitler*, p. 528.

182   **After reporting all the reassuring things**: François-Poncet to Paul-Boncour, January 30, 1933, *Documents Diplomatiques Français*, 1re Serie, Tome 2, pp. 542–43.

183   **The former Reich chief prosecutor**: Erich Ebermayer, *Denn Heute gehört uns Deutschland: Persönliches und politisches Tagebuch* (Hamburg: P. Zsolnay, 1959), p. 13.

183   **"The first stage"**: Joseph Goebbels, diary entry for January 31, 1933, TB, Teil 1, Bd. 2/III, pp. 120–21.

7. COORDINATION

184   **"Because the Reichstag has burned" . . . from all the blood**: Lina Haag, *Eine Handvoll Staub: Widerstand einer Frau 1933–1945* (Frankfurt: Fischer Taschenbuch Verlag, 1995), pp. 8–18.

185   **A few weeks after Lina Haag's arrest**: *Braunbuch über Reichstagsbrand und Hitlerterror*, facsimile of the original 1933 edition (Frankfurt: Roderberg Verlag, 1978), pp. 210–12. Much of the material in the *Braunbuch*, particularly dealing with the Reichstag fire, is unreliable, but the facts of this story are supported by other accounts: see, for instance, Wilhelm Hoegner, *Der schwierige Aussenseiter: Errinerungen eines Abgeordneten, Emigranten und Ministerpräsidenten* (Munich: Isar Verlag, 1959), p. 93.

186   **"It is better to look away"**: Haag, *Eine Handvoll Staub*, p. 23.

186   **Soon enough**: Hett, *Burning the Reichstag*, pp. 69–71.

187   **the constitution of Hitler's Reich**: Ernst Fraenkel, *The Dual State: A Contribution to the Theory of Dictatorship* (New York: Oxford University Press, 1941), p. 3.

187   **Because the Reichstag fire worked out**: Hett, *Burning the Reichstag*; Benjamin Carter Hett, "'This Story Is About Something Fundamental': Nazi Criminals, History, Memory, and the Reichstag Fire," *Central European History* 48, no. 2 (June 2015): 199–224. Until recent years, the prevailing view among historians was that Marinus van der Lubbe indeed acted alone. The most influential writer to take this view was Fritz Tobias: see Tobias, *Der Reichstagsbrand: Legende und Wirklichkeit* (Rastatt: G. Grote'sche Verlagsbuchhandlung, 1962), translated into English, though at half the length, as Tobias, *The Reichstag Fire* (New York: Putnam, 1964). Tobias's view was endorsed by the influential historian Hans Mommsen: Mommsen, "Der Reichstagsbrand und seine politische Folgen," *VfZ* 12 (1964): 365. Massive quantities of original documents that became available only in the mid-1990s have changed the debate, however. See, in particular, Marcus Giebeler, *Die Kontroverse um den Reichstagsbrand: Quellenprobleme und historiographische Paradigmen* (Munich: Martin Meidenbauer Verlagsbuchhandlung, 2010); Hersch Fischler, "Neues zur Reichstagsbrandkontroverse," in *Der Reichstagsbrand und der Prozeß vor dem Reichsgericht*, ed. Dieter Deiseroth (Berlin: Verlagsgesellschaft Tischler, 2006); Alexander Bahar and Wilfried Kugel, *Der Reichstagsbrand: Geschichte einer Provokation* (Cologne: PapyRossa Verlag, 2013). In 2014, the author discovered a document that established beyond doubt that Fritz Tobias, a senior official in one of West Germany's domestic intelligence services, wrote his book on official orders and with a view to rehabilitating former Nazi police officers and creating effective Cold War propaganda. He also fabricated evidence and blackmailed historians who disagreed with him (see Hett, "'This Story Is About Something Fundamental'"). Not all historians are willing to acknowledge the new evidence, however, nor Tobias's regrettable role in the controversy. See Richard J. Evans, "The Conspiracists," *London Review of Books* (*LRB*), May 8, 2014, and "Letters," *LRB*, June 5, 2014, as well as the author's longer response at http://urban.hunter.cuny.edu/~hett/reichstag.html.

189   **In August 1932**: Hermann Pünder, *Politik in der Reichskanzlei. Aufzeichnungen aus den Jahren 1929–1932*, ed. Thilo Vogelsang (Stuttgart: Deutsche Verlags-Anstalt, 1961), p. 141.

190   **The historian Irene Strenge**: This passage follows the main argument in Strenge, *Machtübernahme*.

190   **The Nazis' plan for power**: That the Nazis thought carefully about how to seize power, and planned the process in a legalistic way, is known among historians as an "intentionalist" explanation. It is the kind of explanation that arose and seemed intuitively obvious in the years just after the Second World War. It came to be challenged by what is called the "functionalist" interpretation. Functionalist historians—among them such distinguished scholars as Martin Broszat and Hans Mommsen—objected to what they called the "Hitlercentric" view of the intentionalists, which they saw as an ironic reflection of Nazi propaganda about Hitler's supposed genius and far-seeing mastery of events. Functionalists put much more emphasis on the impact of institutions and structures, and of unplanned and unforeseen events and outcomes, due in part to competition among Nazis

themselves and in part to the inability of even an authoritarian party or state to control everything around it. Starting in the 1960s and gathering speed through the 1970s and 1980s, the intentionalist-functionalist debate was often vitriolic and structured most of the research on all aspects of Nazi Germany. In the 1990s, the debate eased off as the two sides essentially met in the middle, although what might be called a "neo-intentionalist" current has arisen in recent years. Irene Strenge's work could be classed under this heading, along with that of the American historian Timothy Snyder. See particularly Timothy Snyder, *Bloodlands: Europe Between Hitler and Stalin* (New York: Basic Books, 2010).

191   **The plans demonstrated**: Michaelis et al., *Ursachen und Folgen*, Bd. 8, pp. 377–79.

191   **Goebbels's newspaper, *Der Angriff***: Hett, *Burning the Reichstag*, pp. 67–68.

192   **Shortly afterward**: Joseph Goebbels, diary entry for September 16, 1931, TB, Teil 1, Bd. 2/II, pp. 99–100.

192   **Six months later**: Martin Schuster, "Die SA in der nationalsozialistischen "Machtergreifung" in Berlin und Brandenburg 1926–1934" (Berlin: PhD dissertation, 2005), pp. 222–25.

192   **On January 29**: Joseph Goebbels, diary entry for January 30, 1933, TB, Teil 1, Bd. 2/III, p. 119.

192   **On February 1**: Joseph Goebbels, diary entry for February 1, 1933, TB, Teil 1, Bd. 2/III, p. 121.

192   **The new secret police chief**: Diels, *Lucifer Ante Portas*, p. 131.

192   **In a cabinet meeting**: Karl-Heinz Minuth, *Die Regierung Hitler* (Boppard am Rhein: Boldt Verlag, 1983), Bd. 1, pp. 29–30.

193   **Goebbels offered a good example**: Hett, *Burning the Reichstag*, pp. 47–49; Daniel Siemens, *Horst Wessel: Tod und Verklärung eines Nationalsozialisten* (Munich: Siedler Verlag, 2009), pp. 96–98.

193   **Nothing in Goebbels's diary**: Longerich, *Goebbels*, pp. 289–90.

193   **A woman from Braunschweig**: Hedda Kalshoven, *Ich denk so viel an Euch. Ein Deutsch-Holländischer Briefwechsel 1920–1949* (Munich: Luchterhand Literaturverlag, 1995), p. 168.

194   **Looking back years later**: Brüning, *Memoiren*, p. 652.

194   **His model was commercial**: Longerich, *Goebbels*, pp. 81–82.

194   **Goebbels was a quick study**: Pamela E. Swett, *Selling Under the Swastika: Advertising and Commercial Culture in Nazi Germany* (Stanford, CA: Stanford University Press, 2014), p. 42.

194   **Germany's advertising professionals**: Ibid., pp. 42–43.

195   **"how desperately thin"**: Hett, *Death in the Tiergarten*, p. 154.

196   **Elsewhere in Europe**: Mark Mazower, *Dark Continent: Europe's Twentieth Century* (New York: Knopf, 1999), pp. 101–2.

196   **The nationalist conservative writer**: Edgar J. Jung, *Sinndeutung der deutschen Revolution* (Oldenburg: Garhard Stalling, 1933), pp. 42–43 and 46.

197   **Drucker intuitively grasped**: Peter F. Drucker, *The End of Economic Man: A Study of the New Totalitarianism* (New York: John Day, 1939), pp. 18–19.

197   **The best explanation**: Ibid., pp. 13–14.

197   **Nazism could only "accomplish its task"**: Ibid., p. 84.

198   **When the Nazis achieved**: Michaelis et al., *Ursachen und Folgen*, Bd. 8, pp. 129–30.

198   **Early in 1933**: Carl Severing, *Mein Lebensweg*, Bd. 2 (Cologne: Greven Verlag, 1950), pp. 375–76.

198   **The revolutionary socialist**: Ernst Toller, *Eine Jugend in Deutschland* (Reinbek bei Hamburg: Rowohlt, 2006), p. 8.

198   **The sharp-eyed political reporter**: Aust, *Hitlers erster Feind*, pp. 89–90.

199   **In a 1932 book**: Heuss, *Hitlers Weg*, p. 129.

199   **In a direct and material sense**: Aust, *Hitlers erster Feind*, pp. 147–48.

200   **When one of the best of these journalists**: Philip Metcalfe, *1933* (Sag Harbor, NY: Permanent Press, 1988), p. 156.

200   **Soon after becoming chancellor**: Max Domarus, *Hitler: Speeches and Proclamations 1932–1945: The Chronicle of a Dictatorship*, trans. Mary Fran Gilbert (Wauconda, IL: Bolchazy-Carducci Publishers, 1990), 1:252. I have slightly corrected the translation by referring to the German edition of Domarus's compilation.

200   **By 1934**: Richard J. Evans, *The Third Reich in Power* (New York: Penguin, 2005), pp. 148–49.

201   **Yet Hitler had expected more**: Martin H. Sommerfeldt, *Ich war Dabei: Die Verschwörung der Dämonen* (Darmstadt: Drei Quellen Verlag, 1949), pp. 31–32.

202   **At the Lutheran service**: "Staatsakt" in *Verhandlungen des Reichstages*, Bd. 457, p. 4.

202   **The services were followed**: Pyta, *Hindenburg*, p. 822.

202   **"state office must not be mixed"**: "Staatsakt," p. 4.

203   **"the wide square"**: Hoegner, *Der schwierige Aussenseiter*, pp. 92–93. Partial translation in Noakes and Pridham, *Nazism*, 1:159–60.

203   **Hitler opened the debate**: Domarus, *Hitler*, 1:275–85. I have corrected the translation with reference to the German edition.

204   **"It is clear"**: Ibid., 1:287–89.

204   **"You're late in coming"**: Ibid., 1:290–95. I am following the translation of the Schiller text by Flora Kimmich. Friedrich Schiller, *Wallenstein: A Dramatic Poem*, trans. Flora Kimmich, with an introduction by Roger Paulin (Cambridge: Open Book Publishers, 2017).

205   **Heinrich Brüning claimed**: Brüning to Hans Bernd Gisevius, August 20, 1946, IfZ ED 82; Brüning, "Ein Brief," pp. 17–18.

206   **The Nazis called it**: Evans, *Coming of the Third Reich*, p. 381.

206   **In April came the "Law"**: Terms of the law in German Historical Institute, *Deutsche Geschichte in Dokumenten und Bildern*, Bd. 7, http://germanhistorydocs .ghi-dc.org/sub_document.cfm?document_id=2325.

207   **Twelve years later**: "Hitlers Lagebesprechungen am 23., 25., und 27. April 1945," *Der Spiegel*, October 1, 1966; Kershaw, *Nemesis*, p. 814.

8. "WE HAVE TO GET RID OF HIM"

208   **For Fritz Günther von Tschirschky**: Fritz Günther von Tschirschky, *Erinnerungen eines Hochverräters* (Stuttgart: Deutsche Verlags-Anstalt, 1972), pp. 188–89.

208   **Starting at 8:00**: Ibid., pp. 189–91.

209 **When Papen and Tschirschky**: Ibid., pp. 191–94.

209 **It is men**: Orth, *"Amtssitz,"* p. 497.

210 **Papen's staff take this assault**: Ibid., p. 498.

210 **It is just after this**: Ibid., pp. 498–500.

210 **Meanwhile, at 12:30 p.m.**: "Zur Ermordung des Generals Schleichers," *Viertel-jahrshefte fur Zeitgeschichte*, Bd. 1 (1953), pp. 71 and 85–86.

211 **A year later**: Rainer Orth, *Der SD-Mann Johannes Schmidt. Der Mörder des Reichskanzlers Kurt von Schleicher?* (Marburg: Tectum Verlag, 2012), p. 148. Güntel privately gave another, more detailed but in important points consistent account of the murder. Orth makes a plausible case that the SD-man named in his title was Schleicher's killer, perhaps by accident on account of his own nervousness—he might only have been sent to arrest Schleicher.

211 **That afternoon**: Tschirschky, *Erinnerungen*, pp. 194–95; Orth, *"Amtssitz,"* pp. 503–4. There are considerable contradictions in the sources about where Jung's body was found. It seems clear it was taken to a place north of the central city (probably Oranienburg) and, according to former Gestapo officer Hans Bernd Gisevius, that was where his body was found. It might also have been in the north Berlin district of Reinickendorff. Orth, *"Amtssitz,"* pp. 503–4.

212 **Even his commanding officer**: Magub, *Jung*, p. 14.

212 **The much more extroverted**: Tschirschky, *Erinnerungen*, p. 103; Joachim Petzold, *Papen: Ein deutsches Verhängnis* (Munich: Buchverlag Union, 1995), p. 176.

212 **Like other young conservatives**: Magub, *Jung*, p. 81; Petzold, *Papen*, p. 176.

212 **But when Hitler**: Orth, *"Amtssitz,"* p. 445.

212 **On one occasion . . . "We are partly responsible"**: Ibid., pp. 305 and 402.

212 **He became a convinced advocate**: Forschbach, *Jung*, p. 16.

213 **Jung seems to have imagined**: Magub, *Jung*, p. 200.

213 **In part, he disliked**: Ibid., pp. 183, 199, and 201.

213 **In July 1933**: Forschbach, *Jung*, p. 81.

213 **Ballestrem suggested**: Tschirschky, *Erinnerungen*, p. 96.

214 **Tschirschky found**: Ibid., pp. 96–97.

214 **Ketteler and Tschirschky**: Ibid., p. 98.

214 **Over time**: Ibid., pp. 100–104.

214 **The core of the group**: Orth, *"Amtssitz,"* pp. 359–67.

215 **None of these men**: Ibid., pp. 356–57; Forschbach, *Jung*, p. 104; Tschirschky, *Erinnerungen*, p. 135.

215 **Though Papen was oblivious**: Orth, *"Amtssitz,"* p. 900n959.

215 **In April 1933**: Hett, *Burning the Reichstag*, p. 136.

215 **One day, standing in the garden**: Alfred Rosenberg, *The Political Diary of Alfred Rosenberg and the Onset of the Holocaust*, ed. Jürgen Mattäus and Frank Bajohr (New York: Rowman and Littlefield, 2015), p. 36.

215 **It didn't help**: Orth, *"Amtssitz,"* pp. 446–47.

215 **At first, Papen's staff**: Ibid., pp. 359–67; Tschirschky, *Erinnerungen*, pp. 108–9.

216 **Another form of resistance**: Orth, *"Amtssitz,"* pp. 378–80.

216 **They also provided**: Ibid., pp. 396–97.

216 **The vice-chancellery group planned**: Forschbach, *Jung*, pp. 88–89.

216 **The vice-chancellery group put together**: Orth, *"Amtssitz,"* pp. 404–12.

217   **it is likely**: Forschbach, *Jung*, p. 85.

217   **Yet it seems**: Orth, *"Amtssitz,"* p. 419.

218   **By early 1934**: Petzold, *Papen*, p. 176.

218   **The more refined plan**: Tschirschky, *Erinnerungen*, pp. 177–78.

220   **Jung began by**: "Denkschrift Edgar Jung," in Marek Maciejewski, "Edgar Julius Jung und der Nationalsozialismus. Zur Geschichte der 'konservative-revolutionären' Opposition gegen Hitler," in Gerhard Ringhausen and Rüdiger von Voss, eds., *Widerstand und Verteidigung des Rechts* (Bonn: Bouvier Verlag, 1997), pp. 12–21.

221   **"As I came back"**: Tschirschky, *Erinnerungen*, p. 172.

221   **Jung listened to the speech**: Orth, *"Amtssitz,"* p. 463.

221   **Papen's (or Jung's) real message**: Text of Papen's speech in Forschbach, *Jung*, Appendix, pp. 154–74.

223   **The audience had followed**: Tschirschky, *Erinnerungen*, p. 172.

224   **"In the coming years"**: Domarus, *Hitler*, 1:464.

224   **As Edmund Forschbach noted**: Forschbach, *Jung*, pp. 120–21.

225   **If the plans**: Orth, *"Amtssitz,"* pp. 475–76.

225   **He claims**: Papen, *Wahrheit*, p. 344.

225   **Hindenburg's fundamental political goal**: Pyta, *Hindenburg*, p. 845.

226   **There was even worse news**: Ibid., p. 848.

226   **"Who wrote it for him?"**: Joseph Goebbels, diary entry for June 18, 1934, TB Teil 1, Bd. 3/I, p. 65.

226   **They didn't have to look far**: Orth, *"Amtssitz,"* p. 471. See also "Hitler Halts Move to Ban Stahlhelm; Papen Aide Seized," *New York Times*, June 28, 1934.

226   **The chargé d'affaires**: Arnal to Barthou, June 27, 1934, *Documents Diplomatiques Français*, 1er Serie, Teil 6, 795.

226   **On June 22**: Joseph Goebbels, TB June 23, 1934, p. 68.

226   **In these tense days**: Orth, *"Amtssitz,"* pp. 478–79; "Goebbels Berates 'Gentlemen' Critics," *New York Times*, June 22, 1934.

227   **Three days later**: Arnal to Barthou, June 27, 1934, *Documents Diplomatiques Français*, 1er Serie, Teil 6, 795.

227   **In a revealing glimpse**: Joseph Goebbels, diary entry for June 25, 1934, TB Teil 1, Bd. 3/I, p. 69.

227   **That same evening**: Orth, *"Amtssitz,"* p. 480.

228   **The next day . . . in a few days**: Orth, *"Amtssitz,"* p. 480.

228   **Hitler remarked scornfully**: Rosenberg, *Political Diary*, p. 35.

228   **Yet the threat of a coup**: Siemens, *Stormtroopers*, p. 164; Eleanor Hancock, "The Purge of the SA Reconsidered: 'An Old Putschist Trick?'" *Central European History* 44, no. 4 (2011): 671–72.

229   **Tschirschky saw what happened**: Tschirschky, *Erinnerungen*, p. 195.

229   **Hindenburg was highly pleased**: Michaelis et al., *Ursachen und Folgen*, Bd. 10, pp. 195–96.

229   **On July 6**: Joseph Goebbels, diary entry for July 6, 1934, TB Teil 1, Bd. 3/I, p. 76.

230   **"Fragile clues"**: François-Poncet to Barthou, July 18, 1934, *Documents Diplomatiques Français*, 1er Serie, Teil 6, p. 996.

230   **Papen's story**: Petzold, *Papen*, pp. 226–27.

231   **If this were not craven enough**: Papen, *Wahrheit*, pp. 352–66.

231   **In June 1944**: Fabian von Schlabrendorff, *Offiziere gegen Hitler* (Berlin: Siedler Verlag, 1984), p. 109.

235   **"I am German"**: Victor Klemperer, *I Will Bear Witness: A Diary of the Nazi Years*, vol. 2 (1942–1945), trans. Martin Chalmers (New York: Random House, 2001), pp. 63–64.

ACKNOWLEDGMENTS

At the end of a project, it is always a pleasure to thank those who offered crucial help.

First of all, I must thank my agent, Scott Mendel, and my editor at Henry Holt, Paul Golob, without whose encouragement and creative inspiration this book would never have come about. It helps immensely that both gentlemen are a real pleasure to work with.

A book of this nature inevitably rests on the work of countless other scholars. While writing it, I have had the pleasure of reading a great deal of brilliant scholarship on the end of Weimar and the rise of the Nazis. The notes record my debts.

Several colleagues made invaluable contributions to my thinking on this period. Dagmar Herzog gave me the benefit of her tremendous knowledge of German Protestants and the history of sexuality, and she put me on to the work of Richard Karwehl, her own grandfather. My regular lunch conversations with Christoph Kimmich have amounted to an education in themselves. As he has been before, Christoph was also very generous in reading a draft of this book and offering extensive and careful feedback. Helena Rosenblatt kindly gave me advice on my French translations.

I am very grateful to Professor Benjamin Friedman, Professor Barry

Eichengreen, and Professor Edmund Clingan for generously helping me understand some of the finer points of the gold standard and the financial crises of the early 1930s.

My very talented graduate student Ky Woltering helped enormously with research on German Protestants in the Weimar era. With patience and good humor, Ky has managed to get me to understand a bit of theology as it pertains to midcentury politics.

I am also grateful to Jenna Dolan for her careful copyediting of the manuscript. Her work has saved me from many errors.

Needless to say, all remaining errors and wayward judgments are solely my own responsibility.

This is the fourth book that my wife, Corinna, has had to endure. As always, she responded with loyalty, generosity, and good humor. My gratitude can hardly be put into words, but my life would be unimaginable without her.

Given the theme of this book and the times we live in, the dedication speaks for itself.

INDEX

Abegg, Wilhelm, 149
Abel, Werner, 117–18
Action Française, 104
Adenauer, Konrad, 24
advertising, 66, 194
agriculture, 70–72, 85–86, 109, 135, 140, 173, 233
Allies (World War I), 21–22, 48, 57, 82, 115, 118, 120
Alsace-Lorraine, 90
Altona murders ("Bloody Sunday"), 149, 165
Amann, Max, 46, 48
anti-intellectualism (Nazi), 196, 212, 223
antisemitism, xviii, 41, 47, 49–51, 59, 72–73, 99–103, 111–12, 115, 195, 197, 213, 234
Armenian genocide, 115
Armistice (1918), 5, 13, 17, 21–22, 30–31, 41, 45–46, 48, 50–52, 79, 87, 135
Arrow Cross, 118
Asquith, H. H., 18
Atatürk, Mustafa Kemal, 114–15, 145
Aufbau (Reconstruction) group, 115
August 1914 vs. November 1918, ii, 30–31, 52, 110–11, 163–64, 202, 232–33. See also myth of 1914; Revolution of 1918
Auschwitz, 235
Austria, xiv, 29, 42–43, 117, 197
annexation of, 98, 230

customs union proposed, 120–21, 123–24
Austrian legitimists, 228
Austro-Hungarian Empire, 44
autarky, 109–11, 113–14, 220
authoritarianism, 12, 80, 93, 101, 104, 168
automation (rationalization), 86, 94, 113

Babi Yar, 235
Baden, Prince Max von, xi, 15–17, 56
Baedeker Guide to Berlin, 99
Ballestrem, Nikolaus von, 213–14
Bank for International Settlements, 108
Bank of England, 107, 122
banks, 70, 86, 92, 97, 107, 123–24. See also financial system
Banuscher, Johann, 94–95
Baranowski, Shelley, 69
Barth, Karl, 103
Bauer, Max, xi, 31, 34
Bavaria, xii, 22, 43, 47–50, 52, 105, 203, 206
Bavarian Army, 44, 46–48
Bavarian People's Party, xviii, 67–68, 132, 166
Bavarian Reserve Infantry (List) Regiment 16, 44, 46
Bebel, August, 72
Beer Hall Putsch, 53–54, 61, 115, 117, 129, 142, 233
Behrends, Hermann, 210
Belgium, 19–21, 29, 56–57, 90, 98, 112

Bennett, John Wheeler, 227
Berlin, xiii, xvii, 1–3, 23–24, 31, 35, 49,
    62–72, 81, 94–95, 125–28, 148,
    161–64, 185, 207
    transit strike, 166
    uprising of 1919, 49
Berliner Lokal-Anzeiger, 59
Berliner Tageblatt, 37, 97, 199
Berlin police, 187, 192
Best, Werner, 191–92
Bethmann-Hollweg, Theobald von, 21
Bismarck, Prince Otto von, 126, 160
Black Reichswehr, 83
Blomberg, Werner von, 177
"Blood May" (1929), 62–65
"Bloody Sunday." See Altona murders
Boer War, 206
Bolsheviks, 23, 105, 112
border, Germany's eastern, 57, 87, 90, 99,
    111–14, 120, 136
Borsig, Albert, 208
Bose, Herbert von, xi, 208, 210, 214–15,
    217, 230–32, 234
Boxheim Documents, 191–92
Bracht, Franz, 149
Brandenburg (concentration camp), 207
Braun, Otto, xi, 77, 88, 135–36, 139,
    142–43, 149–50, 172, 178, 198, 217
Braunschweig, 90, 129, 138, 193
Brecht, Bertolt, 7, 66, 68
Bredow, Ferdinand von, 164–65, 217–18
Briand, Aristide, xi, xv, 55, 57–58, 60,
    91–92, 98, 119–21, 213
Britain, 10, 27, 33, 56, 60, 92, 106–7, 114,
    114, 119, 121–24, 195–96, 216, 230
    House of Commons, 24–25
    intelligence, 145, 227
    World War I and, 18–19, 22, 233
    World War II and, 231
Brückner, Wilhelm, 35
Brüning, Heinrich, xii, 12, 84–93, 107, 112,
    118–25, 129, 132–44, 146–48, 152–53,
    164, 167, 173, 179, 181–82, 190, 194,
    205, 213, 217–18, 227, 234
Bülow, Bernhard von, 107–8, 112, 121
Buwert, Karl, 1

cabinet
    Brüning's, 89–90, 92, 112, 119–21, 137
    constitution and, 25–26
    fighting, 170
    Hitler's, 179, 181–83, 187, 192–93, 217,
        231
    Papen's, 147, 153–54, 160–61, 165, 177
    presidential vs. parliamentary, 84,
        179–80
    Schleicher's, 166, 168–70, 172, 176,
        179–80
capitalism, 10, 13, 33, 72, 80, 98, 106–8,
    111, 168, 192, 196–97
Catholics, xiv, xviii, 3, 9, 11–12, 26, 67–69,
    77, 84, 87–88, 101–2, 104, 132–33, 146,
    160, 178, 202, 213, 216–17, 220, 222,
    234
censorship, 218, 224
Center Party, xii, xiv, xviii, 21, 24, 31,
    67–68, 77, 79, 83–84, 97, 102, 104–5,
    132, 135–36, 143, 146, 148–49,
    153–54, 159, 166, 178, 182, 203, 205,
    213
Chamberlain, Austen, 58, 60
Chamberlain, Houston Stewart, 14
Chamberlain, Neville, 41
chancellor, constitutional powers of,
    25–27, 83
Chaplin, Charlie, 43
Chicago Daily News, 64
Christianity, 9, 100, 212, 213, 223. See also
    Catholics; Protestants
Christmas Amnesty (1933), 185
cities, 69–72, 99–100, 111, 115, 127–28.
    See also rural-urban divide
citizenship, denial of, 99–100, 113,
    115
civil service, 28, 206
civil war, 14, 16, 61, 73, 129, 132–33,
    152–55, 158, 160–61, 165, 167, 170,
    172, 176–77, 179
Clemenceau, Georges, 18
Cockburn, Claud, 55
Cold War, end of, 9–10
Combat League Against Fascism, 95–96,
    126
Communist International (Comintern),
    xvii, 74, 85, 113
Communist Party of Germany (KPD), xii,
    xiv, xvii, 2–3, 6, 11, 13, 20–21, 23–24,
    36, 47, 49, 64–68, 70, 73–74, 94, 97,
    104–5, 112–13, 118, 122, 125–28, 132,
    134, 138, 144, 148–50, 153–54, 157–59,
    161, 166–68, 174–76, 184–87, 191–95,
    202, 216
    Munich uprising of 1919, 47
    Nazi street battles vs., 36, 64–65, 94, 97,
        127–28, 149
    Nazi violence blamed on, 189–92
    Reichstag fire and, 2–3, 6, 184–85, 187,
        189, 193–94, 201
    Soviet Union and, 112–13
concentration camps, 3, 6, 38, 62, 67–68,
    185, 206–7, 213, 235
confessional divisions, 67–68, 146, 150

conservatives, 11, 21, 28, 32, 59, 70, 77, 130, 133, 163–64, 182–83, 205–7, 219, 228, 230, 234–35
Constitution (Bismarckian, 1871), 27–28
Constitution (Weimar, 1919), 5–7, 11–12, 24–27, 56, 79, 82–84, 102, 138, 147, 175, 198
  Article 24, 156
  Article 42, 156
  Article 43 (impeachment), 152, 178
  Article 48 (emergency powers), 26–27, 83–84, 88, 149
  Article 52, 25
  Article 54, 25
  Article 59 (prosecution of president), 152
  Nazi rise to power and, 154, 156, 159–60, 218
  Reichstag Fire Decree and, 6, 187
Cordemann, Reinhold, 165
Corriere d'Italiano, 117
Cotton, Joseph P., 119
Could We Have Avoided, Won, or Broken Off the War? (Bauer), 31
Council of People's Deputies (1918), 22, 23
Council of the League of Nations, 91
coup d'état, 88, 181, 192
cross-front plan, 164–68
Curtius, Julius, 92, 121
Czechoslovakia, 57, 98

D'Abernon, Viscount, 55
Dachau (concentration camp), 206, 213
Daluege, Kurt, 215
Dawes, Charles, 56
Dawes Plan, 56, 61, 108
Day of Potsdam, 201–3, 205, 217
death penalty, 7
Defense Ministry, xii, xiv–xv, 136–37, 144, 147, 161, 171
deflation, 118–19, 135
democracy
  compromise and, 14, 75
  end of, 3, 216, 232–35
  gold standard and, 107–8
  hostility to, 14, 27, 33–34, 72, 101–4, 139, 194, 212–13
  key insurgencies and, 74–75
  Papen and, 148–50
  Schleicher and, 142
  Stresemann and, 59–60
  Weimar constitution and, 7–8, 26–27
democratic block, 21, 24, 28, 32–33, 79
Denmark, 29
deportations, 6, 99
Depression, 12, 85, 92, 96, 98, 113, 118–26, 133, 138, 140, 150, 160, 199

Der Angriff, 36, 191
Deutsche Rundschau, 212
Dibelius, Otto, 101–2, 202, 217
Diels, Rudolf, xii, 2, 148–50, 189, 192
Die Rote Fahne, 94
Dix, Otto, 7
Döblin, Alfred, 8
Dostoevsky, Fyodor, 116
Doumer, Paul, 121
Drexler, Anton, 20, 50
Dreyfus, Alfred, 195
Drucker, Peter, 197
Duesterberg, Theodor, 90, 138–39, 217
Dunckern, Anton, 209

Eastern Aid (scandals of), 173, 178
eastern Europe, 22, 109, 112, 114, 231, 234
Eastern Front, 77
East European Jews, 71, 99
East Prussia, xiii, 71, 76, 85, 112, 140, 151, 173, 178
Ebermayer, Ludwig, 183
Ebert, Friedrich, xii, xiv, 15–17, 22–24, 56, 65, 75, 142
economic problems, 12–13, 52, 56, 61, 71–72, 82, 84, 86, 90, 107–8, 113–14, 118–24, 129, 133, 150, 176, 218, 231. See also deflation; globalization; inflation; unemployment
eight-hour workday, 7, 80, 82
Einstein, Albert, 8
Eisner, Kurt, 47
elections
  of 1907, 56
  of 1912, 20
  of 1917, 21
  of 1919, xviii, 5, 24, 46
  of 1920, 49
  of 1924, 79–80
  of 1925, xviii, 12, 79
  of 1928, 59, 79–80, 84–85, 89–90, 90, 96, 117
  of 1929, 85, 90
  of 1930, 36, 89–90, 92–93, 96–98, 118, 133
  of 1932, 5, 11, 68, 86, 138, 140, 143–44, 147, 150–54, 158–60, 166, 169, 173, 182
  of 1933, 68, 167, 171, 173–74, 180–81, 187, 201–2, 216–17
elections, presidential, 25
  of 1925, 75, 79–80, 139, 146
  of 1932, 137–40
electoral system, 7, 24–25, 27, 194–95
elites, 9, 19, 72, 98, 104–5, 212, 222, 147
Eltz-Rübenach, Paul von, 182

emergency powers, 6, 11, 26
Enabling Act (1933), 180, 190, 201–6,
     216
Enlightenment, 194, 196
equality, 7, 19, 100, 104–5, 212
Erzberger, Matthias, 31, 50–51
eugenics, 196
Eupen-Malmedy, 90
European integration, 57, 60, 91–92, 109,
     124, 213, 220, 222–24, 233
European Union, 91–92, 220
evangelical Christians, 9, 104
executive orders, 82–84, 88–89, 133, 135,
     147, 152, 168, 176, 190
exports, 69, 109, 111, 124, 220

fascism, appeal of, 105, 116, 118, 220
Fatherland Party, 20, 21, 31
Federal Republic of Germany (West
     Germany), 24, 55
federal system, 22, 212–13
     Nazi attack on, 6, 206, 231
Felseneck (garden colony), 94–95, 127–28,
     189, 193
feminism, 7, 28, 72–73
Fest, Joachim, 13
financial crises, 97, 123
financial system, 107–11, 113, 122. See also
     globalization
Fischer, Rudolf, 142
Flechtheim, Alfred, 66
Flöter, Hans, 1
Fontane, Theodor, 125
food imports, 106, 109, 119, 191
food prices, 69–70, 72, 85, 106, 119
Ford, Henry, 115
foreign loans, 86, 107–9, 119, 123–24
Foreign Ministry (German), xv, 107, 121,
     137, 182
foreign policy, 26, 33, 69, 82–83, 87,
     109–10, 114–15, 121
foreign press, 200, 216, 227
Forschbach, Edmund, 213, 217, 224
Fraenkel, Ernst, 6
France, 33, 55–58, 90–92, 107, 114, 123–25,
     194–96, 216
     loan offer, 119–21, 124
     territories lost to, 29, 53, 56–57, 82,
          90–91, 98, 112
     World War I and, 20, 22, 233
Franco-German reconciliation, 12, 57–58,
     60, 87, 91, 113, 119, 121
François-Poncet, André, xii, 81–82, 87,
     146, 157, 165–66, 172, 174, 178,
     182–83, 211, 229–30
Franco-Prussian war, 76–77, 145

Frank, Hans, 38, 42
Frankfurter Zeitung, 14, 199
Free Conservative Party, xviii, 79
Free Corps (Freikorps), 23–24, 48, 65, 110
Freedom Law, proposed, 106
Freemasons, 13
Freisler, Roland, 103
French Revolution (1789), 196, 212
Freud, Sigmund, 195
Freundeskreis der Wirtschaft (Friends of
     the Economy), 170
Frick, Wilhelm, xii, 4, 6, 90, 142, 152–53,
     175, 181–82, 190, 216–17
Fried, Ferdinand (Friedrich
     Zimmermann), 109, 113–14
Friedrich II, the "Great," King of Prussia,
     125, 202
Friedrich Wilhelm I, King of Prussia, 202
Frischauer, Willi, 2
Fritsch, Werner von, 216, 218, 226
Fromm, Bella, 97
Funk, Walther, 224–25
Fürst, Margo, 62–63
Fürst, Max, 5, 62–63, 207

Galen, Clemens von, 217
Gallipoli (campaign), 114
Gayl, Baron Wilhelm von, 156
gay rights, 7, 28, 68, 100
Gemeinhardt, Max, 63
genocide, 7, 115
Gereke, Günther, 164–65
German Army, xiii, xv, 4–5, 11–12, 21–24,
     26, 29–31, 70, 78, 80–85, 112, 129,
     132–33, 136, 142, 151, 161, 167, 170,
     176, 177, 182, 202, 216–18, 226,
     228–31, 233–34
     High Command, 93, 219, 228–29
     Ministerial Office, 12, 82
German Conservative Party, xviii, 79
German Democratic Party (DDP), xviii,
     24, 49, 67, 80, 89, 96, 129, 132, 134–36,
     157, 170, 205
German Democratic Republic (East
     Germany), 9, 66
German Empire, 27–28, 76, 145
Germania, 146, 178, 213, 224
German Jews, 99–100, 126, 213, 235
German National People's Party (German
     Nationals), xii, xviii–xix, 4, 20, 37, 49,
     59–60, 67, 74–75, 79–80, 90, 96–97,
     101, 104–5, 116, 126–27, 129–30,
     133–38, 144, 146, 153–54, 157–58,
     166, 174, 179–80, 201, 205, 217
German Navy (Imperial), 29, 33, 120, 124
     mutiny of 1918, 22

German People's Party, xv, xviii, 56, 67, 79–80, 205

German Workers' Party (later National Socialist German Workers' Party), xiv, xix, 20, 50–51

Gestapo, xii, 6, 42, 150, 185, 191, 200, 209–10, 216, 224, 228–30

Gewehr, Hans Georg, 189

Gisevius, Hans Bernd, 189

Gleichschaltung (coordination), 206, 216

globalization, 10, 33–34, 106–14, 118, 122, 124–25, 150, 219

Goebbels, Joseph, xii, 2, 37, 109–10, 116–17, 125–28, 130–31, 138–39, 143–44, 149, 152–54, 158, 163–64, 168–71, 175, 180–81, 183, 190–94, 196, 200, 206–7, 216, 218–19, 221, 223–27, 229

Goerdeler, Carl, 217–18

Goethe, Johann Wolfgang von, 28, 71

gold reserves, 98, 107, 122–23

gold standard, 10, 107–8, 111, 113, 121, 123–24

Göring, Hermann, xii, 2–4, 116, 137, 143–44, 151–53, 157, 163, 169, 175, 180–83, 186–87, 192, 196, 201, 205, 209, 215, 218, 228

Gothein, Georg, 32

Graml, Hermann, 90

Great Coalition (1928–30), xiv, 79

Great Dictator, The (film), 43

Greater Berlin Workers' and Soldiers' Council, 23

Groener, Wilhelm, xii, 16, 23–24, 81–82, 137, 140–44

Grosz, George, 7, 68

Güntel, Marie, 210–11

Gürtner, Franz, xii–xiii, 154, 182

Haag, Alfred, 185

Haag, Lina, 184–86, 207

Haber, Fritz, 8

Habsburg Empire, 112

Haffner, Sebastian, 30

Hamburger Echo, 178

Hammerstein-Equord, Kurt von, xiii, 141, 143, 177, 207

Hanfstaengl, Ernst, 40–41, 53, 96, 138

Harden, Maximilian, 126

Hayek, Friedrich, 197

Heiden, Konrad, xiii, 38, 41, 51, 133–34, 198–99

Heine, Wolfgang, 198

Helldorff, Wolf-Heinrich Count von, xiii, 143, 190, 192

Hess, Rudolf, 41, 54, 96

Heuss, Theodor, 14, 55, 126, 199, 217

Heydrich, Reinhard, 191

Hiedler, Johann Georg, 42

Hiedler, Johann Nepomuk, 42

Himmler, Heinrich, xiii, 174–75, 209–10, 228

Hindenburg, Annemarie von, 77

Hindenburg, Gertrude von (née von Sperrling), 77

Hindenburg, Oskar von, xiii, 77, 82, 125, 137, 143, 159, 173–75, 177

Hindenburg, Paul von, xiii–xv, xviii, 7, 78, 84, 114, 145, 158–59, 204
 abdication of Kaiser and, 16
 background of, 75–79
 Brüning and, 84, 88–89, 118, 120–21, 123–25, 133–44, 147, 182
 chancellors controlled by, 11–13, 82
 death of, 219, 229, 231–32
 Hitler and, 3–5, 11, 129–30, 137, 142, 151–65, 170–82, 186, 190, 201, 205–7, 224–26, 234–35
 impeachment threats and, 174, 178–79, 190
 Nazi rule and, 214, 216, 218–19
 Night of the Long Knives and, 229
 Papen and, 146–47, 149, 165, 171–78, 224–26
 presidential elections and, 137–40
 Reichstag Fire Decree and, 6, 187
 Reichstag opening of March 1933 and, 201–2
 SA ban and, 140–41
 Schleicher and, 82–84, 142–43, 151–53, 171–80
 "stab in the back" and, 31–32, 48–49
 Versailles and, 21, 142
 World War I and, 18, 21, 76–79

Hitler, Adolf, xiii. See also National Socialist German Workers' Party
 antisemitism and, 41–42, 46–48, 73, 100, 115, 196
 Atatürk and, 114–15
 Bavarian Army and, 47–50
 Beer Hall Putsch and, 53–54, 61, 115, 233
 big business and, 134
 big lie and, 37–39
 borders and, 112
 Brüning and, 88, 133–34, 137, 143
 chancellorship ambitions of, 152–56, 159, 168–78, 174–75, 190–92
 chancellorship appointment of, xiii, xiv, 3–7, 163, 177–87, 200–201, 207–8, 224–26, 235
 dictatorship of, after death of Hindenburg, xiv, 218–19, 231

Hitler, Adolf (*cont'd*)
  early life of, xiv, 42–49
  education and, 43, 52–53
  electoral path to power and, 11, 61, 96, 98, 129, 138–40, 201–2
  Enabling Act and, 180, 190, 201–2, 206
  failure of opposition to, 14
  Führer title and, xiv, 116, 231
  German citizenship and, 138
  Germans' inability to foresee impact of, 232–35
  globalization and, 106, 113–14
  Goebbels and, xii, 125, 194
  Great Depression and, 85
  Hindenburg's resistance to, 137–38, 142, 152, 154–56, 170, 173–77, 181–82, 190
  Hugenberg and, 61, 129–30
  Iron Crosses and, 45, 54
  irrationality and, 13–14, 45, 196
  Italian Fascists and, 116–18
  justice system and, 200–201
  living space (*Lebensraum*) and, 113–14, 117
  Ludendorff and, 34, 114
  Munich Soviet Republic of 1919 and, 47–48
  nationalist insurgency of 1920s and, 74
  national unity and, 14
  Nazi Party joined and named by, xix, 20, 50–51
  Night of the Long Knives and, 209–11, 228–30
  Papen and, xiv, 170–81
  Papen's Marburg speech and, 222–26, 228
  personality of, 9, 13–14, 39–41, 52–53
  Potempa murderers and, 165, 171
  press and, 200
  propaganda and, 100, 131–32, 194
  Protestant middle-class and, 67–68
  Reichstag fire and, 2–3, 6, 187–88, 200–201
  Reichstag opening of 1933 and, 202–5
  rhetoric and appeal of, 5, 14, 39–41, 49–53, 85, 198–99
  Ribbentrop and, 174
  rise of, 4–6, 9, 11, 61, 234-35
  Schleicher and, 81, 85, 93, 134, 141–43, 151–53, 155, 165–69, 172
  South Tyrol and, 117–18
  Stormtroopers and, 35–38, 140, 151, 190, 219
  Strasser and, xv, 111, 165–66, 168–69
  Stresemann and, 60–61
  total war and, 114
  Valkyrie plot vs., 217, 231–32
  vice-chancellery plot vs., 212–32
  Weimar democracy and, 7–8
  witness at sedition trial (1930) and, 5
  writes *Mein Kampf*, xiv, 5, 38–41, 43–44, 46, 47, 53–54, 199
  World War I and, 17–18, 41, 44–46, 110
  World War II and, 207
  Young Plan and, 61, 106
Hitler, Alois, 42–43
Hitler, Klara (née Pölzl), 42–43
Hitler's Path (Heuss), 199
Hoegner, Wilhelm, 111, 203
Hoffmann, Heinrich, 41
Hoffmann, Max, 76
Holmes, Oliver Wendell, Jr., 27
Hoover, Herbert, 119, 122–23
Hoover Moratorium, 123–25
Horthy, Miklós, 118
Hugenberg, Alfred, xix, 20, 58–61, 74, 80, 85, 87–88, 96–97, 106, 116, 129, 134, 136–37, 140, 177, 179–82, 201, 205, 234
Hungary, 118
hunger, 22, 119, 123, 132
Huxley, Julian, 196

IG Farben, 199
immigrants, 10, 99, 112, 125
Independent Social Democratic Party (Independents), xvii, 16–17, 20, 22–23, 31, 47, 49, 65, 67
individual rights and freedoms, 6, 7, 24, 84, 103, 187, 205, 212, 220, 223
industry, 28, 70, 86, 109, 124, 212–13, 220
inflation, 14, 107
  hyperinflation, 53, 56, 73, 124, 233
Inner Mission, 103–4
interest rates, 98
Interior Ministry (Prussia), xvii, 4, 181, 183, 192
Interior Ministry (Reich), xii, xv, 4, 119, 137, 153, 171, 181, 182, 216
"invisible occupation," 108
Iron Front, 127
irrationality, 13–14, 30, 32, 103, 194–201, 235
Isherwood, Christopher, 68
Italian Fascists, 116–18, 220
Italy, 10, 33, 56, 104, 116–17, 232

Jankowski, Maria, 185–86, 203
Japan, 33
Jehovah's Witnesses, 100
Jews, 5, 7, 13, 28, 36, 39, 42, 46–52, 59, 70, 72–73, 97, 99–100, 102, 111–15, 125–27, 154, 191, 195, 197–98, 206–7.

See also antisemitism, German Jews, Russian Jews
job creation, 164, 180
Jung, Edgar Julius, xiv, 29, 163, 196, 211–32, 234
Justice Ministry (Reich), xii, 154, 182
justice system, Nazi crackdown on, 199–201, 223, 230. *See also* rule of law

Kaas, Ludwig, 178
Kafka, Franz, 8
Kant, Immanuel, 28, 71
Karwehl, Richard, 103
Kästner, Erich, 71
Kellogg, Frank, 57
Kellogg-Briand Pact (1928), 57
Kelsen, Hans, 197
Keppler, Wilhelm, 174–75
Kessler, Count Harry, 96–97, 147–48
Ketteler, Wilhelm von, 214–15, 230
Keynes, John Maynard, 123–24
Kiaulehn, Walter, 6
Kirchner, Ernst Ludwig, 7
Kisch, Egon Erwin, 66, 200, 207
Klemke, Fritz, 94, 127–28, 193
Klemperer, Victor, 235
Knickerbocker, H. R., 110
Königgrätz, Battle of, 76–77
Königsberg, 150, 153
Kreuzzeitung, 28, 104
Krupps (firm), 58
Kubizek, August, 52–53
Kyffhäuser League, 138

labor, compulsory, 191
Labor Ministry, 153, 182
labor unions, 80, 164–66, 216, 218, 233–34
Landvolk (Country People) movement, 72, 74, 85, 106
Lang, Fritz, 7, 126
Lausanne, Treaty of (1923), 115
Law for the Restoration of the Professional Civil Service (1933), 206
League for the Renewal of the German Reich, 80
League of German Girls, 202
League of Nations, 19, 29, 57, 59, 91, 196
Leber, Julius, 217
Le Bon, Gustav, 195
Lederer, Emil, 109
left, 20–23, 56, 64–65, 80, 83, 113, 126, 190, 207
  uprisings of 1918, 23
  uprisings of 1919, 47–49
  uprisings of 1923, 53
Leibstandarte SS Adolf Hitler, 209

Lemkin, Raphael, 7
Lemmer, Ernst, 128
Lessing, Theodor, 72–73
Leuna (chemical factory), 199
Levetzow, Magnus von, 78
Ley, Robert, 164
liberals, 10, 21, 28, 56, 59, 72, 96–97, 102–3, 126, 178, 184–87, 190, 196, 199, 207, 213, 223
Liebermann, Max, 163
Liebknecht, Karl, 16–17, 23–24, 65
Lippe-Detmold, 171, 173–74
List, Julius, 44
Litfass, Ernst, 131
Litten, Hans, 5, 36–38, 207
living space (*Lebensraum*), 5, 113–14, 117
Lloyd George, David, 18, 19, 41
Locarno Treaties (1925), 56–57, 59–61, 75, 90, 91
Lower Saxony, 85
Lubbe, Marinus van der, 2, 188–89, 193, 200–201
Ludendorff, Erich, xi, xii, xiv, 18, 21, 23, 31–34, 48–49, 53–54, 76–78, 85, 114, 194
Luther, Hans, 57–59, 92, 108–9
Luther, Martin, 101, 118, 160
Lutheran Church, 9, 11, 71, 77, 101, 103–4, 202
Luxemburg, Rosa, 23–24, 65

MacArthur, Douglas, 145
MacDonald, Ramsay, 122
Manchester Guardian, 83
Mann, Heinrich, 8
Mann, Thomas, 8, 55, 196
Marburg University League, Papen speech at (1934), 221–28, 231
March on Rome (1922), 53
Marx, Wilhelm, xviii, 79, 83, 146
Marxists, 5, 154, 190, 222
Maschmann, Hans-Hermann, 162
Maschmann, Melita, 162–63
Maurras, Charles, 104
Mayr, Karl, xiv, 48–50
media and press, 28, 100, 126–28, 131–32, 186–90, 193, 199–200, 206–7, 218
Mein Kampf (Hitler), xiv, 5, 38–41, 43–44, 46, 47, 53, 54, 199
Meissner, Otto, xiv, 82–83, 88, 137, 143, 155–56, 159, 165, 174–75, 177, 181
Mendelsohn, Erich, 68
Migliorati (Captain), 117–18
military dictatorship, 85, 167
military spending, 74, 83–84, 107, 124
minority rights, 212

Mises, Ludwig von, 197
Mjölnir (Hans Herbert Schweitzer), 131–32
modernity, 72, 102–3
Mohnke, Wilhelm, 207
Moltke, Count Helmuth James von, 103
Moltke, Count Helmuth von, the Elder, 168
Mommsen, Theodor, 72
monarchists, 16–17, 28, 101, 104, 219, 228
Mosse (press empire), 59
Mowrer, Edgar Ansel, 200
Moyzischewitz, Arno von, 217
Müller, Hermann, xiv, 79, 84–86, 88–89, 146, 181
Müller, Vincenz, 81–82, 93
Munich, 24, 47–54, 61, 96
    Soviet Republic of 1919, 24, 47–49, 52
Murnau, F. W., 8
Mussolini, Benito, 53, 115–17, 224
myth of 1914, 29–32, 105, 202–3. *See also* August 1914 vs. November 1918; "stab in the back" myth
Myth of the Twentieth Century, The (Rosenberg), xv

national assembly of 1919, 24, 32–33
nationalists, 19, 21, 32–34, 39, 56, 58, 59, 72–74, 84, 87, 90–92, 101–2, 104–6, 117, 120–21, 124, 129, 233
nationalization, 99, 109
National Liberals, 56, 79
National Socialist German Workers' Party (Nazis), xii, xiv, xv, xix. *See also* Hitler, Adolf; *and specific events; issues; individuals; and paramilitary forces*
    appeal of program of, 14, 98–106, 113
    autarky and, 109–10
    Berlin and, xii, 70, 125–28
    borderlands and, 112–13
    breakthrough of 1930, 198
    Brüning and, 87, 122–23, 133, 137
    civil war threat and, 161
    Communist street fights vs., 66, 94–96, 127–28, 149
    contempt for truth and reason, 13–14, 195–200
    crackdown on political enemies by, 184–88, 200
    declared sole political party, 206
    demand for power of 1932, 153–60
    Depression and, 85
    early days of, in Munich, 50–54
    elections of 1924 and, 79

elections of 1928 and, 79–80, 89–90, 96, 111, 117
elections of 1929 and, 90
elections of 1930 and, 89–90, 92–93, 96–98
elections of 1932 and, 11, 36, 67–68, 86, 111, 137–39, 143, 150–51, 158–59
elections of March 5, 1933 and, 67-68, 201–2
elections of November 1933 and, 216–17
electorate coalition of, 85, 101
Enabling Act and, 180, 190, 201–6, 216
flag of, 127
foreign influences on, 10, 114–18
German Nationals and, 129–30, 134–36
Germans' inability to imagine worst actions of, 235
globalization and, 106–10, 114, 118
grassroots organizing and, 90
Groener and, 143–44
Hindenburg and, 130, 137, 151–54, 173–74, 176
Hitler's appointment as chancellor and, 4, 162–64, 181–83
Hugenberg and, 61, 80, 129–30
ideology of, 98, 113
justice system and, 200–201
Landvolk and, 72
Lippe-Detmold elections of 1933 and, 173–74
living space (*Lebensraum*) and, 113–14
Munich uprising of 1923, 53–54
myth of 1914 and, 31–32
named, 20, 50
national unity and, 103, 105–7
negative majority and, 175
Night of the Long Knives and, 208–11, 228–30
Ott on war games vs., xiv, 160–61, 166
Papen and, 147–48, 170–74
paramilitary and, 126, 163
plan to take power, 151–54, 190–93
political tactics of, 98–99
post-1933 actions, prefigured in rise of, 14
Potempa murders and, 151, 153, 159, 165, 171, 186
press censorship and, 100–101, 199–200
program and Twenty-Five Points of, 98–106, 113, 199
propaganda and lies of, 37–39, 131–32, 195–99
Protestant middle-class and, 67–68, 101–6
Prussian coup and, 148–50
reasons for rise of, 7–14, 189–90, 232–35

Reichstag debates and, 128
Reichstag fire and, 2–3, 187–89, 193–94
Reichstag opening of 1933 and, 201–6
reparations and, 122
resistance vs., by vice-chancellery cell, 212–28
rule consolidated by, 218–19
Schleicher and, 83, 93, 132–35, 140–44, 147–48, 164–70, 171–74
Stormtroopers trial of 1931 and, 35–37
Strasser and, 110, 168–69, 172
total war and, 114
underestimated by political elite, 5–6
Versailles Treaty and, 29
World War I and, 10–11
Young Plan and, 129
national unity, 98, 103, 135, 163–64, 201–4, 225, 232, 235
Nation at War (Ludendorff), 33–34
naval blockade of 1917–18, 22, 123
Nazi Party. *See* National Socialist German Workers' Party
Neurath, Konstantin von, 182
Niemöller, Martin, 103
Nietzsche, Friedrich, 195
Night of the Long Knives, 208–11, 228–30, 234–35
Nolde, Emil, 7
Norman, Montagu, 122
Nuremberg Laws (1935), 42
Nuremberg trials, 9, 46, 181, 189

Oberer Kuhberg (concentration camp), 185, 207
Oberfohren, Ernst, 130, 205
Ohnesorge, Kurt, 37
Olden, Rudolf, 37–38
Oldenburg-Januschau, Elard von, 177
"On the Meaning and Interpretation of the German Revolution" (Rosenberg), 226
Oranienburg (concentration camp), 207
Orwell, George, 69
Ossietzky, Carl von, 65, 200, 207
Ott, Eugen, xiv, 161, 166–67, 176
Ottoman Empire, 115, 145

Pabst, G. W., 7
pacifists, 72, 184–87, 200, 207
paganism, 222
Pande, Paul, 64
Pan-German League, 58, 129
Papen, Franz von, xi, xiv–xv, 2–5, 12–13, 164–65, 167–68, 170–77, 179, 201, 214
aftermath of 1934 and, 230–31
chancellorship of, 144–61

Hitler's rise to power and, 151, 153–60, 180–82, 201, 234
Hitler's strike vs., 226–28
Marburg speech by, xiv, 219–28
memoirs of, 225, 231
Night of the Long Knives and, 208–11, 229–30
Prussian coup and, 148–50, 172, 183, 187
Reichstag fire and, 2
resistance cell in vice-chancellery of, xiv, 212–29
Ribbentrop and, 174–75, 177
as vice-chancellor under Hitler, xiv, 3–5, 181–82
Papen, Martha von, 214
paramilitary forces, 126–27, 136, 163, 191
"Patriotic Associations," 187
Patriotic Auxiliary Service Law (1916), 19
patriotism, 30, 87, 164, 223
Peace Resolution (1917), 21, 31
Pechel, Rudolf, 163, 212
People's Church (*Volkskirche*), 102–4
People's Community (*Volksgemeinschaft*), 32, 103, 105, 203–4
People's Marine Division, 23
People's Supreme Court (*Volksgerichtshof*), 103, 201
Picasso, Pablo, 7
Pietrzuch, Alfons, 151
Pietrzuch, Konrad, 151
Pietrzuch, Maria, 151
Planck, Erwin, 155, 174, 179, 190
Poincaré, Raymond, 58
Poland, 7, 20, 29, 38, 57, 69–70, 90, 98, 111–12, 136
police, xiii, 62–65, 95, 129, 136, 176, 186–87, 191–93
political enemies, Nazi crackdown on, 184–87, 190, 201, 207
political parties, outlawed, 206, 213, 231
Pomerania, 71, 85
populism, 10, 19, 72–73, 79, 104–5
Potempa murders, 151, 153, 159, 165, 171, 186
Potsdam, xiii, 201–202
president, powers of, 24–27, 83–84
Preuss, Hugo, 24, 26–27, 102
propaganda, xii, 9, 18, 33, 37–39, 100, 114, 127–28, 131–32, 158, 174, 194–99, 218–19, 223, 227
Protestants, 26, 67–69, 71, 87, 88, 90, 96, 101–7, 126, 146, 150, 158, 202, 216, 234
Protocols of the Elders of Zion, 115

Prussia, xi–xii, xv, 4, 11–12, 19, 44, 64, 69, 77, 82, 88, 101–2, 125, 135–36, 142–43, 146, 164, 174, 202, 209
  Papen coup, 148–50, 152, 172, 183
Prussian police, 148–49, 183, 186–87, 215
Prussian secret police (*Gestapa*), 150, 192
Prussian Union, 101
Public Enlightenment and Propaganda, Ministry of, 194, 206, 227
Pünder, Hermann, 190

Quinz, Matheo, 66

racism, 196, 220. *See also* antisemitism
recession of 1928–29, 86
Red Front Fighters' League, 126
Reformed (Calvinist) Church, 101
refugees, 10, 99, 112–13, 125, 234
Reich Association of German Industry, 80
Reich Banner Black-Red-Gold, 63, 126–27, 141
Reich Chancellery, 153, 179
Reichenau, Walter von, 216
Reichsbank (German central bank), 56, 92, 98, 107–9, 111, 123–24, 227
Reichslandbund, 135
Reichsmark, 107, 123
Reichstag, xii, 1–3, 6, 11, 14, 19–21, 24–28, 56, 60, 67–68, 72, 74, 79, 83–84, 88–90, 96–98, 111, 118–19, 121, 128, 130, 133, 136, 143–44, 152–54, 156–58. *See also* elections; *and specific chancellors; and political parties*
  final sessions of, 190, 201–6
  Hitler's dictatorship and, 231
  negative majority and, 175–76
  Schleicher's efforts to end deadlocked, 165–68, 171–72, 175–76, 179–82
Reichstag Council of Elders, 179
Reichstag fire, 1–3, 6, 184–85, 187–90, 193–94, 215
  trial, 200–201, 230
Reichstag Fire Decree (1933), 6, 187, 190, 205
Reich Supreme Court, 201
religious divisions, 26, 30, 69, 105, 218, 234
Renzetti, Giuseppe, 116
reparations, 10, 12, 19, 21, 29, 53, 56–57, 60–61, 84, 86, 88, 106, 108, 119–25
Republican Tragedy, A (Schiller), 144
Reusch, Paul, 212
Revolution of November 1918, xii, 13, 15–18, 22, 29–32, 46, 49, 52, 65, 80, 87, 93, 102, 110–11, 191, 203

Rhineland, 53, 57, 82, 90–91, 120, 211
Ribbentrop, Annelies von, 177
Ribbentrop, Joachim von, 60, 174–75, 177, 180
right, 10, 20–21, 28–29, 31–32, 39, 46, 49, 59, 72, 79, 83–84, 90, 102, 109, 120, 163–64, 173
Röhm, Ernst, xv, 54, 151, 156, 169, 211, 228
Roman law, 101
Roosevelt, Franklin D., 145
Rosenberg, Alfred, xv, 196, 215, 226, 228
Rosenthal, Leo, 36–37
Roth, Joseph, 199
Ruhr Valley, 53, 56, 86, 212
Rule of Inferiors, The (Jung), xiv, 212
rule of law, 147, 200–201, 206–7, 223
Rumbold, Horace, 97, 122
Rundstedt, Gerd von, 218
rural-urban divide, 28, 68–72, 85–87, 87, 90, 102, 105, 111, 124, 233–34
Russian Empire, 99, 112, 115–16, 125
  World War I and, xiii, 20, 22, 76
Russian Jews, 7, 51
Russian Revolution, 22–23, 105, 112, 206. *See also* Soviet Union

Saarland, 57, 90
Sackett, Frederic M., 119, 122
Sanders, Liman von, 145–46
SA Stormtroopers (Brownshirts; *Sturmabteilung*), xiii, xv, 3, 6, 10, 93–96, 126–29, 136, 140–43, 147, 149–52, 155, 158, 163–64, 185–87, 206, 216–19, 224, 226
  attempted murder trial (Eden Dance Palace Trial), 35–38
  Night of the Long Knives and, 209, 211, 228–31
  Reichstag fire and, 3, 189–90, 192–93
  Reichstag opening of March 1933 and, 202–4
  violence of, used to seize power, 189–94
Saxony, 22, 53, 56, 61
Schacht, Hjalmar, 227
Scheidermann, Philipp, 17
Scherl, August, 58–59
Schicklgruber, Maria Anna, 42
Schiller, Friedrich, 77, 144, 204
Schleicher, Elisabeth, 210–11
Schleicher, Kurt von, xii, xiii–xv, 12, 93, 105, 116, 140–56, 201
  background of, 81–85
  Brüning and, 88–89, 93, 120–21, 125, 132–37, 140–43, 153
  chancellorship of, xv, 160–61, 164–78

Hitler's demand for power and, 141–44, 151–56, 158–61, 207, 234
Night of the Long Knives and, 210–11, 217–18, 229
Papen and, 145–53, 158–61
Prussian coup and, 148–50, 183
resignation of, 178–81
Schleswig-Holstein, 72, 85–86, 149
Schmidt-Hannover, Otto, 158, 205, 217
Schmitt, Carl, xv, 156, 201, 213
Schnee, Heinrich, 221
Schopenhauer, Arthur, 39
Schröder, Kurt von, 170–71
Schuhr, Hermann, 95
Schulze, Werner, 95
Schumacher, Kurt, 128
Schumpeter, Joseph, 197
Schwartz, Ernst, 95–96
Schweitzer, Hans Herbert ("Mjölnir"), 131–32
Schwerin von Krosigk, Count Lutz, 38, 181, 182, 214
SD (SS intelligence service), 209–10, 227
Second Book (Hitler), 40, 106
Seldte, Franz, 182
Sello, Erich, 195
Severing, Carl, xv, 62, 136, 142–43, 149, 150, 198, 203, 217
Sèvres, Treaty of, 115
Shabelskii-Bork, Piotr, 115
Siedler, Wolf Jobst, 8
Siemens (firm), 70
"silent dictatorship" (1916), 19
Silesia, 71, 85, 111–12, 125, 151, 208, 213
Sinti and Roma, 100
Slavs, 71
Small Business Party, 67, 105
social class divisions, 26, 30, 68–69
Social Darwinism, 58
Social Democratic Party of Germany (SPD), xi–xv, xvii–xviii, 5, 11, 15, 17, 20–24, 46–49, 56, 59, 63–70, 72, 74–75, 77, 79–80, 83–84, 88–89, 93, 102, 104–5, 113, 117, 125, 127–28, 132–37, 141, 148, 150, 153, 160, 164, 166, 168, 172, 174, 178, 198, 212, 233
Hitler's rise and, 178–79, 216–17
Nazi arrests of, 184–87, 203–4, 193–94
Reichstag opening of March 1933 and, 202–5
socialists, 17, 26, 46, 52, 67–68, 72, 80, 101–2, 105, 168, 178, 185–86, 198
social welfare, 72, 82, 98–99, 104–5
Soldiers' Council, 46
Sommerfeldt, Martin, 201
Sonnenburg concentration camp, 207

South Tyrol, 117–18
Soviet model, 65
Soviet Red Army, 207
Soviet Republic of Munich, 47
Soviet Union, xvii, 8, 9, 23, 74, 91, 97, 109, 113–15
Spain, 104
Spartacus Revolt, 23, 74
Special Courts, 147, 151
Spengler, Oswald, 110
SS (Protection Squads; Schutzstaffel), xiii, 163, 187, 191, 202–5, 207, 209–10, 217, 226, 230
"stab in the back" myth, xi, xiv, 13, 29–33, 41, 48–49, 202–3, 232
Stalin, Joseph, xvii, 8, 113, 192
Stampfer, Friedrich, 5
Stapel, Wilhelm, 71–72
"state of emergency," 152–54, 156–58, 161, 175–76, 178–79
State Party, xviii, 96–97, 128, 132
Stauffenberg, Count Claus von, 231–32
Steel Helmet, 4, 90, 116, 127, 129, 136, 138, 163, 182, 187, 208, 217
Steiner, Zara, 86–87
Sternheim, Thea, 97
St. Germain, Treaty of, 98, 121
Stimson, Henry, 122
Stinnes, Hugo, 110
Strasser, Gregor, xv, 88, 90, 107, 110–11, 126, 143, 152–53, 159, 160, 164–66, 168–70, 172–74, 217, 229
Strasser, Otto, 217
Strauss, Richard, 7
Strenge, Irene, 190
Stresemann, Gustav, xi, xv, xviii, 19, 54–61, 73, 79, 85, 91–92, 98, 102, 108, 121, 133, 136, 146, 170, 204–5, 233
Struggle for Berlin (Goebbels), 125
Sudeten region, 98
Supreme Constitutional Court (Staatsgerichtshof), 149, 172
Szálasi, Ferenc, 118

Tägliche Rundschau, 173
Tannenberg, Battle of, xiii, 16, 76, 135
Tardieu, André, 120
tariffs, 69, 72, 106, 119
taxes, 89, 118–19, 122
Taylor, A. J. P., 9
Technical Working Community, 166
Telegraph Union, 59
terrorism, 10, 14, 72
Thaler, Werner, 1
Thälmann, Ernst, 132, 138–39
Thirty Years' War, 77, 118

Thoma, Ludwig, 70
Thuringia, 53, 90, 133–34, 152, 169, 173
toleration policy, 133
Toller, Ernst, 198
Torgler, Ernst, 128
totalitarian state, xiv, 33, 103, 213, 216
total war, xiv, 19, 33–34, 85, 114
trade, 69, 106–7, 109, 113–14, 119, 233
Transport Ministry, 137, 182
Treblinka, 235
Treitschke, Heinrich von, 78
Tresckow, Henning von, 231–32
Treviranus, Gottfried, 5, 90, 111–12, 137, 227
Troeltsch, Ernst, 48
Tschirschky, Fritz Günther von, xv, 208–9, 211–15, 221, 224, 229–30
Tucholsky, Kurt, 71
Turkey, xiv, 10, 114–15, 145, 174, 230
Twenty-Five Points, 98–99, 105–6, 113, 199

UFA (film studio), 59
Ukraine, 20, 114
Ullrich, Volker, 45
Ullstein (press empire), 59
unemployment, 73, 86, 94–95, 113, 119, 123–24, 132–33, 140, 160, 164, 173, 180
unemployment insurance, 82, 89, 118, 123
United States, 10, 24–25, 33, 57, 60, 73, 91, 106–7, 112, 119–20, 145, 216
    Constitution, 24
    Federal Reserve, 107
    World War I and, 233
    World War II and, 231
University of Berlin, 8, 55
University of Leipzig, 55
Unruh, Friedrich Franz von, 14
Upper Silesia, 90

Valkyrie, Operation, xiii, 217, 231–32
Verhey, Jeffrey, 32
Versailles, Treaty of, 12, 24, 29, 32, 48–52, 56, 82–83, 92, 98, 116, 121, 135, 142, 196, 204, 231
veterans, 90, 128
vice-chancellery resistance group, 211–32
Vienna, 47
Villwock, Heinrich, 95
violence, 11, 36–38, 90, 94–96, 119, 126–29, 140, 147, 149–51, 162–63, 165, 189–90, 212

Voigt, Wilhelm, 28
Völkischer Beobachter, xv, 1, 151, 164, 226
Volkov, Shulamit, 72
Vorwärts, 5
Vossische Zeitung, 199

wages, 74, 80, 80, 111, 134, 233
wall, protective, 109
Wallenstein (Schiller), 77, 204
Wall Street crash of 1929, 85–86
Washington Naval Treaty (1922), 33
Weber, Thomas, 45
Wecke, Walther, 192
Weill, Kurt, 7, 68
Weimar coalition, 21
Weitz, Eric, 66
Wells, H. G., 19
Wels, Otto, 204–5
Wessel, Horst, 193
Western Front, 21, 45
Westphalia, 145
West Prussia, 85, 90, 111, 128
White Russians, 115
Wiedemann, Fritz, 46
Wiener Allgemeine Zeitung, 2
Wilhelm II, 15–17, 19, 21–22, 27, 56, 135, 138, 145, 202
Wilson, Woodrow, 19, 21, 24
Winkler, Heinrich August, 139
Wirth, Joseph, 119
Wolf, Markus, 66
Workers' movement, 21, 23–24, 218
working class, 65, 68–69, 80–81, 101, 105, 127, 133, 162, 198
World Stage, The (Weltbühne), 200
World War I, xii–xiv, xvii, 10–11, 13, 17–22, 28–34, 41, 44–46, 56, 70, 76, 85, 87, 104, 107, 109–10, 115, 128, 145, 174, 195–96, 212, 232–33
World War II, 7, 22, 46, 85, 109, 114, 128, 207–8, 230, 235
Württemberg parliament, 185

young conservative movement, 211–12
Young Plan, 57, 60–61, 88–89, 106, 108, 120, 129
Ypres, Battle of, 44

Zehrer, Hans, 165
Ziegler, Leopold, 218
Zuckmayer, Carl, 30

ABOUT THE AUTHOR

BENJAMIN CARTER HETT is the author of *Burning the Reichstag, Crossing Hitler,* and *Death in the Tiergarten.* He is a professor of history at Hunter College and the Graduate Center of the City University of New York, and holds a PhD in history from Harvard University and a law degree from the University of Toronto. Born in Rochester, New York, he grew up in Edmonton, Alberta, and now lives in New York City.